Mastering Data Engineering with BigQuery

Building Scalable Analytics and ML Pipelines with BigQuery

Shanthababu Pandian

www.orangeava.com

First Published: March 2026

Published By: Orange Education Pvt Ltd, AVA®

Address: 9, Daryaganj, Delhi, 110002, India

275 New North Road Islington Suite 1314 London,
N1 7AA, United Kingdom

ISBN (PBK): 978-93-49887-71-8

ISBN (E-BOOK): 978-93-49887-50-3

Scan the QR code to explore our entire catalogue

www.orangeava.com

Get a Free eBook

We hope you're enjoying your recent book purchase! Your feedback is incredibly valuable to us and helps other readers discover books that truly make a difference.

If you found this book useful or enjoyable, we'd greatly appreciate it if you could leave a short review with a 5-star rating on Amazon. Your review supports our work and allows us to reach more learners worldwide.

As a thank-you, we're happy to offer you a **free digital copy of this book** plus a **30% discount code** for your next purchase on our official websites:

www.orangeava.com

www.orangeava.in (For the Indian Subcontinent).

☑ **How it works:**

Leave your review on Amazon, take a screenshot of the confirmation or use the following link to submit the claim and email it to **info@orangeava.com.** Once received the required detail, we will send your rewards within 24 hours, **along with one month free subcription to the book on AVA SkillShelf!**

Claim Form
https://rebrand.ly/4d2477

Thank you for your support—it truly means a lot to us.

Downloading the code bundles and colored images

Please follow the links or scan the QR codes to download the
Code Bundles and Images of the book:

https://github.com/ava-orange-education/Mastering-Data-Engineering-with-BigQuery

The code bundles and images of the book are also hosted on
https://rebrand.ly/2e4a70

In case there's an update to the code, it will be updated on the existing GitHub repository.

Errata

We take immense pride in our work at **Orange Education Pvt Ltd,** and follow the best practices to ensure the accuracy of our content to provide an indulging reading experience to our subscribers. Our readers are our mirrors, and we use their inputs to reflect and improve upon human errors, if any, that may have occurred during the publishing processes involved. To let us maintain the quality and help us reach out to any readers who might be having difficulties due to any unforeseen errors, please write to us at:

errata@orangeava.com

Your support, suggestions, and feedback are highly appreciated.

Dedicated to

My Beloved Siblings:
Shri Shanthakumar Pandian,
Shri Shanthamaheswaran Pandian,
and Smt Shanthi Meenakshisundaram

About the Author

Shanthababu Pandian is a seasoned technology leader with over 24 years of experience in the IT industry, specializing in Artificial Intelligence (AI), Machine Learning (ML), Generative AI (GenAI), and Data Science. He holds a bachelor's degree in Electronics and Communication Engineering, along with three master's degrees (M. Tech, MBA, and M.S.) from premier Indian institutions. He has also completed a postgraduate program in AI & ML from the University of Texas, and a postgraduate certification in Data Science from IIT Guwahati. He is currently pursuing a PhD in Artificial Intelligence at Anna University, Chennai. His strong academic foundation enhances his ability to design and implement innovative, data driven solutions across healthcare, finance, and retail sectors.

Shanthababu has extensive experience in data engineering, analytics, and AI solution development, delivering impactful projects for clients in the UK and US. He excels in architecting and deploying complex data models, implementing AI governance frameworks, and developing Business Intelligence (BI) and AI-powered products. He has effectively led geographically distributed teams, collaborating with senior stakeholders to deliver initiatives aligned with business objectives while mitigating delivery risks. His strategic mindset, combined with hands-on technical expertise, enables seamless execution of end-to-end project lifecycles using agile methodologies.

A recognized thought leader, Shanthababu has delivered 50+ national and international talks on AI, ML, and data science, engaging both academic and industry audiences. He is a prolific author with over 100 publications, including articles and books, and actively contributes to the AI and data science communities. As a technical reviewer for leading global publishers, he has reviewed more than 75 books on data, AI, cloud technologies, and programming.

About the Technical Reviewers

Dr. Sankaraiah Sreeramula is the Founder and Chief Executive Officer at Turilytix. AI, spearheads transformative efforts in business efficiency through cutting-edge advancements in machine learning, artificial intelligence, automated analysis, and visual intelligence. With a career spanning over 18 years, Dr. Sankaraiah has developed AI-driven solutions across a diverse array of industries, including FMCG, retail, finance, and manufacturing, collaborating with some of the world's leading companies in semiconductors, pulp, and paper. Recognized globally for his innovative contributions, he was honored as the innovative leader in 2023, and the top innovative leader driving Generative AI and global inspirational leader in 2024.

Dr. S. Neelavathy Pari is an Assistant Professor (Senior Grade) in the Department of Computer Technology, Anna University, Chennai. She specializes in security of Wireless Networks, Cloud Computing, Data Structures and Algorithms, Soft Computing as well as Emerging Computer Technologies. With over 20 years of academic and research experience, she has contributed extensively to curriculum development, interdisciplinary research, and technology-driven education.

Vatsal Mishra is an accomplished Data Engineer with over 9 years of experience specializing in data pipeline architecture, GenAI applications, and software development. With a strong foundation in Electronics and Communications Engineering from the Indian Institute of Information Technology, he has developed expertise in Python, Apache Spark, Kafka, Java and cloud data technologies, including GCP, Snowflake, and AWS. Vatsal has a proven track record in leading data engineering initiatives at prominent organizations, including Google and Urban Company, where he designed scalable data platforms.

Preface

The world of DATA ENGINEERING is undergoing a profound transformation, driven by rapid advancements in cloud technologies, machine learning, and large-scale distributed data systems. Organizations across industries now rely on modern data platforms to unlock real-time insights, support intelligent applications, and build resilient, future-ready architectures. Thus, this book emerges as a comprehensive guide for learners seeking to master data engineering on Google Cloud Platform (GCP), whether you are a beginner exploring cloud data tools, or a practitioner enhancing your pipeline design skills, or an architect building enterprise-grade data ecosystems.

Designed to bridge foundational concepts with hands-on implementation, the content delves deeply into GCP's most powerful services, including BigQuery, Dataflow, Pub/Sub, Dataproc, and Cloud Composer. Readers will gain practical experience with end-to-end data architectures, from ingestion and storage to processing, orchestration, analytics, and machine learning. Along the way, the book highlights GCP's unique strengths such as serverless scalability, advanced query engines, real-time pipelines, and built-in security, while emphasising techniques for performance optimisation, cost efficiency, and governance. Through step-by-step tutorials, real-world use cases, and industry best practices, each chapter equips readers to apply concepts confidently in production environments.

Drawing from my experience of more than 24 years in IT, AI, data engineering, and cloud solution delivery, this book consolidates practical wisdom gained from architecting complex platforms for global enterprises. My journey across Azure, AWS, and GCP ecosystems has shaped the holistic perspective reflected in these pages. The goal is not only to teach technology but to empower readers to build secure, scalable, and trusted data solutions that align with modern business and regulatory needs. This book aims to inspire readers to harness the full potential of Google Cloud, transforming raw data into intelligence, and building the next generation of cloud-driven innovations.

Chapter 1: Introduction to Data Engineering on Google Cloud

This chapter lays the foundation for understanding how data engineering powers modern, data-driven organizations. It introduces the core principles of data engineering, and explains why it has become essential for enabling actionable insights in today's digital economy. The narrative highlights Google Cloud Platform's unique position as a scalable, innovative provider of big data solutions, contrasting its capabilities with those of AWS and Azure to help readers appreciate GCP's strengths. The chapter also explores the relevance of Big Data in current business ecosystems.

Chapter 2: Google Cloud Platform Essentials

This chapter provides a guided introduction to the Google Cloud ecosystem, ensuring readers gain confidence in navigating and using GCP's tools effectively. It begins with setting up a GCP account and understanding the layout of the cloud console, followed by creating a project, setting up billing, and configuring IAM for secure access management. Readers learn how enterprise environments leverage multi-project architectures to manage workloads at scale. The chapter closes with an overview of GCP's core services, and how they align with big data and analytics workloads, preparing readers for more advanced implementations.

Chapter 3: Data Storage in GCP

Focusing on the backbone of every data platform storage, this chapter examines GCP's powerful services for housing structured and unstructured data. It introduces Cloud Storage and BigQuery as the primary storage options, detailing how projects, datasets, tables, and views fit into BigQuery's architecture. Readers learn to load, query, and manage data through the BigQuery Web UI, while exploring advanced features such as Data Canvases, Schedulers, and BigQuery Data Forms. The chapter concludes by explaining optimization techniques like partitioning and clustering, enabling readers to build scalable and cost-efficient storage solutions.

Chapter 4: Processing Data with Cloud Dataproc

This chapter simplifies the world of distributed processing by introducing Cloud Dataproc, GCP's managed Hadoop and Spark service. It starts by revisiting the fundamentals of Hadoop and Apache Spark, and then moves into creating and managing Dataproc clusters for large-scale data tasks. Readers gain insight into optimizing Spark jobs for performance and cost, while learning how Dataproc integrates with Cloud Storage, BigQuery, and other GCP services. The chapter provides a practical understanding of how Dataproc can automate workflows, and streamline big data processing in real-world applications.

Chapter 5: Data Pipelines with Dataflow

Centred on building scalable data pipelines, this chapter introduces Google Cloud Dataflow and its Apache Beam programming model. Readers learn how Dataflow handles both batch and streaming workloads through unified pipeline development. The chapter explores pipeline creation, transformation logic, advanced windowing, and performance tuning, enabling efficient real-time and batch data processing. Real-world scenarios illustrate how Dataflow supports mission-critical analytics and event-driven systems

Chapter 6: Orchestrating Workflows with Cloud Composer

This chapter explores the importance of orchestration in automated data ecosystems, and introduces Cloud Composer, GCP's managed implementation of Apache Airflow. Readers are guided through the concepts of workflow orchestration and the design of Directed Acyclic Graphs (DAGs) to automate pipeline execution. The chapter covers task scheduling, dependency management, and the use of custom operators to enhance workflow flexibility. It also addresses scaling considerations for enterprise environments, enabling readers to build reliable, production-ready orchestration systems.

Chapter 7: Analytics with BigQuery

This chapter unlocks BigQuery's full analytical power by diving into SQL capabilities, query optimization, and advanced data manipulation techniques. Readers learn how to write efficient SQL using window functions, arrays, structs, and other advanced features. The chapter explains how to implement automation using stored procedures, along with disaster recovery strategies that ensure high availability and resilience. It wraps up by introducing BigQuery BI Engine, and exploring how it enhances analytical performance as well as integrates with visualization tools to deliver fast, actionable insights.

Chapter 8: Managing Data Integration with Cloud Pub/Sub

Dedicated to real-time data movement, this chapter introduces Cloud Pub/Sub as GCP's backbone for event-driven architectures. It explains how Pub/Sub enables asynchronous messaging through topics and subscriptions, and how it integrates seamlessly with Dataflow for large-scale stream processing. Readers explore design patterns for building resilient, fault-tolerant, real-time ingestion systems that support modern enterprise workloads, making this chapter pivotal for understanding streaming data architectures.

Chapter 9: BigQuery Machine Learning (BQML)

This chapter showcases how machine learning can be seamlessly embedded within a data warehouse using BQML. It explains the fundamentals of ML in BigQuery, the supported model types, and the use cases where in-warehouse ML becomes most powerful. Readers learn to create, train, and evaluate ML models using SQL, perform hyperparameter tuning, and generate predictions directly from BigQuery. Advanced sections explore time-series forecasting with ARIMA, building recommendation systems, and integrating BQML models with TensorFlow and other external frameworks for more sophisticated applications.

Chapter 10: BigQuery Performance Optimization

Performance and cost efficiency are central themes of this chapter, which explains how to fine-tune BigQuery workloads for scalable analytics. Readers learn how to enhance query speed through partitioning and clustering, implement schema design best practices, and reduce storage costs through intelligent structuring. The chapter also focuses on data validation, quality checks, and version control to ensure reliable, maintainable, and repeatable data environments—skills critical for production-grade data systems.

Chapter 11: Data Security and Compliance on GCP

This final chapter emphasizes the critical role of security and governance in building trustworthy data platforms. It explores BigQuery security features, including access control, roles, and encryption, while also addressing data masking and compliance practices. Readers learn how to apply governance frameworks involving cataloguing, classification, stewardship, retention policies, and data quality monitoring. The chapter ensures that by the end of the book, readers are well-equipped to design secure, compliant, and regulation-aligned data architectures on GCP.

DID YOU KNOW

Did you know that Orange Education Pvt Ltd offers eBook versions of every book published, with PDF and ePub files available? You can upgrade to the eBook version at **www.orangeava.com** and as a print book customer, you are entitled to a discount on the eBook copy. Get in touch with us at: **info@orangeava.com** for more details.

At **www.orangeava.com**, you can also read a collection of free technical articles, sign up for a range of free newsletters, and receive exclusive discounts and offers on Print Books and eBooks.

PIRACY

If you come across any illegal copies of our works in any form on the internet, we would be grateful if you would provide us with the location address or website name. Please contact us at **info@orangeava.com** with a link to the material.

ARE YOU INTERESTED IN AUTHORING WITH US?

If there is a topic that you have expertise in, and you are interested in either writing or contributing to a book, please write to us at **business@orangeava.com**. We are on a journey to help developers and tech professionals to gain insights on the present technological advancements and innovations happening across the globe and build a community that believes Knowledge is best acquired by sharing and learning with others. Please reach out to us to learn what our audience demands and how you can be part of this educational reform. We also welcome ideas from tech experts and help them build learning and development content for their domains.

REVIEWS

Please leave a review. Once you have read and used this book, why not leave a review on the site that you purchased it from? Potential readers can then see and use your unbiased opinion to make purchase decisions. We at Orange Education would love to know what you think about our products, and our authors can learn from your feedback. Thank you!

For more information about Orange Education, please visit **www.orangeava.com**.

Table of Contents

Chapter 1
Introduction to Data Engineering on Google Cloud

Introduction

Data engineering lies at the core of modern data enterprises and acts as the engine that transforms raw, disparate data into actionable insights across many industries. In an era where every decision is increasingly data-driven, formulating effective solutions begins with the ability to collect, process, and analyze vast volumes of data.

This chapter introduces data engineering and explains its core concepts, while highlighting its importance in modern data warehousing. It also outlines the role of Google Cloud Platform (GCP) in delivering scalable and efficient solutions for big data processing. The chapter sets the foundation for building robust data pipelines and analytics systems by comparing major cloud platforms such as GCP, AWS, and Azure and emphasizing GCP's unique strengths in managing and processing large-scale data.

This chapter will explore data engineering, why it is vital for today's businesses, and how leveraging cloud solutions can enhance data workflows. We will also walk through practical examples and real-world use cases that illustrate the creation of robust data pipelines and analytical systems.

Structure

In this chapter, we will discuss the following topics:

- Importance of Understanding Big Data and its Current Relevance
- Understanding Big Data and its Significance
- Current Relevance of Big Data
- Evolution of Data Engineering

- Significance of Data Engineering in Modern Organizations
- Core Concepts in Data Engineering
- Major Components and Activities
- Data Engineering in a Data-Driven Business Landscape
- On-Premises Data Engineering
- Cloud Platforms for Data Engineering
- Google Cloud Platform (GCP) and its Unique Advantages
- Comparing GCP, AWS, and Azure for Data Engineering

Importance of Understanding Big Data and Its Current Relevance

Understanding Big Data is essential in today's technology-driven landscape because it offers different levels of transformative insights and competitive advantages. Here is an in-depth look at why Big Data is essential and how its relevance continues to grow:

Definition of Big Data

Big Data describes extremely large and complex datasets that cannot be efficiently processed using traditional data management tools. These datasets can be structured, semi-structured, or unstructured. Based on their characteristics, Big Data is commonly defined through the three **V**'s, which are as follows:

Volume

In terms of a straightforward statement, this is defined as the massive amounts of data generated from various sources. In the realm of social media, **Volume** refers to the vast amount of data continuously generated across websites, portals, and online applications. For B2C companies, this includes an enormous pool of user generated content that must be analyzed for relevance and insights.

Consider how Facebook, YouTube, Instagram, and Twitter users and their everyday activities lead to these platforms creating billions of posts, images, videos, tweets, and interactions. The scale of data being produced every minute is staggering and highlights the immense **volume** that defines Big Data in the social media landscape. This volume would vary with respect to individual domains such as manufacturing, healthcare, education, banking, and financial services.

Velocity

This is nothing but the rapid data generation and real-time processing requirements aspects. In social media, ~900 million photos are uploaded daily to Facebook, ~500 million tweets are posted on Twitter, ~400,000 hours of video are added to YouTube, and ~3.5 billion searches are performed on Google[1].

This represents an exceptional flood of data and resembles a digital explosion. Big Data technologies playing a crucial role in managing this relentless influx, while ensuring that data is ingested efficiently and processed in real time to prevent bottlenecks and enable timely insights. A classic example of velocity aspects is machine-generated data, such as IoT-generated data from machines and equipment, which is an enormous amount of data in a fraction of a second and transmitted to the data platform for analytics and machine learning operations.

Variety

Variety in Big Data encompasses the diverse forms of structured and unstructured data generated by humans and machines. Structured data like defined columns and rows is commonly added and easily categorized. However, unstructured data such as emails, voicemails, handwritten notes, and audio recordings also play a crucial role in the data landscape.

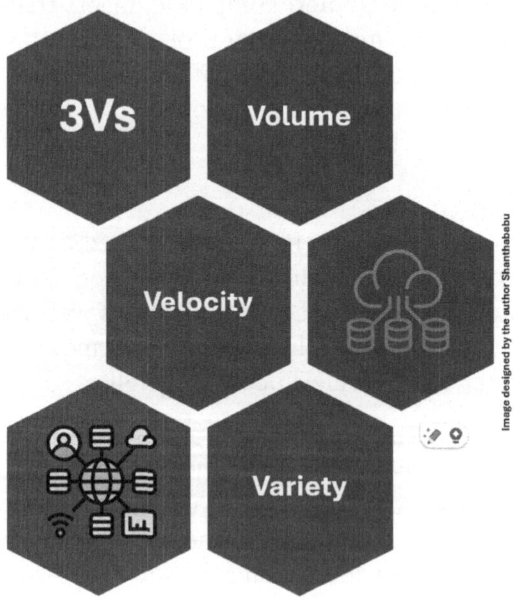

Figure 1.1: *Three V's of Big Data*

1. **Google Search statistics**: Google Search – Wikipedia (search volume info) **General internet/society data (related stats)**: How Much Data Do We Create Every Day? – Bernard Marr article

Understanding Big Data and Its Significance

Understanding Big Data and its significance will help data engineers, data scientists, and analysts deliver their tasks effectively after understanding the nature of the data and resident values, extracting them as insights to plan for deliverables, and meeting the business stakeholders' expectations.

Informed Decision-Making

The Big Data platforms must have specific features and characteristics that enable efficient data processing, analysis, and insight generation to achieve the following benefits:

- **Actionable Insights:** Big Data analytics enables organizations to extract actionable insights from vast datasets from various upstream applications, which transforms raw data into strategic intelligence to enhance their business in various aspects. This can lead to better decision-making at all levels, from operational adjustments to strategic planning.
- **Predictive Analytics:** By analyzing historical data, organizations can predict future trends and customer needs and interests, identify potential risks, seize opportunities before their competitors by continuing to predict and forecast potential opportunities across different regions. This helps them plan for future opportunities and assess market sustainability.

Driving Innovation and Efficiency

- **Enhanced Customer Experience:** Continuously collecting data and constantly analyzing consumer behavior and preferences helps businesses in various ways, such as in enhancing product experiences, tailoring products based on customer needs, providing the best services, building marketing strategies, and promoting personalized customer experience awareness.
- **Process Optimization:** Big Data allows organizations to identify inefficiencies in operations related to manufacturing, people, and supply chains. This helps organizations in optimizing processes, reducing costs, and improving on-time service delivery.

Figure 1.2: *Understanding Big Data and Its Significance*

Competitive Advantages

- **Market Trends:** Understanding Big Data equips organizations with the ability to monitor market dynamics and instantly adapt to transformations by continuous data collection from various sources from organizations and doing data analytics and predicting the market trends and getting hold of them and running the business is crucial in this digital era. This agility is crucial in fast-paced industries.
- **Data-Driven Culture:** Nowadays, most companies that effectively leverage big data cultivate a data-driven culture, foster innovation strategies, stay ahead in competitive markets, and can sustain in the market in the long term.

Current Relevance of Big Data

Explosion of Data Sources: All industries are collecting data across various divisions and have found a way to utilize it for various business purposes; ultimately, data sources are expanding on a daily basis.

- **Digital Transformation:** The rise of IoT devices, social media, e-commerce, and mobile technologies has contributed to increasing data. Each generates data in different forms, such as structured, semi-structured, and unstructured. Companies that have started using data for business development and strategy roadmap have access to diverse datasets from the enterprise level, ranging from transactional records to user-generated content at different layers in the organization.
- **Real-Time Analytics:** With technological advances, businesses can now process, acquire, and analyze data in real time, which enables immediate responses to emerging trends and challenges to address customer needs and enhance services. This data could be man-made or machine-made.

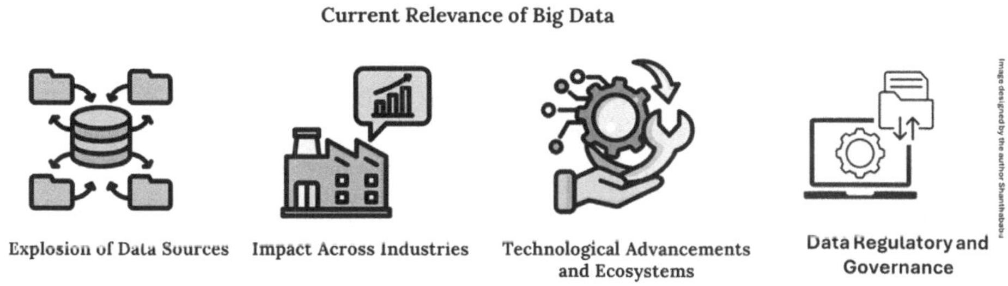

Figure 1.3: *Current Relevance of Big Data*

Impact across Industries: The emergence of several data sources and their impact across industries are limitless. The following industries are driving the major influence in this area:

- **Healthcare:** Big Data improves patient outcomes by enabling personalized medicine, predictive diagnostics, and efficient resource management.
- **Finance:** In the financial sector, Big Data drives fraud detection, risk management, and algorithmic trading, which enhances both security and profitability.
- **Retail:** Retailers harness Big Data to optimize inventory, forecast demand, and deliver personalized marketing, which directly impacts sales and customer loyalty.
- **Manufacturing:** Integrating Big Data analytics in manufacturing leads to predictive maintenance, improved quality control, and optimized supply chain management.

Technological Advancements and Ecosystems: Technological advancements such as cloud computing and AIML are taking industries to new levels and cultivating possibilities that were not feasible a few decades ago. Now, let us explore the key characteristics of this ecosystem:

- **Cloud Computing:** Cloud platform service providers like Google Cloud, AWS, and Azure provide a scalable solution for processing Big Data. These platforms offer managed services such as data storage, data warehouses, streaming analytics, and machine learning to simplify the complexity of Big Data operations.
- **Artificial Intelligence and Machine Learning:** As these technologies evolve, they become more effective at processing vast datasets to drive automation, enhancing decision-making, prediction and forecasting, and generating valuable insights from the data.

Regulatory and Governance Implications: When dealing with data, data privacy and security play pivotal roles in regulatory and governance compliance and its implementation.

- **Data Privacy and Security:** With increased data collection emerges the need for proper data governance frameworks that can be implemented while building data platforms, handling data, and implementing analytics and advanced analytics ecosystems. Understanding Big Data also means addressing data privacy regulations like GDPR, PII, and HIPAA, which ensures that organizations maintain data privacy and compliance as they leverage data for growth.
- **Ethical Considerations:** The way data is collected, stored, and analyzed raises ethical questions and challenges that organizations must address to build trust with consumers and stakeholders for ethical use and management of data.

Evolution of Data Engineering

Data engineering has evolved from traditional ETL systems to highly scalable, real-time, and AI-driven architectures. As data volumes continue to grow, modern data engineering will focus on quality, security, privacy, and efficiency, which will allow businesses to extract insights faster and with greater accuracy.

Data engineering has undergone significant transformations over the years and has evolved from essential data storage and processing techniques to modern real-time systems. Here is an in-depth look at each stage of this evolution:

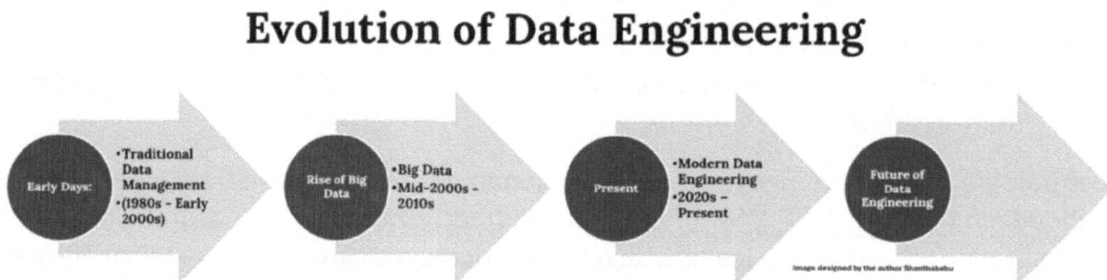

Figure 1.4: *Evolution of Data Engineering*

Early Days: Traditional Data Management (1980s - Early 2000s)

- **Relational Databases (RDBMS):** Early data engineering was dominated by structured data stored in relational databases like Oracle, MySQL, and SQL Server.
- **Enterprise Data Warehouses (EDW):** Organizations started building large-scale data warehouses (for example, IBM DB2, Teradata) for analytical workloads.
- **ETL Pipelines:** Data was extracted from operational systems, transformed, and loaded (ETL) into centralized data warehouses like IBM DB2 and Teradata.

- **Batch Processing:** Most data processing is batch-oriented, using tools like Informatica and Apache Nifi.
- **Data Reporting and Business Intelligence (BI):** SQL-based analytics tools like IBM Cognos and SAP BusinessObjects were used to generate reports.

Rise of Big Data (Mid-2000s - 2010s)

- **Hadoop Ecosystem:** The explosion of data has led to the adoption of distributed systems such as Apache Hadoop, which allows for scalable storage and batch processing with MapReduce.
- **Big Data and Distributed Computing:** Apache Hadoop has introduced a new distributed data storage and processing paradigm called HDFS (Hadoop Distributed File System). It became a popular storage layer and MapReduce enabled parallelized batch processing of large datasets.
- **NoSQL Databases:** NoSQL databases like MongoDB, Cassandra, and HBase were used to handle semi-structured and unstructured data. These databases offered flexible schemas and high scalability.
- **Data Warehouses and BI:** Cloud-based data warehouses such as Amazon Redshift and Google BigQuery simplify data analytics and business intelligence (BI) reporting by enabling seamless integration with tools like SSRS, PowerBI and Tableau, providing scalable, high-performance, real-time insights.

Real-Time Data Processing and Streaming (2010s - 2020s)

- **Shift to Real-Time Data Pipelines:** Tools like Apache Kafka, Apache Flink, and Apache Spark Streaming enable real-time data ingestion and processing. **Google Cloud Pub/Sub and AWS Kinesis** offer cloud-native event streaming solutions.
- **Data Lakes:** Organizations started leveraging cloud-based data lakes such as **AWS S3 and Azure Data Lake** to store massive raw data in a cost-effective manner. Enabled **schema-on-read** (as opposed to schema-on-write in traditional data warehouses).
- **ML and AI Integration:** Data engineering began integrating with machine learning workflows and used feature stores as well as MLOps pipelines.

Modern Data Engineering (2020s - Present)

- **Cloud-Native and Serverless Architectures:** Serverless data processing with AWS Glue, Google Cloud Dataflow, and Snowflake offers scalability and cost efficiency.
- **Data Mesh and Data Fabric:** Decentralized approaches like Data Mesh empower domain-driven data ownership, while improving accessibility and

governance. **Data Fabric** uses AI-driven metadata management to provide a unified view of all data assets.

- **DataOps and Automation:** Data pipelines are increasingly automated with CI/CD for data (DataOps), improving reliability and agility. **Apache Airflow, Azure Data Factory and Azure Synapse** automate workflow orchestration.
- **Edge and IoT Data Processing:** The rise of edge computing enables real-time analytics at the source, which reduces latency in data-driven decision-making.

Future of Data Engineering

- **AI-Driven Data Engineering:** Automated data pipeline management, anomaly detection, and self-healing data architectures powered by AI.
- **Privacy-Preserving Data Processing:** Increased adoption of differential privacy, homomorphic encryption, and federated learning to ensure data security.
- **Real-Time Graph Processing and Knowledge Graphs:** More businesses will leverage graph databases (for example, Neo4j, TigerGraph) to analyze complex data relationships.
- **Federated Learning and Privacy-Enhancing Technologies:** Secure data processing techniques like differential privacy and federated learning will become more mainstream, going forward.
- **Quantum Data Processing:** While it is still in the research phase, quantum computing has the potential to revolutionize complex data processing tasks. Although in its early stages, it may revolutionize data processing, especially in optimization and cryptography.

Characteristics of Data Engineering: Stages of Evolution

The following table describes the characteristics of data engineering at various stages of its evolution:

Stages of Evolution	Key Characteristics
Traditional Data Management (1980s - Early 2000s)	• Structured data with strict schema requirements
	• Centralized storage using relational databases
	• Batch ETL process for data movement
	• Business Intelligence (BI) reporting with SQL-based queries

Stages of Evolution	Key Characteristics
Rise of Big Data (Mid-2000s - 2010s)	• Emergence of distributed storage and computing
	• Handling of semi-structured and unstructured data
	• The rise of NoSQL databases for flexible schemas
	• Cloud-based data warehouses for scalable analytics
Real-Time Data Processing and Streaming (2010s - 2020s)	• Transition from batch to real-time data processing
	• Event-driven architectures with streaming frameworks
	• Cloud-native data lakes for storing raw, unstructured data
	• Machine learning (ML) and AI integration
Modern Data Engineering (2020s - Present)	• Cloud-native, serverless, and scalable data architectures
	• Decentralized data management (Data Mesh)
	• AI-driven automation for data pipeline management
	• Edge computing for ultra-low latency data processing
Future of Data Engineering (Beyond 2025)	• AI-driven Data Engineering
	• Privacy-preserving data Processing
	• Real-Time Graph Processing and Knowledge Graphs
	• Quantum Data Processing

Table 1.1: *Characteristics of Data Engineering Stage of Evolution*

Challenges in Data Engineering: Stages of Evolution

The following table describes the challenges confronted at the various evolutionary stages of data engineering:

Stages of Evolution	Key Challenges
Traditional Data Management (1980s - Early 2000s)	• Scalability was limited due to high costs and rigid architectures.
	• Data silos made integration across departments difficult.
	• ETL processes were time-consuming and error-prone.
Rise of Big Data (Mid-2000s - 2010s)	• Batch processing still dominated and limited real-time analytics.

Stages of Evolution	Key Challenges
	• Managing Hadoop clusters was complex and required specialized skills.
	• NoSQL databases lacked standardization, which made interoperability challenging.
Real-Time Data Processing and Streaming (2010s - 2020s)	• Complexity in managing real-time data pipelines at scale
	• Higher infrastructure costs due to continuous processing
	• Data governance and security challenges with decentralized architectures
Modern Data Engineering (2020s - Present)	• Data privacy concerns with decentralized architectures
	• Increased complexity in managing multi-cloud and hybrid environments
	• There is a need for AI-driven observability to detect and prevent data quality issues.
Future of Data Engineering (Beyond 2025)	• Ethical and regulatory concerns around AI-driven data engineering
	• Security risks associated with federated learning and quantum computing
	• Need for standardized frameworks for edge computing and real-time analytics

***Table 1.2**: Challenges During Various Stages of Evolution in Data Engineering*

The Data Explosion and Business Transformation

Over the past two decades, digital transformation has led to an explosion of unprecedented data volume, velocity, and variety explosion. Organizations now face the challenge of managing terabytes of data generated from:

- Customer transactions and interactions
- Social media activity
- Sensors and IoT devices
- Log files and operational data

Data engineering has been tasked with building the systems and architectures that ingest, clean, and transform this data into formats suitable for analysis. Today, effective data engineering is a critical competitive differentiator as it enables organizations to harness data for predictive analytics, machine learning (ML), and real-time decision-making.

Significance of Data Engineering in Modern Organizations

Data engineering is the backbone of modern organizations in an era dominated by data. Organizations are adopting data engineering and analytics as they understand the importance of data and its valuable hidden insights. Data engineering involves designing, constructing, and maintaining scalable systems that ingest, transform, and store vast amounts of relevant data, which enables organizations to extract actionable insights and drive business decisions (see the block diagram in *Figure* 1.4). Here is an in-depth exploration of data engineering and its significance in today's business landscape:

Understanding Data Engineering

Data engineering is the new discipline in modern data warehouse exercises. It involves designing and building robust data platforms that transform raw data into valuable information after many data operations. This is achieved by incorporating the business rules and adapting the data security and privacy policies and serving data as the **ideal data set** for downstream applications like data science, analytics, AI products, data warehouse and exposing as API for external customer demands.

The program encompasses the following activities:

- **Data Collection**: Collect data from various sources, such as upstream applications, and define the **tables** and **columns** after detailed discussion with stakeholders and the business team.
- **Data Ingestion:** Data Ingestion is the process of **collecting, importing, and loading data** from various sources into a **data storage system** for further processing or analysis. Technically, this is called a **staging layer**. This data can come from **databases, APIs, IoT devices, logs, files, real-time streams, or other cloud storage**. The ingestion process could be in batches, real-time, or a hybrid of both.
- **Data Transformation:** Data transformation is the process of converting raw data into a structured format ready for analysis by applying a set of methods like cleaning, filtering, aggregation, normalization, and formatting for analytics and machine learning model building. This step is crucial in **ETL (Extract, Transform, Load)** pipelines and ensures that data is consistent, accurate, and usable. This layer is the **processing or transformation layer.**

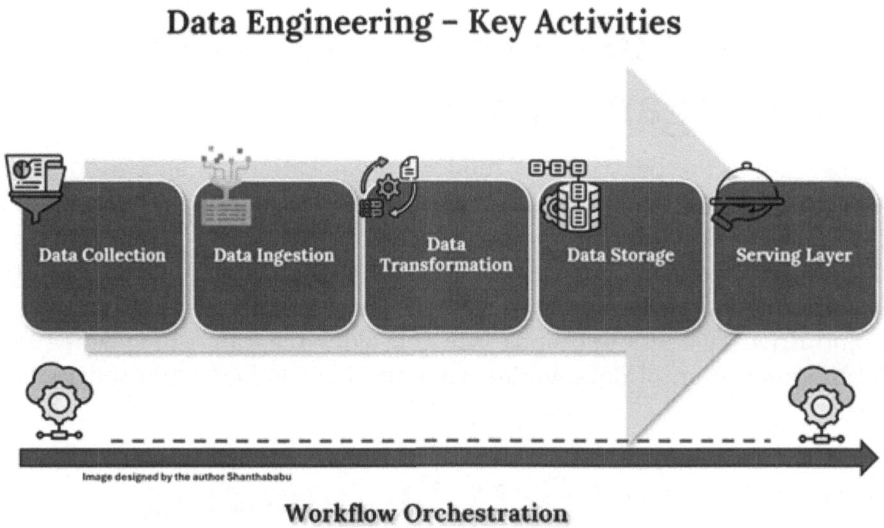

Figure 1.5: *Key Activities in Data Engineering*

- **Data Storage:** Using databases, data warehouses, or data lakes to store processed data efficiently for future retrieval and analysis. This layer is called the **storage layer.**
- **Serving Layer:** From the data storage, the data is served to different applications such as data science, data analytics, AI-powered products, data warehouse, and API for external application usage.
- **Workflow Orchestration:** Automating the data pipeline processes with tools that schedule, monitor, and manage the data flow

These activities ensure that data is reliable, timely, and ready for advanced analytics, Machine Learning (ML), and business intelligence applications.

Data Engineering in Modern Organizations

Data engineering plays a critical role in modern organizations by designing and managing scalable data pipelines that collect, process, and store large volumes of data. It ensures high data quality, reliability, and accessibility to support analytics and advance analytics, as well as enables real-time and batch data processing. Data engineering helps organizations make faster, data-driven decisions.

Enabling Data-Driven Decision Making

- **Actionable Insights:** By transforming raw data into a structured and analyzable format after applying the filters and business rules, data engineering makes it possible for organizations to perform complex analyses and generate insights and predictive modeling. These exercises help the organization to predict customer behavior or optimize operational processes and the derived insights drive strategic decisions and roadmap.

- **Real-Time Analytics:** Modern organizations require immediate access to data, so real-time analytics are in place. Data engineering pipelines that support real-time or near-real-time processing enable businesses to react swiftly to market changes or emerging trends in time understand the market demand and customer interest, as well as strengthen the supply chain process.

Scalability and Flexibility

- **Handling Big Data:** With the increasing growth of data in terms of volume, velocity, and variety, traditional data systems often fall short when it comes to handling it. Moreover, exponential growth needs to be tackled by handling the data in appropriate ways. Data engineering leverages the distributed computing and cold and hot storage capabilities provided by the various cloud services to scale processing power and storage, which ensures that data can be managed efficiently on the data platform and can be used to build data analytics and machine learning solutions.
- **Adaptability:** As businesses evolve, so do organizations' enormous data needs. Ultimately, data engineering helps in designing flexible data pipelines, which allows organizations to add new data sources, adjust processing methods, enhance performance dynamically, and integrate with various analytics tools without overhauling the entire system.

Enhancing Data Quality and Reliability

- **Data Cleansing and Validation:** When insights are extracted from the vast volume of data, the quality and reliability of data are the significant parameters to strengthen the outcome of the data analytics and machine learning (ML) solutions. Therefore, the automated data quality checks and validation rules embedded in the pipeline ensure that only accurate and consistent data is passed on to analytics and AI-powered systems.
- **Governance and Security:** In addition to data quality and reliability, data engineering frameworks should incorporate robust governance practices to comply with industry regulations such as PII, GDPR, and HIPAA. They should protect sensitive information through encryption, access controls, and audit trails to instill confidence in customers about the confidentiality of their data.

Optimizing Operational Efficiency

- **Automation:** More automation certainly enhances performance and is cost-effective. Basically, this will be done by automating repetitive tasks like data extraction, cleaning, and loading, so that organizations can free up valuable resources. This allows data engineers and analysts to focus on high-impact activities like developing more complex pipelines, creating advanced models, or refining business strategies.

- **Cost Efficiency:** A cost-effective solution is always the thump rule for service providers' customer-retention strategies. Cloud-based data engineering solutions like Google Cloud Platform, AWS, or Azure offer pay-as-you-go pricing and scalable infrastructure. This minimizes capital expenditure and operational costs, which makes it feasible for businesses of all sizes to harness the power of Big Data by scaling as per the demand.

Driving Innovation through Advanced Analytics

- **ML and AI:** Of course, Big Data and data engineering lay the groundwork for ML and AI-powered applications by ensuring that high-quality, curated data is available for model training and inference. This integration transforms descriptive analytics into predictive and prescriptive analytics, leading to innovative solutions across industries.
- **Customer Personalization:** There is always a high demand for customization, and personalization helps sustain the market as well as provide reliable service for critical customers. Therefore, in data engineering, data pipelines that aggregate customer interactions across multiple touch points and help in personalized marketing and generate product recommendations, toileted output, and improved customer service are the key differentiators in today's competitive landscape.

Data engineering has evolved into a critical discipline that supports AI, ML, and real-time analytics. Mastering these core concepts allows data engineers to build **scalable, secure, and efficient** data architectures.

Let us understand the core concepts in data engineering,

Core Concepts in Data Engineering

Data Modeling: Data modeling stage one, when planning for a data platform, is the process of structuring and organizing data to optimize storage, retrieval, and integrity in a database or data warehouse.

Types of Data Models:

- **Conceptual Model:** High-level representation focusing on business requirements
- **Logical Model:** Defines relationships between data elements without considering storage specifics

- **Physical Model:** Details how data is stored in databases, including tables, columns, and indexing strategies

Common Data Modeling Techniques:

- **Star Schema:** Uses fact tables linked to multiple dimension tables for efficient querying
- **Snowflake Schema:** A normalized version of the star schema to reduce redundancy
- **Entity-Relationship Model (ER Model):** Represents entities and their relationships in a structured manner

Tools for Data Modeling: ER/Studio, Toad Data Modeler, Lucidchart, SQL Power Architect.

Data Warehousing

A **data warehouse** is a centralized repository designed for analytical queries and reporting. It stores structured data optimized for read operations.

Characteristics of Data Warehouses:

- Subject-oriented (focused on business areas like sales, finance)
- Integrated (collects data from multiple sources)
- Time-variant (stores historical data for trend analysis)
- Non-volatile (data doesn't change after being loaded)

Popular Data Warehouses: Snowflake, Amazon Redshift, Google BigQuery, and Microsoft Azure Synapse Analytics.

Comparison with Data Lakes:

Features	Data Warehouse	Data Lake
Data Type	Structured	Structured, Semi-structured, Unstructured
Storage Cost	High	Low
Processing	SQL-based	Supports SQL, ML, and analytics
Use Case	BI and Analytics	Big Data, AI, and ML

***Table 1.3**: Comparing Data Warehouse vs. Data Lakes*

ETL and ELT Processes (Extract, Transform, Load)

A traditional data processing approach that involves extracting data from source systems, transforming it (cleaning, formatting), and then loading it into a data warehouse.

- **Example Tools:** Apache Nifi, Talend, Informatica, SSIS, ADF, and so on.
- **ELT (Extract, Load, Transform):** is a modern approach in which data is first loaded into a data warehouse or data lake, and transformations occur later using the warehouse's processing power.
- **Example Tools:** dbt (data build tool), Apache Spark, BigQuery, Snowflake, ADF, Synapse, and so on.
- **Ideal Scenarios for Use: ETL and ELT** are preferred when dealing with structured data and traditional BI workloads.
- **ELT** is better for handling large, unstructured datasets with cloud-based architectures.

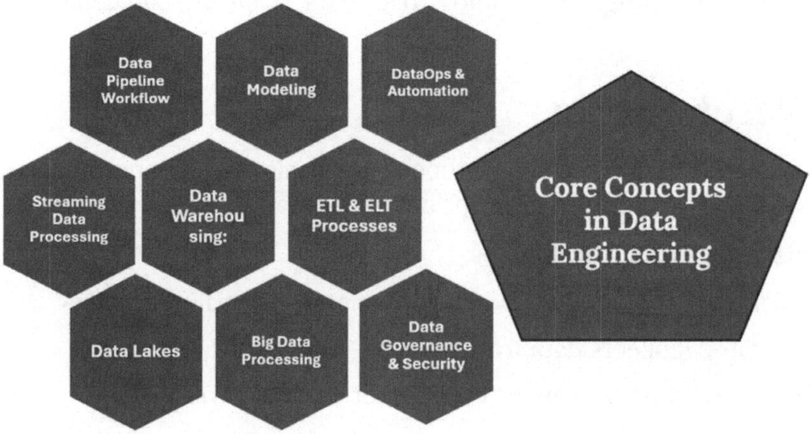

Figure 1.6: *Core Concepts in Data Engineering*

Big Data Processing

Big Data processing involves managing large-scale structured and unstructured data that traditional databases cannot handle efficiently.

Key Technologies and Frameworks:

- **Apache Hadoop** is an open-source framework for distributed storage and parallel processing of large-scale data. It uses the Hadoop Distributed File System (HDFS) and MapReduce.
- **Apache Spark** is an open-source, distributed computing framework that enables fast, in-memory data processing for Big Data analytics, ML, and real-time streaming applications.
- **Azure Synapse** is a cloud-based analytics service that integrates Big Data and data warehousing, enabling scalable, real-time analytics with SQL, Spark, and data integration capabilities.

Data Lakes

A **data lake** is a centralized storage repository that can hold structured, semi-structured, and unstructured data in its raw format. These scalable storage repositories store raw, structured, semi-structured, and unstructured data in its native format, enabling flexible analytics, AI, and ML workloads.

Key Benefits:

- **Scalability**: It stores vast amounts of raw data at a low cost.
- **Flexibility**: It supports various analytics, ML, and AI workloads.
- **Schema-on-read**: Unlike warehouses, data is structured when it is read and not when it is written.

Popular Data Lake Solutions: AWS S3, Azure Data Lake, Google Cloud Storage, Delta Lake

Data Pipelines and Workflow Orchestration

A **data pipeline** is an automated process for moving and transforming data from source to destination. It automates data movement, transformation, and processing across systems and results in efficient, reliable, and scalable data workflows.

Key Components:

- **Ingestion Layer:** Extracts data from sources (APIs, logs, databases)
- **Processing Layer:** Transforms data (cleansing, de-duplication, aggregation)
- **Storage Layer:** Stores processed data in warehouses or lakes

Workflow Orchestration Tools: ADF, Apache Airflow, Google Cloud Workflows and Cloud Compose automate scheduling and monitoring of data workflows.

Streaming Data Processing

Streaming data processing deals with real-time event-driven data such as IoT sensors, financial transactions, and social media feeds. The real-time ingestion, transformation, and analysis of continuous data streams using event-driven architectures and frameworks enable instant insights and decision-making.

Key Technologies:

- **Apache Kafka:** A real-time messaging system for event streaming
- **Apache Flink, Apache Spark Streaming:** Real-time data processing frameworks
- **AWS Kinesis, Google Pub/Sub:** Cloud-based event streaming platforms

Data Governance and Security

Data Governance involves **data quality, access control, compliance, and security** to ensure reliable and trustworthy data.

Key Practices:

- **Data Quality Management:** Ensuring completeness, consistency, and accuracy
- **Access Control:** Implementing role-based access controls (RBAC)
- **Data Lineage**: Tracking how data moves through the system
- **Compliance**: Ensuring adherence to PII, GDPR, HIPAA, and SOC 2 regulations

DataOps and Automation

DataOps applies **DevOps principles to data engineering** to bring about agility, automation, and collaboration.

Core Principles:

- **Continuous Integration and Continuous Deployment (CI/CD)** for data pipelines
- **Automated Testing and Monitoring** to ensure data reliability
- **Infrastructure as Code (IaC)** using Terraform or CloudFormation

Tools: dbt (Data Build Tool), Great Expectations (data validation), Monte Carlo (Data Observability).

Major Components and Activities

Data Pipelines and Workflow Orchestration: A data pipeline is a set of automated processes that move data from one system to another. It typically involves the following:

- **Data Ingestion:** Collecting data from diverse sources (APIs, databases, streaming platforms)
- **Data Transformation:** Cleaning, aggregating, and converting data into a usable format
- **Data Storage:** Depositing data into data warehouses, lakes, or marts for analysis

Workflow orchestration tools such as ADF and Apache Airflow allow data engineers to schedule, monitor, and manage pipelines. For instance, a pipeline might extract daily sales data from a transactional database, perform necessary data cleaning and transformations, and finally load the processed data into a data warehouse for reporting.

Practical Example: Imagine a retail company that wants to analyze daily sales performance. A data pipeline could:

- Use a scheduled job to extract sales records every night.
- Clean the data by handling missing values and normalizing currency formats.
- Aggregate data to generate metrics such as total daily sales and average transaction value.
- Load the results into a business intelligence tool for dashboarding and insights.

Two common paradigms in data processing are **ETL and ELT, which are explained as follows:**

ETL (Extract, Transform, Load) and Its Importance: ETL (Extract, Transform, Load) is a fundamental data integration process that moves data from multiple sources, processes it into a structured format, and loads it into a data warehouse or data lake for analysis.

- **Extract**: Collects raw data from various sources like databases, APIs, files, and logs
- **Transform**: Cleans, enriches, and standardizes the data to meet business requirements
- **Load**: Stores the transformed data in a target system (warehouse, lake, or analytical database)

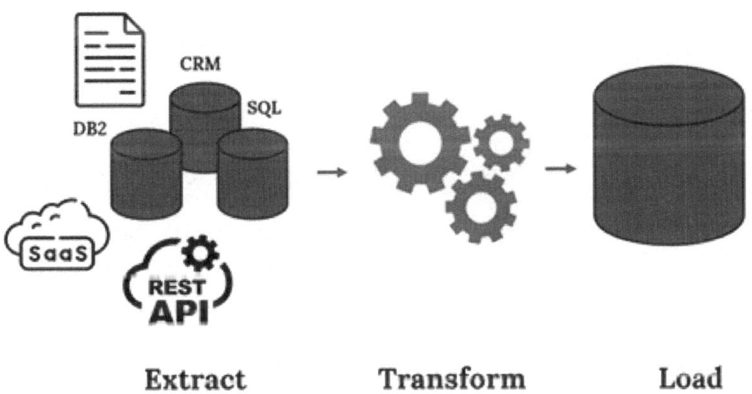

Figure 1.7: *Extract, Transform, Load*

Importance of ETL in Data Engineering

- **Data Consolidation**: Combines data from multiple sources into a single repository for a unified view
- **Data Quality and Accuracy**: Ensures that data is cleansed, validated, and formatted before analysis

- **Optimized Query Performance**: Prepares data for faster, more efficient querying in data warehouses like Snowflake, Redshift, or BigQuery
- **Supports Business Intelligence (BI) and Analytics:** Powers dashboards, reports, and predictive analytics for decision-making
- **Automated Workflows**: Enable scheduled, repeatable processes to keep data pipelines running efficiently

Popular ETL Tools: Apache, Informatica, Talend, AWS Glue, Azure Data Factory (ADF), and Google Dataflow.

Practical Example: A media streaming service might use an ELT approach by loading raw click stream data into a cloud data warehouse like BigQuery and then running SQL queries to transform and analyze viewer engagement.

ELT (Extract, Load, Transform) and Its Importance: This is a modern data integration process where raw data is first **extracted** from source systems, **loaded** directly into a data warehouse or data lake, and then **transformed** inside the destination system.

- **Extract:** Collects raw data from multiple sources (databases, APIs, cloud storage)
- **Load:** Stores the raw data in a **data warehouse (for example, Snowflake, BigQuery, Redshift) or a data lake** for scalable processing
- **Transform:** Performs data cleaning, aggregation, and structuring using the computing power of the warehouse or lake

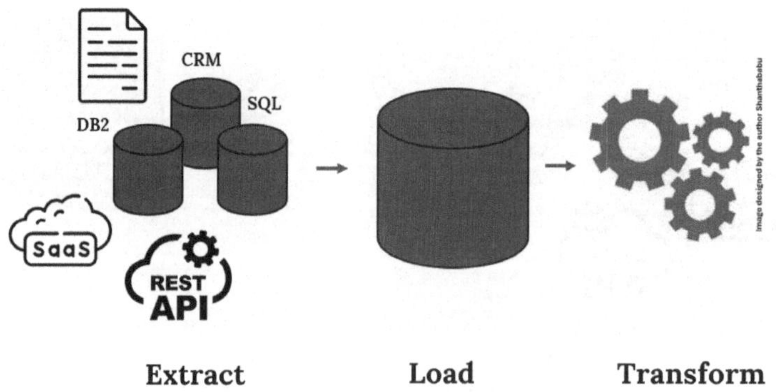

Figure 1.8: *Extract, Load, Transform*

Importance of ELT in Data Engineering

- **Faster Data Ingestion:** As transformation happens after loading, data is available for immediate use.
- **Scalability and Cost-Efficiency:** Leverages **cloud-based warehouses** (Snowflake, BigQuery) for distributed, cost-effective processing

- **Flexibility for Unstructured Data:** It is suitable for **semi-structured and unstructured data** (JSON, Parquet, Avro) that is commonly used in **data lakes.**
- **Enables Real-Time Analytics:** Supports **real-time data transformation** for faster insights
- **Better for Big Data and AI/ML Workflows:** Raw data is available for multiple transformations, which benefits AI and ML models.

Popular ELT Tools: dbt (data build tool), Google BigQuery, Snowflake, Amazon Redshift, Apache Spark, Azure Data Factory (ADF), Google Dataflow.

Comparison between ETL and ELT

The following table considers a comparison between ETL and ELT:

Features	ETL (Extract, Transform, Load)	ELT (Extract, Load, Transform)
Processing Order	Extract → Transform → Load	Extract → Load → Transform
Transformation Timing	Data is transformed before it is loaded into the target system.	Data is loaded first, then transformed inside the data warehouse or lake.
Data Storage	Structured data is stored in a Data Warehouse.	Raw data is stored in a Data Lake or Data Warehouse.
Performance	Slower, as transformation happens before loading	Faster, as raw data is immediately available
Scalability	Limited scalability, depends on ETL processing infrastructure	Highly scalable, leverages cloud-based processing
Use Case	Best for structured data, business intelligence, and reporting	Best for big data, real-time analytics, and ML
Best For	Traditional BI and analytics, smaller datasets	AI/ML pipelines, data lakes, large-scale analytics
Common Tools	Informatica, Talend, Apache NiFi, AWS Glue, Azure Data Factory	dbt, Google BigQuery, Snowflake, Amazon Redshift, Apache Spark

Table 1.4: *Comparison between ETL and ELT*

Practical Example: A **media streaming service** might use an **ETL** approach to generate daily **subscription reports**. It **extracts** structured data from MySQL (user subscriptions, payments), **transforms** it by aggregating watch time and revenue per user, and **loads** it into Snowflake for **BI dashboards**. This ensures high-quality, structured data for business intelligence and executive decision-making.

Data Quality, Governance, and Security

As data flows through pipelines, ensuring its accuracy, consistency, and security is crucial. Therefore, considering the following metrics is essential for this purpose:

- **Data Quality**: Implementing validation rules, de-duplication processes, and error-handling mechanisms
- **Data Governance**: Defining policies for data access, usage, and regulation compliance (for example, GDPR, HIPAA)
- **Security**: Protecting data at rest and in-transit through encryption, access controls, and audit logging

Practical Example: Consider the example of a global e-commerce platform that collects real-time data from website interactions, mobile apps, and customer service channels. Here is how data engineering will play a crucial role in this case:

- **Data Ingestion:** The platform uses tools like Apache Kafka or cloud-native services (for example, GCP Pub/Sub) to capture real-time streaming data from user activities.
- **Data Transformation:** An ETL pipeline cleans the data by removing duplicates, filling in missing values, and standardizing formats. It also aggregates data to compute key metrics like average session duration and conversion rates.
- **Data Storage:** The transformed data is stored in a cloud data warehouse (such as Google BigQuery or AWS Redshift) optimized for analytical queries, which enables the business to generate reports and dashboards quickly.
- **Analytics and Insights:** Data analysts and data scientists use this well-curated data to build predictive models that forecast demand trends and identify customer segments, while directly influencing marketing strategies and inventory management.

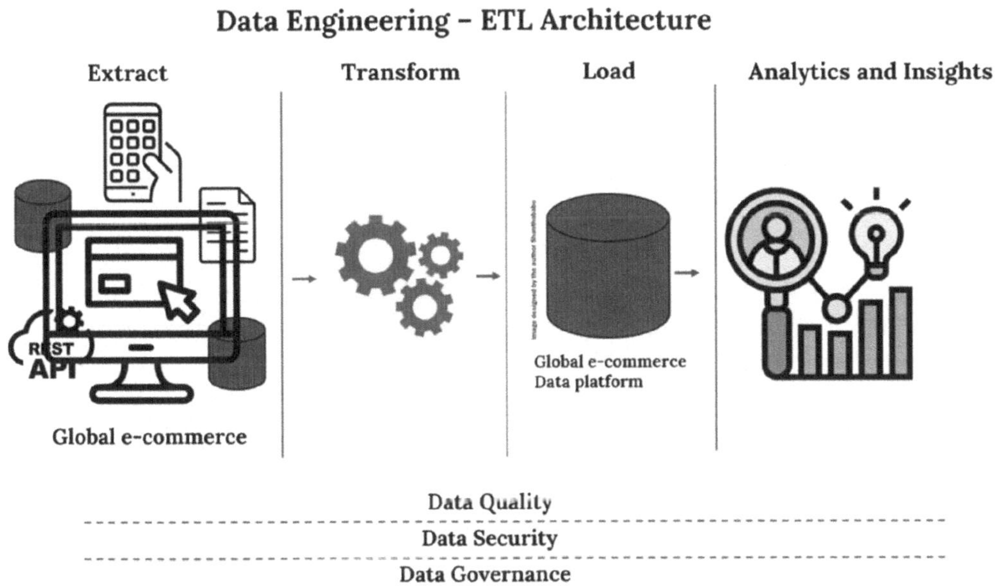

Figure 1.9: *ETL Architecture for Global E-Commerce*

This integrated data engineering process ensures that the e-commerce platform can operate efficiently and adapt to changing customer behaviors and market conditions.

Data Engineering in a Data-Driven Business Landscape

In today's digital economy, data engineering is the backbone of data-driven businesses, as it enables efficient data collection, storage, processing, and analysis. As companies generate massive volumes of data, a robust data engineering framework is essential to turn raw data into actionable insights for decision-making, automation, and innovation.

In a data-driven business landscape, data engineering is not just about managing data but empowering businesses to innovate, compete, and grow. With the right tools and strategies, organizations can unlock the full potential of their data and drive meaningful outcomes.

Impact on Business Performance

- **Faster Decision-Making**: Enables real-time Business Intelligence (BI) dashboards
- **Cost Optimization**: Reduces storage and compute costs with a cloud-based architecture
- **Personalized Customer Experiences**: AI-driven recommendations and targeted marketing

- **Operational Efficiency**: Automates repetitive tasks, improving productivity

Industry Use Cases

There are many industry use cases; let us explore a few of them here:

- **Finance:** Financial institutions leverage data pipelines to detect fraudulent transactions by analyzing real-time patterns, which reduces risk and ensures compliance.
- **Healthcare:** Hospitals and research institutions use data engineering to integrate patient records, genomic data, and treatment outcomes to support both clinical decision-making and research.
- **Retail:** Retailers harness data pipelines for inventory management, dynamic pricing strategies, and customer behavior analysis to improve operational efficiency and customer satisfaction.

On-Premises Data Engineering

On-premises data engineering refers to managing and processing data within an organization's private infrastructure rather than using cloud-based solutions. This approach is essential for high-security, compliance-driven, and low-latency environments such as finance, healthcare, and government organizations.

Key Components of On-Premises Data Engineering

- **Data Storage:** Uses on-prem databases (for example, PostgreSQL, MySQL, Oracle, SQL Server) and HDFS for big data storage.
- **ETL Pipelines:** Apache NiFi, Talend, and Informatica for data extraction, transformation, and loading.
- **Big Data Processing:** Apache Hadoop and Apache Spark are used for distributed computing on large datasets.
- **Workflow Orchestration:** Apache Airflow, Luigi for scheduling and automating data pipelines.
- **Streaming and Event Processing**: Apache Kafka, Flink for real-time data processing.
- **Data Security and Compliance:** Implements role-based access control (RBAC), encryption, and audit logging to ensure regulatory compliance (GDPR, HIPAA, SOC 2)

Advantages of On-Premises Data Engineering

- **Full Control Over Data and Security**: Ideal for industries with strict compliance requirements.

- **Low Latency Processing**: Data stays within the local network, which reduces processing delays.
- **Customizable Infrastructure**: Organizations can fine-tune hardware and software according to their needs.
- **Cost Optimization for Large-Scale Workloads**: It avoids long-term cloud subscription fees.

Challenges and Considerations

- **High Initial Infrastructure Costs:** Requires upfront investment in hardware and maintenance
- **Scalability Limitations:** Expanding on-prem infrastructure takes time compared to cloud auto-scaling
- **Operational Complexity:** Requires dedicated IT teams for system administration, updates, and security patches
- **Limited Disaster Recovery Options:** For redundancy, on-site backups or hybrid solutions must be implemented.

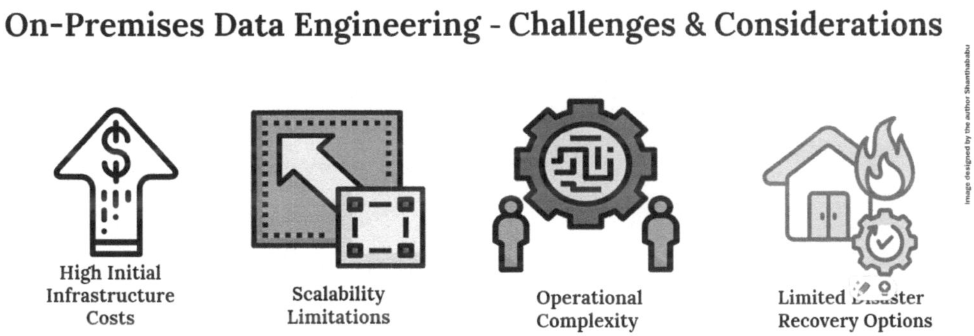

Figure 1.10: *On-Premises Data Engineering: Challenges and Considerations*

Cloud Platforms for Data Engineering

Why the Cloud? Cloud platforms provide scalability, cost savings, managed services, and AI-driven insights, which makes them the preferred choice for modern data engineering workflows. Businesses can accelerate innovation while maintaining security, reliability, and efficiency.

The rise of cloud computing has revolutionized data engineering by offering the following advantages:

- **Scalability and Elasticity**: Ability to handle vast data volumes without the need for significant upfront hardware investment

- Cloud platforms auto-scale based on workload demands, which eliminates hardware constraints.
- Enables horizontal scaling for distributed data processing.
- Examples include AWS Auto Scaling, Azure Scale Sets, and GCP Autoscaler.

* **High Availability and Disaster Recovery:** High availability and disaster recovery are significant advantages of cloud-based data engineering.
    - Multi-region backups, automatic failover, and redundancy ensure the reliability of data.
    - **Example**: Google Cloud Storage's geo-redundancy.
* **Cost Efficiency**: Pay-as-you-go models that reduce capital expenditure
    - There is no upfront investment in infrastructure; businesses pay only for what they use.
    - Optimized storage costs with tiered pricing models (for example, Amazon S3 Glacier, Azure Blob Storage Archive)

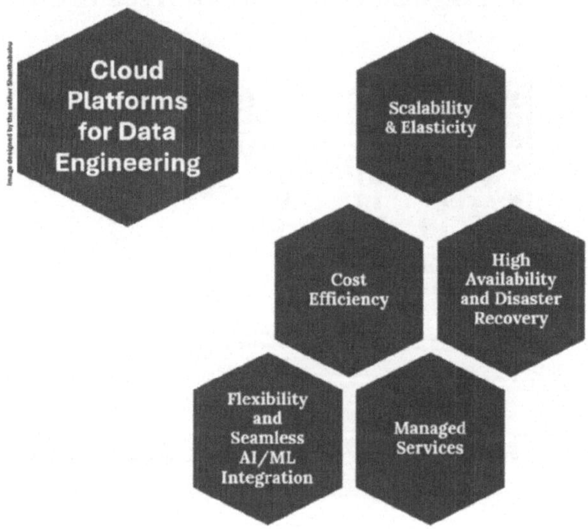

Figure 1.11: *Cloud Platform for Data Engineering*

* **Managed Services**: Reduced operational overhead with services like managed databases, serverless compute, and integrated analytics tools
    - Cloud providers offer managed ETL, data warehousing, and ML solutions.
    - Reduces operational overhead, which allows engineers to focus on data workflows

    - **Examples**: AWS Glue, Google Dataflow, Azure Synapse Analytics.

- **Flexibility and Seamless AI/ML Integration**: On-demand resources that can be scaled up or down based on workload.
    - Native support for ML with automated model training and deployment.
    - **Examples**: AWS SageMaker, Google Vertex AI, Azure ML.

Overview of Leading Cloud Platforms

The three major cloud providers: Google Cloud Platform (GCP), Amazon Web Services (AWS), and Microsoft Azure offer robust solutions for data engineering, which are detailed as follows:

- **Google Cloud Platform (GCP):** Renowned for its serverless and highly scalable solutions, GCP provides services such as BigQuery for analytics, Dataflow for stream and batch processing, and Pub/Sub for messaging. Its tight integration with ML tools further enhances data-driven insights.
- **Amazon Web Services (AWS):** AWS is known for its breadth of services, including Redshift for data warehousing, Glue for ETL, and Kinesis for real-time data streaming. The AWS ecosystem supports a wide variety of use cases, from IoT to enterprise analytics.
- **Microsoft Azure:** Azure offers tools like Azure Synapse Analytics, Data Factory, and Stream Analytics. Its deep integration with other Microsoft products makes it an attractive option for organizations that are already embedded in the Microsoft ecosystem.

GCP and its Unique Advantages

Overview of GCP's Data Engineering Services: GCP has positioned itself as a leader in big data processing, while emphasizing scalability, simplicity, and innovation. Its key services include:

- **BigQuery:** A fully managed, serverless data warehouse that supports SQL queries on petabytes of data in seconds. BigQuery is particularly effective for interactive analytics and large-scale data exploration.
- **Dataflow:** A unified programming model for both stream and batch data processing. Built on Apache Beam, Dataflow allows data engineers to create efficient pipelines without having to manage the underlying infrastructure.
- **Pub/Sub is a messaging service designed for real-time analytics and event-driven systems.** It facilitates reliable and asynchronous communication between decoupled systems.

- **Dataproc:** It is a managed Spark and Hadoop service that simplifies big data processing and analytics tasks by automating cluster management.

Practical Example: Building a Data Pipeline on GCP

Let us walk through a scenario where a company needs to process and analyze streaming data from IoT devices:

- **Data Ingestion:** IoT devices send telemetry data to a GCP Pub/Sub topic. Pub/Sub efficiently handles high-throughput, low-latency messaging.
- **Data Processing:** A Dataflow pipeline developed using Apache Beam consumes messages from Pub/Sub. The pipeline performs necessary transformations such as filtering out noise, aggregating sensor readings, and converting data formats.
- **Data Storage and Analysis:** The processed data is loaded into BigQuery, where it is stored in a structured format. Analysts can then run SQL queries to generate real-time dashboards and historical trend analyses.
- **Visualization and Insights:** Integration with tools like Google Data Studio(Looker Studio) allows users to create interactive reports that drive business decisions.

GCP Advantages

GCP's advantages in the context of big data processing include:

- **Serverless Architecture:** Services like BigQuery and Dataflow reduce the need for manual infrastructure management and allow engineers to focus on developing pipelines.
- **Scalability:** GCP's infrastructure can automatically scale to handle varying data loads, which makes it ideal for real-time analytics.
- **Cost Efficiency:** Pay-as-you-go pricing models and managed services minimize operational costs.
- **Innovation and Integration:** Deep integration with Google's AI and machine learning services (such as TensorFlow and AutoML) facilitates the transition from descriptive to predictive analytics.

Comparing GCP, AWS, and Azure for Data Engineering

AWS offers a comprehensive suite of data engineering tools such as:

- **Amazon Redshift:** A fast, scalable data warehouse solution

- **AWS Glue:** A managed ETL service that simplifies data preparation
- **Amazon Kinesis:** For real-time data streaming and analytics
- **Amazon EMR:** A managed Hadoop and Spark service for big data processing

The AWS ecosystem is robust, with a vast array of complementary services. However, the learning curve and integration complexity can be steeper compared to GCP's streamlined, serverless approach.

Azure Data Engineering Solutions: Microsoft Azure provides a comprehensive suite of data engineering tools such as:

- **Azure Synapse Analytics:** An integrated analytics service that combines big data and data warehousing
- **Azure Data Factory:** A cloud-based ETL service to build data integration solutions
- **Azure Stream Analytics:** Real-time data streaming and event processing

Azure shines in environments already integrated with Microsoft products, but its ecosystem may not offer the same level of serverless simplicity found in GCP.

Comparative Analysis: GCP vs. AWS vs. Azure

The following table provides a comparative analysis of GCP, AWS, and Azure:

Features/ Criteria	GCP	AWS	Azure
Serverless Architecture	Highly advanced with BigQuery and Dataflow	Comparatively limited serverless options; requires more manual setup	Serverless options exist but are less mature
Ease of Use	Streamlined and intuitive, ideal for rapid prototyping	Comprehensive but can be complex	Seamless for Microsoft environments but variable
Scalability	Automatically scales to handle massive data volumes	Robust scaling options with a broad service portfolio	Excellent scalability, especially for hybrid scenarios
Cost Efficiency	Competitive pricing with pay-as-you-go and managed services	Broad pricing models; cost management can be challenging	Competitive pricing: Benefits for Microsoft licensees
Innovation	Tight integration with AI/ML tools and continuous innovation	Extensive ecosystem with frequent new releases	Integrated with Microsoft's enterprise solutions

***Table 1.5:** Comparative Analysis of GCP, AWS, and Azure*

Building Robust Data Pipelines

Here, we will discuss building robust data pipelines in terms of practical considerations such as architectural components and best practices.

Practical Considerations

Architectural Components

When designing a data pipeline, consider the following components:

- **Data Ingestion:** Selecting appropriate tools (for example, Pub/Sub for real-time, Cloud Storage for batch uploads)
- **Data Processing:** Deciding between stream processing (Dataflow, Kinesis) versus batch processing (Dataproc, EMR)
- **Data Storage:** Choosing storage solutions based on access patterns—data lakes (Cloud Storage, S3) versus data warehouses (BigQuery, Redshift, Synapse)
- **Data Access and Analytics:** Integrating with business intelligence tools, SQL engines, and Machine Learning (ML) frameworks

Best Practices and Challenges

Data Quality and Consistency

- **Validation:** Incorporate data validation steps to catch anomalies early on in the pipeline.
- **Monitoring:** Logging and monitoring tools can help in tracking pipeline health and performance (Stackdriver on GCP, CloudWatch on AWS, Monitor on Azure).

Error Handling and Resilience

- **Retry Mechanisms:** Implement retries and fallbacks for transient errors.
- **Data Lineage:** Maintain precise records of data provenance to troubleshoot issues and ensure auditability.

Security and Governance

- **Access Controls:** Enforce strict role-based access control (RBAC) and encryption protocols.
- **Compliance:** Ensure that data-handling practices comply with regulatory standards such as PII, GDPR and HIPAA.

Future Trends in Data Engineering

As the field evolves, data engineering is likely to embrace several emerging trends such as:

- **Serverless and Managed Services:** Continued innovation in serverless architectures will further reduce operational overhead.
- **Real-Time Analytics:** The growing demand for immediate insights will drive improvements in streaming data platforms.
- **Machine Learning Integration:** Closer integration between data pipelines and machine learning workflows will enable predictive and prescriptive analytics.
- **DataOps and Automation:** Adopt DataOps practices to improve collaboration, agility, and the continuous delivery of data products.

Conclusion

This chapter explains Big Data and its significance in today's digital landscape. Big Data drives innovation and requires meticulous data engineering to manage, process, and analyze vast amounts of structured and unstructured data.

We explored the evolution of data engineering, which has transitioned through multiple stages, while addressing key challenges such as scalability, real-time processing, and governance. Modern organizations rely on data engineering to optimize data pipelines, storage, and analytics for decision-making.

We understood the key concepts in data engineering, including ETL/ELT pipelines, data warehousing, streaming data processing, and cloud-based solutions. Businesses can operate with on-premises data engineering, offering security and control, or adopt cloud platforms like AWS, Azure, and GCP for scalability and cost efficiency.

Among cloud providers, Google Cloud Platform (GCP) offers unique advantages such as BigQuery, Dataflow, and AI-driven analytics, which make it a strong competitor to AWS and Azure for data engineering workloads.

In the next chapter, we will discuss Google Cloud Platform Essentials, as well as how to set up a GCP account and navigate the console. We will also provide an overview of GCP's core services in relation to Big Data and analytics.

CHAPTER 2
Google Cloud Platform Essentials

Introduction

In the previous chapter, we introduced Big Data and understood its importance in today's digital world. We explored and understood how data engineering has evolved to handle challenges such as scalability, real-time processing, and governance. We reviewed key concepts like ETL/ELT, data warehousing, streaming, and cloud-based architectures, while noting that organizations can use on-premises systems or cloud platforms such as AWS, Azure, or GCP. We also explored GCP's strengths like BigQuery, Dataflow, and AI-driven analytics, which make it an important option for processing Big Data workloads.

This chapter provides a comprehensive understanding of how to work with Google Cloud Platform (GCP) and elaborates how to set up your first GCP account and navigate the GCP Console Dashboard. It explains the significance of projects in GCP and how they relate to organizations, billing accounts, payment profiles, and subaccounts. The chapter also covers essential cost-management features such as budgets, alerts, and billing exports, along with a cost table overview for GCP. Additionally, it explores Identity and Access Management (IAM) for secure access control and discusses how to design a scalable multi-project architecture suitable for enterprise applications. Finally, the section concludes with an overview of GCP's core services that support Big Data processing and analytics.

By the end of this chapter, you will be equipped with the foundational knowledge to effectively use GCP.

Structure

In this chapter, we will discuss the following topics:

- Understanding the GCP Account
- Setting Up Your First GCP Account
- Understanding the GCP Console Dashboard
- Project in GCP and Its Significance
- Understanding GCP Billing
- Relationships between
    - Organizations-Projects-Cloud Billing Accounts
    - Payment Profiles
- Understanding Subaccounts in GCP
- Budget, Alerts, and Billing Export
- Cost Table for Google Cloud Platform (GCP)
- Understanding Identity and Access Management (IAM) in GCP
- Designing a Multi-Project Architecture for Enterprise-Scale Applications on GCP
- Overview of GCP's Core Services for Big Data and Analytics

Understanding the GCP Account

A GCP (**Google Cloud Platform**) account is your gateway to accessing Google's cloud services. It allows individuals, developers, and organizations to **build, deploy, and manage applications and data infrastructure** globally on Google's distributed cloud environment.

Many powerful Google cloud computing services are available to demonstrate various activities, along with a scalable, secure, and globally distributed platform environment. We will discuss them in the upcoming chapters.

We need a GCP account for several reasons that are detailed as follows:

- **Access Powerful Cloud Services:** It gives you access to Google's robust infrastructure, including computing, storage, databases, networking, and AI services, without needing physical servers globally in Google's distributed cloud environment. It is cost effective and comes with ease of implementation of cloud platforms for a customer's digital transformation needs. This helps them run their business without any intervention and is highly scalable and secured.

- **Scalable Resources:** While the data platform builds and manages applications and data infrastructure, it might expand depending on the size of the volume of data. As all these services are paid, cost efficiency is a significant factor to consider. Based on the demand, we can expand the environment and computations. GCP supports scalability as your needs grow and allows you to process a large volume of data, while encouraging sustainability.
- **Big Data and AI Capabilities:** As we discussed the various significances of Big Data in Chapter 1, we know that GCP offers powerful Big Data and AI capabilities through services like **BigQuery** for large-scale analytics and **Vertex AI** for end-to-end machine learning workflows. These tools enable real-time insights and predictive modeling, as well as result in intelligent automation at scale.
- **Global Reach and High Performance:** It is established that we need high-performance systems and a global reach environment to run heavy and critical AI models such as ML, DL, and computer vision. These systems have critical applications in banking, financial, insurance, healthcare and retail domains. As client businesses run on the typical infrastructure that should perform well without any obstructions, Google powers apps like Gmail, YouTube, and Google Search to ensure speed, reliability, and availability.

***Figure 2.1:** GCP Capabilities*

- **Secure and Compliant:** Google Cloud provides built-in security, compliance, and identity management features to protect your data, maintain it, and demonstrate data analytics and AI models. GCP ensures security and compliance through IAM roles, encryption, VPCs, and audit logging. It supports global standards such as GDPR, HIPAA, and ISO to protect data and meet regulatory requirements.

Setting Up Your First GCP Account

Step 1: Create a Google Account (if you do not have one).

To access GCP, you need a **Google account**. You can use the same login if you have used Gmail or other Google services before.

To create a Google account:

- Go to: https://accounts.google.com/signup

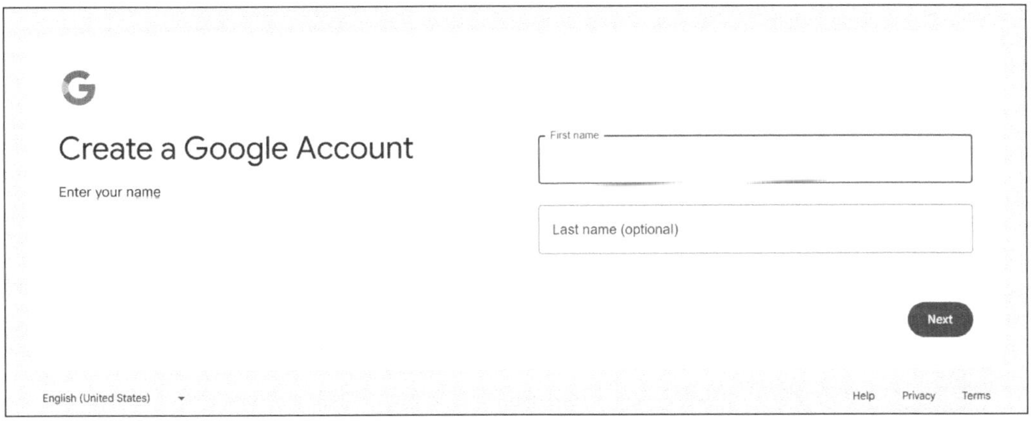

Figure 2.2: *Creating a Google Account*

Step 2: Sign Up for Google Cloud Platform (GCP).

a. Visit the GCP homepage at https://cloud.google.com.

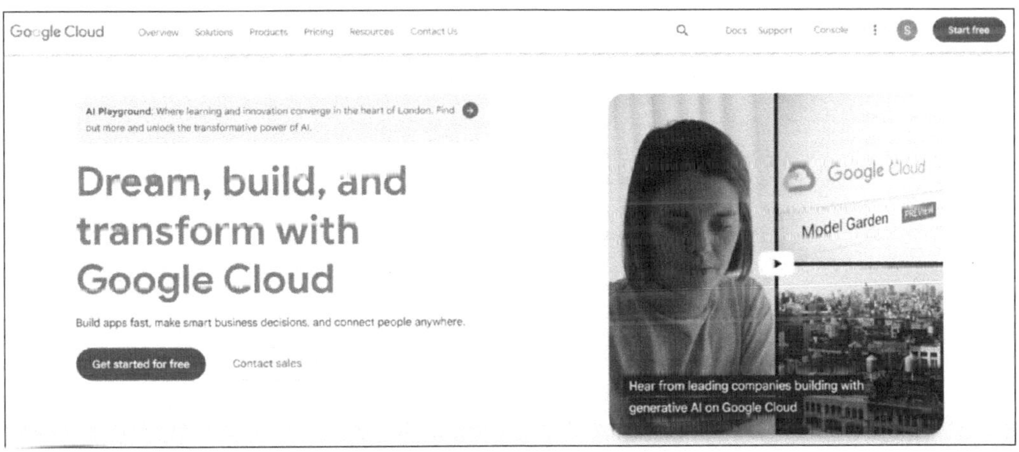

Figure 2.3: *Signing up for GCP*

Click **"`Get started for free`"** or **"`Try Free`"** button. You must complete the successive steps to enter account information.

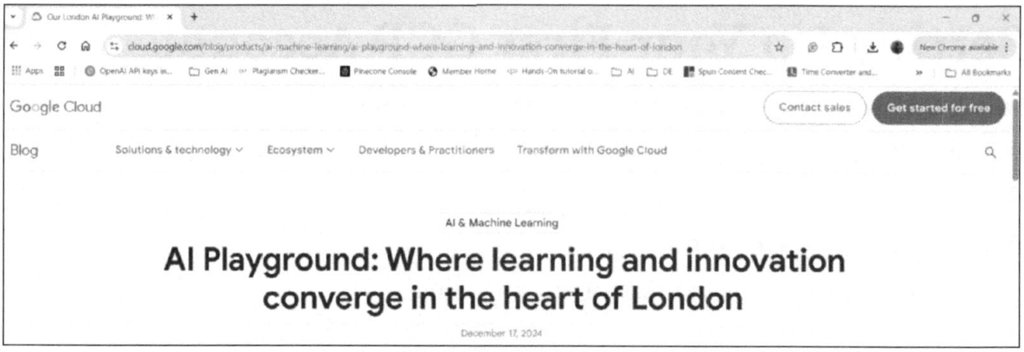

Figure 2.4: *Accessing GCP*

b. Refer to the first step for account information and select the country where you are based.

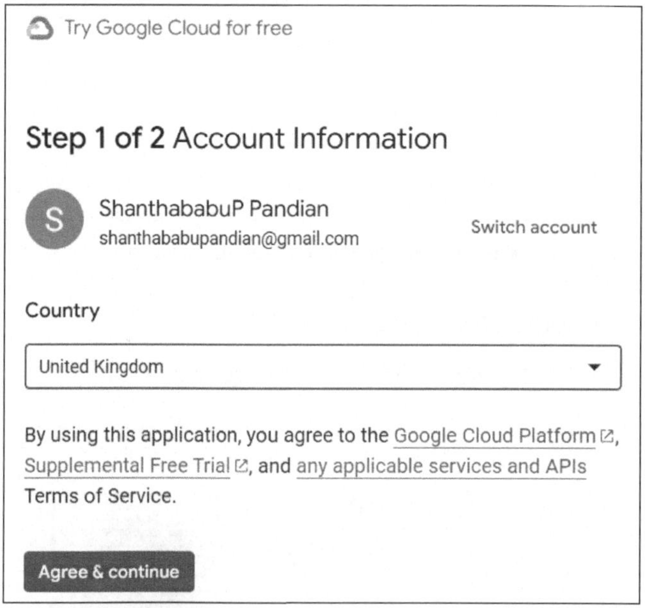

Figure 2.5: *Entering Account Information*

c. Click the "**`Start free`**" button to configure the payment profile. You can create a payment profile from an individual or a business perspective.

Individual Profile: The individual payment profile is intended for personal use. Here, billing is typically associated with a single user who manages payments for services like Google Cloud. This type of profile is ideal for freelancers, developers, or anyone using Google services on a personal basis. All billing, receipts, and tax information are recorded under the individual's name.

Business Profile: Companies or organisations use a business payments profile for centralized billing, which allows multiple authorized users to work on projects. It also supports role-based access and account delegation. It is designed to handle tax information and invoicing at the business level, which makes it suitable for managing corporate expenses and financial records.

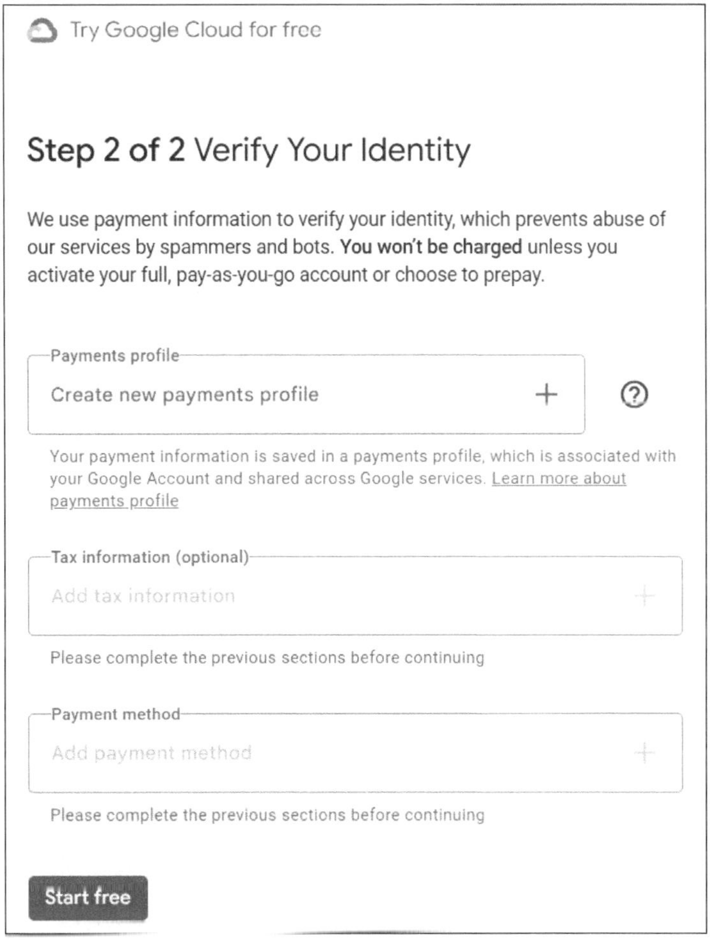

Figure 2.6: *Verifying User Identity on GCP*

d. Configure the payment profile and click "**`Create`**".

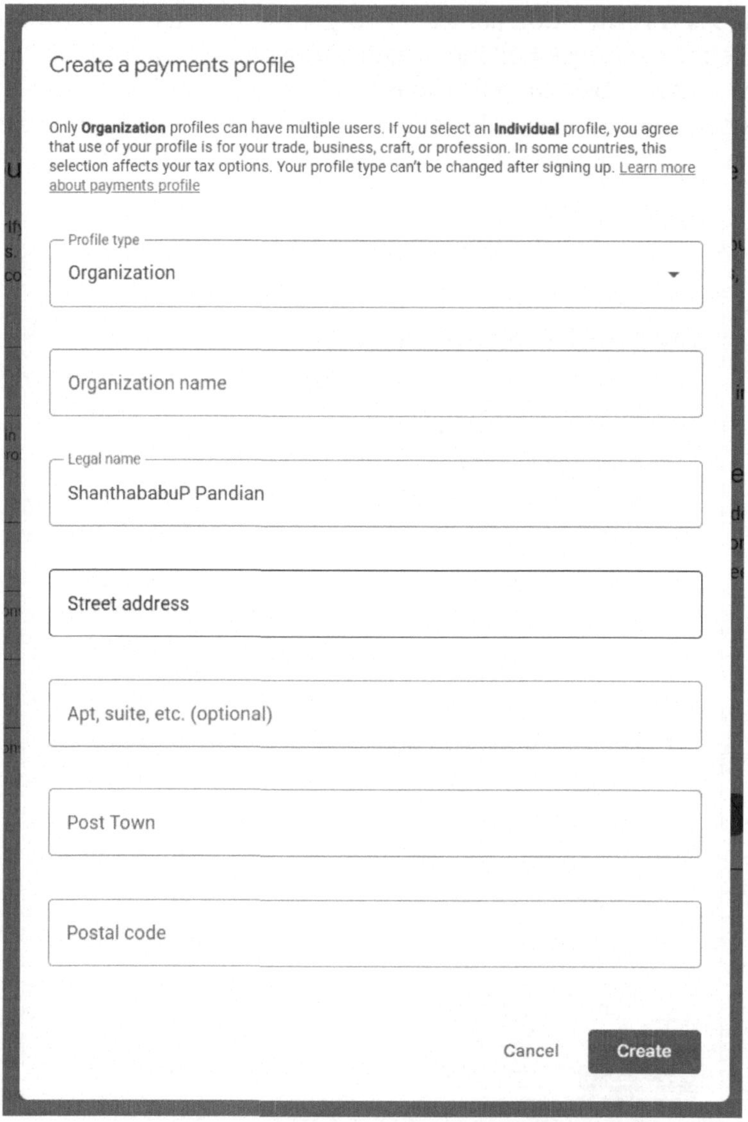

Figure 2.7: *Creating a Payments Profile*

e. Configure the payment method, click "**`Start Free`**", and provide your credit/debit card details. Enter billing information (a valid credit/debit card is required for identity verification, but Google also offers $300 in free credits for the first 90 days). You may have a look at your currently available free credits in the Google website.

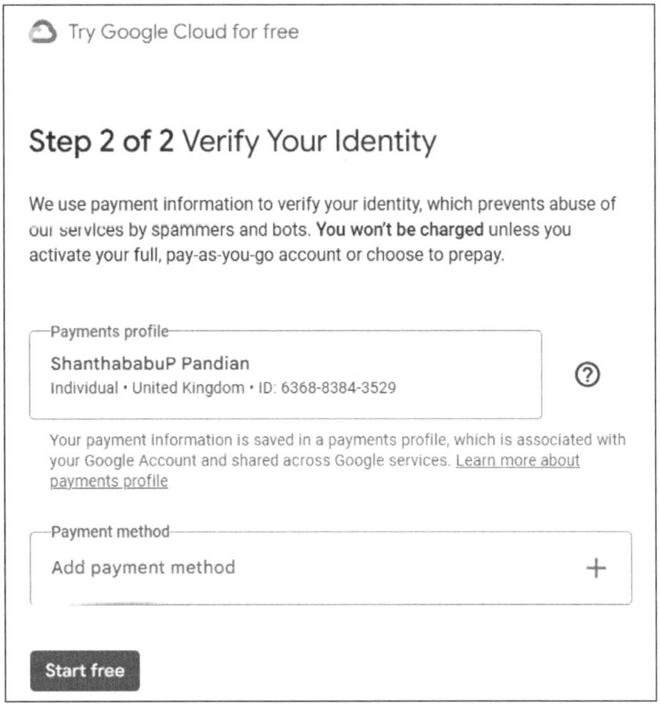

Figure 2.8: *Adding Payment Method*

f. Once you click "**Start Free**", the portal will take you to the "**Additional Details Configuration**" page. Then, click "**Done**".

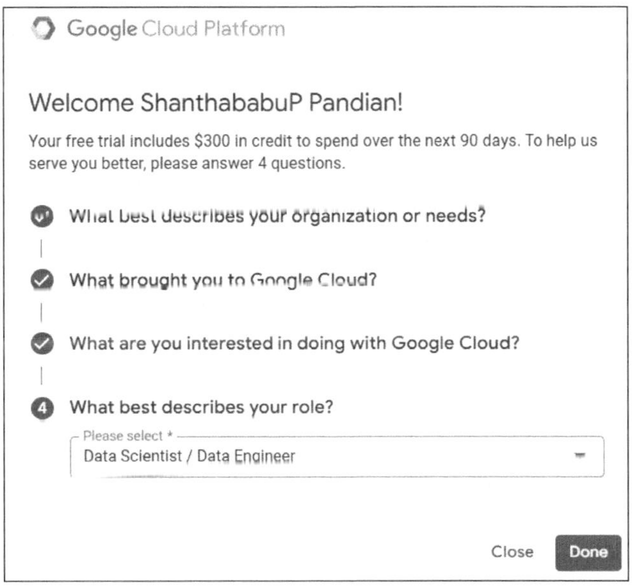

Figure 2.9: *Additional Configuration*

g. This portal takes you to the GCP Ready-to-Use page, as shown in *Figure* 2.10.

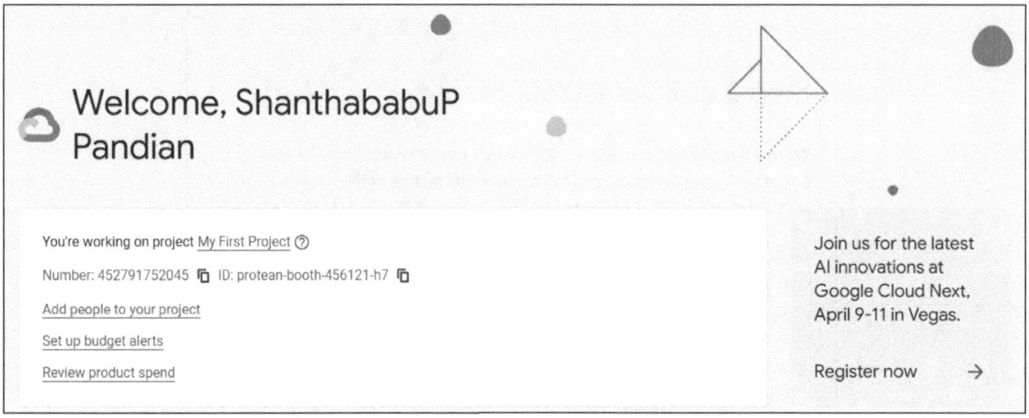

Figure 2.10: *A Ready-to-Use GCP Interface*

h. Click "**`My First Project`**", as shown in *Figure* 2.10. The portal will direct you to the page shown in *Figure* 2.11.

Figure 2.11: *GCP Master Page*

> **Note:** *You will* **not be charged** *until your credits run out or you explicitly upgrade to a paid account.*

i. Once your account is ready, go to the console directly using the https://console.cloud.google.com.

You can now access the **GCP Console Dashboard**, which gives you an overview of your projects, resources, and billing details.

Understanding the GCP Console Dashboard

We can see the following features in the dashboard for every successful login. The Google Cloud Console dashboard is shown in *Figure 2.11*.

Project Info: As you can see in the following image, an "**`Add people to this project`**" button is present, which allows for collaboration and provides access to people with different roles.

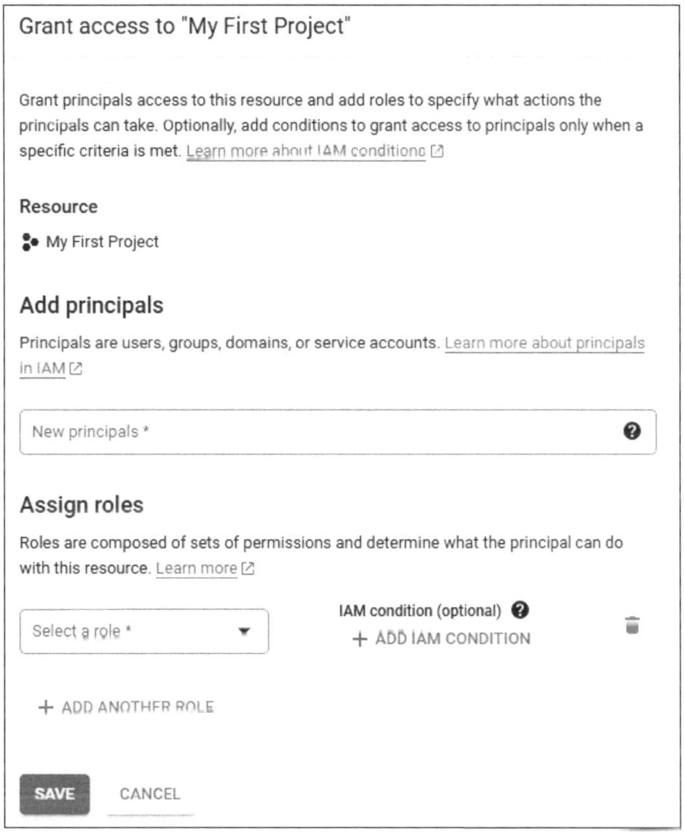

Figure 2.12: *Granting Access to the Project*

APIs Section: The dashboard's APIs section features a graph showing the number of requests per second. The link with the graph leads users to the APIs overview for further configuration and monitoring, as shown in *Figure 2.11*. Click "**`Go to API overview`**", and the portal will take you to the page shown in *Figure 2.13*:

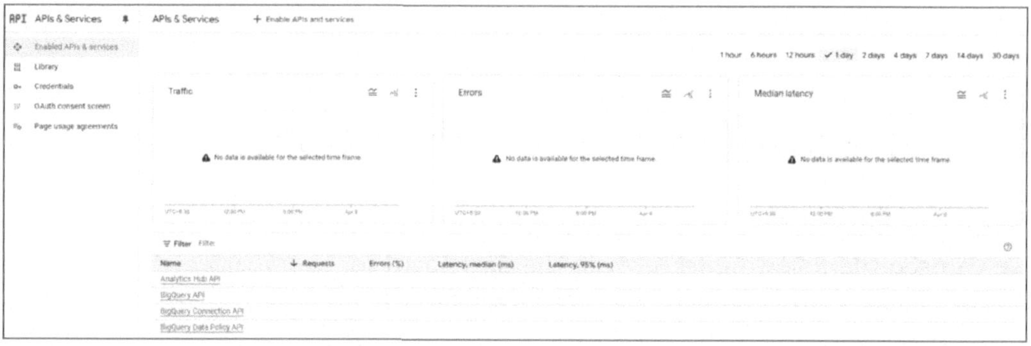

***Figure* 2.13:** APIs *Overview in* GCP

The "**`Enabled APIs & Services`**" section under the **`APIs & Services`** menu in the Google Cloud Console page monitors the usage and performance metrics of APIs enabled for a Google Cloud project.

The central panel displays the following **three metric charts**:

- **Traffic**: This chart shows the volume of requests made to the enabled APIs over a selected period.
- **Errors**: This chart indicates any failed API calls or responses with error codes.
- **Median Latency**: This shows the average time for an API request to be processed and responded to.

Below the charts is a table listing the currently **enabled APIs**, along with the Requests, Errors (%), Latency (ms), and Latency 95% ms) parameters for each API in the list. Some of the key APIs are listed here:

- Analytics Hub API
- BigQuery API
- BigQuery Connection API
- BigQuery Data Policy API

Google Cloud Platform Status: To the right, you will see a Google Cloud Platform status card that reports the status of the services. If everything is fine, it will display "**`All services are normal`**" and show a button that links to the Cloud status dashboard. It provides more detailed insights into system health.

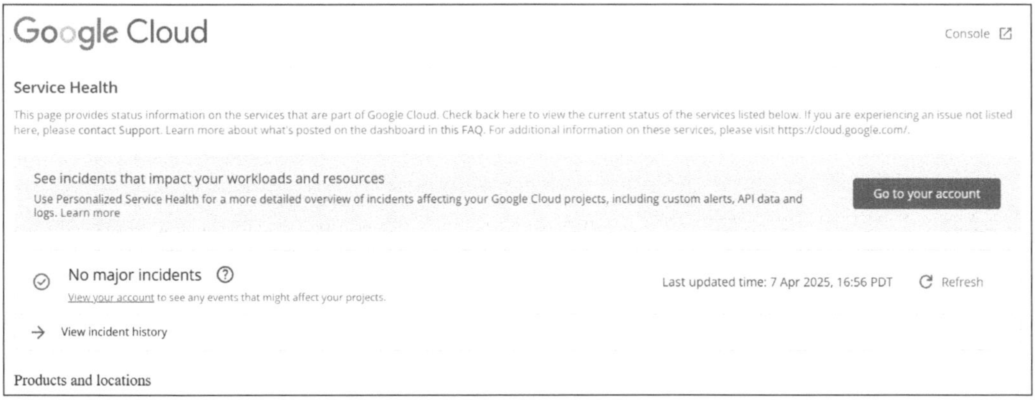

Figure 2.14: *Google Cloud Platform Status*

Billing Section: The Billing section reports an estimated charge of GBP £x.xx for the billing period from **`<<Month>>`** **`<<Date>>`** to **`<<Month>>`** **`<<Date>>`**, **`<<Year>>`**. It includes a button to take a billing tour and a link to view detailed charges.

Figure 2.15: *GCP View Detailing Billing Charges*

Monitoring Panel: The adjacent Monitoring panel provides essential operational tools such as **creating a custom dashboard, setting alerting policies**, and **creating uptime checks**. There also exists a direct link to access all monitoring dashboards.

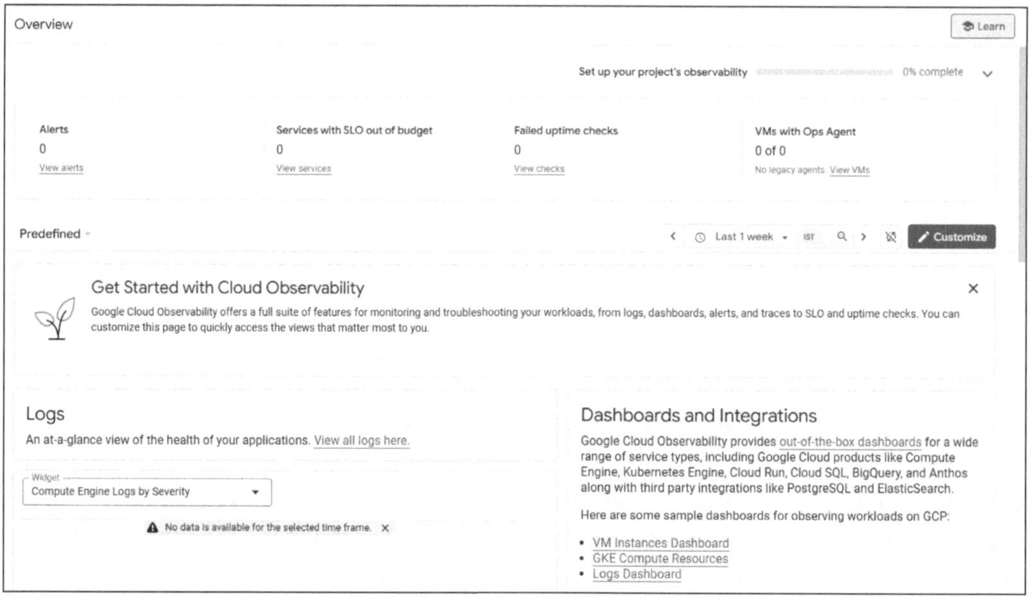

Figure 2.16: *GCP Monitoring Dashboards*

Error Reporting Section: Here, the dashboard displays several detected errors and prompts users to learn how to set up error reporting with a help link.

Getting Started Panel: This panel presents various quick-start options and onboarding activities. These include exploring and enabling APIs, deploying a prebuilt solution, adding logging to running apps, monitoring errors, VM QuickStart, creating a Cloud Storage bucket, and setting up a Cloud Run function. It also includes a prompt to install the Cloud SDK and a link to explore all tutorials.

Figure 2.17: *GCP Getting Started Panel*

Resources Panel: The Resources panel provides convenient shortcuts to widely used Google Cloud services that are listed as follows:

- BigQuery (for data warehousing and analytics)
- SQL (managed MySQL, PostgreSQL, and SQL Server)
- Compute Engine (VMs, GPUs, TPUs, and Disks)
- Storage (multi-class multi-region object storage)
- Cloud Functions (event-driven serverless functions)
- Cloud Run (a fully managed application platform).

News Section: The News section presents updates relevant to the cloud ecosystem.

On the left side, the navigation sidebar includes sections like **Cloud Hub, Cloud Overview, Solutions, and Recently Visited (marked as "NEW").**

The sidebar also showcases **Pinned Products**, including frequently used services such as **APIs and Services, Billing, IAM and Admin, Marketplace, Vertex AI, Compute Engine, Kubernetes Engine, Cloud Storage, BigQuery, VPC Network, Cloud Run, SQL, Security, and Google Maps Platform.**

At the top of the interface is a project selector showing the current project name "XYZ" and a search bar that lets users search for resources, documentation, products, and more.

Under the user avatar in the top-right corner, user interface elements include a cloud shell, account controls, and settings options.

Project in GCP and Its Significance

In the Google Cloud Platform, a project is the core organizational entity used to group and manage all Google Cloud resources and services. Think of it as a **container/ package** that holds everything you build and run on GCP for a project-specific.

A **GCP Project** is a **logical namespace** for organizing cloud resources such as virtual machines, storage buckets, databases, APIs, and networking configurations. It acts as a boundary for **permissions**, **billing**, **quotas**, and **resource isolation**.

Each project has:

- Project Name: A readable and valid name
- Project **ID**: A unique identifier across GCP (used in APIs)
- Project **Number**: A system-generated numeric identifier
- Associated **billing account** and **IAM policy**

Significance of a Project in GCP

- **Resource Management:** Every GCP resource (VM, Cloud Storage, BigQuery, and so on) must belong to a specific project. This allows you to organize and manage resources independently for different applications, teams, and environments (for example, dev, test, prod).
- **Access Control with IAM:** IAM (Identity and Access Management) policies are applied at the project level. This lets you control who can access resources within a project and is ideal for ensuring secure access and enforcing the principle of least privilege.
- **Billing and Cost Tracking:** Projects are linked to billing accounts, which makes it easy to track spending per project. You can create budgets, alerts, and cost exports for individual projects.
- **Quota Enforcement:** Google Cloud sets quotas and limits at the project level to protect against unexpected usage and manage resource availability across customers.
- **Audit Logging and Monitoring:** Projects enable centralized audit logs, error reporting, and monitoring dashboards, which helps with security compliance, debugging, and operations.
- **API and Service Management:** You can enable or disable APIs per project, which provides better control and isolation of services.
- **Isolation Between Projects:** Projects are isolated from each other. A mistake or misconfiguration in one project doesn't affect the others, which makes it ideal for multi-environment setups (for example, dev versus prod).

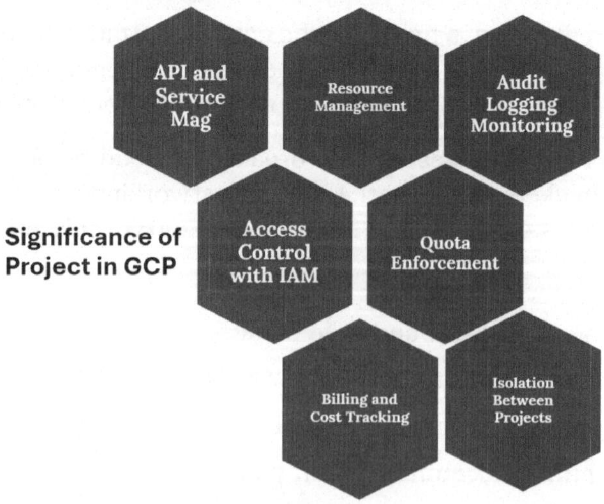

Figure 2.18: *Significance of a Project in GCP*

Understanding GCP Billing

In **Google Cloud Platform (GCP)**, billing is a fundamental component that tracks your resource usage, calculates costs, and manages payments for the services you use. Each GCP project must be linked to a billing account, which serves as the financial entity that is responsible for covering the expenses of the cloud resources consumed.

These billing accounts can be either self-service (paid via **credit or debit card**) or invoiced (suitable for enterprises with negotiated agreements). A single billing account can be associated with multiple projects, which allows for centralized cost management across teams or departments.

GCP offers budgeting and alerting tools to help manage costs effectively. You can set spending limits for each project and configure alerts that notify you via email or Pub/Sub when your expenditure crosses certain thresholds, such as **50%, 90%, or 100%** of your budget.

This proactive monitoring prevents unexpected billing surprises. GCP also provides detailed billing reports and a Cost Table that allows you to analyze costs by service (like **BigQuery, Compute Engine**) or by **project**, which helps you identify usage patterns and opportunities to optimize.

For advanced financial tracking, GCP enables billing data export to **BigQuery**, which allows users to build custom dashboards using tools like **Looker Studio**. This helps teams monitor and forecast their spending with greater precision. Billing operations are tightly integrated with Identity and **Access Management (IAM),** which grants fine-grained control over who can view or manage billing data. Roles such as **Billing Account Viewer** or **Billing Account Administrator** can be assigned to ensure secure and appropriate access.

GCP Billing is not just about invoicing; it is a comprehensive cost governance, optimization, and accountability system across your cloud environment. For effective cloud cost management, using features like budgets, alerts, cost analysis tools, and access controls in tandem is important.

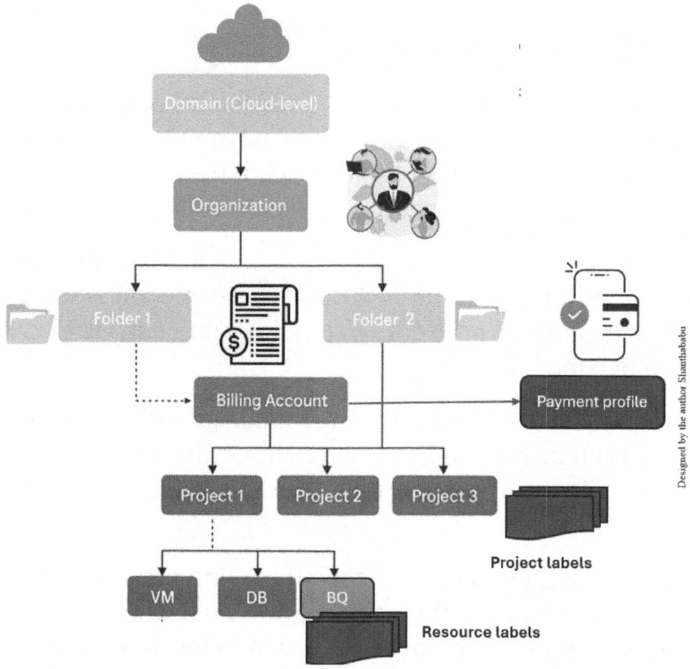

Figure 2.19: *GCP Billing*

Figure 2.19 illustrates the hierarchical structure of Google Cloud Platform (GCP) resources and their relationship with billing components.

At the top level is the **domain,** which represents the cloud identity or G Suite domain that owns the cloud resources. Directly under the domain is the **organization**, which serves as the central administrative unit for managing all resources in the cloud environment under the particular organization.

Within the organization are **folders** such as "Folder 1", "Folder 2" and so on, which help in organizing and managing related projects from different groups. Additionally, folders provide a way to apply policies and delegate administrative responsibilities for the people under the project.

Beneath the folders are **projects**, which are the fundamental units in GCP where all the services and resources are mapped, provisioned, and tightly integrated.

Example: Project 1, Project 2, and Project 3. Each project can contain various GCP Resources such as Virtual Machines (VM), Databases (DB), and BigQuery (BQ) datasets, which are the actual cloud services used by applications or users.

A central **billing account** is linked to the organization level or specific folders and manages the financial aspects of the resources being used across all projects, depending on their computational capacity and scalability configuration perspective. This billing account is in turn connected to a **payment profile**, which we had created earlier in this chapter. The payment profile stores payment methods, tax information, handles invoicing, and does much more.

The relationship between the billing account and projects ensures that resource usage is tracked and billed appropriately, which enables effective cost management and accountability within the organization.

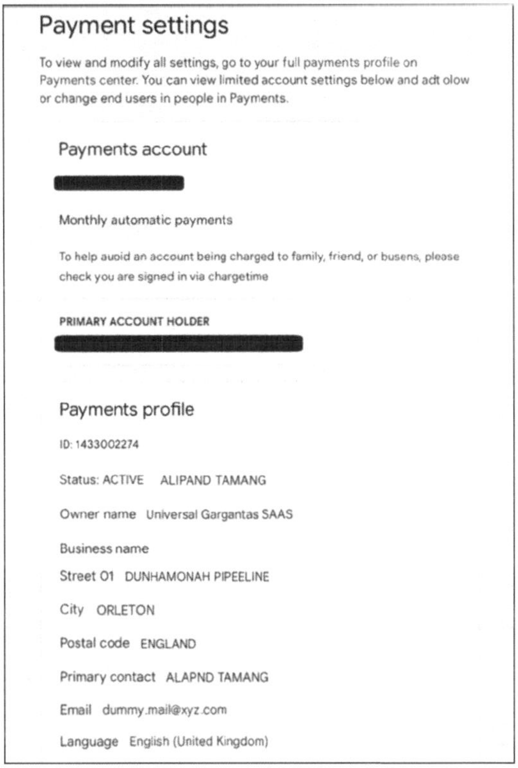

Figure 2.20: GCP Payment Settings

We can assess the billing account from the account management page, as shown in *Figure 2.21*, which shows the projects linked to your billing account.

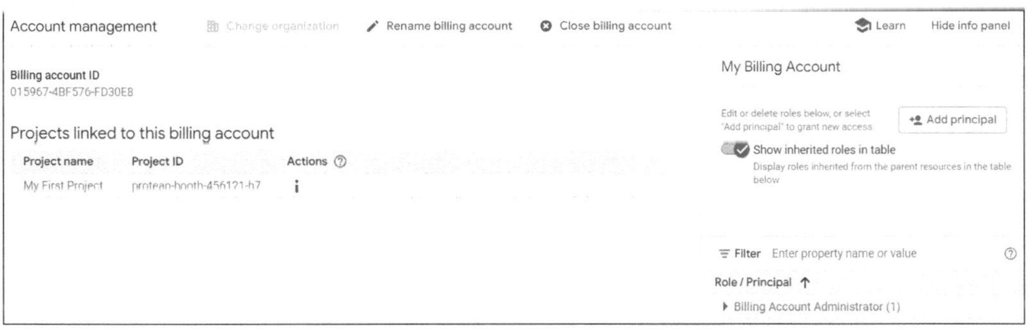

Figure 2.21: GCP Account Management

We can assess the overview of billing details from the account management page, as shown in *Figure 2.22*.

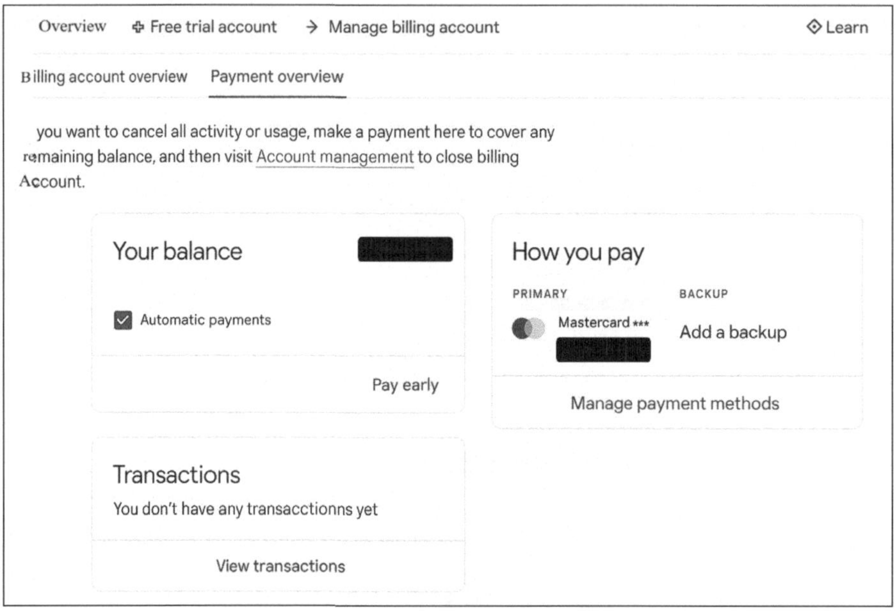

Figure 2.22: *GCP Billing Details*

Relationships between Organizations-Projects-Cloud Billing Accounts, and Payment Profiles

Figure 2.23 clearly shows how billing and ownership responsibilities are structured in Google Cloud. It illustrates the logical separation and interaction between resource ownership, financial responsibility, and payment configuration within the Google Cloud ecosystem. At the cloud level, an **organization** is the root entity that **owns** multiple resources, including projects and billing accounts, as the arrows indicate. Under this organization, we can have several **projects,** such as Project 1, Project 2, and Project n, each of which is associated with a **billing account**. The arrows demonstrate that the billing account pays for all related projects.

Google Cloud Platform offers two types of cloud billing accounts: **self-serve sccounts** and **invoiced accounts.**

A ***self-serve account*** is designed for **individuals, small businesses**, or **startups**, which allows users to pay automatically using a credit card or bank account on a pay-as-you-go basis. It is simple to set up and charges are processed according to the services consumed. On the other hand, an ***invoiced account*** is typically used by

larger organizations or **enterprises**. In this model, Google sends a monthly invoice detailing the usage and the payment is made manually within a set credit term. This account type typically requires special approval and is ideal for customers who require centralized billing and financial operations. These account types cater to a wide range of users, from individual developers to large-scale enterprises.

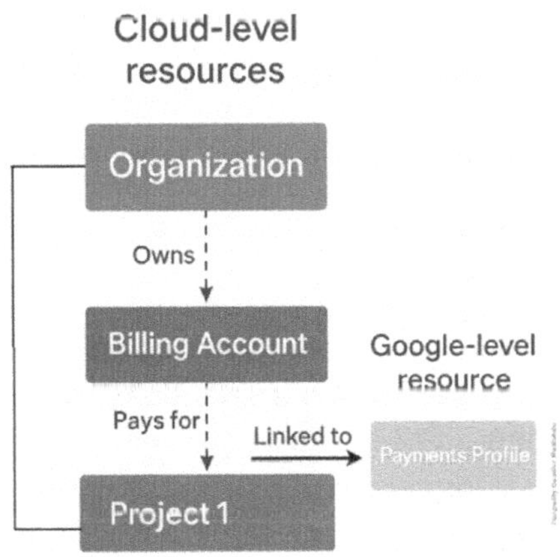

Figure 2.23: *GCP Relationships between Organizations-Projects-Cloud Billing Accounts-Payment Profiles*

The Billing Account is also **linked to** a **payments profile**, which is key in GCP. This linkage is represented by a black bi-directional arrow, which indicates a mutual connection. The payment profile contains the actual payment information such as credit card or bank details and governs how funds are managed for the billing account.

Understanding Subaccounts in GCP

Subaccounts: Subaccounts are very flexible and designed primarily for resellers to manage and track customer-related charges for chargeback purposes. If you are a reseller, you can create subaccounts to represent each customer's usage and organize their charges separately for their convenience.

A Cloud Billing subaccount functions as a dedicated billing account and is managed under a reseller's parent Cloud Billing account. All charges associated with the subaccount are consolidated and paid through the reseller's parent account. **It is important to note that the parent billing account must be set up for invoicing.**

Functionally, a subaccount operates much like a regular Cloud Billing account. You can link projects to it, configure billing data exports, and assign IAM roles independently. Charges from related projects are grouped and subtotalled on the reseller's invoice or across multiple invoices. If we split the invoicing, it is enabled. This setup allows for complete isolation of access control policies, which makes it easier to manage and separate customer environments securely.

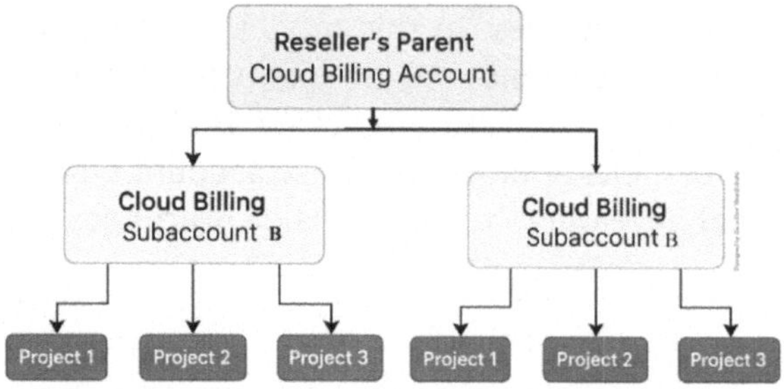

Figure 2.24: *GCP Reseller Subaccount Billing Details*

Budgets and Alerts

Budgets in GCP: A budget in Google Cloud is a provision in GCP that limits the spending that you set for your billing. It could be for a specific project or service. It lets you track and manage your cloud spending and helps prevent unexpected charges. However, the services do not stop the budget exceeds the limit; ultimately, you do get alerts that notify you when the expenditure crosses a certain threshold.

Alerts in GCP: Once your billing amount reaches your budget level, you can set up alerts like **email notifications** or **Pub/Sub messages**. These alerts help you monitor and respond to cost spikes in real time.

Step 1: Select "**`Budgets and Alerts`**" from the left panel and you will be taken to the Budgets and Alerts screen, where you have to click "**`Create Budget`**" and the portal will take you to the budget configuration screen shown in *Figure 2.26*.

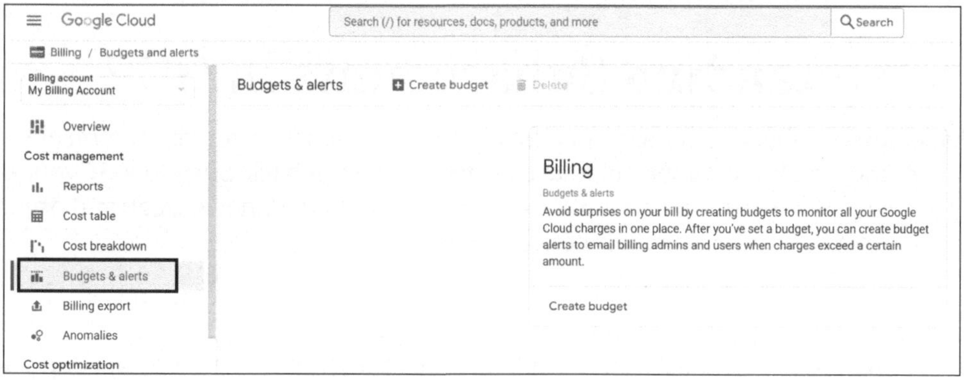

Figure 2.25: *GCP Budgets and Alerts*

Step 2: We need to configure the details for the budget creation screen. Once it is done, click "**`Next`**".

- **`Name`**
- **`Time Range`** (Monthly/Quarterly/Yearly/Custom Range
- **`Project`** (Specific project(s)/All projects)

- **`Services`** (Specific service(s)/All services)
- **`Discount`** (avail any discounts)
- **`Promotions`** (availing any promotional offers)

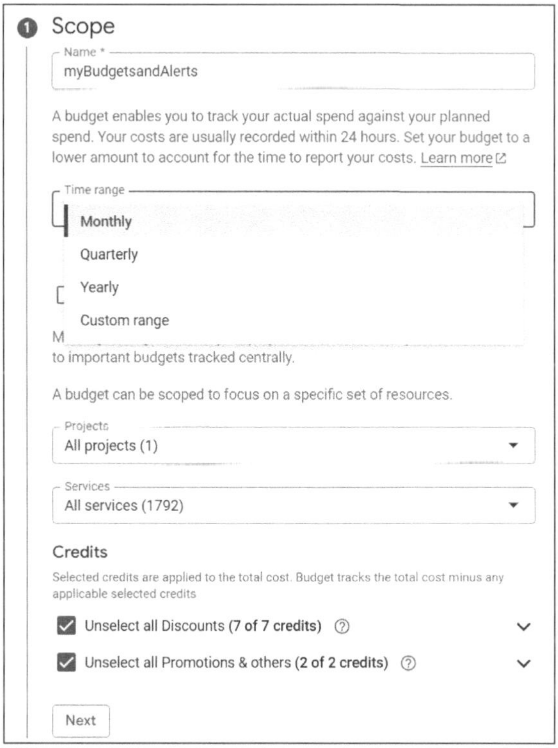

Figure 2.26: *GCP Budgets and Alerts*

Step 3: You must specify the budget amount and click "**`Next`**".

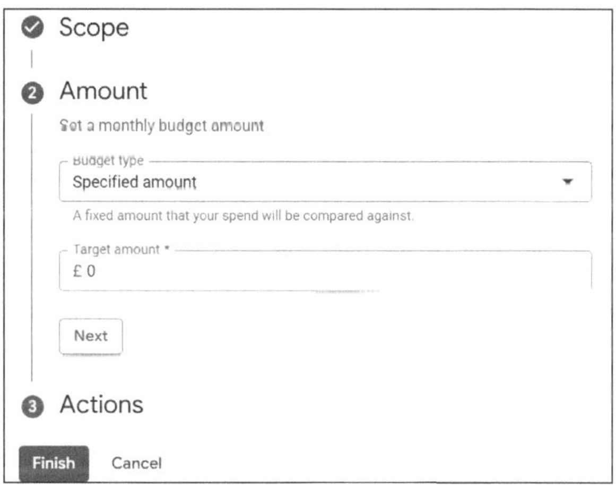

Figure 2.27: *Setting Up a Budget*

Step 4: You must set alert threshold rules and send email alert notifications after the actual or forecasted spending exceeds a percentage of the specified budget. You can specify the alert after 25%, 50%, 75%, and 100% of the amount spent. You must also check the email alerts for admins, users, and project owners and allocate a budget for a Pub/Sub topic.

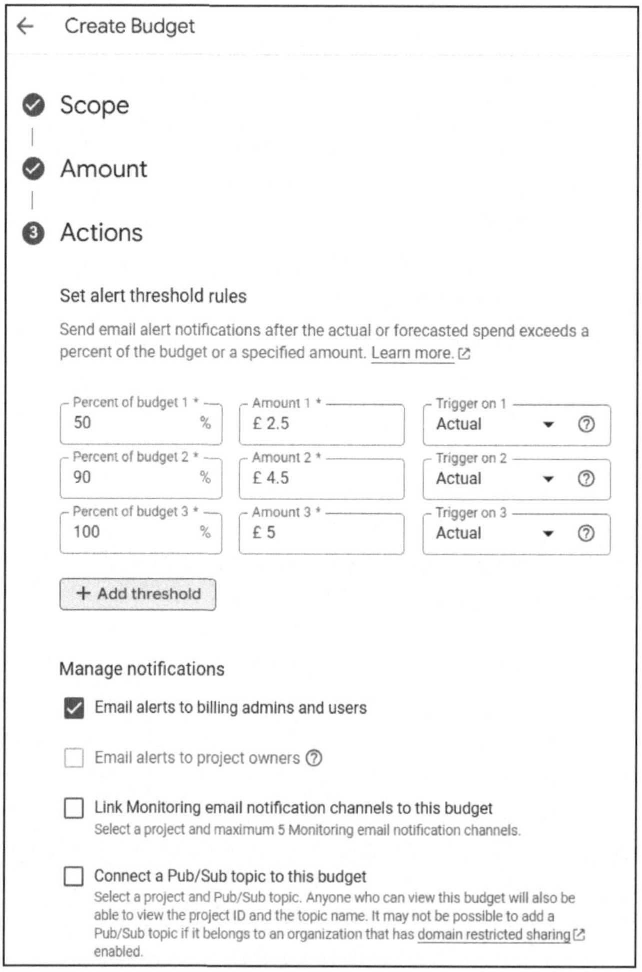

Figure 2.28: *Allocating GCP Budgets and Enabling Alerts*

The budgets and alerts are ready for the project, as shown in *Figure 2.29*.

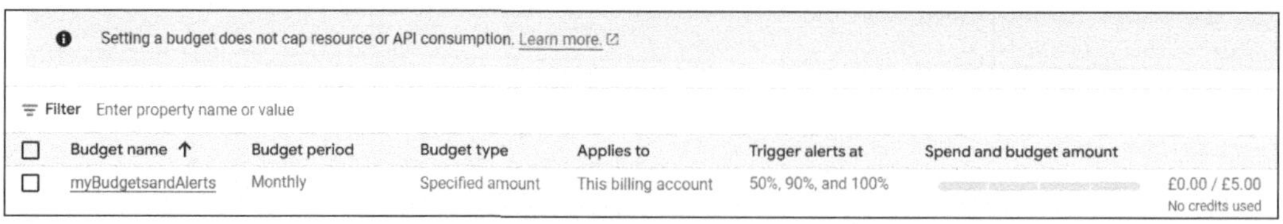

Figure 2.29: *GCP Budgets and Alerts Ready*

You can monitor costs in real-time and even integrate budget data with **`BigQuery`** or **`Looker Studio`** for advanced analysis and reporting.

Billing Export

Billing export in GCP is a feature that allows you to export detailed billing and cost data from your Cloud Billing account to Google Cloud services like BigQuery or Cloud Storage. This provides deeper visibility into your cloud spending. The benefits are as follows:

- Complete visibility into your actual and forecasted spend, depending on your configuration
- Easy BI tool integration enables advanced analysis, reporting, and automation.
- Supports cost optimization and resource efficiency for project-specific and controls the expenses
- Facilitates internal chargeback or cost centre billing

Step 1: Click **"`Billing export`"** in the left panel, the portal will load the Billing export screen shown in *Figure* 2.30.

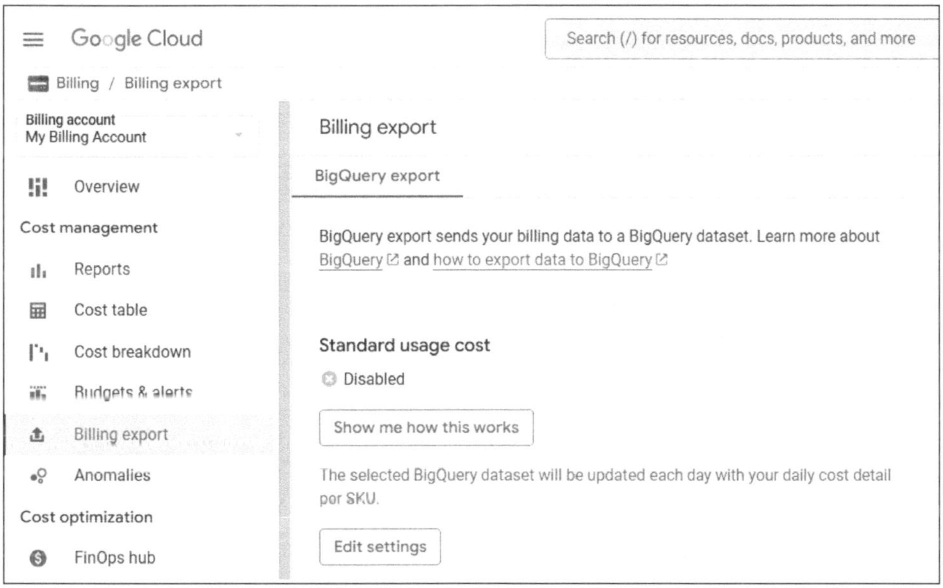

***Figure 2.30:** GCP Billing Export*

Step 2: Click "**`Edit settings`**" button, as shown in *Figure* 2.30. The portal will take you to the BigQuery export screen. We have to configure the project and the Dataset. You can load an existing or create a new dataset.

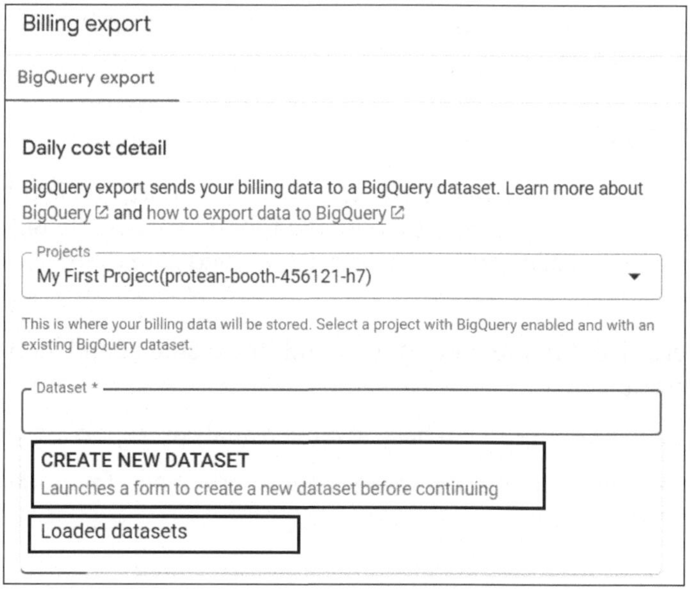

Figure 2.31: *GCP BigQuery Export*

Step 3: When you click "**`Create new dataset`**", the system will pop up the screen, as shown in *Figure* 2.32. You have to configure the following features:

- **Project ID**: The currently selected project
- **Dataset ID**: A required field where you name your dataset
  (must contain only letters, numbers, and underscores)
- **Location Type:**
  - **Region**: Allows dataset colocation with other Google services (not selected)
  - **Multi-region**: Allows BigQuery to use a group of locations to improve quota and availability
- **External Dataset:** Option to link to an external dataset
- **Tags**: Tags help you manage and enforce policies on your resources.
  They consist of a unique tag key and a set of tag values.
- **Advanced Options:**
  - Encryption:
    - Google-managed encryption keys (keys owned by Google)
    - Cloud KMS key (user-managed encryption via Google Cloud KMS)
- **Case Insensitive:** To enable case-insensitive table names

- **Default table expiration:** Enable table expiration and specify the number of days. Any new tables created in this dataset will be automatically **deleted** after the specified number of days after creation. This is useful for temporary data that does not need to be preserved.
- **Other Options:**

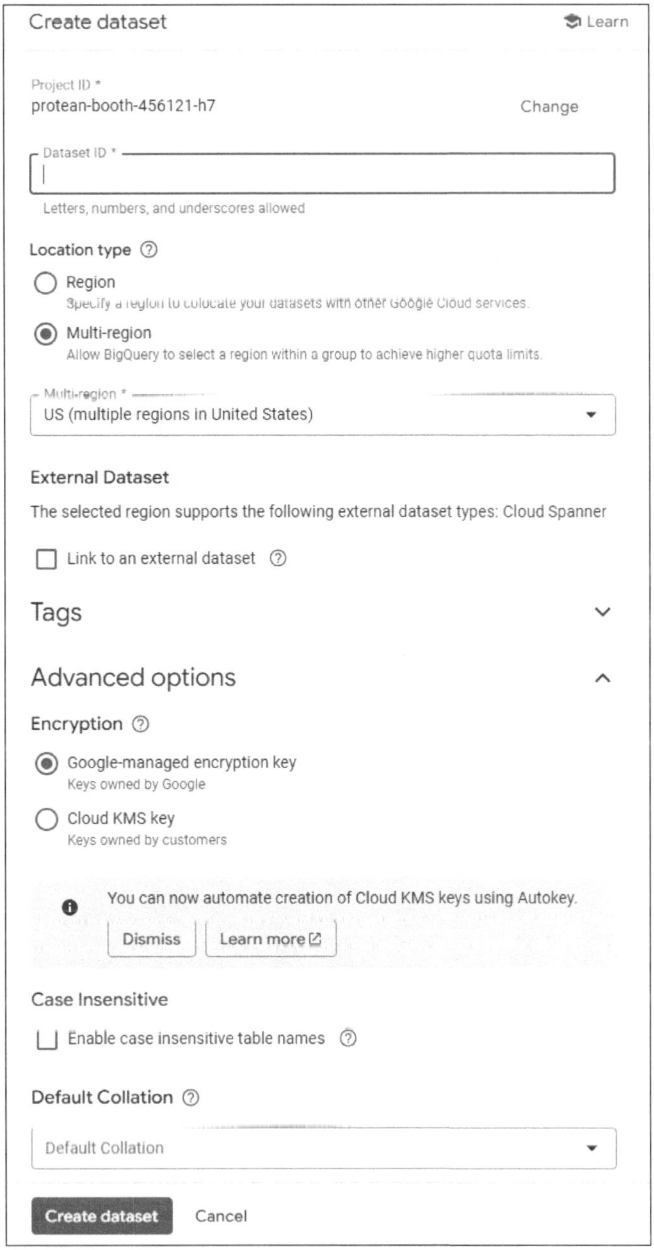

Figure 2.32: *Creating a New Dataset*

Step 4: Once the dataset is created, connect it to the project, as shown in *Figure 2.33*:

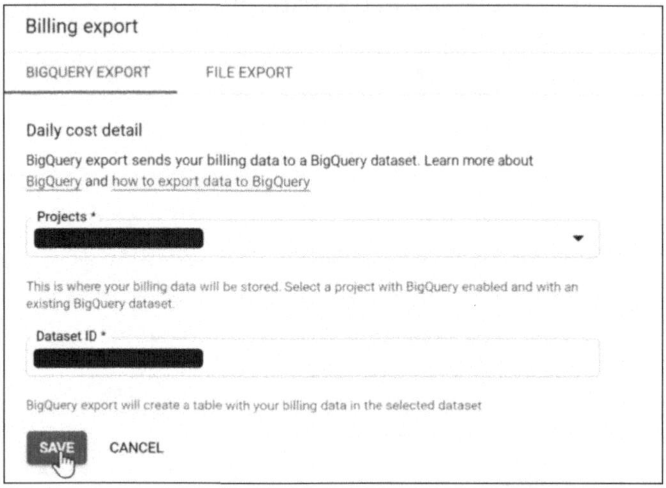

Figure 2.33: *Connecting a Dataset to a Project*

Step 5: We can also enable pricing. This selected BigQuery dataset will contain your SKU prices and can be updated whenever you change your pricing preferences. This feature helps us understand and plans for our budget.

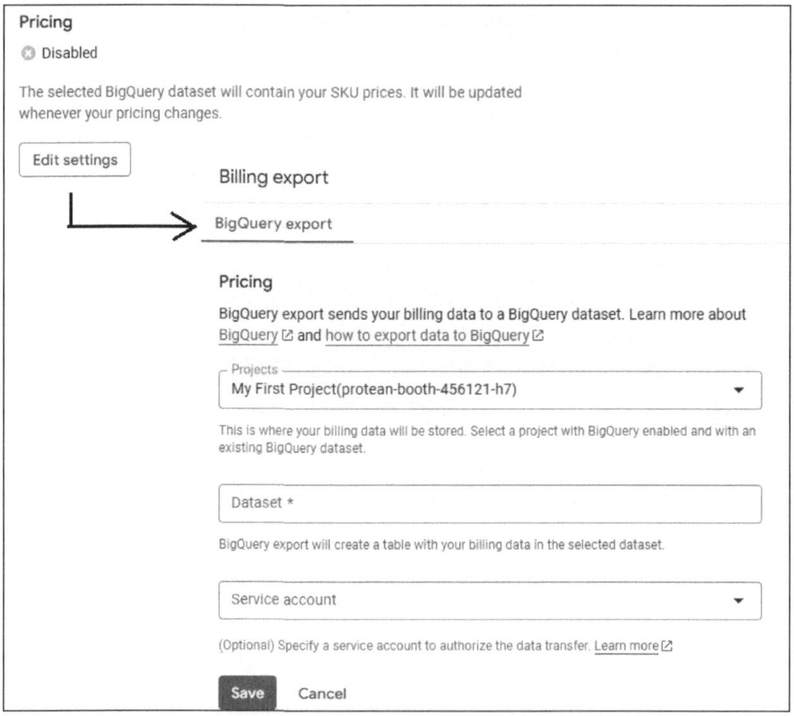

Figure 2.34: *Enabling Pricing*

Step 6: We have to enable the data transfer API in BigQuery. Once this is done, the data will be saved in your BigQuery dataset.

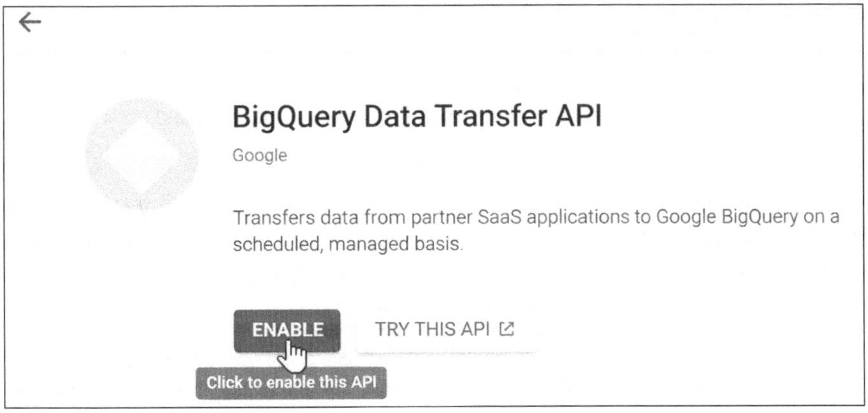

Figure 2.35: *GCP Data Transfer API to BigQuery*

Cost Table for Google Cloud Platform (GCP)

The Cost Table in GCP provides a detailed view of your cloud spending and breaks down usage costs by categorizing them in various dimensions such as a **service, a project, an SKU**, and more. Billing Reports and Billing Export to BigQuery are the key features for understanding, analyzing, and optimizing cloud costs.

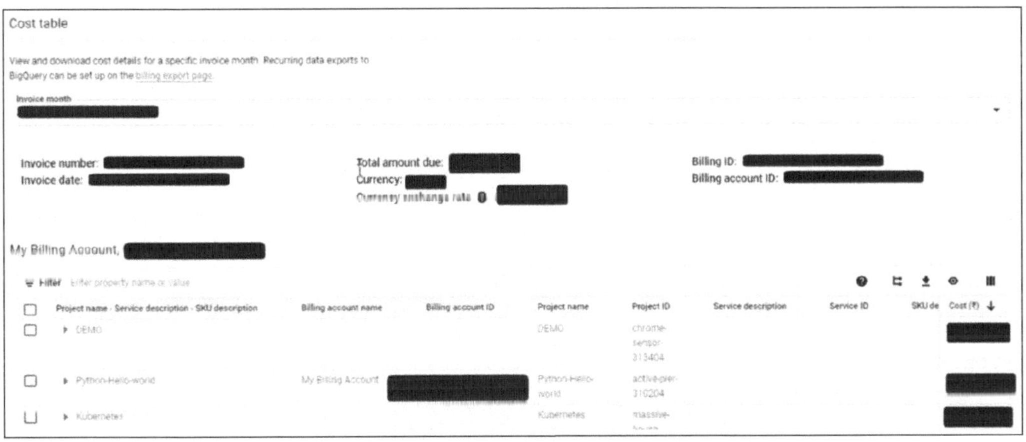

Figure 2.36: *GCP Cost Table*

Overall, GCP Budgets, Alerts, Billing and Cost tables provide valuable visibility and control over cloud expenses, which helps teams avoid surprises, make informed financial decisions, and maintain cost efficiency across their cloud environment.

Understanding Identity and Access Management (IAM) in GCP

Identity and Access Management (**IAM**) in GCP is a framework that allows administrators to manage the identity of who has **what access (roles/permissions) to which resources**. This ensures secure and appropriate access across your GCP environment.

This is to control who can do what on your GCP resources using a centralized and consistent authorization approach. It unifies access control for Google Cloud services into a single system and presents consistent operations across the resources.

The idea here is that permission to access a resource isn't granted directly to the end user. Instead, permissions are grouped into roles, and roles are granted to authenticated members. An IAM policy defines and enforces the roles granted to specific members, and this policy is in turn attached to a resource.

IAM uses **role-based access control (RBAC),** where:

- **Members** can be users, service accounts, or groups.
- **Roles** are collections of permissions.
- **Policies** bind members to roles for specific resources.

Figure 2.37 illustrates how to manage IAM in GCP with clear steps.

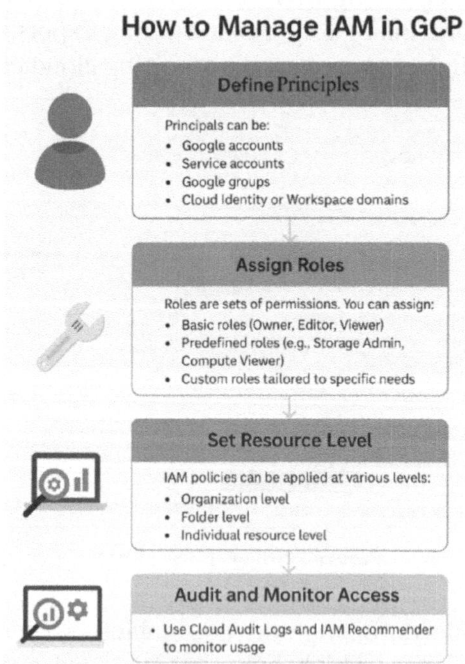

Figure 2.37: IAM *in* GCP

Significance of IAM in GCP

- **Security:** IAM ensures that only authorized users and services can access specific resources, which reduces the risk of data leaks or unauthorized access.
- **Granular Control:** With fine-grained permissions, you can provide just enough access for users to perform their roles.
- **Organizational Management:** IAM helps enforce access policies across large teams and complex project hierarchies to support scalability and governance.
- **Compliance and Auditing:** IAM enables you to meet regulatory requirements by tracking who accessed what and when, which is helpful during audits and policy enforcement.
- **Automation and Integration:** IAM policies can be integrated with CI/CD pipelines and infrastructure-as-code tools for automated security enforcement.

Designing a Multi-Project Architecture for Enterprise-Scale Applications on GCP

Designing a multi-project architecture for enterprise-scale applications on Google Cloud Platform (GCP) requires a well-structured approach that supports **scalability, security, cost control, compliance, and efficient operations**.

Here is a breakdown of the best practices and components involved in such an architecture. *Figure* 2.38 illustrates the overall architecture.

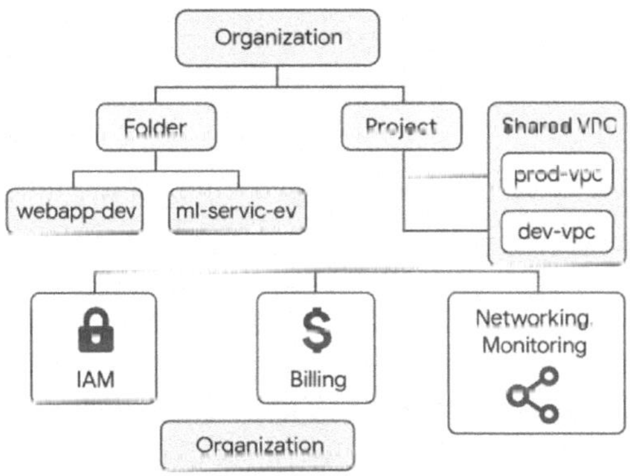

Figure 2.38: *Multi-Project Architecture for Enterprise-Scale Applications in GCP*

Organizational Structure: In GCP, the Organizational Structure starts with the Organization Node, which is the root container for all GCP resources in an enterprise.

Under it, Folders group projects by departments, teams, or environments, which allows for centralized policy management and access control inheritance.

- **GCP Organization Node**
  - Root node that ties together all GCP resources for an enterprise
  - Required to set up IAM policies and enable centralized billing
- **Folders**
  - Used to group projects by department, environment (dev/test/prod), business unit, or region
  - Apply policies (IAM, org policies) at the folder level to inherit across projects

Project Structure: In GCP, the Project Structure involves creating separate projects for each application, service, or environment (like dev, test, prod) to ensure isolation, manage permissions, and track costs effectively. Each project acts as a boundary for resources, policies, and billing.

- **Project-per-Application / Microservice**
  - Each application or major component resides in a separate project.
  - Promotes isolation, ease of access control, and cost tracking
- **Project-per-Environment**
  - Separate projects for dev, staging, and prod environments
  - Enhances deployment safety and auditability
- **Example:**

```
org-name
│
├── folders
│   │
│   ├── projects
│   ├── fin-app-dev
│   └── fin-app-prod
│
├── engineering
│   │
│   ├── eng-service1-dev
│   └── eng-service1-prod
```

Figure 2.39: *Project Structure in GCP*

Identity and Access Management (IAM): In GCP, IAM enables you to control who (users or service accounts) has access to which resources (roles/permissions). It follows the principle of least privilege and grants fine-grained access control at the project, folder, or resource level.

- **Principle of Least Privilege:** Assign roles at the narrowest scope (preferably project or resource-level).

- **Custom Roles:** Use custom IAM roles for fine-grained access when predefined roles are too broad.
- **Service Accounts:** Use per-service or per-application service accounts for automation and workloads.
- **Organization Policies:** Enforce constraints like restricting service account key creation, domain restrictions, or allowed regions.

Shared VPC and Networking: It allows multiple projects to securely share a common Virtual Private Cloud (VPC) network from a central host project. This enables centralized network control, efficient resource management, and consistent security policies across service projects.

- **Shared VPCs**
    - Centralized VPC hosted in a host project
    - Service projects (app-specific projects) are attached to the shared VPC.
    - Enables centralized control over network and firewall rules
- **Peering and Private Services Access**
    - Connect to projects or use Private Google Access for security and performance.

Billing and Cost Management: GCP provides centralized control through a single billing account linked to multiple projects, which enables clear visibility and accountability. Budgets, alerts, and labels help monitor spending and optimize resource usage efficiently.

- **Centralized Billing Account:** Link all projects to a single billing account.
- **Budgets and Alerts:** Set budgets per project and use alerts for cost monitoring.
- **Labels:** Apply consistent labels for cost attribution.
    - For example, team: engineering, env: prod

Monitoring, Logging, and Security: In GCP, Monitoring, logging, and security are managed using tools such as Cloud Monitoring, Cloud Logging, and Security Command Centre to ensure visibility, performance tracking, and threat detection. These tools help centralize insights across projects for proactive issue resolution and compliance.

- **Cloud Logging and Monitoring (formerly Stackdriver)**
    - Centralize logs across projects with log sinks.
    - Use Monitoring Workspaces for cross-project visibility.
- **Security Command Centre (SCC)**
    - Enterprise security monitoring with threat detection

- **Cloud Audit Logs**
    - Enable Admin Activity, Data Access, and System Event logs.

CI/CD and Deployment Strategy: GCP leverages tools such as Cloud Build, Cloud Deploy, and Artefact Registry to automate application build, testing, and deployment workflows. This ensures faster, more reliable, and consistent releases across multiple environments and projects.

- **Cloud Build, Cloud Deploy, Artefact Registry**
    - Containerized deployment using GKE or Cloud Run
    - Automated pipelines per project and environment
- **Infrastructure as Code (IaC)**
    - Use Terraform with GCP modules for consistent provisioning.

Compliance and Governance: GCP is enforced using organization policies, VPC Service Controls, and access transparency to meet regulatory requirements and prevent data exfiltration. These tools ensure secure, policy-driven management across all cloud resources.

- **Policy Constraints:** Restrict usage to approved services or regions.
- **VPC Service Controls:** Define perimeters to prevent data exfiltration between services.
- **Access Transparency:** Monitor how Google supports access to data (for sensitive workloads).

Naming Conventions and Automation: GCP ensures consistency, clarity, and scalability across projects and resources. Automated tools like Terraform help enforce these standards while simplifying infrastructure provisioning and management.

- **Consistent Naming:** for example, `[env]-[team]-[service]-[region]: prod-finance-billing-us`
- **Automation Tools:** Use Deployment Manager or Terraform to automate project setup.

Overview of GCP's Core Services for Big Data and Analytics

Google Cloud Platform (GCP) offers a comprehensive suite of services tailored for Big Data and analytics, which enables organizations to efficiently store, process, analyze, and visualize massive datasets.

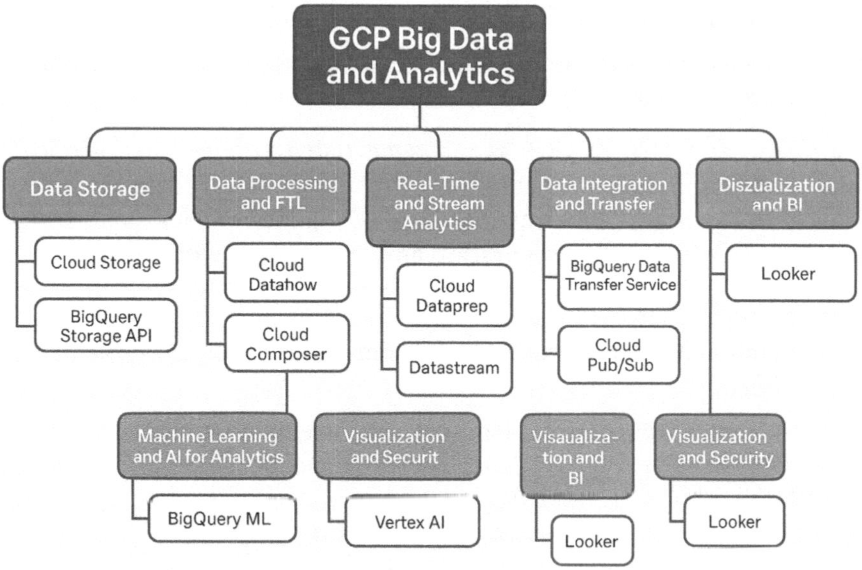

Figure 2.40: *Overview of GCP's Core Services for Big Data and Analytics*

Data Storage and Data Lake: Data Storage in GCP refers to services like **cloud storage**, which offer scalable, durable object storage for structured and unstructured data. A **data lake** is a centralized repository built on such storage that allows you to store raw data in its native format, which is ready for processing, analytics, or ML operations.

- **Cloud Storage**
    - Object storage for structured and unstructured data
    - Used for data lakes, backups, and media storage
    - Supports lifecycle management, versioning, and integration with other GCP services
- **BigQuery Storage API**
    - Offers high-throughput access to BigQuery-managed storage
    - Enables data sharing across services with low latency

Data Warehousing and Querying: In GCP, data warehousing is primarily handled by BigQuery, a fully managed, serverless data warehouse. It allows you to run fast, SQL-based analytics over petabytes of structured data with built-in machine learning and real-time querying support.

- **BigQuery**
    - GCP's serverless, highly scalable data warehouse
    - Supports SQL queries over petabytes of data

- Features built-in ML (BigQuery ML) and GIS analytics
- Allows federated queries from external sources (Cloud Storage, Google Drive, and many more)

Data Processing and ETL in GCP is managed using services like Cloud Dataflow and Cloud Dataprep, which enable real-time and batch data transformations. These tools help Extract, Transform, and Load (ETL) data efficiently across pipelines, while supporting scalable data preparation and enrichment workflows.

- **Cloud Dataflow**
    - Fully managed service for real-time and batch processing via Apache Beam
    - Handles ETL, data enrichment, and stream analytics
- **Cloud Dataprep (by Trifacta)**
    - Visual, no-code data wrangling and preparation
    - Ideal for business users and analysts
- **Cloud Composer**
    - Managed Apache Airflow service
    - Used for orchestrating complex data pipelines and workflows

Data Integration and Transfer: Data integration and transfer in GCP are facilitated by tools like BigQuery Data Transfer Service, Cloud Pub/Sub, and Datastream.

These services enable seamless, automated, real-time data movement from various sources like SaaS apps, databases, or streaming data into Google Cloud for analytics and processing.

- **BigQuery Data Transfer Service**
    - Automates data movement from SaaS apps (for example, Google Ads, YouTube, Salesforce) to BigQuery
    - Schedule-based ingestion with minimal setup
- **Cloud Pub/Sub**
    - Asynchronous messaging service for real-time ingestion
    - Useful in event-driven architectures and streaming pipelines

Real-Time and Stream Analytics

- **Cloud Dataflow (Streaming)**
    - Real-time data processing and transformation
    - Integration with Pub/Sub for ingestion and BigQuery for output

- **Datastream**
  - Serverless change data capture (CDC) service
  - Syncs data in near real-time from MySQL, PostgreSQL, and other sources to BigQuery or Cloud Storage

Machine Learning and AI for Analytics: These services work together to ingest, process, and analyze data in real time, while enabling instant insights and actions on continuously flowing data.

- **BigQuery ML**
  - Allows users to build and train ML models using SQL directly in BigQuery
  - Supports linear models, time series forecasting, clustering, and more
- **Vertex AI**
  - End-to-end platform for ML lifecycle
  - Integrates with BigQuery, Dataflow, and Looker for AI-driven analytics

Visualization and BI: In GCP, visualization and BI are delivered through tools like Looker and Looker Studio (formerly Data Studio). These tools enable users to create interactive dashboards and reports, while providing real-time insights by connecting directly to data sources like BigQuery.

- **Looker (formerly Data Studio)**
  - Modern BI tools for creating interactive dashboards and reports
  - Deep integration with BigQuery and other GCP sources
  - Supports data modeling via LookML

Data governance and security in GCP are managed through services like data catalogs and cloud Data Loss Prevention (DLP). These services help organize, classify, secure, and monitor data by enabling metadata management, access control, and protection of sensitive information.

- **Data Catalog**
  - Metadata management tool for data discovery and governance
  - Supports tagging, lineage, and access control
- **Cloud DLP (Data Loss Prevention)**
  - Scans and classifies sensitive data in BigQuery, Cloud Storage, and other sources
  - Helps enforce compliance and protect PII

Conclusion

This chapter provides a comprehensive understanding of the essentials of Google Cloud Platform (GCP) for data engineering. It began with the importance of data engineering in today's data-driven world and introduced GCP as a robust, scalable, and secure cloud platform. We learned how to create and configure a GCP account, navigate the console, and manage projects, billing, and IAM effectively. We explored the role and significance of GCP Projects, while learning how they serve as the central unit for resource management, cost tracking, and security enforcement. We also examined GCP's billing system, budgets, alerts, and export options for cost governance and analysis. A detailed view of multi-project architecture emphasized best practices for enterprise-scale solutions. Finally, the chapter offered a deep dive into GCP's core Big Data and analytics services, and addressed topics such as storage, ETL, real-time processing, ML, and governance. With this knowledge, you are now well-prepared to build scalable data pipelines and manage cloud resources efficiently using GCP.

The next chapter will discuss how storing data effectively is a cornerstone of any data engineering strategy and storage solutions, while focusing on BigQuery and Cloud Storage. Additionally, it covers advanced features like Data Canvases, Schedulers, and BigQuery Data Forms, which will help the readers build a scalable and cost-efficient data storage architecture.

CHAPTER 3
Data Storage on GCP

Introduction

The previous chapter provided a comprehensive foundation for understanding the essentials of Google Cloud Platform (GCP) for data engineering. You learned how to create and configure a GCP account, as well as manage projects, billing, and IAM effectively.

This chapter will discuss how storing data effectively is a cornerstone of any data engineering strategy and storage solutions, while focusing on BigQuery and Cloud Storage. Additionally, it covers advanced features like Data Canvases, Schedulers, and BigQuery Data Forms, which will help readers build a scalable and cost-efficient data storage architecture.

Data is at the heart of modern enterprises for various reasons. Storing, managing, and analyzing massive volumes of structured and unstructured data should be understood as a strategic necessity across industries, instead of being considered a mere feature of corporate organizations.

All cloud providers provide data storage facilities, but Google Cloud Platform (GCP) offers comprehensive storage services well-tailored to different data types, which are useful in processing needs and achieving cost-efficiency.

Structure

In this chapter, we will discuss the following topics:

- GCP's Most Essential Storage Technologies
- Significant Characteristics of Google Storage

- Understanding Encryption at Rest and in Transit
- Understanding GCP Storage Classes
- Exploring Google Cloud Storage Services (Key Features and Use Cases)
- Working with Cloud Storage and Cloud SQL Service

GCP's Most Essential Storage Technologies

GCP Storage refers to the suite of **cloud-based storage solutions** offered by Google Cloud Platform (GCP) that allow users to store, manage, and access data reliably and securely across the globe. It has a set of various storage services for different domain-specific needs. This storage service is a **RESTful** online file storage service web service for storing and accessing data on Google's infrastructure and other external cloud providers and applications. It allows users to store and retrieve data at any time. It supports various scenarios such as website content, archival, and disaster recovery data.

The most significant characteristics of Google storage are as follows:

Single API for All Storage Classes

One of Google Cloud Storage's advantages is that it offers a single, unified API for accessing and managing all storage classes under the GCP environment, such as ***Standard, Nearline, Coldline, and Archive***. This means you can use the **same API commands** to upload, download, copy, move, or manage your files for all storage classes.

Advantages:

- **Simplicity:** When moving data between various classes in the GCP environment, developers and administrators do not need to rewrite code or manage different tools.
- **Flexibility:** Transitioning between storage classes based on simple changes in access patterns among storage classes without having to move objects to a new bucket.
- **Cost Optimisation:** We can access data and dynamically shift it to lower-cost classes from higher-cost ones without disrupting the applications. Ultimately, we will be able to optimize costs effectively (for example, from Standard to Coldline).
- **Consistency:** During shifts, the applications, scripts, and workflows stay the same, even as storage strategies evolve over time.

11 Nines of Durability: GCP replicates data across multiple physical locations to enhance availability. In case a copy is lost or corrupted, you can access another from standby data centres. Data might be lost during processing or in unexpected scenarios. However, the probability of losing data in the GCP environment is rare, as it comes with 99.999999999% durability for object storage. This means that ***even during rare hardware failures, your data will be still safe***.

Strong durability of **99.999999999% (11 nines)** is achieved through automatic replication of data across multiple physical locations within a region. This architecture enables continuous integrity checks and self-healing mechanisms that automatically detect and repair data errors, ensuring long-term data reliability and availability.

- **How to Achieve Automatic Replication:** When you store a file, GCP keeps multiple copies in different physical places based on the ***regional*** and ***multi-regional replication*** options.
    - **Regional Storage:** Replication happens across **multiple zones** within **one region,** like in Mumbai or London. This option is suitable for local apps with low latency needs.
    - **Multi-Regional Storage:** This occurs when replication happens **across multiple regions**, like across Europe or Asia. This option is suitable for global apps with super-high availability needs.
- **Self-Healing Capabilities:** This characteristic is more profound than other cloud providers. If one copy is damaged, the others are used to restore it immediately without requiring any manual action.

  Example: Storing critical medical records in Cloud Storage is a wise application. Even if a data centre experiences a disaster (fire, power outage), your data remains untouched because it is replicated and automatically repaired in the background.

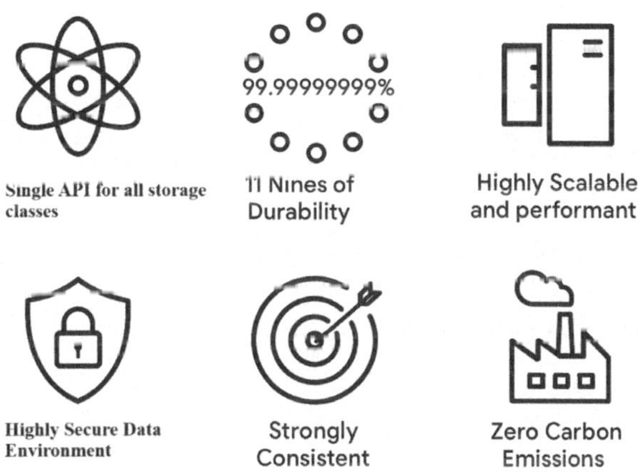

***Figure 3.1:** GCP's Significant Characteristics*

- **Highly Scalable and Performant:** It can automatically handle growing data needs. This means you can start with minimal storage and expand the capacity without worrying about running out of space or provisioning new hardware. You also do not have to anticipate any disruption, downtime, or manual effort while scaling up. On the other hand, GCP allows you to access data rapidly, whether you are uploading, downloading, or querying data from applications. Even though millions of users are accessing data files from the application simultaneously, the system **maintains low latency (fast responses)** and **high throughput (large data transfer rates)**. Additionally, performance tuning such as **caching, load balancing, and smart routing** takes place automatically behind the scenes.

  Why It Matters:

  - There is no need to predict storage needs upfront; just add data and GCP scales.
  - Handles sudden traffic spikes, such as data from millions of IoT sensors and sentiment analysis feeds

  Example: An e-commerce Site during a Sale

  An online store launched a massive holiday sale. The user traffic jumped from 5,000 daily users to 500,000 overnight. Users can upload product reviews, place orders, and download invoices from the site. Tools like GCP Cloud Storage and Firestore automatically scale to handle this load without any manual upgrades to ensure smooth performance during peak traffic.

- **Highly Secure Data Environment:** Data protection is critical in the cloud. GCP provides this in two different stages: **encryption at rest** and in **transit**, and additional security using IAM access control. Data is always protected, whether it is sitting in storage, moving between services, or in transformation, and only authorized users can access it.

  Why It Matters:

  - **Encryption at Rest:** Data is automatically encrypted before being stored in GCP storage services.
  - **Encryption in Transit:** Data is encrypted as it travels over the network.
  - **IAM (Identity and Access Management):** Lets you decide who can view, edit, or delete your data, and under what conditions (for example, read-only access for interns)

Example: A company stores confidential financial documents in GCP. Each employee gets role-based access, with the **CFO** able to edit and **analysts** able to view the data only. All files are encrypted in an encrypted format, which ensures privacy and regulatory compliance with GDPR, HIPAA, and PII.

Encryption at Rest and in Transit

In Google Cloud Platform (GCP), **encryption at rest** refers to encrypting data stored on disk, whether in databases, file storage, or backups, based on the project's convenience. Data saved within GCP services is automatically converted into unreadable code using strong encryption standards like **AES-256** before being written to disk. Even if someone gains unauthorized access to the physical storage device, they will not be able to read the data without the encryption keys.

GCP handles this automatically, but also offers options like **customer-managed encryption keys (CMEK)** for organizations that want to control their own encryption keys.

For example, if a company stores sensitive financial records in Cloud Storage, the data remains protected from theft or leakage even if the hardware is compromised.

On the other hand, **encryption in transit** protects data as it travels between systems during processing and transformation. GCP uses encryption protocols like TLS (**Transport Layer Security**) and **HTTPS** to secure this data in motion, which ensures that attackers cannot intercept or alter it during transmission. **This is especially important when using public networks or when applications need to send data across regions**.

For instance, when a user uploads a critical document(s) to Cloud Storage via a web application, the file(s) are encrypted during transfer from source to destination, so no one on the network can snoop on their contents. Together, encryption at-rest and in-transit provide **end-to-end protection,** and ensure that data remains secure from storage to transmission.

- **Global-Availability:** GCP's infrastructure spans the globe, which facilitates data storage close to the user's location or geography for a speed and reliability perspective. This GCP is a distributed architecture, ensuring high availability and performance.

  Why It Matters:

  - Reduces latency (delay) by serving data from nearby regions based on the user's preference.
  - Provides immediate attention and increases uptime by rapidly routing around failures or slow connections.
  - Supports disaster recovery by replicating across regions, which reduces data loss panic.

  Example: You run a video streaming platform. A user in **Japan** gets video content from a **Tokyo centre**, while another user in **New York** gets it from a

U.S. data centre—both users can enjoy fast and smooth playback without any interruptions this way.

- **Strongly Consistent:** This characteristic is determined by the consistency of the data. Once data is written, it is immediately available to read and causes no confusion or delays. This leads to predictability and accuracy. It simplifies the application design, so that the developers do not need to write complicated retry logic or deal with data synchronization issues.

  What Exactly Happens:

  - As soon as a file upload finishes successfully, anyone can read that file and get the latest version, without waiting for a long time.
  - If you update or delete a file, all users across the world immediately see the updated file from the application, or they can understand that the file has been deleted or removed.
  - There's no "***eventual consistency***" delay, like other cloud services, where users might temporarily see old data for a few seconds or minutes, a kind of buffer storage.

  Example: Suppose you upload a new product image to your e-commerce website. Right after uploading the image to GCP Cloud Storage, all customers visiting your website immediately see the latest product image. There is no waiting, no cache confusion, and no old versions floating around.

Zero Carbon Emissions: GCP is committed to ensuring that the operation of its infrastructure does not contribute to greenhouse gas emissions. Google Cloud Storage has a ***zero-carbon emissions footprint***, which results in environmentally sustainable cloud operations. The energy that powers Google's data centres comes from 100% renewable energy sources such as wind energy, solar energy, and hydropower.

Google Cloud aims to power its operations with clean energy. By 2030, Google plans to achieve 24/7 carbon-free energy in all its data centres. To measure and manage carbon emissions, Google Cloud offers the **Carbon Footprint tool**, which helps customers understand and reduce their cloud-related carbon footprint. This tool provides a breakdown of emissions by ***project, service, and region, allowing customers to identify areas for improvement***.

Understand the GCP Storage Classes

GCP provides different classes of storage that help us with various factors such as performance, data access frequency level, and cost-effectiveness. Each storage class is designed for specific use cases, from frequently accessed to rarely accessed data.

Standard storage is ideal for frequently accessed data, or "**HOT-data storage**". It offers the highest availability and performance, which makes it perfect for storing files that need to be accessed frequently and for short-term requirements. It is commonly used for web content, mobile applications, and streaming media. It provides options to add geographic redundancy for higher availability across global services in dual-regions or multi-regions. Standard storage has ***no minimum storage duration, no retrieval fees***, and offers a typical monthly availability of **>99.99% in multi/dual regions** and **99.99% in single regions.**

Nearline storage is designed for data accessed **on average once a month or less**. It is a low-cost, extremely durable storage class that is suitable for occasionally accessed analytics datasets. It offers a **thirty-day minimum storage** period at **a minimal retrieval fee**, which makes it more cost-effective than standard storage when data is not being accessed often. It still provides fast access times and is an excellent fit for scenarios with acceptable lower availability. The typical monthly availability for it is **99.95% in multi/dual regions** and **99.9% in single regions**.

Coldline storage is an even more cost-effective option for storing data you access **less than once a quarter**. It is ideal for infrequently accessed content such as disaster recovery backups or archival datasets. It has a **ninety-day minimum storage period** and **higher retrieval costs**, which are balanced by its lower storage price. Like other classes, it offers high durability and worldwide accessibility. Coldline is most effective for data that needs to be stored for long periods but is not frequently used. It is available for **99.95% in multiple/dual regions** and **99.9% in single regions**.

Archive storage is the lowest-cost storage class in GCP, designed explicitly for data accessed **less than once a year** or **that has a minimum storage duration of 365 days.** It is perfect for regulatory or legal archives, compliance data, and long-term backups. It provides **the highest data access and operation costs. Still, it offers the lowest cost per GB for storage and millisecond-level access, which makes** it suitable even for emergency disaster recovery scenarios. Its availability mirrors that of Coldline, with **99.95% in multi/dual regions** and **99.9% in single regions**.

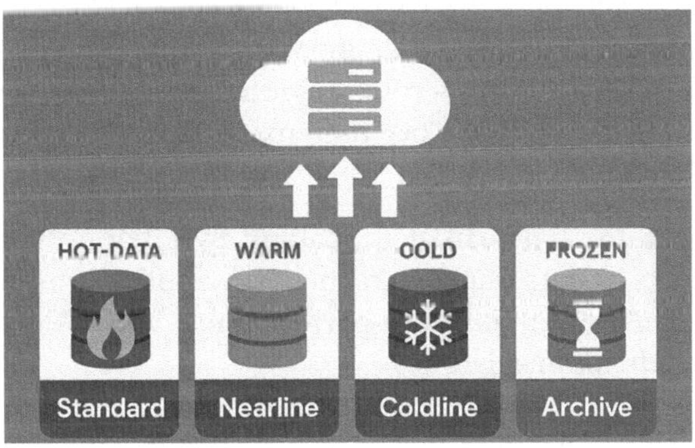

Figure 3.2: GCP Storage Classes

Google Cloud Storage Services

Google Cloud Platform (GCP) provides a suite of storage solutions designed for different use cases, which range from simple object storage to globally distributed relational databases (RDBMS systems). Each service is optimized for performance, scalability, and security aspects. Here is an in-depth analysis of each storage service, including architecture, use cases, pricing considerations, and best practices.

Figure 3.3: *Google Cloud Storage Services*

Cloud Storage

This is an **object storage service.** This highly durable and scalable object storage service is ideal for storing unstructured data like ***emails, social media posts, documents, audio files, video files, and sensor data***. It is designed to offer high availability, scalability, and durability at a large scale. With features like **lifecycle automation**, **custom dual-region buckets**, and the **11 nines durability**, it is ideal for backup, disaster recovery, static website hosting, big data, and AI/ML storage. It also ensures robust **security through encryption**, IAM, and object versioning.

Key Features

- **Point-in-Time Recovery (PITR):** This feature allows you to restore data to a specific moment, while offering protection against accidental deletions or overwrites. This is especially useful for compliance, audits, or recovering from operational errors.
- **Automated Daily Backups and Replication:** Cloud Storage supports automatic backups and replication **across regions** or **zones**, while ensuring data availability and durability. This minimizes data loss and supports disaster recovery planning.
- **Read Replicas for Performance Scaling:** By creating **read-only replicas** of storage objects or data buckets, read-heavy applications like media streaming or content delivery can improve performance. It can be improved and scaled effectively with minimal latency.
- **Connection Pooling via Cloud SQL Proxy:** Although this feature is specific to Cloud SQL, it is relevant when Cloud Storage is accessed through SQL

instances. Cloud SQL Proxy efficiently manages and pools connections, while ensuring secure and scalable data access.

- **Storage Transfer Service and High-Speed Import/Export:** It provides a **Storage Transfer Service** that allows for fast data migration from AWS S3, Azure Blob, or on-prem systems. It supports scheduling, incremental transfers, and bandwidth-optimised large-scale migrations.
- **Lifecycle Management and Automation:** Lifecycle policies enable automated transitions between storage classes (for example, from Standard to Archive) and automatic deletions after a set period (for example, 365 days), which reduces storage costs and manual maintenance.
- **Custom Dual-Region Storage:** With **Custom Dual-Region** options, you can configure buckets to replicate data between **two specific regions** (for example, nam4 = us-central1 (Iowa) + us-east1 (South Carolina)), while optimizing for latency and disaster recovery across geographies.
- **High Durability (11 Nines) and Multi-Region Redundancy:** It offers **99.999999999% (11 nines)** durability by replicating data across multiple locations. Depending on your access needs and fault tolerance, you can choose from multi-regional, regional, or dual-regional storage options.
- **Advanced Security and Access Control:** Data is encrypted at rest (AES-256) and in transit (TLS). IAM policies and optional ACLs provide fine-grained access control. Features like object versioning and retention policies enhance compliance and recovery.

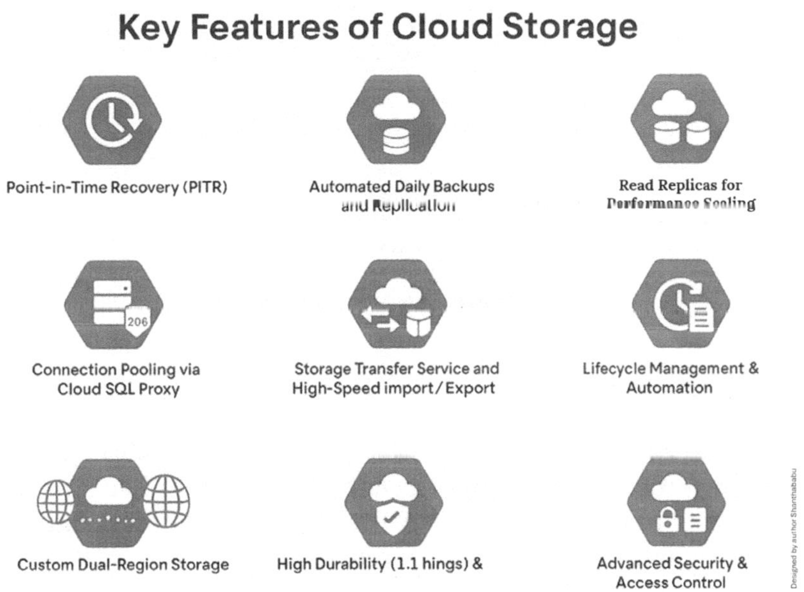

Figure 3.4: *Key Features of Cloud Storage*

Use Cases

Here are the best use cases for GCS:

- **Backup and Disaster Recovery**: We can build a secure system that securely stores automated backups with versioning and geo-redundancy. We can also provide a solution for instant recovery with lifecycle policies from a cost optimization perspective.
- **Static Website Hosting**: We can host static assets globally with low latency via HTTP/S endpoints and integrate with Cloud CDN and load balancers for high availability.
- **Big Data and AI/ML Storage**: It can build a central repository for training datasets and model artefacts, integrated with BigQuery, Vertex AI, and enable direct analysis in BigQuery and AI services without data movement.
- **Media Storage and CDN** (works with Cloud CDN): It can store and deliver videos/images globally with edge caching. It supports transcoding workflows and adaptive bitrate streaming.

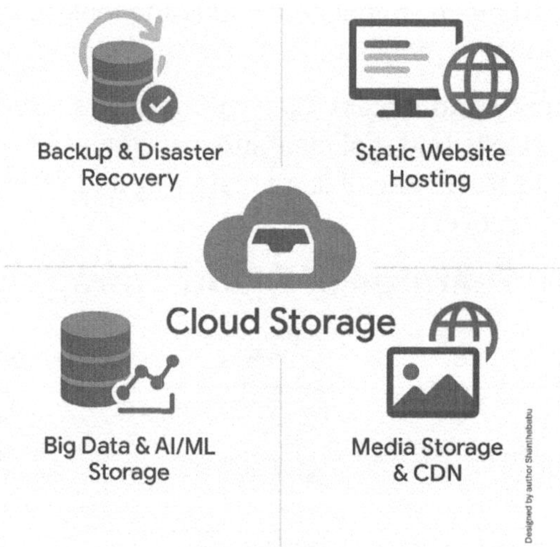

***Figure* 3.5:** *Use Cases for Cloud Storage*

Cloud SQL

It is a fully managed relational database service supporting **MySQL, PostgreSQL**, and **SQL Server** with built-in high availability, automated backups, and strong security features. Optimized for OLTP workloads, it offers low latency, vertical and horizontal scaling, and seamless integration with serverless services like **Cloud Functions** and **App Engine**. IAM-based authentication, VPC-only access, and encryption at rest and in transit ensure enterprise-grade performance and security. It is ideal for transactional systems, SaaS backends, analytics dashboards, and e-commerce platforms.

Key Features:

- **Various SQL Supports**: It supports MySQL, PostgreSQL, and SQL Server
    - **MySQL**: Fully compatible with standard MySQL (5.7, 8.0), including stored procedures and triggers
    - **PostgreSQL:** Supports extensions like Postgis, pgAudit, and IAM-based authentication
    - **SQL Server**: Supports the enterprise, standard, and web editions with Windows Authentication (via AD integration)
- **High availability**: It provides high availability regional replication with automatic failover to maintain a standby instance in a different zone within the same region, with automatic failover (**typically <30 sec downtime**) during outages.
- **Replicas**: It has high-scale, read-heavy workloads with up to ~**5 replicas** across regions. Async replication with near-real-time sync has a latency period of only a few seconds.
- **Encryption**: It provides **at-rest** AES-256 encryption, which is Google-managed or customer-supplied keys via Cloud KMS. **When in transit,** it enforces SSL/TLS for all connections.
- **Network and Security:** Regarding network isolation, it restricts access to VPC-only (no public internet exposure) and prevents data exfiltration via security perimeters. It provides IAM Database Auth with **PostgreSQL** only and users can log in with Google Cloud IAM credentials and no password management.
- **High Scalability:** It provides both scalabilities. **Vertical scaling** can increase vCPUs/RAM with zero downtime, and **Horizontal Scaling** reads and replicas distribute query load, which is helpful for analytics/reporting. Additionally, Cloud SQL does not support native sharding.
- **Point-in-Time Recovery (PITR)**: It offers automated maintenance with configurable windows and auto-applied minor version upgrades. It also provides daily backups, **Point-in-Time Recovery (PITR)** for up to 7 days, and on-demand backups stored in **Cloud Storage** for easy recovery and protection.
- **OLTP workloads:** offering low latency (typically under 10ms) and supporting up to **30,000 concurrent connections**, depending on instance size. However, it is **not designed** for massive write scaling (beyond 50K writes/sec), sharding, or data warehousing. For such use cases, **BigQuery** or **Cloud Spanner** will be more suitable.

***Figure* 3.6:** *Key Features of Cloud SQL*

Use Cases

The following are the best use cases for Cloud SQL:

- **Backend for Transactional Applications (ERP, HRM):** This storage is ideal for OLTP workloads requiring ACID compliance and complex queries. It supports common enterprise systems with reliable uptime (99.95% SLA).
- **Analytics Dashboards with BI Tools**: Read replicas enable high-performance reporting without impacting production workloads by offloading reporting queries from the primary database. These replicas also integrate directly with analytics and visualization tools such as Looker, Tableau, and Data Studio.
- **SaaS Product Metadata Storage:** Since this is a managed service, it eliminates database administration overhead. Automatic scaling handles customer growth seamlessly, which makes it perfect for SaaS products.
- **Integration with Cloud Functions, App Engine, and Cloud Run:** It provides private VPC connectivity, which ensures secure serverless-to-database communication and connection pooling that is optimized for serverless's ephemeral nature
- **E-Commerce Platforms:** They can handle spikes during sales events with vertical scaling, while point-in-time recovery prevents accidental data loss.

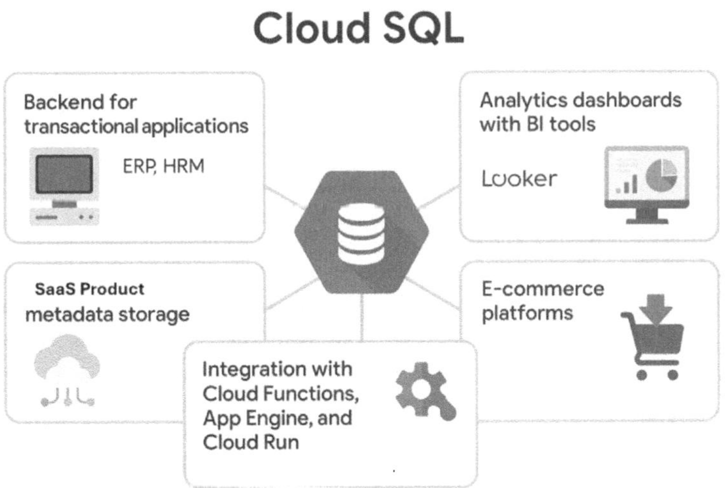

Figure 3.7: *Use Cases for Cloud SQL*

Cloud Bigtable

Cloud Bigtable is a fully managed, scalable NoSQL database on Google Cloud, which is designed for high-throughput, low-latency workloads. It can handle petabyte-scale data with sub-10ms latency, which makes it ideal for applications like real-time analytics, IoT telemetry, and personalization engines. BigTable automatically shards data for horizontal scaling and ensures strong consistency at the row level. It supports time-series data with versioning, while enabling efficient storage of chronological metrics. Seamless integration with BigQuery, Dataflow, and AI/ML tools allows developers to build powerful data pipelines. BigTable is also HBase API-compatible, which simplifies migration and integration with existing Big-Data ecosystems.

Key Features

- **Scalability:** It supports **petabyte-scale** datasets while maintaining low latency, approximately single-digit milliseconds. It automatically shards data across nodes based on row keys, while enabling seamless horizontal scaling. This makes it ideal for applications that grow rapidly and require consistent performance at a large scale.
- **Performance:** It is designed for **high-throughput workloads** and can handle millions of operations per second with low latency. It is well-suited for applications like real-time analytics, recommendation engines, and IoT telemetry processing that demand fast read/write speeds at scale.
- **Integrations:** It integrates smoothly with **BigQuery** for analytics, **Dataflow** for stream/batch processing, and **AI/ML tools** for model training on massive

datasets. This ecosystem support allows developers to build complete data pipelines and ML workflows on GCP.

- **Strong Consistency:** It ensures **strong consistency at the row level**, which means that every read returns the most recent write. This is critical for real-time accuracy applications like fraud detection or inventory management.
- **Time-Series and Versioned Data:** It supports **timestamped versions of each cell**, which enables efficient storage and retrieval of time-series data. This significant feature makes it valuable for use cases like monitoring, metrics storage, and event tracking, where multiple versions of data need to be retained.
- **Apache HBase API and Dataflow Integration:** This is **API-compatible with Apache HBase**, which makes migration and integration with HBase-based applications easy. It also connects well with **Apache Beam/Dataflow**, supporting real-time and batch processing pipelines without complex configuration.

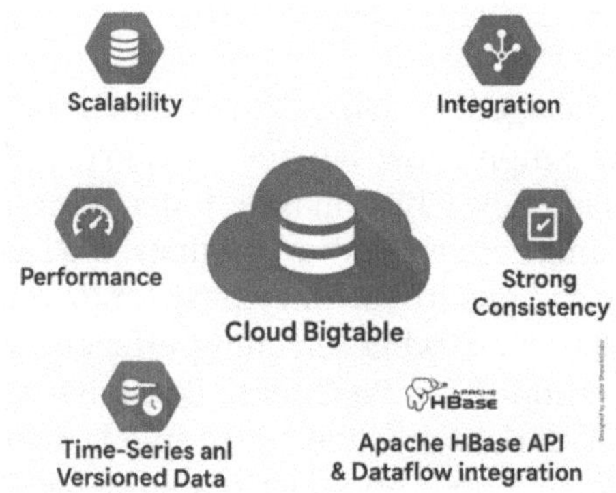

Figure 3.8: *Key Features of Cloud Bigtable*

Use Cases

Here is a list of the best use cases for Cloud Bigtable:

- **Sensor Data Ingestion:** It can handle high-velocity data streams from millions of devices with consistent low latency. Therefore, it is perfect for **IoT** telemetry-based applications. Moreover, its time-ordered data structure feature enables efficient storage and retrieval of device metrics.
- **Financial Tick Data and Stock Market Feeds:** Due to their ultra-low latency, the systems are well-suited to handling financial market tick data, where millions of price updates are generated per second, and sub-10 ms latency is critical. It also preserves the ordered sequence of market events, which is essential for trading algorithms and real-time analytics.

- **Real-Time Analytics:** Its low latency supports instant queries across petabyte-scale datasets for operational insights. It can also integrate with Spark/Hadoop for large-scale processing without compromising on performance.
- **Personalization Engines:** These engines facilitate microsecond-level access to behavioural data for content suggestions. They also store and update user profiles in real-time for recommendation engines.
- **Time-Series Data:** We can design an optimized structure for chronological data with efficient time-range queries. This is ideal for IoT device logs, application monitoring, and industrial telemetry.
- **Fraud Detection:** We can design the best analysis of transaction patterns across massive datasets and identify anomalies by using machine learning models on fresh data for fraud detection-based applications.

Figure 3.9: *Use Cases for Cloud Bigtable*

Cloud Datastore (Now Firestore in Datastore Mode)

Datastore is a **serverless NoSQL document database** that automatically scales with your application's needs. It is now unified with Firestore, but is still available in Datastore mode for App Engine users. It provides automatic scaling and is ideal for semi-structured data.

Key Features

- **ACID Transactions at Entity Group Level:** It supports **ACID-compliant transactions** within an entity group, while ensuring that multiple operations on related data are either fully completed or fully rolled back. This maintains data integrity in scenarios like updating user profiles or atomising orders.
- **Indexed Queries (with Automatic Index Creation):** It automatically creates indexes for most queries, while enabling **fast lookups** and **efficient filtering** without manual tuning. Developers can also define custom composite indexes, which allow them to explore **complex and high-performance queries**.

- **Integration with Firebase and GCP SDKs:** It integrates natively with **Firebase** and is ideal for mobile and web app development. Additionally, it supports the Google Cloud SDKs, which allows developers to interact with the database programmatically across serverless, App Engine, and containerised environments.
- **Support for Offline Sync (Firestore):** When used in **Firestore mode**, Datastore supports offline data persistence and synchronization for mobile and web apps. This allows users to continue using apps without internet access and automatically syncs data once connectivity is restored.
- **Serverless (No Infrastructure Management):** It is a **fully serverless database**, which means developers do not need to manage servers, storage, or scaling. Google Cloud automatically handles capacity provisioning, replication, and high availability behind the scenes.
- **Scalability:** It is built to scale automatically, handling high volumes of reads and writes without performance degradation. It is suitable for growing applications with unpredictable workloads such as chat apps, metadata stores, or gaming backends.

Figure 3.10: *Key Features of Cloud Datastore*

Use Cases

Here is the list of the best use cases for Cloud Datastore:

- **User Profile Management:** This service is well-suited for storing user profiles with attributes like preferences, activity history, and authentication metadata-based applications. Its flexible, schema-less structure allows for easy updates and expansion that run in tandem with app features and their evolved versions. ACID transactions ensure consistency during profile updates and are reliable for user-centric applications.
- **Content Management Systems (CMS):** They support content types such as articles, images, tags, and metadata in a document-oriented model. Their automatic indexing and fast query performance enable efficient content retrieval and filtering. They also allow developers to adapt data structures

without rigid schema constraints, which makes them ideal for dynamic CMS environments.

- **Chat Apps with Real-Time Updates:** With Firestore mode, Datastore offers real-time synchronization across devices and provides instant message delivery and updates. Offline persistence enables users to send messages even without a network connection and syncs them once the device reconnects. This makes it an excellent choice for modern mobile and web chat applications.
- **Shopping Carts and App Settings:** It can handle frequent updates to shopping cart contents, session data, and user preferences. Its low-latency reads and writes ensure fast checkout processes and dynamic personalization. The flexible schema also simplifies storing varied settings across different app modules.
- **Gaming Leaderboards and App Metadata:** Gaming applications use Datastore to store player scores, achievements, and other in-game data with high scalability. It supports real-time updates for leaderboards and ensures availability under peak load conditions. Its integration with mobile SDKs makes it seamless to implement for mobile or web-based games.
- **Applications Requiring Flexible Schemas:** Datastore's schema-less design allows for agile development without complex migrations for applications with evolving or variable data structures. Developers can add fields or change formats on the fly, which makes Cloud Datastore ideal for startups, prototypes, and apps with frequently changing requirements.

Figure 3.11: *Use Cases for Cloud Datastore*

Cloud Spanner

Cloud Spanner is Google's flagship relational database and combines NoSQL and traditional RDBMS traits. It offers global horizontal scaling, strong consistency, and SQL semantics. It is a globally distributed, horizontally scalable relational database that combines the benefits of SQL with NoSQL-like scalability and large-scale enterprise applications needing SQL with NoSQL Scalability: Spanner combines the structured querying power of SQL with the scalability of NoSQL, supporting enterprise apps that must process massive datasets with complex relationships, like ERP, CRM, or multi-tenant SaaS platforms.

Key Features

- **ANSI SQL Support with Joins, Indexes, and Transactions:** It supports full ANSI SQL, which enables developers to write familiar queries with support for joins, secondary indexes, and ACID transactions. This allows users to scale relational workloads globally without having to rewrite applications in NoSQL syntax.
- **Automatic Schema Migration (Online DDL):** It supports schema changes, such as adding columns, altering indexes, or modifying constraints, which can be performed online without downtime. This feature ensures high availability and continuous deployment, even in live-traffic production environments.
- **Query Partitioning for Performance:** It uses **query partitioning** to parallelize operations across nodes and improves performance for large data sets. It is beneficial for analytical queries and exporting large datasets to BigQuery.
- **Integration with Dataflow, BigQuery, and Looker:** It integrates seamlessly with **Dataflow** for streaming and batch ETL, **BigQuery** for analytics, and **Looker** for data visualization. This creates a powerful, connected data ecosystem within Google Cloud for end-to-end processing and insights.
- **Global Consistency:** Cloud Spanner provides strong consistency across multiple regions through Google's TrueTime API. This guarantees that data is always up-to-date globally, which allows users to deploy it for real-time applications with globally distributed users and writes.
- **Horizontal Scaling:** It automatically **shards data across compute nodes**, which allows for linear scaling without manual partitioning. This allows you to seamlessly scale read and write throughput, even as workloads grow significantly.
- **High Availability (99.999% SLA):** With automatic replication, failover, and a distributed architecture, Cloud Spanner offers an industry-leading **99.999% uptime SLA**. This makes it suitable for mission-critical applications like banking systems, telecom platforms, and global SaaS products.

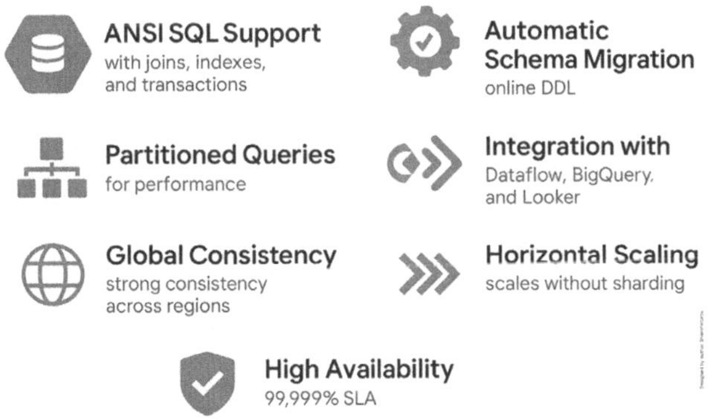

Figure 3.12: *Key Features of Cloud Spanner*

Use Cases

Here are the best use cases for Cloud Spanner:

- **Global Financial Applications:** Since it supports **ACID-compliant** transactions and strong consistency, it is ideal for banking systems that require accurate and reliable transaction processing. Its global replication ensures low-latency access and high availability for cross-border financial operations.
- **Retail Inventory and Order Systems:** Retail platforms benefit from Spanner's ability to manage millions of product updates, orders, and customer interactions across regions. It enables **real-time inventory tracking**, supports promotional scaling, and ensures transactional integrity for purchase flows.
- **Massive Multiplayer Games:** Gaming platforms use Spanner to handle **millions of concurrent users** (Real-Time User Data) with real-time player stats, game progress, and leaderboards updates. Its low latency, horizontal scalability, and no-downtime schema updates are critical for live service games.
- **Telecom Subscriber Management:** It can manage subscriber data, call records, billing, and provisioning across regions, with real-time updates and global consistency. It handles **high throughput** and **concurrent sessions efficiently**, which makes it ideal for telecom-grade backend systems.
- **Financial Systems Requiring ACID Compliance:** Applications such as credit scoring, transaction logging, and reconciliation require strong guarantees of data accuracy, which Spanner delivers through ACID transactions at scale. It ensures secure and traceable record-keeping across vast datasets.
- **Global Inventory and Supply Chain Management:** It enables real-time tracking of **inventory levels, shipments, and vendor coordination** across countries. Its multi-region availability and strong consistency ensure that every stakeholder sees the same data in real time, reducing errors and delays.

Figure 3.13: *Use Cases for Cloud Spanner*

Here is a comparative analysis of the discussed Google Cloud Storage Services:

Features / Services	Cloud Storage	Cloud SQL	Bigtable	Datastore/ Firestore	Cloud Spanner
Data Type	Unstructured Objects	Structured RDBMS	Wide-column NoSQL	Document-based NoSQL	Relational + Distributed
Schema	None	Strict schema	Flexible, per row	Schema-less	Strict SQL
Scale	Massive (exabytes)	Limited by VM size	Virtually unlimited	Auto-scaled	Global (auto-shard)
Consistency	Strong	Strong	Strong (per row)	Strong/ Eventual	Strong (global)
Managed Backups	Manual or Lifecycle	Automatic + PITR	Snapshot-based	Auto-Backup	Auto + PITR
Integration	BigQuery, AI, CDN	Looker, ADF, App Eng.	Dataflow and Kafka	Firebase, App Engine	Looker and Dataflow

Table 3.1: *Comparative Analysis of Google Cloud Storage Services*

BigQuery

BigQuery is Google Cloud's fully-managed, serverless, and highly scalable enterprise data warehouse designed for analytics. It enables users to store, query, and analyze petabyte-scale datasets using ANSI SQL and supports real-time analytics, machine learning, and business intelligence through integrated tools.

Key Features

- **Standard SQL Support:** This fully supports ANSI-compliant SQL syntax, including complex joins, window functions, subqueries, JSON functions, and nested/repeated fields (for semi-structured data).

- **Blazing-Fast Query Engine:** It leverages **Dremel** for high-speed query execution. It follows a distributed architecture, which can scan billions of rows in seconds.
- **Dremel** is Google's highly scalable, distributed query engine that powers BigQuery. It is designed to analyze massive read-only datasets in real time using a multi-level execution tree. This leads to fast and interactive query performance across petabytes of data.
- **Federated Querying:** It has the capability of federated querying capabilities that can query data stored in Cloud Storage (CSV, Avro, JSON, Parquet, ORC), Google Sheets, Bigtable, Cloud SQL, and external connections via BigQuery Omni (cross-cloud queries on AWS/Azure).
- **BigQuery ML (BQML)** is a powerful feature that allows users to build, train, and deploy ML models directly within BigQuery using SQL. It supports models such as ***linear regression, logistic regression, K-means clustering, XGBoost, TensorFlow*** models, and **AutoML** integration.
- **BigQuery BI Engine:** This is an **in-memory analysis service** that accelerates dashboard performance and efficiency in Looker, Data Studio, and third-party BI tools.
- **Partitioning and Clustering:** It helps improve performance by **partitioning** data into segments such as date, region, country, and category. It can also organize data within partitions by specific fields such as customer ID and region.
- **Streaming Data Ingestion:** This feature supports real-time data streaming using insert APIs or Pub/Sub. It is ideal for use cases like fraud detection, activity tracking, and monitoring.
- **Security and Access Control:** It facilitates **IAM roles** at the project, dataset, and table levels and also supports **column-level security, data masking, audit logs**, and **VPC Service Controls**.

Figure 3.14: *Key Features of BigQuery*

Use Cases

- **Customer Behaviour Analysis:** BigQuery enables businesses to analyse large volumes of customer interaction data such as **web clicks, app usage**, and **transaction history** to uncover insights about preferences, churn risk, and buying patterns. It also supports advanced segmentation and personalisation strategies in real time.
- **Real-Time Fraud Detection:** Thanks to streaming ingestion and powerful SQL processing, BigQuery can process transaction data as it arrives to ***detect anomalies***. This enables ***fraud detection models*** to flag suspicious activity in seconds, ideal for ***banking***, ***payments***, and ***cybersecurity***.
- **IoT Telemetry Analytics:** It handles massive telemetry data streams from IoT devices and supports time-***series analysis***, ***alerting***, and ***operational dashboards***. Its integration with Pub/Sub and Dataflow makes it ideal for smart cities, connected vehicles, and industrial monitoring.
- **Predictive Reporting:** Using BigQuery ML, teams can train and deploy models like ***regression*** or ***clustering*** directly on their data warehouse. This results in predictive insights such as future sales, demand forecasting, or customer lifetime value, without having to manually move data to external platforms.

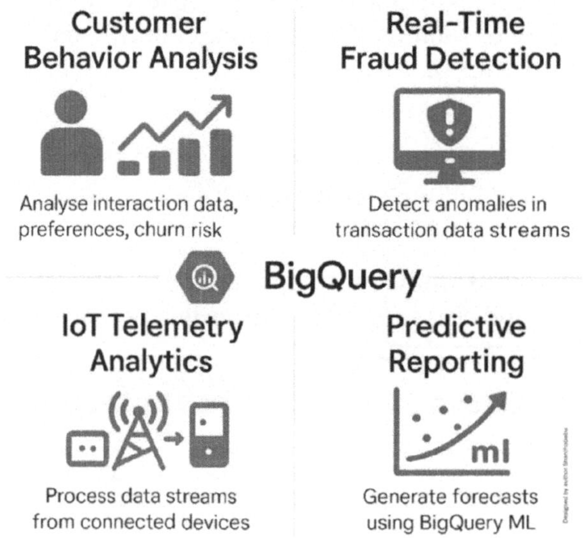

Figure 3.15: *Use Cases for BigQuery*

Working with Cloud Storage Service

Let us discuss how we can work with cloud storage services. GCP provides two different methods, such as the **Console UI** and the **`gsutil` CLI** tool:

- **Console UI:** This UI provides a web-based interface that allows users to manage buckets and objects with point-and-click ease manually. It is best suited for small-scale tasks like uploading files, setting permissions, and viewing storage metrics—ideal for users who prefer not to use command-line tools.
- **`gsutil` CLI: `gsutil`** is a powerful command-line tool used in the Cloud SDK for Google Cloud Storage. It is perfect for automating and scripting bulk operations such as uploading, downloading, syncing, and managing permissions on large sets of files. It is ideal for ***developers, sysadmins***, or ***data engineers*** working with large datasets or repetitive tasks.

Creating Cloud Storage

Step 1: Log in to GCP (https:// console.cloud.google.com/).

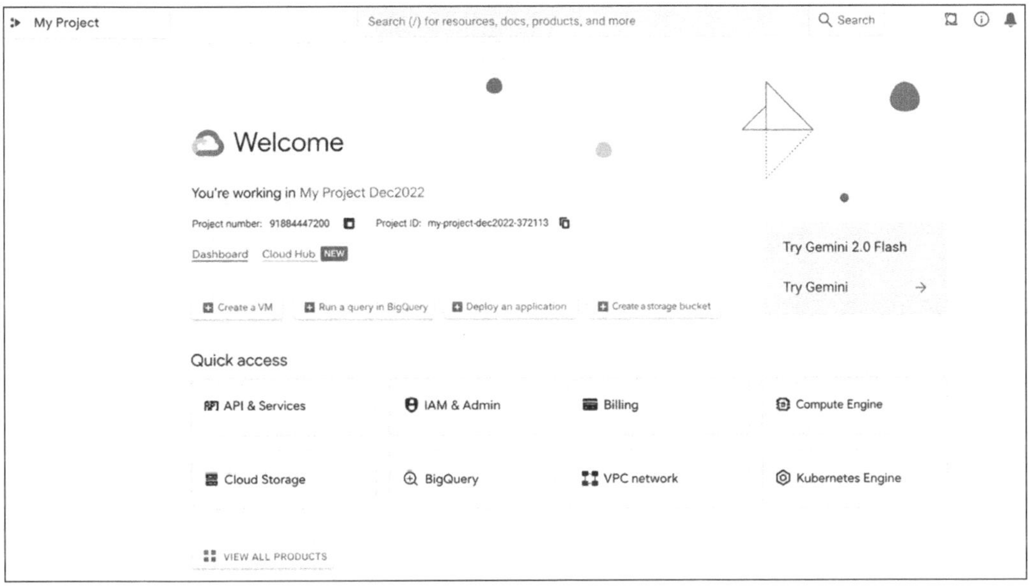

Figure 3.16: GCP - *Homepage*

Step 2: Go to the navigation menu on the left side of the console, select "**`Cloud Storage`**" as shown in *Figure* 3.17 and click "**`Buckets`**".

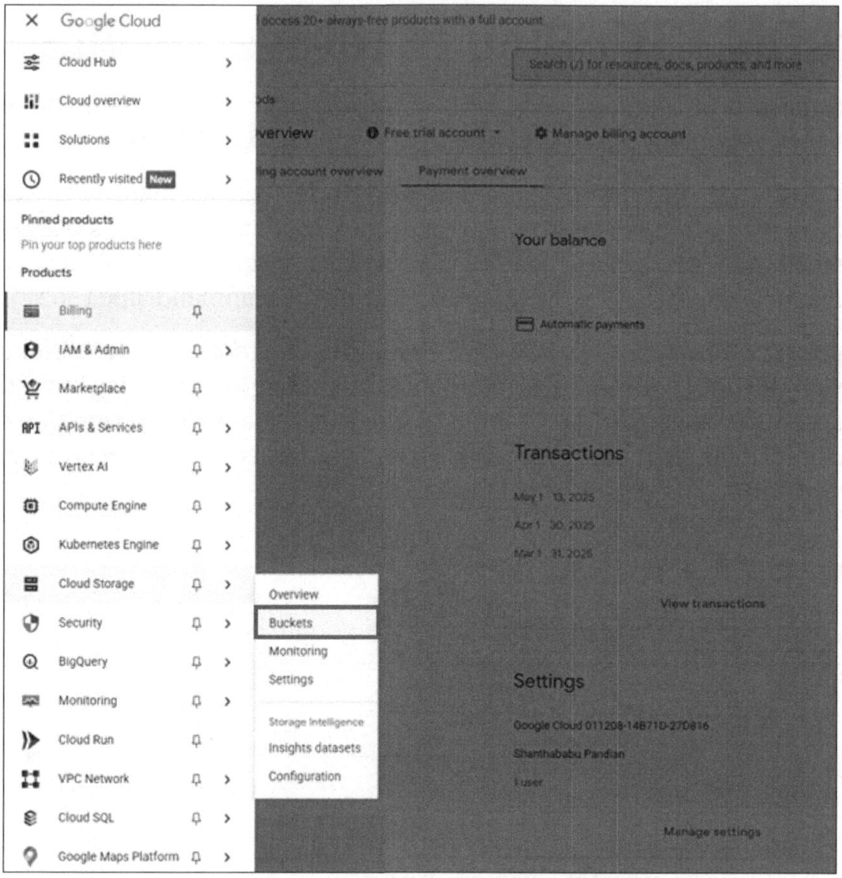

Figure 3.17: *GCP – Navigation Menu – Cloud Storage*

Step 3: Once you click "**`Buckets`**", the portal takes you to the page shown in *Figure* 3.18. Click "**`Create bucket`**".

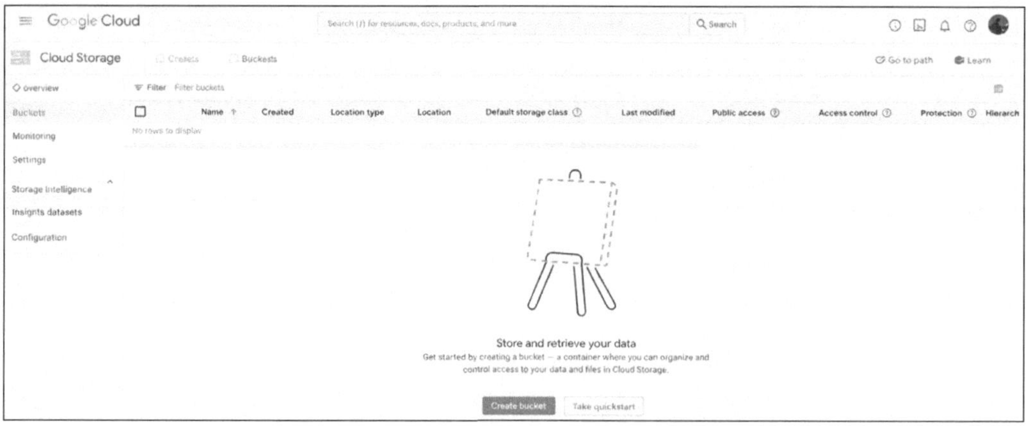

Figure 3.18: *GCP – Cloud Storage – Bucket(s)*

Step 3: Once you click "**`Create bucket`**", the portal takes you to the page shown in *Figure* 3.19. Here, you have to configure the following items one by one:

- Name of the bucket
- Choose where to store your data
- Choose how to store your data
- Choose how to control access to objects
- Choose how to protect object data

Step 4: Enter the name of the cloud storage; it must be a globally unique, permanent name. Then, click "**`Continue`**" as shown in *Figure* 3.19.

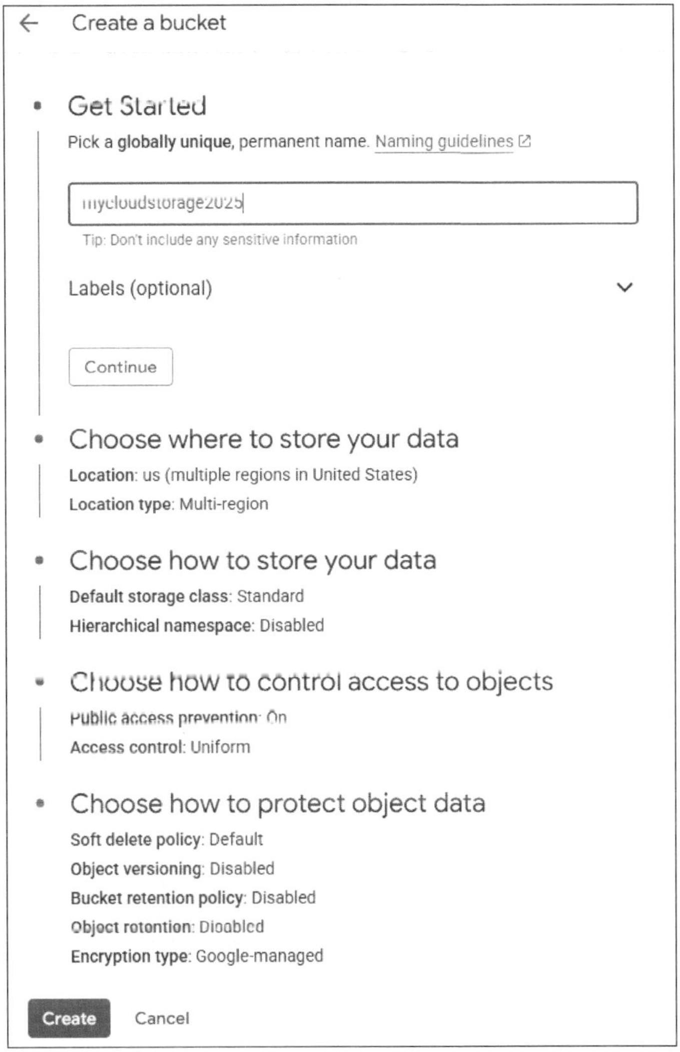

Figure 3.19: GCP – *Cloud Storage – Bucket Configuration (Name)*

Step 5: Choose Where to Store Your Data

This choice defines the geographic placement of your data and affects cost, performance, and availability. It cannot be changed later. Based on our requirements, we must choose either Multi-region, Dual-region, or Region as the location type.

- **Location Type**
  - Multi-Region
    - Highest availability across the most significant areas; we can add cross-bucket replication via Storage Transfer Service.
    - As data is added or changed, replicate it to another bucket. This enables you to store a copy that follows different bucket settings, for example, region, storage class, and so on.
- **Dual-Region**
  - High availability and low latency across 2 regions
  - Add turbo replication (Continent and Regions).
- **Region**
  - Lowest latency within a single region

Based on your requirement, select any one location type from the provided options. Then, click "**`Continue`**", as shown in *Figure* 3.20.

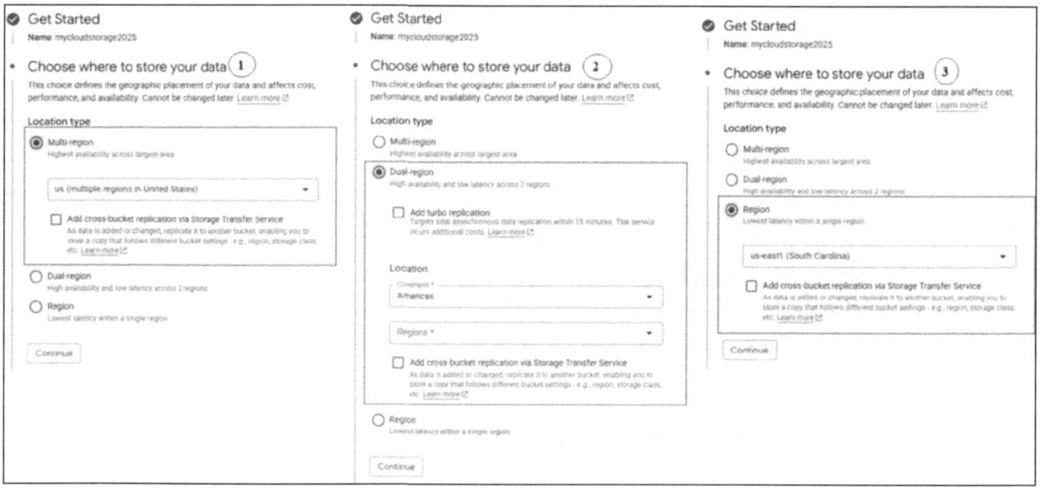

Figure 3.20: GCP – *Cloud Storage – Bucket Configuration (Choose Where to Store Your Data)*

Step 6: Choose How to Store Your Data

Once you have configured "**`Choose where to store your data`**" you must configure how to store it; the GCP environment provides Autoclass, sets a default class, and optimizes storage for data-intensive workloads.

This feature sets storage, retrieval, and operations costs with minimal uptime differences. You can choose whether objects are managed automatically or specify a default storage class based on how long you plan to store your data and your workload or use case.

- **Auto-Class:** Automatically transitions each object to a ***Standard*** or ***Nearline*** class based on object-level activity to optimize cost and latency. This is recommended if the usage frequency may be unpredictable. The default class can be changed at any time.
- **Setting a Default Class:** This helps to apply the class to all objects in your bucket unless you manually modify the class per object or set object lifecycle rules. This works the best when the usage is highly predictable.
    - Standard: Best for short-term storage and frequently accessed data
    - Nearline: Best for backups and data which is accessed less than once a month
    - Coldline: Best for disaster recovery and data which is accessed less than once a quarter
    - Archive: Best for long-term digital preservation of data which is accessed less than once a year
- Optimizing Storage for Data-Intensive Workloads
    - Enable Hierarchical Namespace on This Bucket: You can optimize storage for AI/ML and analytics with a file system-like hierarchical structure. This permanent option comes with atomic folder renames, faster folder listing, and more enhancements that are otherwise unavailable in Cloud Storage's standard buckets with a flat namespace.

Once you have completed the "**`Choose how to store your data`**" configuration, click "**`continue`**", as shown in *Figure 3.21*.

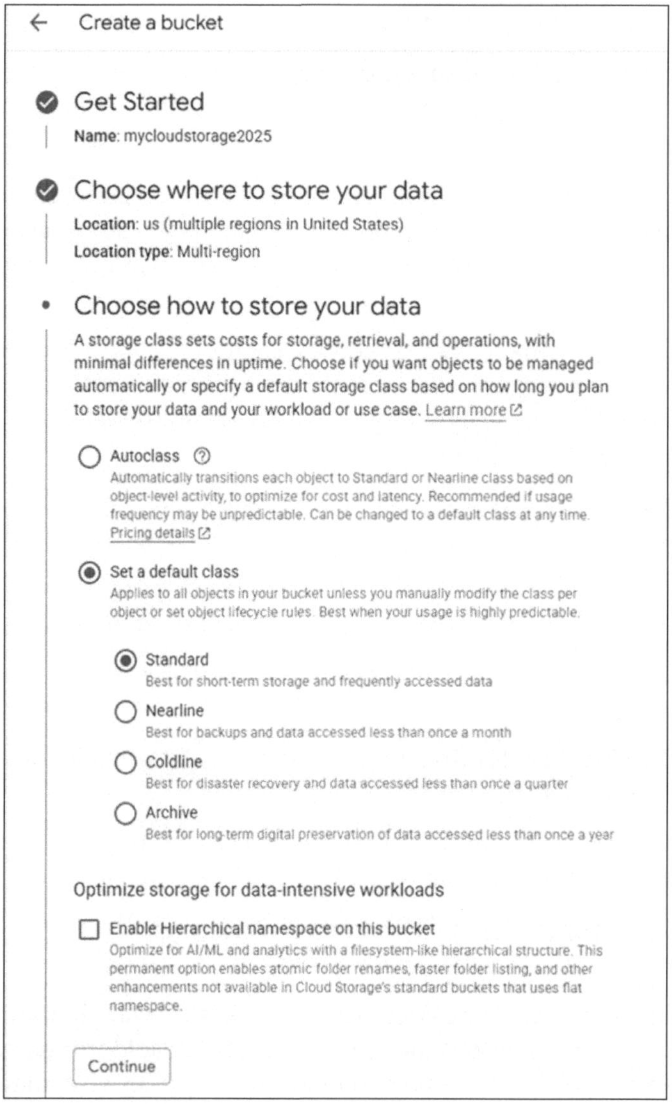

Figure 3.21: GCP – *Cloud Storage – Bucket Configuration (Choose How to Store Your Data)*

Step 7: Choose How to Control Access to Objects

Once you have chosen how to store your data and the configuration is completed, you must configure the "**`Choose how to control access to objects`**" configuration. This is mainly to prevent public access and restrict data that comes via the Internet. The said functionality prevents this bucket from being used for web hosting.

There are two access controls available in this menu, which are:

- **Uniform**: Use only bucket-level permissions (iam) to ensure uniform access to all objects in the bucket. This option becomes permanent after 90 days.

- **Fine-grained**: Specify access to individual objects using object-level permissions (ACLs) and bucket-level permissions (IAM).

Based on your requirements, select the access control and click "**`Continue`**", as shown in *Figure* 3.22.

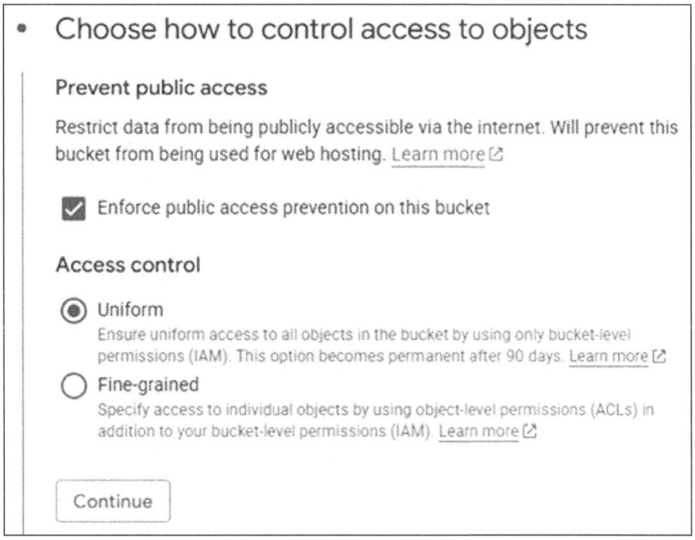

***Figure 3.22**: GCP – Cloud Storage – Bucket Configuration (Choose How to Control Access to Objects)*

Step 8: Choose How to Protect Object Data

Cloud storage always protects your data, but you can also choose from these additional data protection options to add additional layers of security. GCP provides this feature. Once you have configured "**`Choose how to control access to objects`**", you must configure how to protect object data, as shown in *Figure* 3.23:

Data Protection Options: Soft Delete Policy (For Data Recovery): When enabled, this bucket and its objects will be kept for a specified period after they are deleted. They can also be restored during this time.

- **Use Default Retention Duration**: All buckets have a 7-day soft delete duration by default unless your organization administrator has customized it.

- **Set Custom Retention Duration**: Specify how long this bucket and its objects should be retained after they are deleted. Setting a "**`0`**" duration disables soft delete, which means that any deleted objects will be deleted permanently.

Object Versioning (For Version Control): This is used to restore deleted or overwritten objects. To minimize the cost of storing versions, we recommend limiting the number of noncurrent versions per object and scheduling them to expire after a number of days.

Retention (For Compliance): This prevents the deletion or modification of the bucket's objects for a specified period of time.

Data Encryption: GCP provides the following features for data encryption:

- **Google-Managed Encryption Keys (Default):** Google automatically manages encryption keys for data at rest, using AES-256 encryption with built-in key management and automatic key rotation. The encryption keys are owned and controlled by Google, ensuring secure and seamless data protection without user intervention.
- **Cloud KMS Key (Customer-Managed):** You can encrypt data using your own Cloud Key Management Service (KMS) keys, which you (the customer) own and manage by setting key rotation schedules.

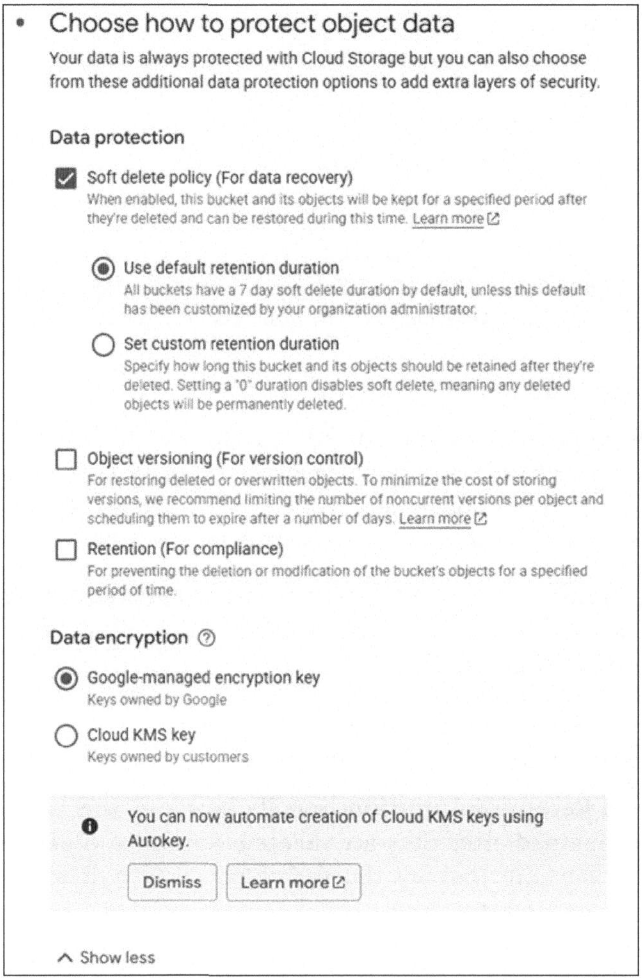

Figure 3.23: *GCP – Cloud Storage – Bucket Configuration (Choose How to Protect Object Data)*

Step 9: Create a Bucket.

Once all the configurations are completed, click "`Create`". A window will pop up on the portal, as shown in *Figure* 3.24.

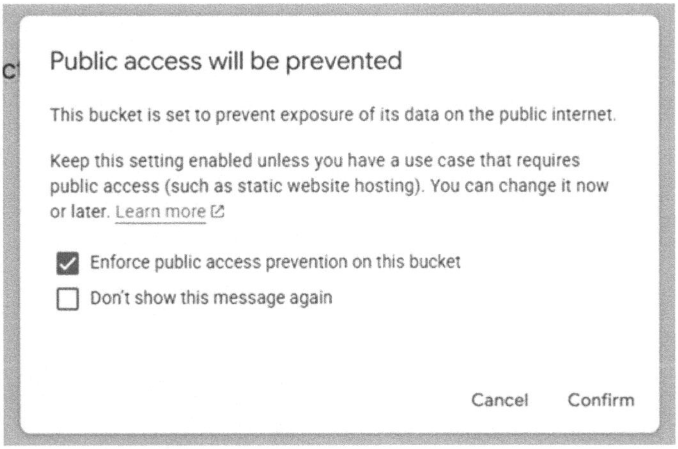

***Figure* 3.24:** GCP – *Cloud Storage – Bucket Configuration (Final Step)*

Public Access Will Be Prevented: You have two options here. This bucket is set up to avoid the exposure of its data to the public internet. Enable this setting unless you have a use case requiring public access (such as static website hosting). You can change it now or later.

- Enforce public access prevention on this bucket (Best option).
- Do not show this message again.

Once you confirm, the storage or bucket is ready to use. This portal will bring you to the screen shown in *Figure* 3.25, where you can see the bucket(s) created for your project.

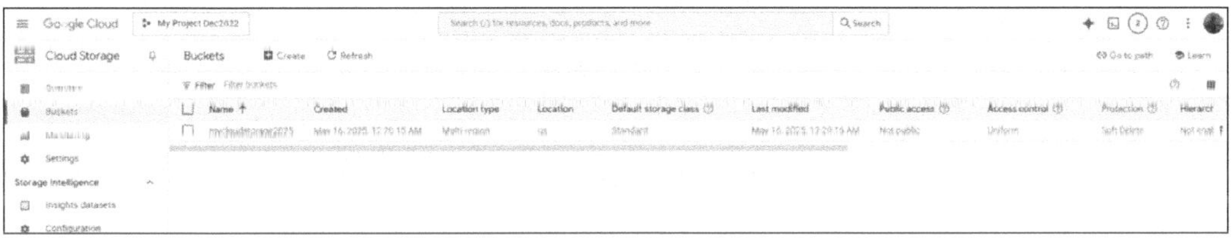

***Figure* 3.25:** GCP – *Cloud Storage – Bucket Ready to Use*

Let us add an object to the bucket now.

Step 10: Add Object(s) to the Bucket.

When you click the name of the bucket (or) storage, the portal will take you to the screen shown in *Figure* 3.26.

Figure 3.26: *GCP – Cloud Storage – Bucket Ready to Add Object (s)*

Step 11: Select the file(s) to upload/store from local folders.

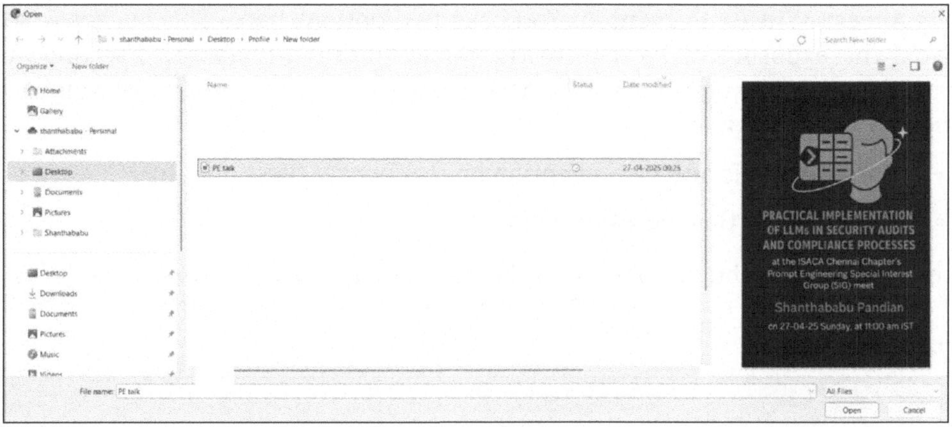

Figure 3.27: *Selecting the File into GCP – Cloud Storage – Bucket*

Step 12: The file is stored in the cloud storage.

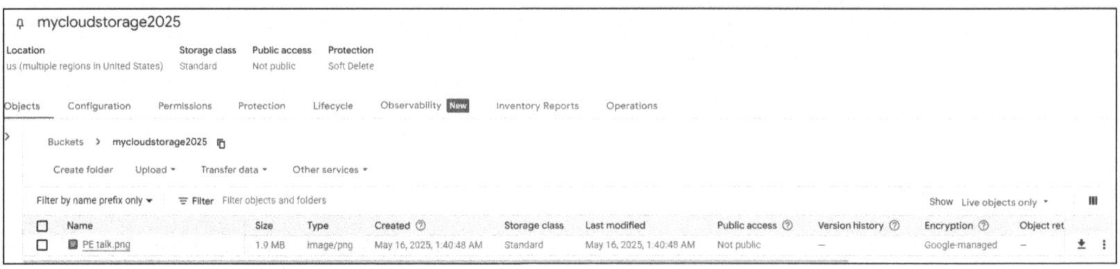

Figure 3.28: *File Stored in GCP – Cloud Storage – Bucket*

Step 13: Review the stored object details. Click the file name, and you will get the screen shown in *Figure* 3.29.

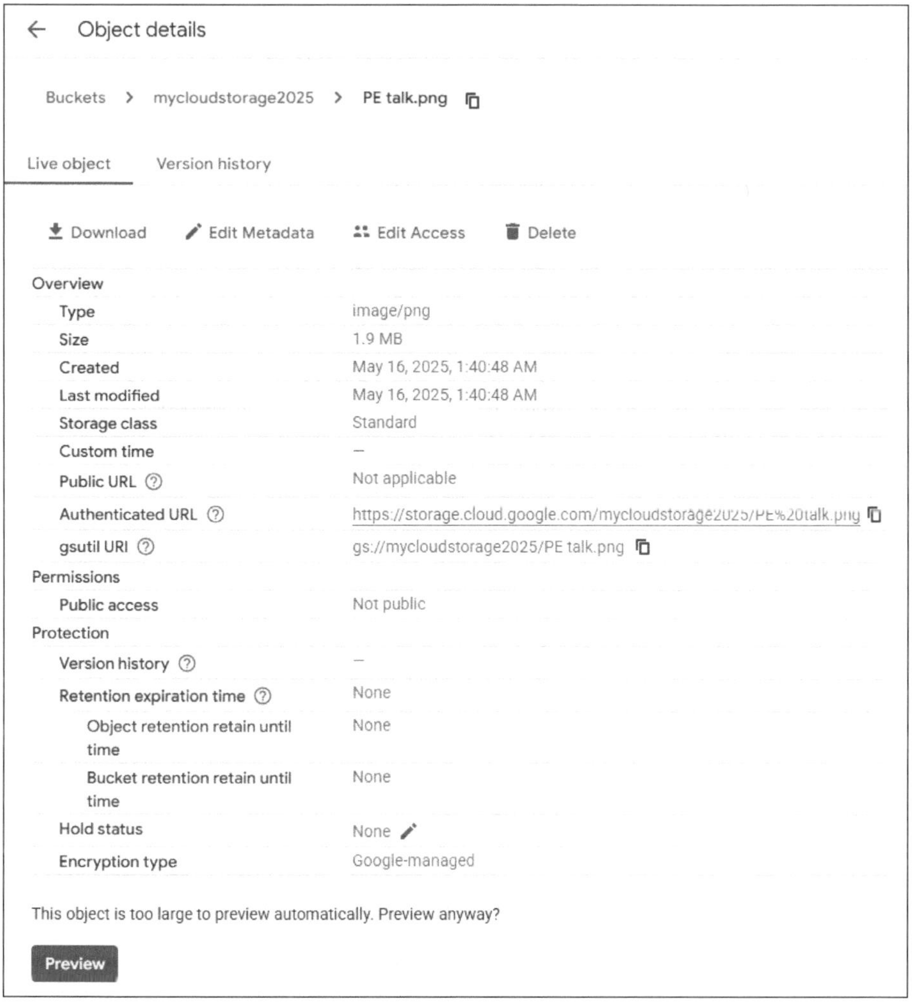

Figure 3.29: *Review the Stored Object Details in GCP – Cloud Storage – Bucket*

Step 14: You can delete the object directly by selecting the check box and clicking "`Delete`".

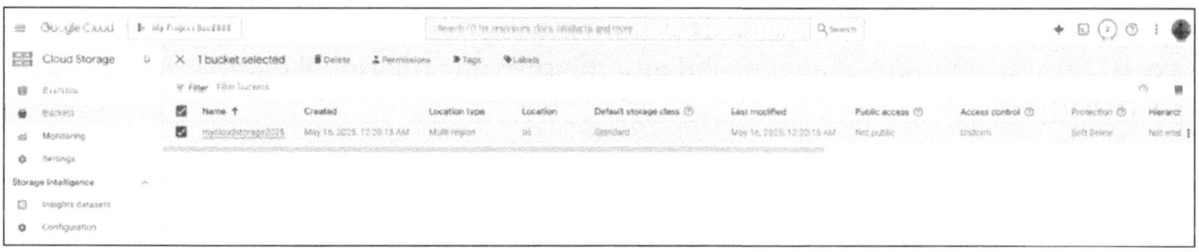

Figure 3.30: *Deleting GCP – Cloud Storage – Bucket*

Step 15: The system will ask for a delete confirmation. To do so, enter "**DELETE**" in the textbox and click "**Delete**", as shown in *Figure* 3.31.

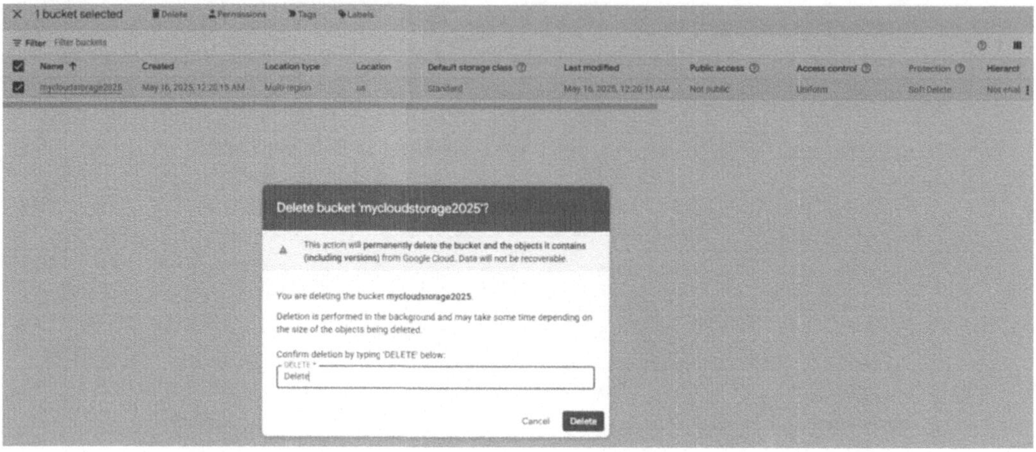

Figure 3.31: *Confirmation for Deleting GCP – Cloud Storage – Bucket*

Now, the Cloud Storage bucket is deleted successfully. Refer to *Figure* 3.32 for this step.

Figure 3.32: *Cloud Storage Bucket Deleted Successfully*

Working with Cloud SQL Service

As discussed earlier, "**Cloud SQL**" is a fully managed database service that makes it easy to set up, maintain, manage, and administer your relational databases on Google Cloud Platform.

Step 1: Go to the navigation menu on the left side of the console, select "**Cloud SQL**" as shown in *Figure* 3.33 and click "**Instance**".

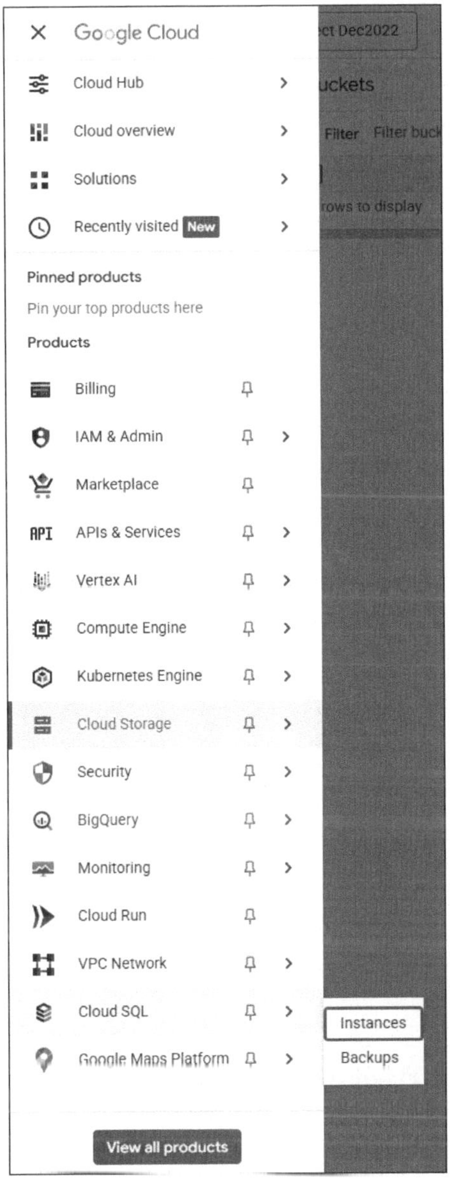

Figure 3.33: *Cloud SQL*

Step 2: Once you select the "`Instance`" sub-menu, the portal will take you to the screen in *Figure* 3.34. Then, click "`Create Instance`".

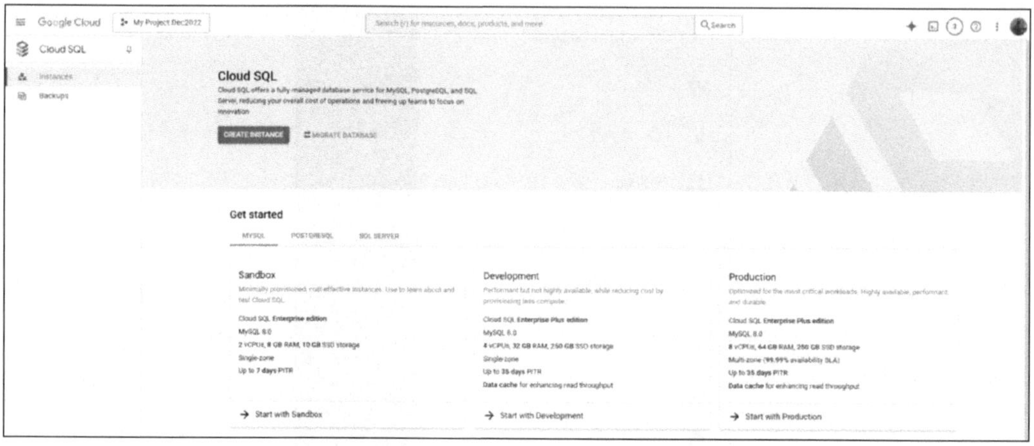

Figure 3.34: *Cloud SQL Master Page*

Step 3: Once you select the "**`Create Instance`**" button, the portal will take you to the screen shown in *Figure* 3.35 and you can select any one option from "**`MySQL`**", "**`PostgreSQL`**" and "**`SQL Server`**".

Note: *For demonstration purpose, we are selecting "MySQL" in this example:*

Figure 3.35: *Cloud SQL -DB Options*

Step 4: Click "**`MySQL`**," and the portal will take you to the screen in *Figure* 3.36. You must click "**`Enable`**" to proceed.

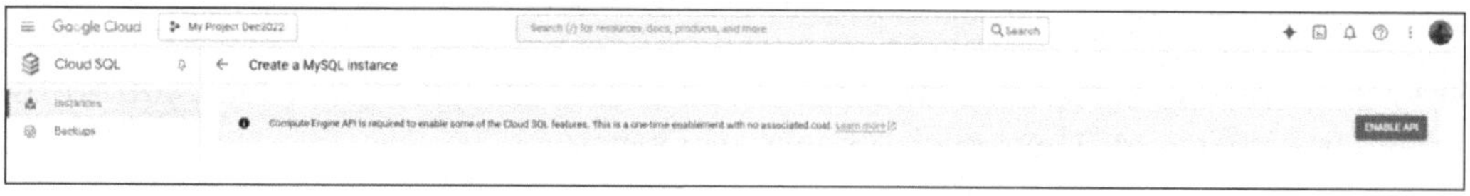

Figure 3.36: *Cloud SQL -MySQL – Enable API*

Step 5: Once you enable the API, the portal will show the available edition in *Figure* 3.37. You can observe the edition and its features.

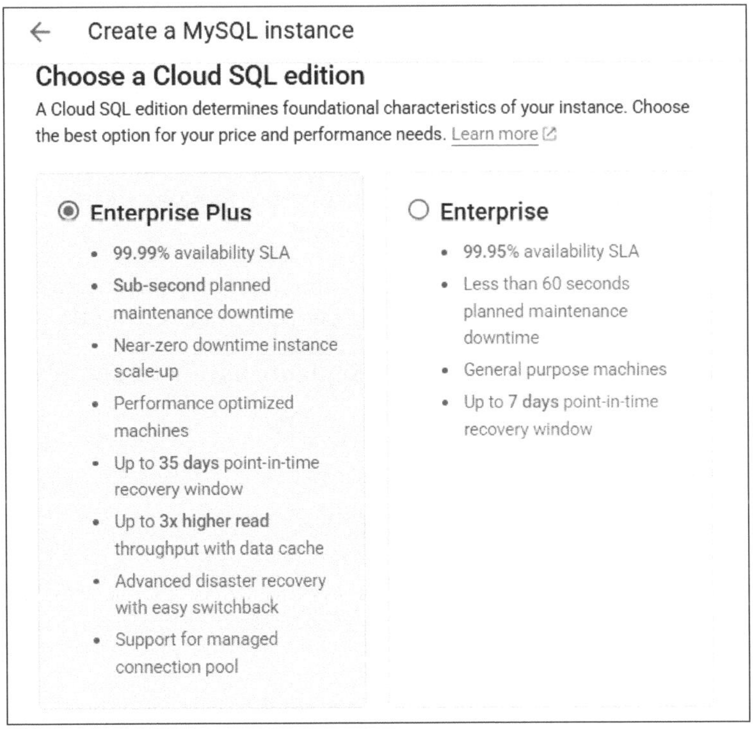

***Figure 3.37**: Cloud SQL -MySQL – Available Edition*

Step 6: You must configure the parameters mentioned here, as shown in *Figure* 3.38.

- **Edition Preset**: This option selects a predefined configuration for the SQL instance based on workload type (Production, Development, and Sandbox) and compares Enterprise and Enterprise Plus plans across different workload types.
- **Instance Info**
    - **Database Version**: You can select a specific version for the list (MySQL x.x).
    - **Option** to view and select minor versions via the dropdown.
    - **Instance ID**: Unique identifier for the Cloud SQL instance. Must use lowercase letters, numbers, and hyphens (starting with a letter).
    - **Password**: Set a password for the root user. You can either enter one manually or click on "**`Generate`**". You also have the option to check "No password" if you plan to use IAM-based auth or Cloud SQL Auth Proxy. There is also a set of password policies in place that you need to follow.
- **Regional and Zonal Availability:** Keep your data close to the needed services for better performance.

  - **Region**: This provides a list of regions you can select based on your requirements. This determines where the instance is physically located (permanent once set).
  - **Zonal Availability**:
    - **Single Zone**: Lower cost, but no failover in case of outage (not recommended for production)
    - **Multiple Zones** (Highly Available): Recommended for production; automatically fails over to another zone within the selected region

- **Customize Your Instance**: You can configure advanced settings like:
  - CPU and memory allocation
  - Disk type and size
  - Backup and maintenance schedule
  - Flags, labels, connection settings, and so on

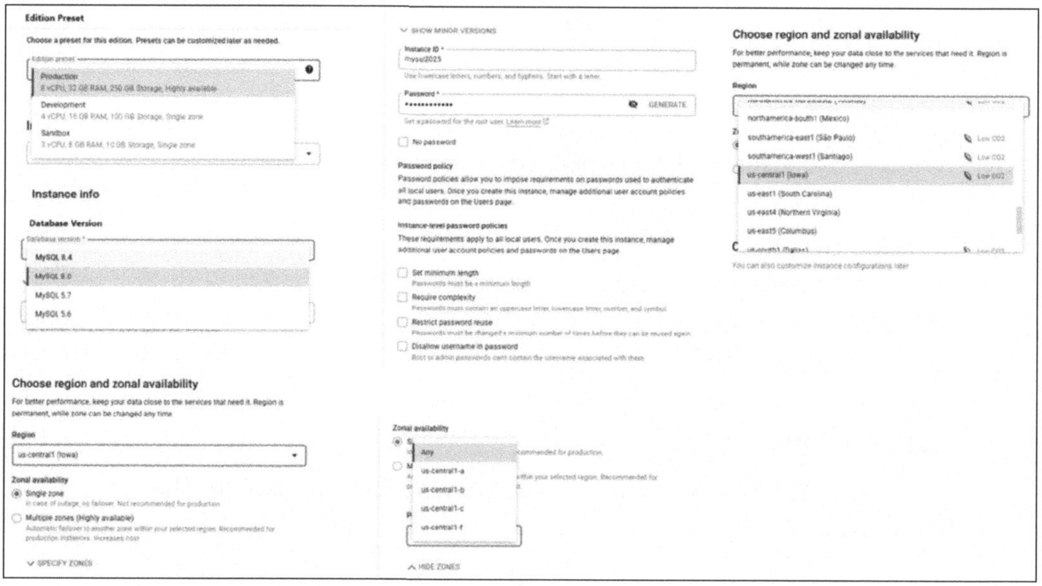

Figure 3.38: *Cloud SQL for MySQL – Configuration Parameters*

Once you have configured all the required parameters, click "**`Create Instance`**", as shown in *Figure* 3.39.

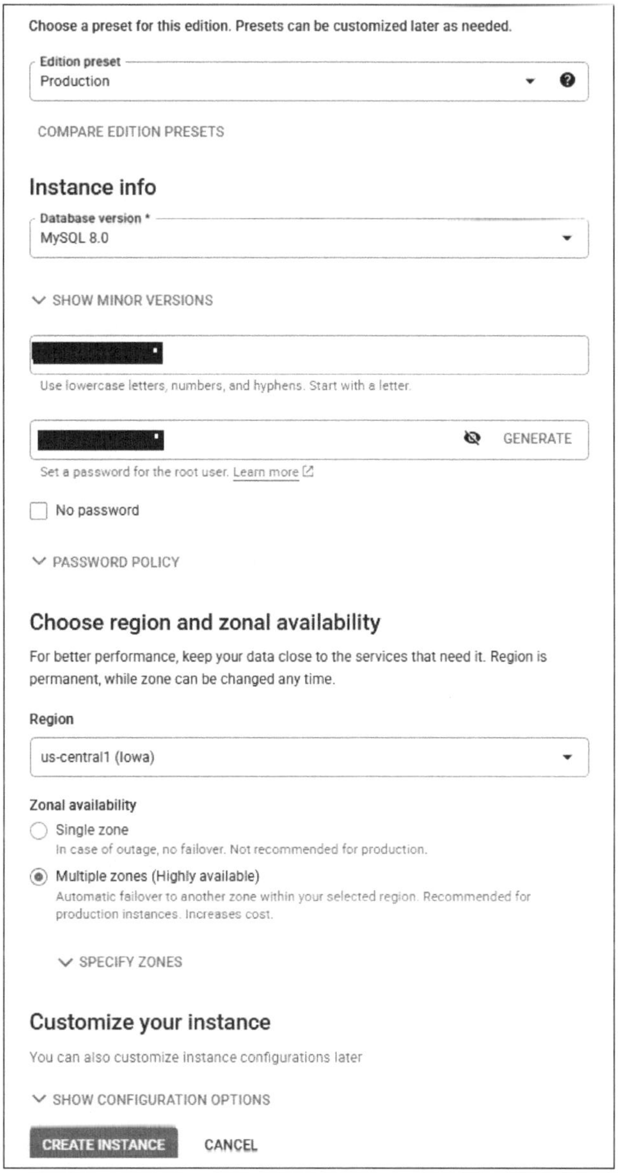

Figure 3.39: *Cloud SQL - MySQL – Configuration Completed*

Once the instance is successfully configured, the portal takes you to the screen shown in *Figure* 3.40, where you can access the Google Cloud SQL navigation panel from the Google Cloud Console.

- **Overview:** Displays instance summary, status, resource usage, and key metrics

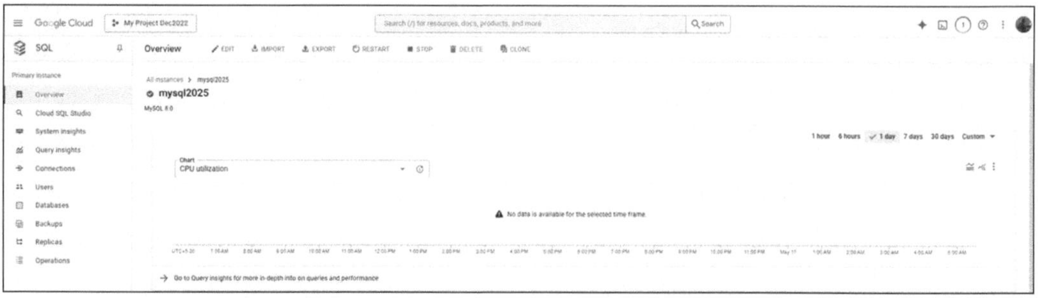

Figure 3.40: *Cloud SQL - MySQL – Environment (Overview)*

- **Cloud SQL Studio**: A built-in SQL editor that allows you to run SQL queries directly from the browser on your Cloud SQL databases
- **System Insights**: Provides visibility into database performance, including CPU, memory, storage, and query performance

Figure 3.41: *Cloud SQL - MySQL – Environment (System Insights)*

- **Query Insights**: Helps you analyze slow or expensive queries with detailed query statistics and performance trends. It also helps you detect and diagnose performance issues in your instance by examining queries using both historical and near real-time data. You must enable it to understand database load, identify slow-running queries, view active queries, and gain visibility into apps that connect to this instance. It also offers telemetry for 7 days at no additional cost.

Figure 3.42: *Cloud SQL - MySQL – Environment (Query Insights)*

- **Connections**: Manage instance connectivity, including IP whitelisting, SSL configuration, and connection strings (public/private IPs, VPCs).

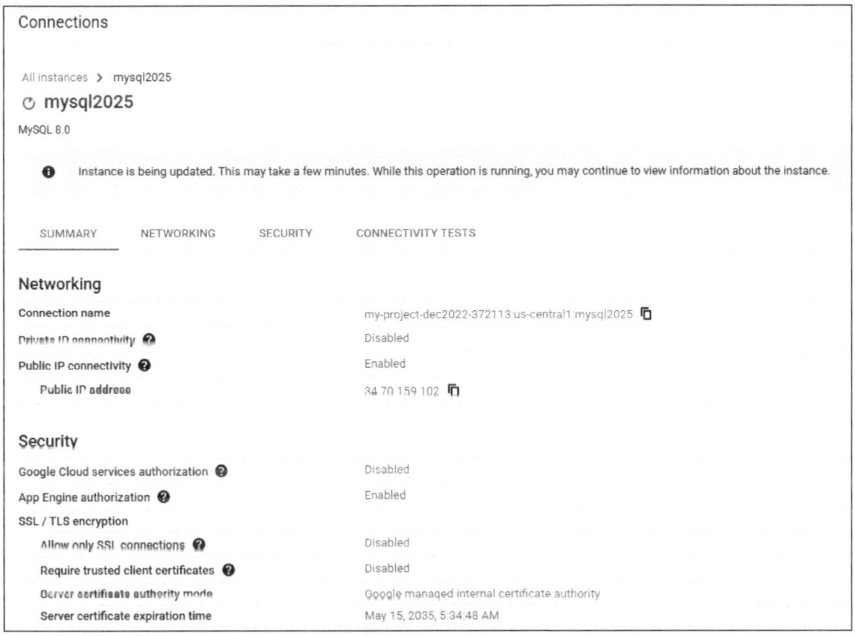

Figure 3.43: *Cloud SQL - MySQL – Environment (Connection Details)*

- **Users**: Manage database users and their authentication methods (password, IAM, and so on).

- **New User**: Click "**Add User Account**" as shown in the figure here.

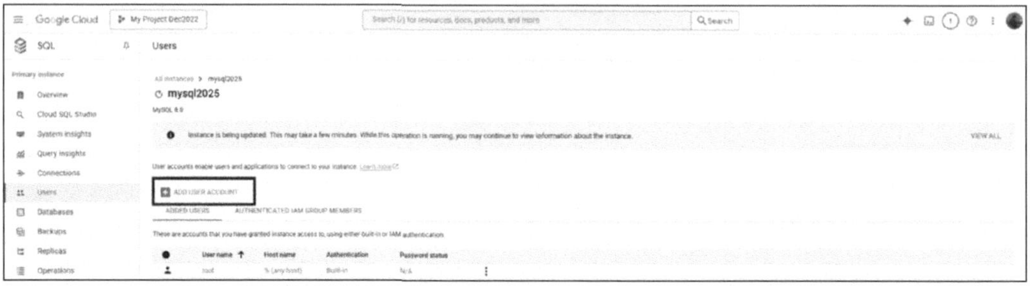

Figure 3.44: *Cloud SQL - MySQL – Environment (User Management)*

The system will pop up the new user adding screen, as shown in *Figure* 3.45. You must provide a username and password and also set IP restrictions, if any.

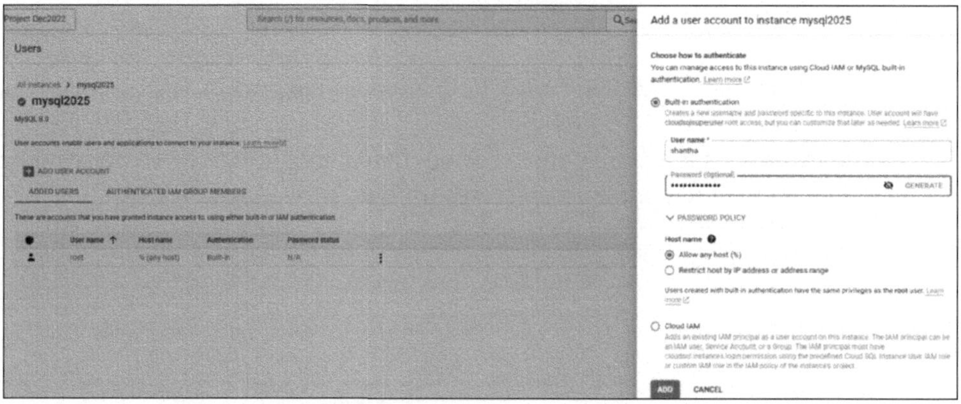

Figure 3.45: *Cloud SQL - MySQL – Environment (New User)*

Once you have provided a valid username and password and clicked "**Add**", the new user will be added to the list of existing users on the server. *Figure* 3.46 shows the same.

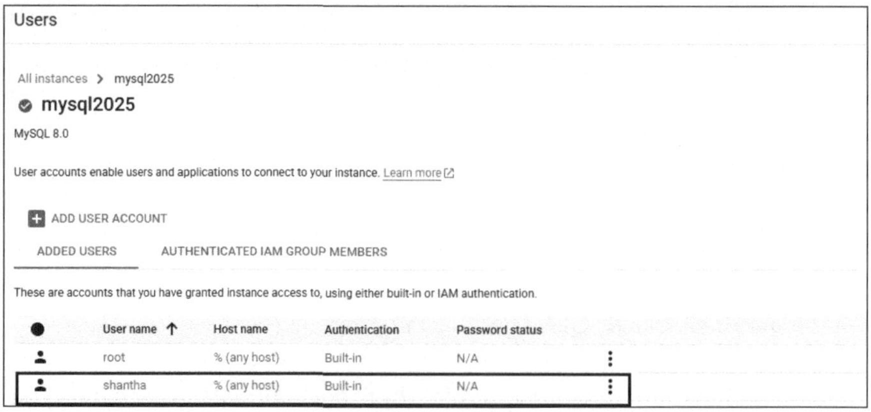

Figure 3.46: *Cloud SQL - MySQL – Environment (List of Users)*

- **Databases:** This menu will help you to view and manage individual databases within your Cloud SQL instance (for example, create, delete, rename databases), as shown in *Figure 3.47*.

Figure 3.47: *Cloud SQL - MySQL – Environment (Databases)*

Let us create a database and a table. The system will take you to the following pop-up window when you click "**`(+) Create Database`**" on the main page. You must provide the Database Name, leave the rest of the parameters as default, and click "**`Create`**".

Figure 3.48: *Cloud SQL - MySQL – Environment (Create New Database)*

The new database is called "**`mydatabase`**" and is ready to use, as shown in *Figure 3.49*.

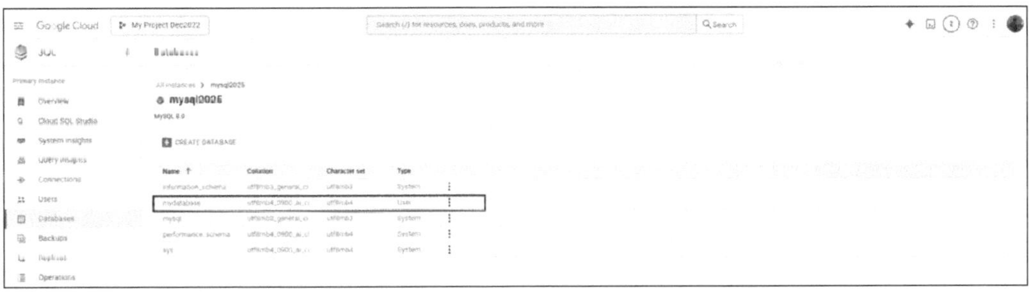

Figure 3.49: *Cloud SQL - MySQL – Environment (New Database is Ready to Use)*

- **Working on Database Objects:** To work on the database, go to Cloud SQL Studio and select the database in the right panel, as shown in *Figure 3.50*:

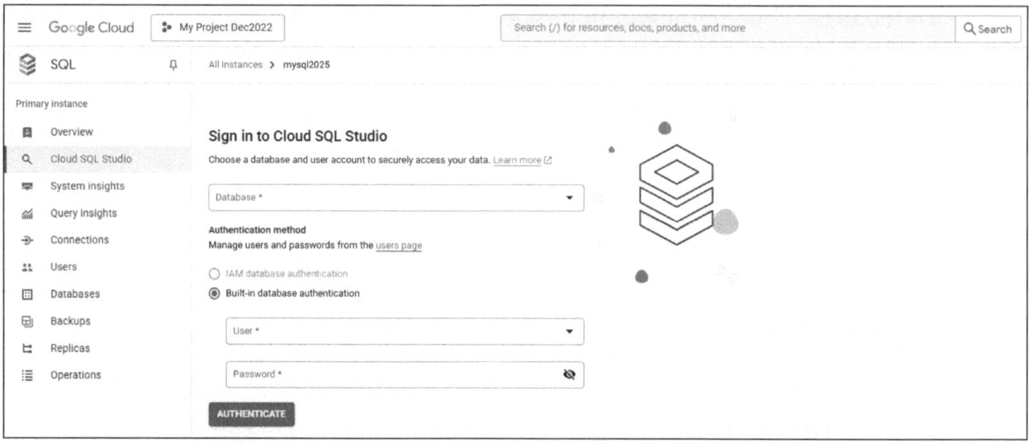

Figure 3.50: *Cloud SQL - MySQL – Environment (Cloud SQL Studio)*

Select the Database from the list, provide the username and password and click "**AUTHENTICATE**", as shown in *Figure* 3.51.

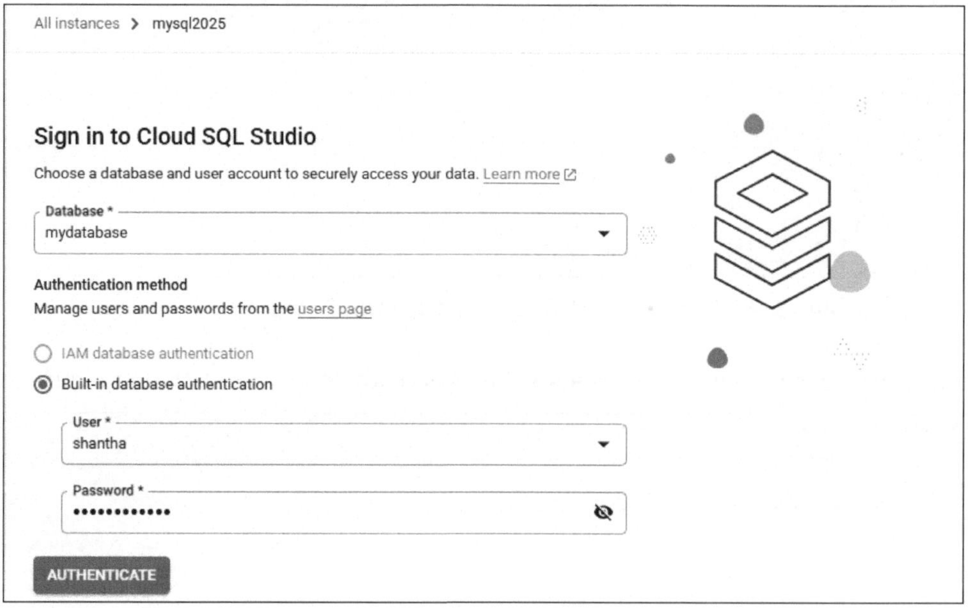

Figure 3.51: *Cloud SQL - MySQL – Environment (Cloud SQL Studio- Log into the Database)*

Once the authentication is successful, the system will take you to the explorer, as shown in *Figure* 3.52.

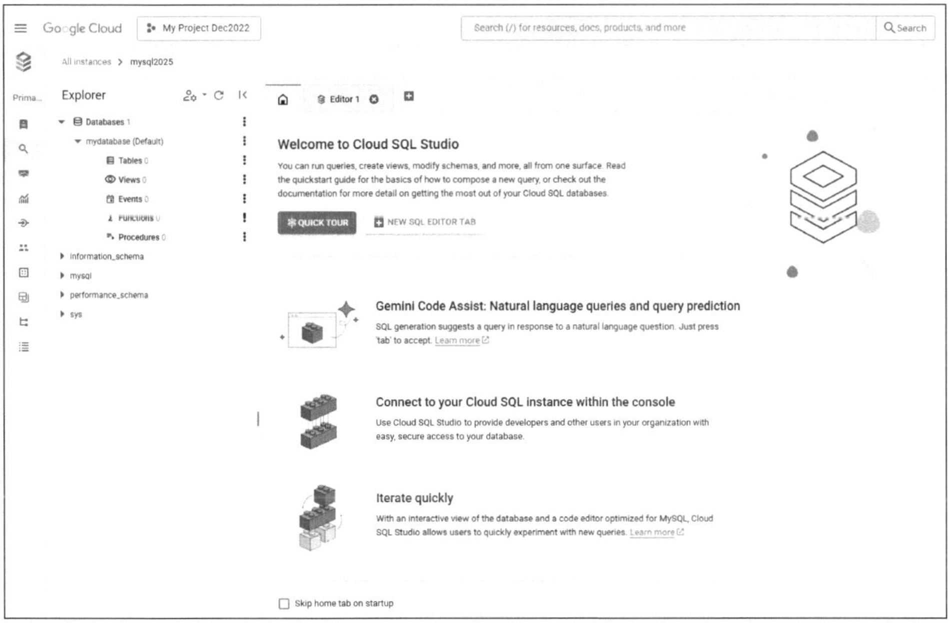

***Figure 3.52:** Cloud SQL - MySQL – Environment (Cloud SQL Studio- Database Explorer)*

You can create a table and insert data through the editor, as shown in *Figure* 3.53. This is very similar to the MySQL environment, where you can perform DDL, DML, and DCL.

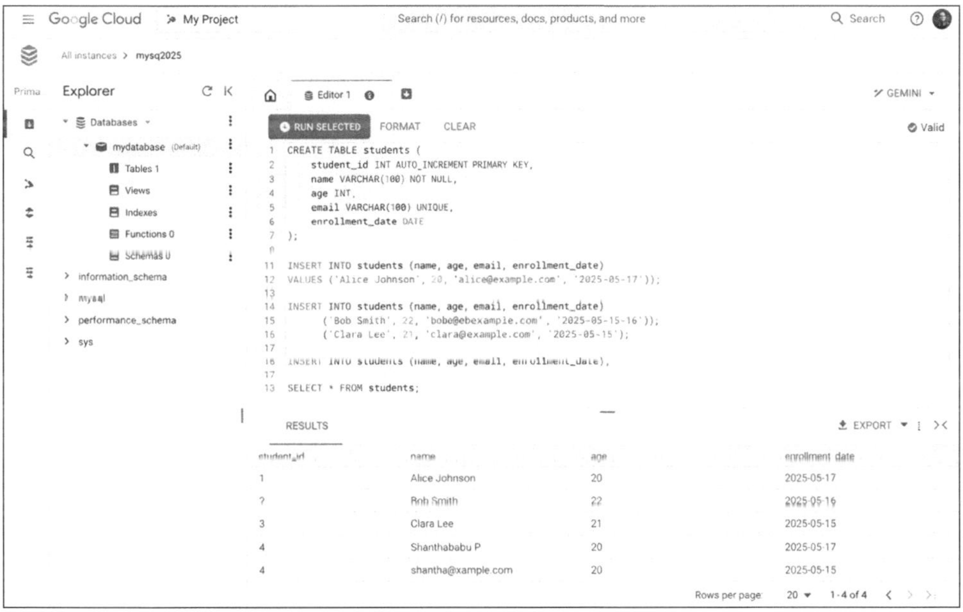

***Figure 3.53:** Cloud SQL - MySQL – Environment (Cloud SQL Studio- MYSQL Environment- Editor)*

- **Backup:** This menu will help you to view and manage automated and on-demand backups, configure retention policies, and monitor backup statuses, as shown in *Figure* 3.54.

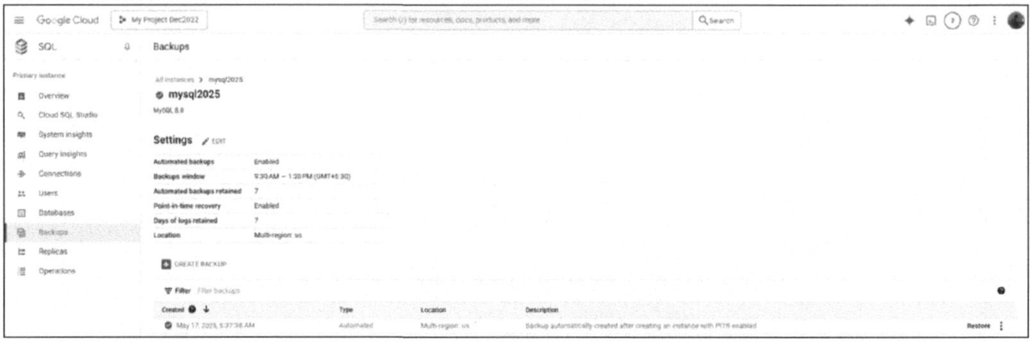

***Figure* 3.54:** *Cloud SQL - MySQL – Environment (Cloud SQL Studio- Backups)*

- **Replicas:** This menu will help you set up and monitor read replicas for scaling or failover purposes.

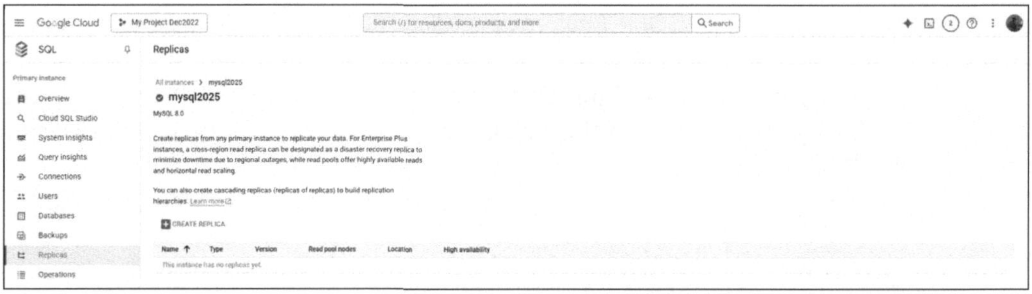

***Figure* 3.55:** *Cloud SQL - MySQL – Environment (Cloud SQL Studio- Replicas)*

- **Operations:** This menu will help you to view the history of instance-level operations such as restarts, updates, and configuration changes.

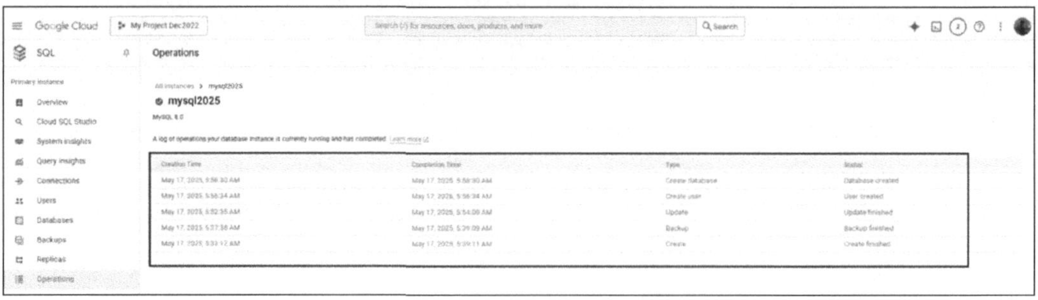

***Figure* 3.56:** *Cloud SQL - MySQL – Environment (Cloud SQL Studio- Operations)*

Delete Operations

You cannot delete this instance because deletion protection is enabled; you can observe this in *Figure* 3.57 (the delete option is disabled). To delete, you have to edit the instance and turn off deletion protection first (editable in the Data Protection section).

Figure 3.57: *Cloud SQL - MySQL – Environment (Cloud SQL Studio- Delete Operations)*

Figure 3.58 shows the **`Edit Instance →Data Protection`** configuration. To enable the delete option, you have to disable the prevent instance deletion.

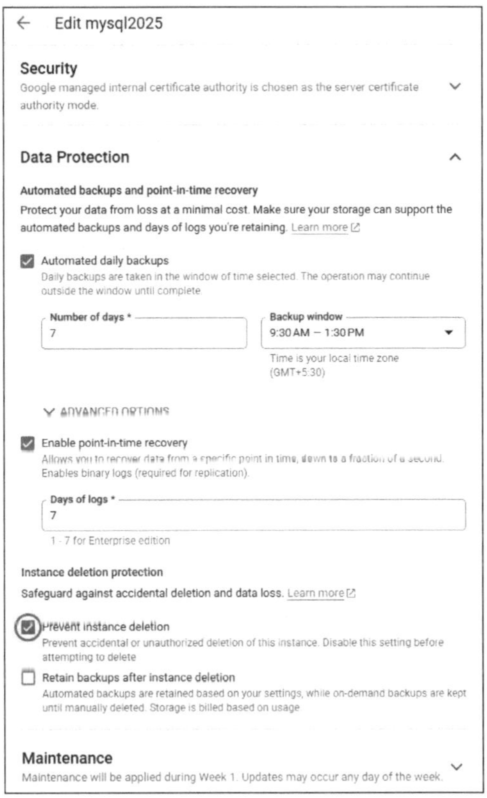

Figure 3.58: *Cloud SQL - MySQL – Environment (Cloud SQL Studio- Prevent Instance Deletion)*

Once prevent instance deletion is enabled, the delete option will also be enabled for deletion. Please refer to *Figure* 3.59 and click "**`Delete`**" in the menu.

***Figure* 3.59:** *MySQL–Environment* (Cloud SQL Studio- Delete Operation Enabled)

The system will pop up the window below for confirmation. You have to provide the instance ID and click "**`Delete`**" to delete it permanently, as shown in *Figure* 3.60.

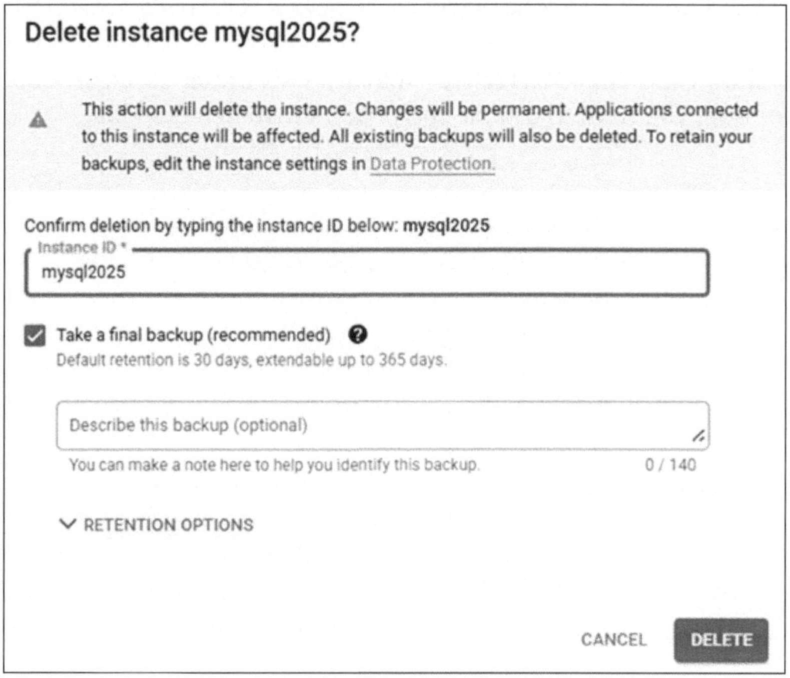

***Figure* 3.60:** *MySQL–Environment* (Cloud SQL Studio-Delete Operation)

Cloud SQL provides PostgreSQL and SQL Server instances. Instance creation is similar to MYSQL, which we had created earlier. *Figure* 3.61 shows the available editions.

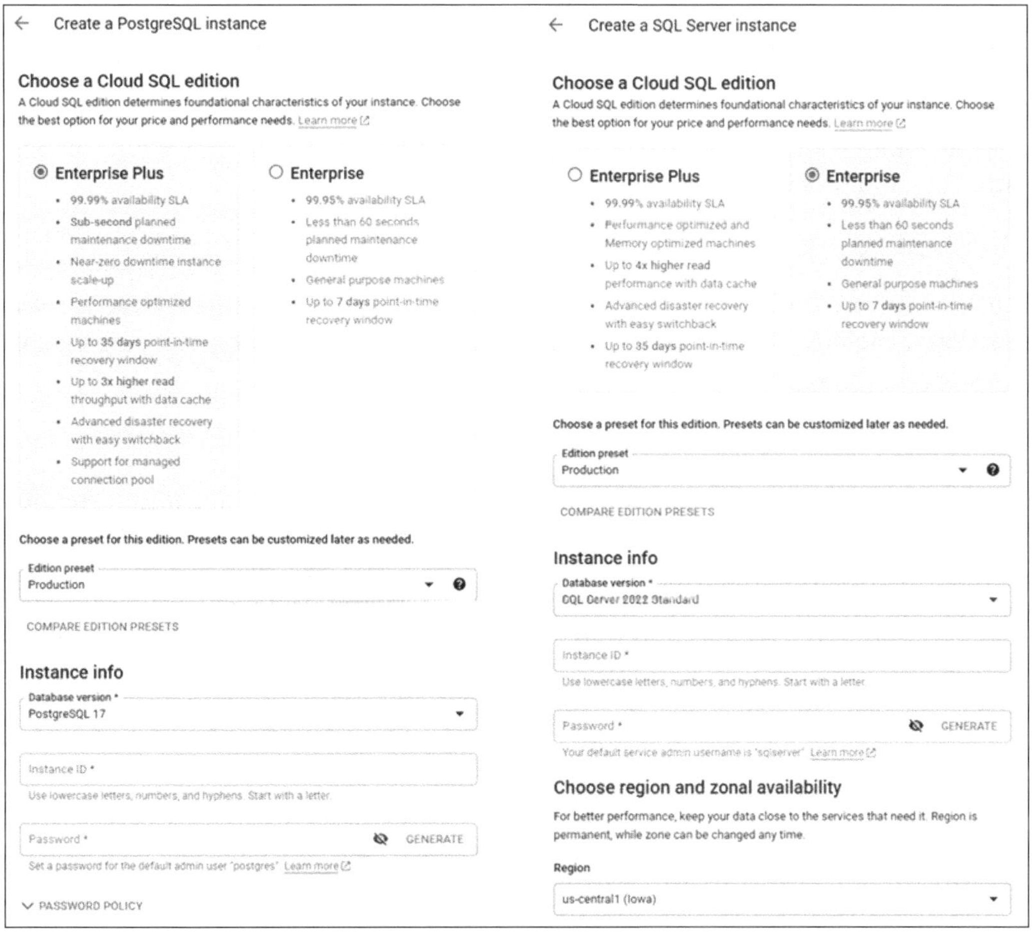

Figure 3.61: *PostgreSQL and SQL Server Instances*

We will exclusively discuss BigQuery in detail in *Chapters* 7, 9, *and* 10.

Conclusion

We have discussed Google Cloud Platform's (GCP's) essential storage technologies and their significant characteristics, such as 11 nines of durability, high scalability and performance, highly secure data environment, global availability, zero carbon emissions, and so on. We learned about the encryption mechanisms at rest and in transit.

We explored GCP storage classes and gained a detailed understanding of the standard, nearline, coldline, and archive storage options.

We investigated various Google Cloud services, including Cloud Storage, Cloud SQL, Cloud Bigtable, Cloud Datastore, Cloud Spanner, and BigQuery, along with their key features and use cases.

We also demonstrated a detailed workshop on Cloud Storage and Cloud SQL Services with steps and procedures.

We also conducted a detailed workshop on ***Cloud Storage and Cloud SQL*** services, covering step-by-step procedures and practical demonstrations. This chapter equips readers with the necessary skills to ***configure, manage, and optimize these services effectively, enabling them to meet real-world data storage, security, and performance*** objectives in cloud-based environments.

The next chapter will discuss how Big Data processing is simplified with GCP's managed Hadoop and Spark services, Cloud Dataproc. It introduces the basics of these frameworks, while guiding readers through creating and managing clusters for large-scale data processing. From automating workflows to optimizing Spark jobs for performance, readers will learn how Dataproc integrates seamlessly with other GCP tools, and enables powerful big data solutions for various business needs.

CHAPTER 4
Processing Data with Cloud Dataproc

Introduction

In the previous chapter, we discussed Google Cloud Platform's (GCP's) essential storage technologies and their significant characteristics. We also understood the encryption mechanisms at rest and in transit, explored GCP storage classes, and gained a detailed understanding of standard, nearline, coldline, and archive storage. We investigated various Google Cloud services such as Cloud Storage, Cloud SQL, Cloud Bigtable, Cloud Datastore, Cloud Spanner, and BigQuery, along with their use cases and key features.

We demonstrated a detailed walkthrough of Cloud Storage and Cloud SQL services, outlining key steps and procedures. It equips readers with the requisite skills to configure, manage, and optimize these services effectively, enabling them to achieve specific objectives related to data storage, security, scalability, and performance in cloud-based environments.

We will explore the basics of these frameworks and how to create and manage clusters for large-scale data processing. We will also explore automating workflows to optimize Spark jobs for performance. Finally, we will learn how Dataproc integrates with other GCP tools to enable powerful big data solutions tailored to business needs.

This chapter provides a detailed exploration of Cloud Dataproc, while guiding you from foundational concepts to advanced optimization strategies and seamless integrations with other GCP services.

Structure

In this chapter, we will discuss the following topics:

- Data Processing in the Big Data Era
- Dataproc
- Reasons for Dataproc as a Choice
- Dataproc Cluster Architecture
- Creating and Managing Clusters for Big Data Processing Using Dataproc
- Various Usage Patterns of Google Cloud Dataproc Clusters

Data Processing in the Big Data Era

Data processing refers to collecting, transforming, organizing, and analyzing raw data to extract meaningful insights. In the **Big Data era**, this process involves multiple stages such as handling massive, diverse, and fast-moving datasets, which are often referred to as the **3Vs**:

- **Volume**: The amount of data generated is in terabytes, petabytes, or more.
- **Velocity**: Data is being produced and needs to be processed in near real-time.
- **Variety**: Data comes in many formats—structured, semi-structured, and unstructured (for example, logs, social media, sensors).

As organizations continue to generate vast amounts of data, processing the load efficiently becomes a critical challenge. Cloud platforms address this challenge with components specific to cloud service providers.

Before going into `Dataproc`, let us understand a few things relevant to Big Data.

Hadoop: Apache Hadoop is an open-source framework designed for the distributed storage and processing of large datasets across clusters of computers. It uses the **Hadoop Distributed File System** (**HDFS**) for **scalable storage** and the **MapReduce programming model** for parallel processing. Hadoop is optimized for batch processing and handles fault tolerance efficiently, which makes it ideal for Big Data applications.

Google Cloud Dataproc simplifies Hadoop deployment by providing a managed service that automates cluster provisioning, configuration, and tuning, which reduces operational overhead by a significant degree.

It consists of:

- **HDFS (Hadoop Distributed File System)**: A distributed file system designed to run on commodity hardware

- **YARN (Yet Another Resource Negotiator)**: Manages cluster computing resources
- **MapReduce**: A programming model for processing large datasets

Apache Spark: Apache Spark, also part of the Hadoop ecosystem, is a fast, in-memory data processing engine that supports batch and real-time analytics. Unlike Hadoop's MapReduce, Spark uses **Resilient Distributed Datasets (RDDs)** and **DataFrames** for efficient iterative processing and Machine Learning (ML) tasks.

When integrated with Dataproc, Spark clusters can be quickly spun up while leveraging Google Cloud's scalability and integration with other GCP services like **BigQuery** and **Cloud Storage**. Dataproc's autoscaling and preemptible VM support further optimization costs and performance for Spark workloads.

Dataproc

Concerning GCP, ***Dataproc*** is a fully managed and scalable service for running **Apache Hadoop, Apache Spark, and other big data tools**. It carries out these processes with minimal operational overhead, while leveraging cloud scalability and GCP-native integrations.

Dataproc provides a fully managed environment for running Hadoop and Spark without the burden of infrastructure setup and maintenance. Its key advantages include:

- Quick cluster creation (90 seconds or less)
- Pay-per-use pricing
- Integrated with other GCP services like BigQuery, Cloud Storage, and Pub/Sub

Significance of Cloud Dataproc

As discussed earlier, Dataproc is a fully managed and scalable service that simplifies running Apache Spark, Hadoop, Hive, and other Big Data tools on a GCP environment. Its significance lies in the following aspects:

- **Simplified Big Data Processing:** Dataproc abstracts away the complexities of infrastructure management, which allows users to focus on data processing tasks without manually having to manage cluster configurations and other factors.
- **Speed and Agility:** With near-instant cluster provisioning, Dataproc enables fast experimentation, testing, and deployment of data workflows within 90 seconds.
- **Cost Efficiency:** It provides a pay-as-you-go pricing model with minute-level billing and the option to use preemptible VMs, which reduces the overall cost

of running large-scale data workloads. This is preferable for low cost and high benefits for data processing for Big Data solutions.

- **Integration with Google Cloud Ecosystem:** It can work seamlessly with services like Cloud Storage, Bigtable, BigQuery, and Vertex AI. This results in complete, cloud-native medium and complex data pipelines, analytics platforms, and AI-based solutions.

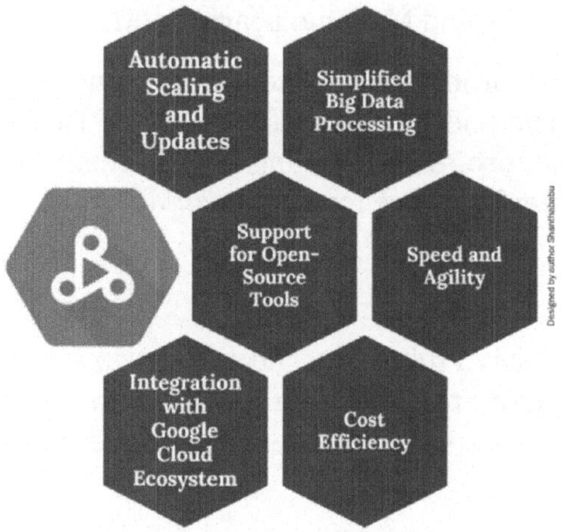

Figure 4.1: *Significance of Cloud Dataproc*

- **Support for Open-Source Tools:** It maintains compatibility with popular open-source Big Data tools, while ensuring flexibility and ease of migration for the existing workloads.
- **Automatic Scaling and Updates:** Clusters can scale automatically based on workload demand. The platform also regularly updates open-source components, which improves performance and security.

Reasons for Dataproc as a Choice

Cloud Dataproc is a good choice because it simplifies big data processing on GCP by allowing users to run open-source tools like Apache Spark and Apache Hadoop on a managed service. It helps reduce costs, improve speed, and lower complexity compared to on-premises or cloud services. Additionally, this results in streamlined cluster operations, and simplifies management.

Here is a more detailed explanation of why Dataproc is a good choice:

- **Cost Efficiency:** It provides the following features to save costs:
  - **Lower Costs:** It is priced at a low cost per virtual CPU hour and offers second-by-second billing with a low, one-minute minimum billing period. Therefore, you pay only for what you use.

  - **Cost Savings:** It allows you to turn off clusters when not in use, which further reduces costs and leads to effective utilization.
  - **Preemptible Instances:** This feature allows you to include preemptible instances in your Dataproc clusters with lower compute prices, which reduces costs even more.
- **Speed and Performance:** These are the significant parameters in any service provider. Dataproc specifically facilitates the following features for faster speed and effective performance:
  - **Fast Cluster Creation:** It can create, scale, and shut down clusters often within seconds or minutes, which is much faster than on-premises or other cloud solutions.
  - **Improved Speed:** It can improve data insights' speed and overall quality.
  - **Data Access:** It provides easy access to data and helps build data applications connecting to other Google Cloud services like **BigQuery, Vertex AI**, and **Cloud Storage.**
- **Simplified Management:**
  - **Automated Tasks:** It eases and automates tasks like provisioning and cluster management, which simplifies its management and use.
  - **Direct Control:** Users can customize clusters and tune workloads for optimal performance.
  - **Managed Service:** Since this is a managed service, you do not have to worry about maintaining the underlying infrastructure.
  - **Integration with GCP:** It is capable of integrating well with other Google Cloud services.
  - **Serverless Option:** It is serverless, which further simplifies the process by abstracting away the infrastructure and providing an easy-to-use interface for running Apache Spark jobs.

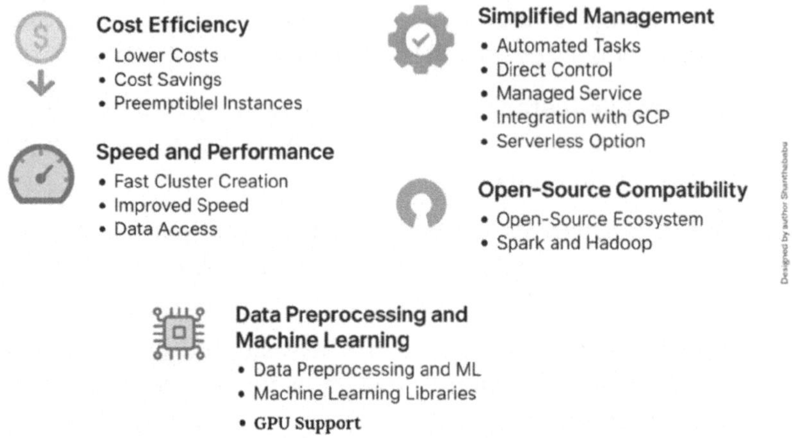

Figure 4.2: *Reasons to Prefer Cloud Dataproc*

- **Open-Source Compatibility:** By default, it has open-source compatibility, which provides the following features:
  - **Open-Source Ecosystem:** It allows you to use open-source tools, algorithms, and programming languages on cloud-scale datasets.
  - **Spark and Hadoop:** It supports running Apache Spark and Apache Hadoop, which are popular open-source Big Data platforms.
- **Data Preprocessing and Machine Learning:** We need extensive data for data processing and ML. Dataproc provides massive support for this through:
  - **Data Preprocessing and ML:** It can be used for data pre-processing and ML model training.
  - **ML Libraries:** We can use Dataproc to build ML models with various libraries like TensorFlow and RAPIDS.
  - **GPU Support:** This allows you to add GPUs to your clusters, which reduces the time it takes to train ML models

Dataproc Cluster Architecture

Dataproc cluster architecture involves creating a distributed computing environment for big data analytics using Apache Hadoop, Spark, and other open-source frameworks. It can be configured as a static (persistent) cluster or an ephemeral cluster, with available options for single-node clusters, High Availability (HA), and various network configurations.

Let us explore the Dataproc cluster architecture, as shown in *Figure* 4.3, as well as its functions and purposes.

Dataproc Cluster

The **Dataproc Cluster** comprises Compute Engine instances and managed services that perform Big Data processing using tools like Spark, Hadoop, Hive, and so on. It is a central component for processing large-scale data via the open-source tools mentioned earlier. It is built upon Compute Engine VMs and is managed via a scalable, automated framework orchestrated by Google Cloud.

Dataproc Agent: The Dataproc Agent acts as the control plane for managing the entire cluster. It automatically provisions, monitors, scales, and deletes clusters as needed by jobs. As shown here, it is the orchestrator or control plane for managing the cluster lifecycle.

- Creation
- Autoscaling
- Termination
- Monitoring

Key Functions

- Coordinates tasks across master and worker nodes
- Acts as the control plane of the cluster
- Orchestrates instance creation and termination
- Configures open-source components (Spark, Hadoop)
- Handles autoscaling and high availability
- Monitors health metrics and lifecycle operations
- Interacts with Google Cloud APIs for resource provisioning

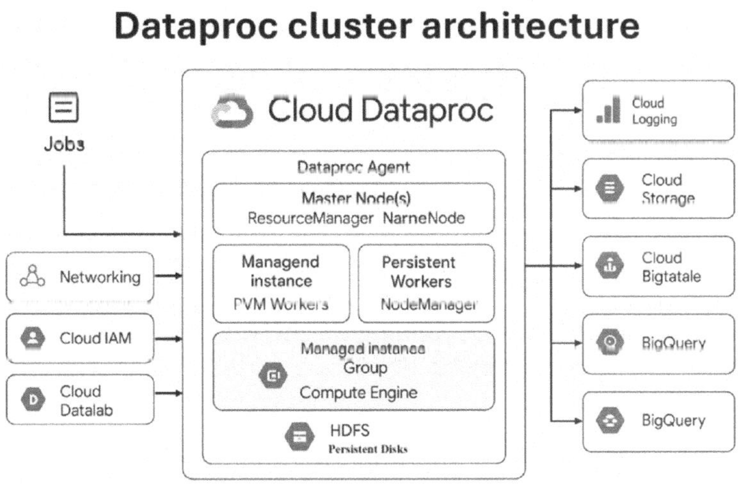

Figure 4.3: *Cloud Dataproc Cluster Architecture*

Compute Engine Instances: The Core Compute Layer of Dataproc

Compute Engine instances form the computational backbone of a Dataproc cluster, while providing the requisite infrastructure to process big data workloads. These virtual machines are grouped into different roles, with each being responsible for specific tasks within the cluster.

Master Node(s) are typically larger, persistent VMs hosted on Compute Engine and act as the central brain of the cluster. They run critical services such as the YARN Resource Manager, which manages resource allocation and job queues; the HDFS Name Node, which maintains the filesystem namespace and metadata; and the Spark Driver, which initiates and coordinates Spark jobs in client mode. Master nodes handle job scheduling, resource distribution, and metadata management, which ensuring that the cluster operates efficiently and reliably.

- **Purpose**
    - Acts as the central coordinator of the Dataproc cluster
    - Manages metadata, resource allocation, and job scheduling
- **Responsibilities**
    - Runs **the YARN `ResourceManager`** to manage cluster-wide resource allocation
    - Runs **the HDFS `NameNode`** to manage the file system namespace and metadata
    - Runs **Spark Driver** to orchestrate job execution in client mode
    - Schedules and distributes jobs to appropriate worker nodes
    - Monitors job progress, track application status, and handle task retries
    - Coordinates with other Google Cloud services (for example, Logging, Monitoring)

Persistent Workers are long-running Compute Engine instances responsible for executing the actual data processing tasks. These nodes host the YARN Node Manager, which oversees resource utilization at the node level; the HDFS Data Node, which stores the physical blocks of data; and the Spark Executors, which carry out distributed computation. Persistent Workload Groups are designed to support fault-tolerant operations and scale horizontally depending on the workload. They are essential for reliably executing distributed data jobs.

- **Purpose**
    - Perform actual data processing tasks in the cluster
    - Serve as long-lived compute nodes for distributed workloads

- **Responsibilities**
    - Run **YARN NodeManager** to manage local resources and containers
    - Run **the HDFS DataNode** to store the actual blocks of HDFS data
    - Run **Spark Executors** to execute the Spark job tasks assigned by the driver
    - Execute compute-intensive operations like ETL, transformation, and ML processing
    - Ensure data redundancy and fault tolerance in storage and execution
    - Scale horizontally to accommodate increased data or job volume

Pre-emptible VM Workers (PVM Workers) are cost-effective, temporary Compute Engine instances that run within a Managed Instance Group. They are ideal for non-critical, fault-tolerant, or batch processing tasks, as they can be pre-empted (terminated) by Google Cloud when resource capacity is needed elsewhere. Despite their impermanence, PVM Workers are highly valuable due to their significant cost savings, as they are up to 80% cheaper than regular VMs. These instances enable organizations to scale compute resources efficiently, while optimizing their cloud spend.

- **Purpose**
    - Provide cost-efficient compute capacity for batch or fault-tolerant jobs
    - Allow for temporary scaling of the cluster for heavy workloads
- **Responsibilities**
    - Run the same execution roles as Persistent Workers (NodeManager, Executors)
    - Operate within a **Managed Instance Group** for easy autoscaling
    - Handle non-critical or interruptible job segments
    - Automatically terminates when Google Cloud reclaims capacity
    - Reduce overall compute costs by using discounted, short-lived VMs

Data Storage: HDFS on Persistent Disks

In a Dataproc cluster, **HDFS** (Hadoop Distributed File System) is configured to run on Google Cloud Persistent Disks attached to each Compute Engine VM.

This setup provides a temporary, high-performance distributed storage layer to execute Spark and Hadoop jobs. Local HDFS is primarily utilized for storing intermediate data, such as Spark shuffle files, temporary Hive warehouse outputs, and partial computation results.

It results in fast read/write operations, which is critical for efficient job execution and low-latency processing. However, this storage is not intended for long-term durability. Once jobs are complete, the data is typically moved to more durable and scalable storage solutions like **Cloud Storage** or **BigQuery**.

In essence, HDFS on persistent disks is a transient data cache that accelerates cluster processing without external I/O overhead.

- **Purpose**
    - To provide temporary distributed storage for intermediate data generated during Spark, Hadoop, and Hive job execution
    - To act as a high-performance local cache for job-related data before it is moved to durable storage like Cloud Storage or BigQuery
    - Apache Spark creates shuffle files as part of distributed computations.
    - Maintain **intermediate results** generated during job execution
    - Hold **temporary Hive warehouse data** used by Hive jobs
    - Enable **fast read/write operations** for big data processing by utilizing local persistent disks
    - Serve as **ephemeral storage** that accelerates I/O without incurring cloud storage latency
    - Support **node-level fault tolerance** by temporarily persisting data locally to the VM

GCP Platform Services (Left Side Integration, Refer to *Figure* 4.3**)**

Google Cloud Platform (GCP) services are critical in supporting and securing Dataproc cluster operations. Cloud Networking ensures seamless communication between nodes within the cluster by leveraging **Virtual Private Cloud** (VPC), which provides private IP addresses, subnets, and customizable firewall rules for secure and isolated networking.

Cloud IAM (Identity and Access Management) offers granular control over permissions, while managing access for users and service accounts to submit jobs, interact with GCP services, and perform data read/write operations.

Additionally, **Cloud Datalab**, an interactive Jupyter-based environment, enhances productivity by allowing users to directly connect to Dataproc clusters to submit PySpark or Spark SQL notebooks. This enables real-time data exploration and job execution in a familiar notebook interface.

Table 4.1 explains the GCP Platform Services (Left Side Integration) as follows:

GCP Services	Purpose	Responsibilities
Cloud Networking	Enables secure, internal communication between Dataproc nodes and other GCP services	Configures and manages **VPC networks** Assigns **private/internal IPs** Defines **subnets** Sets up firewall rules- Supports Shared VPCs
Cloud IAM	Provides role-based, secure access control for users and services interacting with Dataproc	Defines and enforces **roles and permissions** Manages **user, group, and service account** access Integrates with OAuth2 and policies Supports audit logging and compliance
Cloud Datalab	Offers a notebook-based interactive interface for job development and data analysis	Provides **Jupyter notebook environment** Submits **PySpark/Spark SQL jobs** to Dataproc Integrates with **Cloud Storage** and **BigQuery** Supports visualization and ML integration

***Table* 4.1**: *GCP Platform Services (Left Side Integration)*

External Integration Targets (GCP Service Ecosystem, refer to *Figure* 4.3)

Google Cloud Dataproc seamlessly integrates with several GCP services to extend its data processing, analytics, ML, and storage capabilities. These integrations enhance the overall performance and usability of Dataproc clusters by facilitating data movement, job orchestration, and real-time monitoring across the platform.

- **Cloud Logging** is a comprehensive, integrated log management system that collects operational logs from various sources such as Spark executors, YARN resource managers, and cluster components. It helps monitor job progress, system events, node startup/shutdown activities, and Spark driver diagnostics. With support for real-time search, alerting, and long-term log retention, it has become a critical tool for auditing, debugging, and maintaining cluster health.
- **Cloud Storage** acts as the default object storage layer for Dataproc clusters. It replaces traditional HDFS in cloud-native workflows and is used extensively for storing input datasets, exporting processed results, staging job configuration files, and archiving logs. As a scalable, multi-region storage service, Cloud Storage offers high durability, availability, and integration with other GCP services.
- **Cloud Bigtable** is a high-throughput NoSQL database that is well-suited for storing wide-column data and handling time-series analytics. It enables real-time read/write capabilities at scale, which makes it ideal for use cases like IoT data processing, telemetry, and low-latency analytics. Dataproc jobs can write outputs directly to BigTable, while supporting applications that require rapid access to processed results.

- **BigQuery** is Google's serverless, fully managed data warehouse. It plays a key role in analytical workflows. It supports SQL-based interactive and batch analytics on massive datasets. Dataproc jobs can directly export structured output to BigQuery tables or leverage federated queries that read from Cloud Storage. BigQuery also supports ML via **BigQuery ML**, which makes it a preferred destination for transformed data in AI-driven data pipelines. BigQuery often appears multiple times in architecture diagrams to reflect its diverse integration pathways, whether as direct job output or as federated querying from external sources.

Table 4.2 explains External Integration Targets (GCP Service Ecosystem) as follows:

GCP Services	Purpose	Responsibilities
Cloud Logging	Provides real-time **log collection, diagnostics, and monitoring** for Dataproc operations	Collects logs from **Spark drivers**, **executors**, **YARN**, and **cluster components** - Enables real-time monitoring, alerting, and auditing - Supports log retention and search
Cloud Storage	Acts as the **primary cloud-native storage layer** for Dataproc jobs and data pipelines	Stores **input/output datasets**, **job configurations**, and **logs**- Replaces HDFS in cloud-native workflows- Enables data ingestion/export- Offers durable, scalable, multi-region storage
Cloud Bigtable	Serves as a **NoSQL wide-column data store** optimized for **real-time, low-latency analytics**	Stores **time-series data**, **IoT streams**, and **log data**- Handles high-throughput read/write operations- Receives Dataproc pipeline outputs for real-time querying
BigQuery	Functions as a **serverless data warehouse** for structured, SQL-based **advanced analytics**	Supports **SQL queries** over large datasets - Ingests structured output from Dataproc - Enables federated querying from Cloud Storage - Integrates with BigQuery ML for machine learning

Table 4.2: *External Integration Targets (GCP Service Ecosystem)*

End-to-End Workflow

The Dataproc workflow begins when a user submits a job using tools like **Cloud Datalab, API, CLI**, or the **GCP Console**. Before the job runs, **Cloud IAM** checks whether the user has the correct permissions.

Once authorized, the **Dataproc Agent** takes over and automatically sets up the required cluster by provisioning the **Master and Worker Nodes**.

The **Master Node** then analyzes the job and distributes tasks to the **Persistent Workers** and **Preemptible VM Workers**, which handle the actual data processing using **Spark** or **Hadoop**.

During execution, the temporary data is stored in **HDFS (on persistent disks)** or **Cloud Storage**.

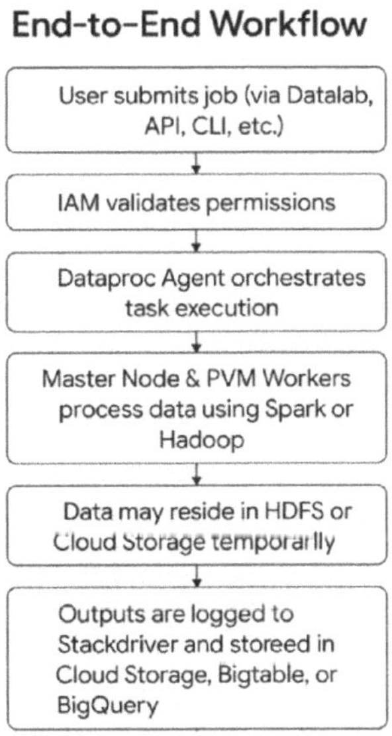

Figure 4.4: *Cloud Dataproc End-to-End Workflow*

Once the job is complete, the results and logs are saved and routed to various destinations, which are mentioned here:

- **Cloud Storage** for general-purpose storage
- **Cloud Bigtable** for real-time NoSQL workloads
- **BigQuery** for SQL-based analytics
- **Cloud Logging** for monitoring, debugging, and auditing.

In some advanced scenarios, the processed data can be passed to **Vertex AI** for ML tasks, while establishing a fully integrated data-to-ML pipeline.

Highlights from the Updated Architecture

Table 4.3 explains the architecture components and their purpose as follows:

Component	Purpose
Dataproc Agent	Controls cluster operations
Master Node	Schedules jobs, manages metadata (`ResourceManager`, `NameNode`)
Persistent Workers	Execute data processing tasks.
PVM Workers	Low-cost, fault-tolerant execution for non-critical jobs
HDFS	Temporary distributed filesystem (backed by persistent disk)

Component	Purpose
Cloud Networking	Enables private communication between cluster nodes
Cloud IAM	Manages secure access across services
Cloud Datalab	Notebook interface to interact with Dataproc
Stackdriver Logging	Logs events, job status, and resource usage
Cloud Storage	Is an Input/output storage layer
Bigtable	Real-time analytics and lookup store
BigQuery	Is an SQL-based data warehouse for advanced analytics

Table 4.3: *Architecture Components and Their Purposes*

Creating and Managing Clusters for Big Data Processing Using Dataproc

Step 1: Log in to **GCP**. Then go to the left navigation and select "**`Analytics`**" from the menu, you will get the list of available components on the main panel. Now, select the "**`Dataproc`**" component as shown in *Figure* 4.5.

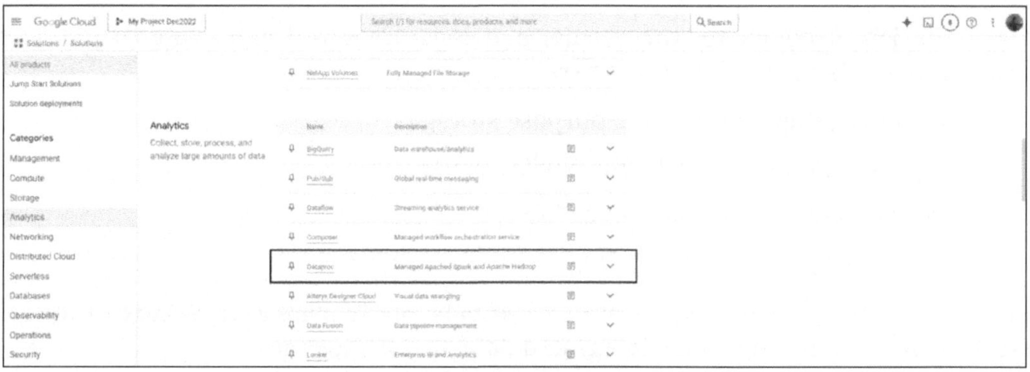

Figure 4.5: *Cloud Dataproc–Cluster Creation*

Step 2: Once you select DataProc, the portal takes you to the screen shown in *Figure* 4.6. Before you can start using it, you have to enable the APIs. To do this, click "**`Enable APIs`**".

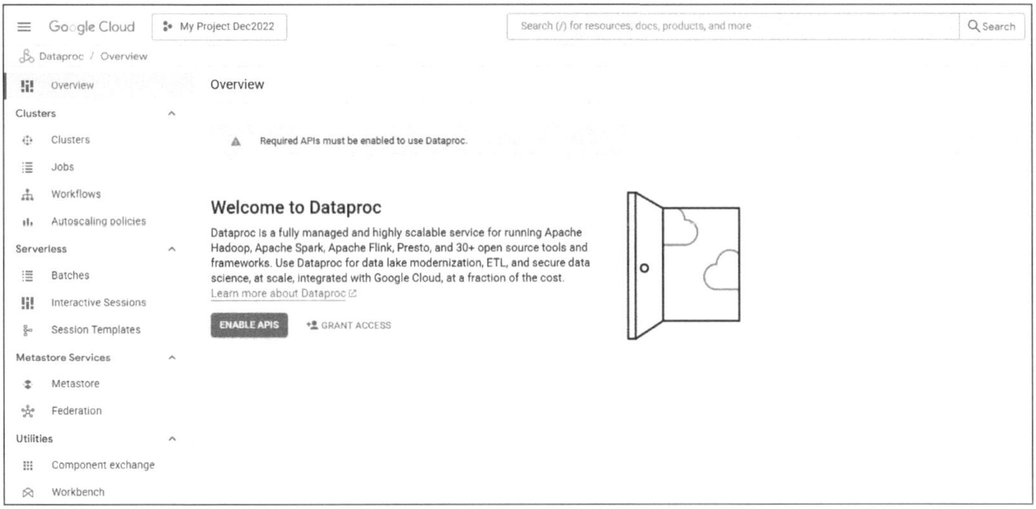

Figure 4.6: *Cloud Dataproc–Cluster (Enable APIs)*

Step 3: You must confirm that the APIs are enabled; then, you will be able to create the cluster.

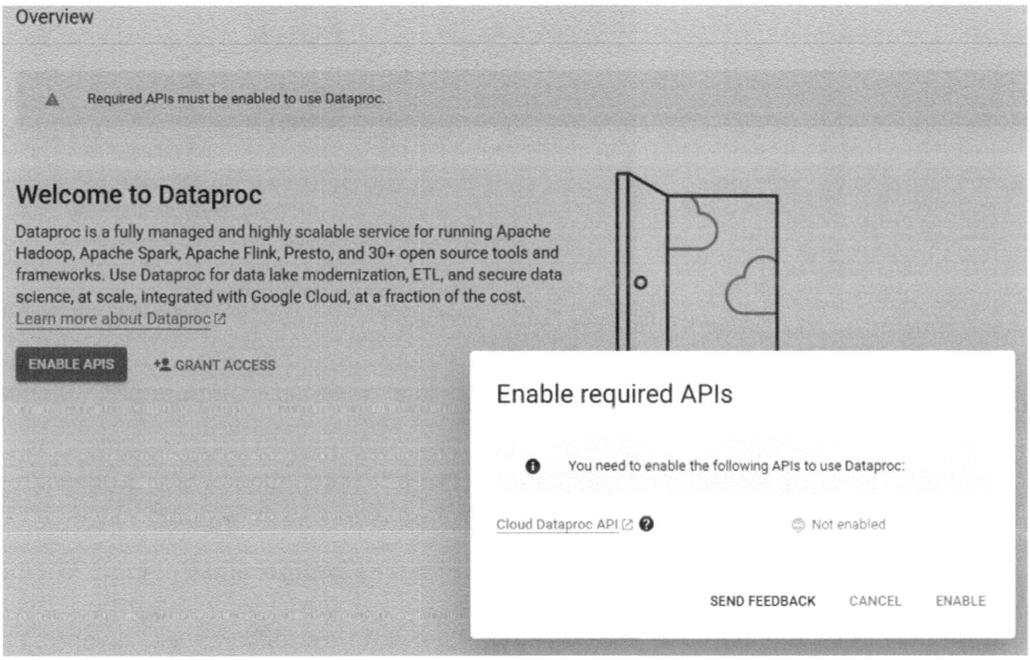

Figure 4.7: *Cloud Dataproc–Cluster (APIs Enable Confirmation)*

Step 4: After the confirmation, the portal will take you to the Dataproc-Cluster window. There, you have to click "`Create Cluster`" as shown in *Figure* 4.8.

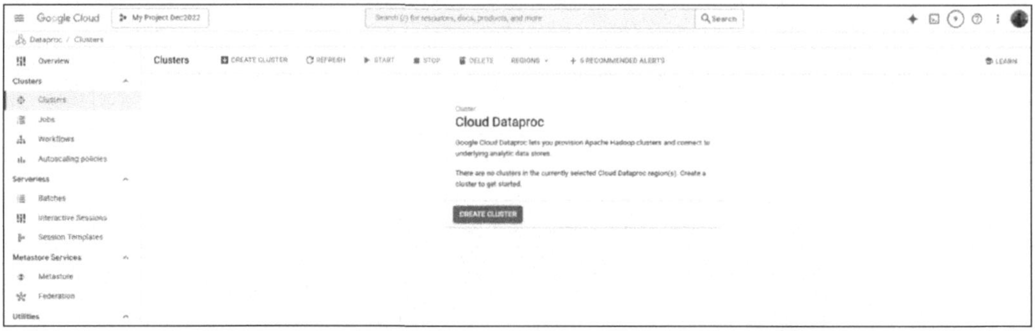

Figure 4.8: Cloud Dataproc–Cluster (Create Cluster)

Step 5: After you have followed Step 4, the portal will provide two options: Cluster on Compute Engine and Cluster on GKE (Google Kubernetes Engine).

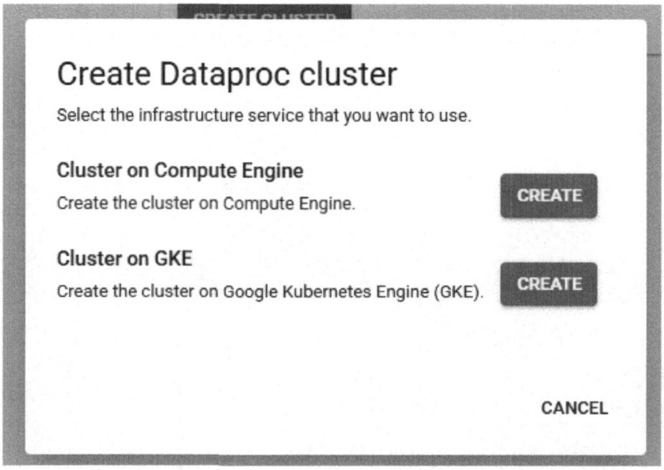

Figure 4.9: Cloud Dataproc Cluster-Options

- If you are trying to install **HBase or use optional components**, **choose `"Cluster on Compute Engine"`**.
- For modern container-based deployments that align with Kubernetes workflows, consider **GKE**, but expect limited component support.

Creating a Dataproc cluster on GKE (**Google Kubernetes Engine**) and Compute Engine (**VM-based**) are two distinct deployment models that Google Cloud's Dataproc service provides. Here is a comparison to help you understand their differences, advantages, and when to use which tool:

Table 4.4 explains Dataproc on Compute Engine vs. Dataproc on GKE (Kubernetes) as follows:

Features	Dataproc on Compute Engine	Dataproc on GKE (Kubernetes)
Deployment Target	Managed VMs (Compute Engine)	Kubernetes cluster (GKE nodes)
Cluster Type	Traditional Hadoop/Spark clusters	Containerized Spark jobs on Kubernetes
Management Style	VM-based lifecycle management	Kubernetes-native pod-based scheduling and scaling
Infrastructure Setup	GCP provisions VMs automatically	Requires an existing GKE cluster or a Dataproc GKE-enabled pool
Cost Efficiency	Pay-per-VM, suitable for long-running jobs	Better for containerized, short-lived, and batch workloads
Resource Isolation	Less granular (per node)	Fine-grained (per pod/container)
Custom Images/ Software	Can use custom VM images	Using Docker containers for Spark jobs
Auto-scaling	Node-level (add/remove VMs)	Pod level (add/remove Spark executor pods)
Job Orchestration	Uses Dataproc Job API and workflows	Uses Dataproc K8s Operator or SparkOperator

Table 4.4: *Dataproc on Compute Engine vs. Dataproc on GKE (Kubernetes)*

Based on the different use cases, you can use either of these options to get maximum benefits. Here is the list of use cases:

Table 4.4 explains Use Case Comparison for Compute Engine and GKE (Kubernetes) as follows:

Use Case	Best Fit
Long-running batch jobs	Compute Engine
Fast startup, short jobs, elastic scaling	GKE
Multi-tenant and microservices environment	GKE
Traditional Hadoop ecosystem compatibility	Compute Engine
Fine-grained control over Spark executors	GKE
Existing Kubernetes-based architecture	GKE

Table 4.5: *Use Case Comparison for Compute Engine and GKE (Kubernetes)*

In short,

- **Use Dataproc on Compute Engine,** if you need a classic Hadoop/Spark setup, robust VM isolation, or minimal Kubernetes knowledge.

- **Use Dataproc on GKE** to build modern, container-native applications with dynamic resource allocation and fast scaling requirements.

Step 6: For our demonstration, we will select "**`Cluster on Compute Engine`**." The portal will take you to the screen shown in *Figure* 4.10.

- Set up Cluster (mandatory).
- Configure node (partially important, good to have).
- Rest is optional.

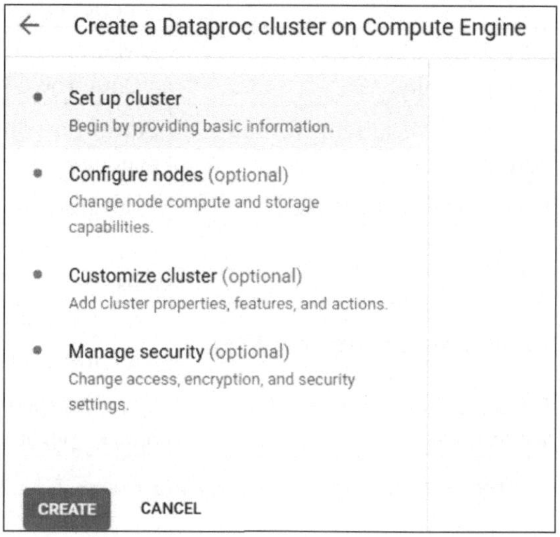

Figure 4.10: *Cluster on Compute Engine – Configuration*

Step 7: Set up your cluster. Here are the mandatory parameters; the rest are optional:

- Name
- Cluster Name
- Location
  - Region
  - Zone
- Cluster type
  - Standard (1 master, N workers)
  - Single Node (1 master, 0 workers): Provides a single node that acts as both master and worker; suitable for proof-of-concept or small-scale processing
  - High Availability (3 masters, N workers): Hadoop High Availability mode provides uninterrupted YARN and HDFS operations despite single-node failures or reboots.

- Select the components for your cluster (one or multiple) based on your requirements, as shown in *Figure 4.11*:
  - Hive, WebHCat, Jupyter Notebook, Zeppelin Notebook, Trino, ZooKeeper, Ranger
  - Flink, Docker, Solr, Hudi, Iceberg and Delta

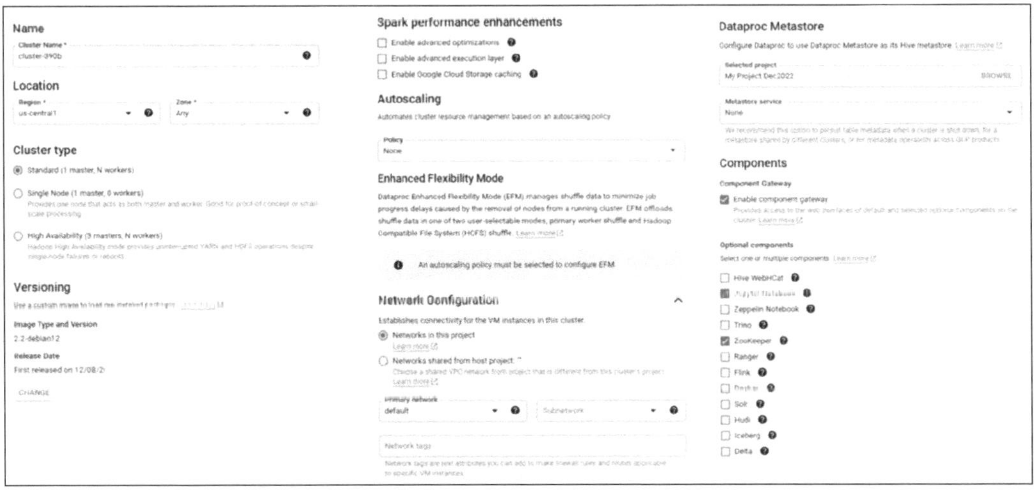

Figure 4.11: *Cluster on Compute Engine – Configuration (Set Up Cluster)*

Leave the rest as it is.

Mainly, you have to provide the details of the Master and Worker nodes.

Step 8: **Configure the Master Node:** In the Google Cloud Dataproc cluster creation wizard. The master node is a critical component that hosts the YARN Resource Manager, HDFS ***NameNode***, and all job drivers, and is responsible for coordinating resource management and job execution across the cluster.

- **Series**: The machine type selection dropdown in Google Cloud, used while configuring a Dataproc cluster (or any GCE VM), highlights the availability of third-generation virtual machine series. It highlights the third-generation VM series and offers several high-performance instance types across different CPU platforms.
  - **C3**: Powered by Intel's Sapphire Rapids CPU platform and optimized for compute-intensive workloads such as HPC, rendering, and analytics
  - **C4**: Powered by the Intel Emerald Rapids CPU platform; offers better performance and energy efficiency than C3 and is ideal for high-throughput compute
  - **C4A**: Powered by Google Axion CPU platform; ARM-based architecture built by Google; Designed for energy efficiency and performance at scale and is suitable for containerized workloads and cloud-native apps

- **N4**: Powered by Intel Emerald Rapids CPU platform and offers balanced general-purpose VMs suitable for various workloads, including databases, web applications, and enterprise apps; Successor to the N2 series

- **Machine Type: Selection** dropdown for the **N4 VM series** in Google Cloud Platform (GCP), which is part of the third-generation general-purpose virtual machines. The machine types shown are **N4-standard instances**, optimized for balanced compute and memory workloads.

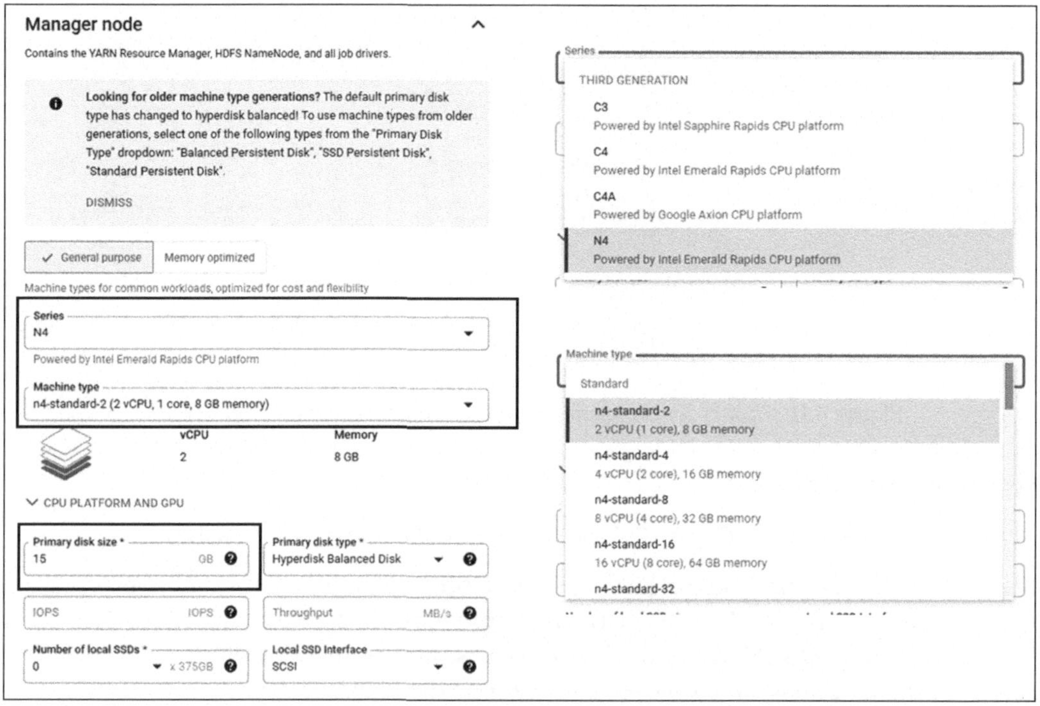

Figure 4.12: *Cluster on Compute Engine–Configuration (Manager Node)*

Step 9: Worker nodes in a Google Cloud Dataproc cluster handle data storage and processing tasks. Each node runs a **YARN NodeManager** and an **HDFS DataNode**, which enables parallel computation and distributed storage. The number of worker nodes determines the cluster's scalability and performance. Depending on workload requirements, they can be configured with different machine types, disk sizes, and SSDs.

Configure the Workers node, which contains a YARN Node Manager and a HDFS Data Node. Here, the HDFS replication factor is 2.

Worker nodes in the Google Cloud Dataproc Cluster creation wizard, explicitly using the N4 VM series.

Each worker node runs the following:

- **YARN NodeManager**: Handles resource allocation and job execution on each node
- **HDFS DataNode**: Stores data blocks
- **HDFS Replication Factor**: Set to 2 (each data block is stored on two nodes)

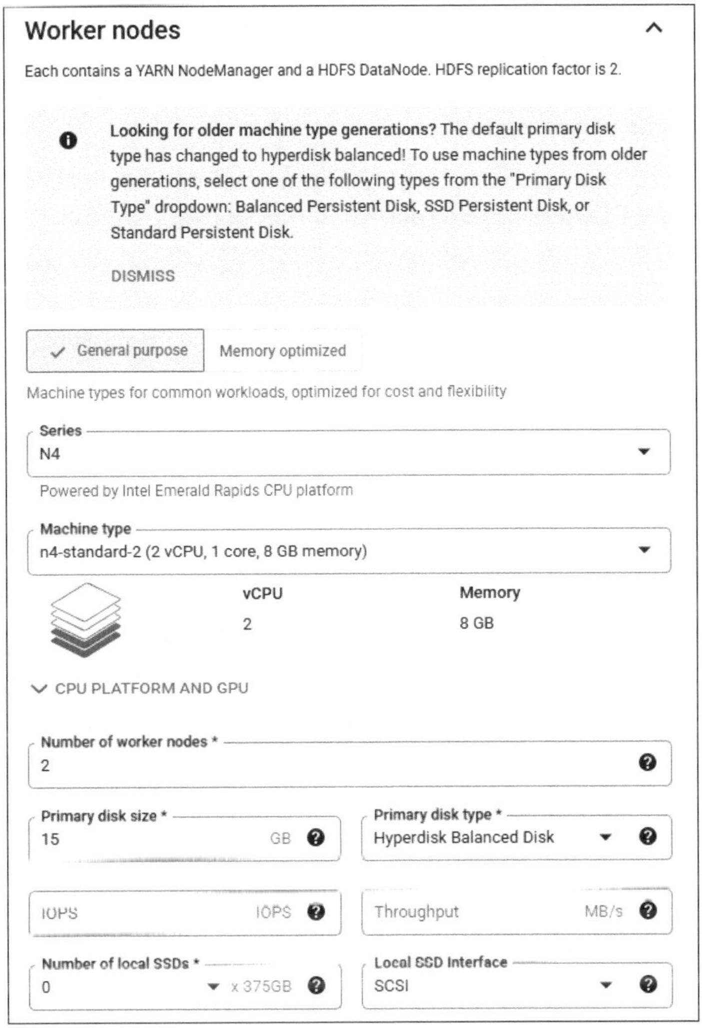

Figure 4.13: *Cluster on Compute Engine–Configuration (Worker Node)*

- **Secondary Worker Nodes:** These nodes in Dataproc are used for pre-emptible (temporary) compute capacity to save costs. They do not store HDFS data; they only handle task execution like Spark/Hadoop jobs. These nodes can be added or removed dynamically to scale the workload and are ideal for batch jobs that can tolerate interruption.

- **Sole-Tenancy:** It allows you to run VMs on dedicated physical servers for your project. This ensures hardware isolation, which enhances security, compliance, and licensing control. This is useful in regulated industries requiring non-shared infrastructure. You can set node affinity policies to control VM placement on hosts.
- **Shielded VMs:** Shielded VMs offer enhanced security features like secure boot, vTPM, and integrity monitoring. They protect against rootkits and firmware-level threats and are ideal for workloads requiring strong OS and kernel verification. They are enabled by default on many GCP images to **create trusted VM environments.**

Step 10: Once the required configurations are completed, click "`Create`". The portal will take you to the Clusters page as shown in the following figure:

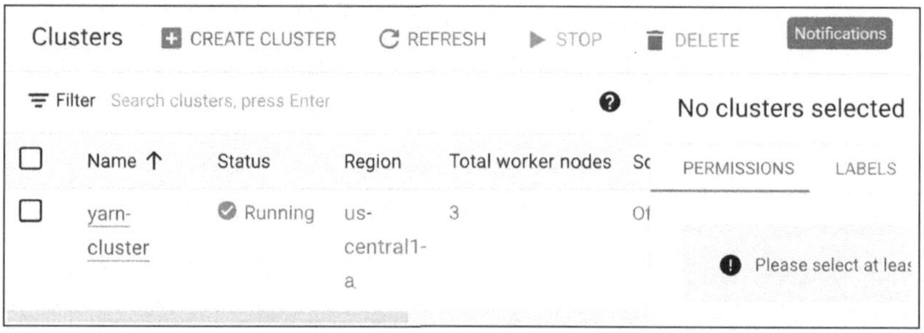

Figure 4.14: *Dataproc-Clusters*

Step 11: Click the cluster name. Then, the portal will take you to detailed sections such as Monitoring, Jobs, VM Instance, and so on, as shown in *Figure* 4.15:

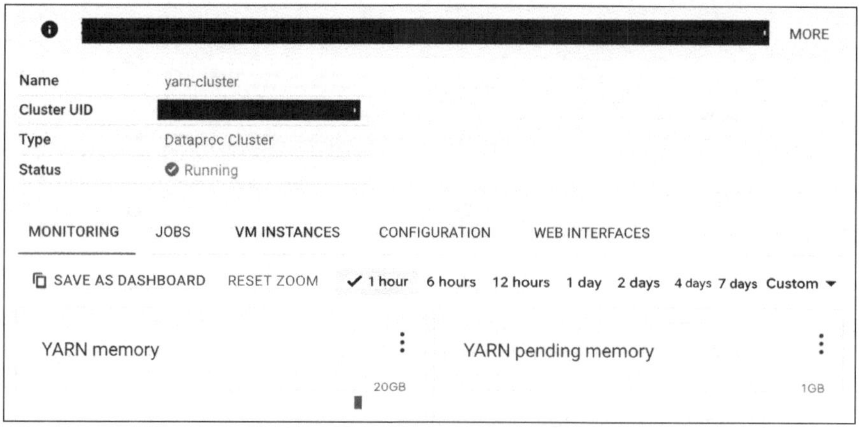

Figure 4.15: *Dataproc-Clusters-Dashboard*

Figure 4.16 shows the VM instances such as Master and Workers in the Dataproc cluster.

***Figure 4.16**: Dataproc–Clusters–VM Instance (Master and Workers)*

The highlighted **SSH** (Secure Shell) in *Figure* 4.16 is a clickable option next to the **Master Node** under the "`VM Instances`" tab of the Dataproc Cluster interface.

- **SSH** lets you securely connect to a **Virtual Machine (VM)** from your browser or terminal.
- When you click on `SSH` next to yarn-cluster-m (the master node), a secure terminal session opens directly into that VM.
- This is useful for:
    - Manually running **Spark, Hadoop, or Hive** commands
    - Debugging jobs
    - Viewing logs and system metrics
    - Accessing installed components and configurations

Benefits of SSH Access:

- Encrypted communication
- Direct command-line control
- No need for external SSH keys or local terminal setup when used via browser

Step 12: Once you click `SSH`, the portal will take you to the terminal as shown in the following figure:

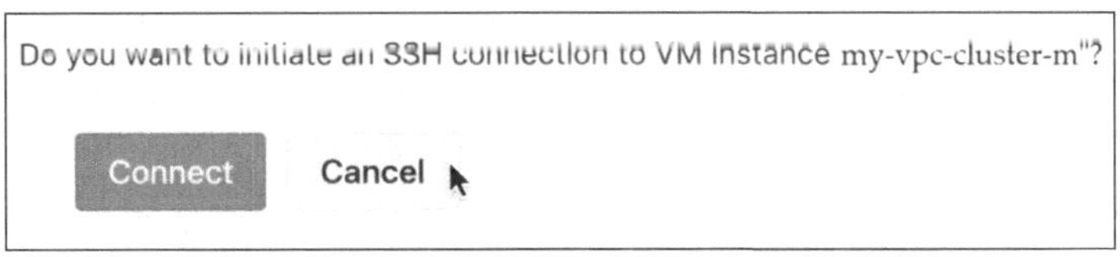

***Figure 4.17**: Connecting to SSH (Secure Shell)*

Once you click "**Connect**", the portal takes you to the cluster, where you can perform your activities.

You can set up a VPC to enable secure communication between the Dataproc master and worker nodes. However, VPC is outside the scope of this book.

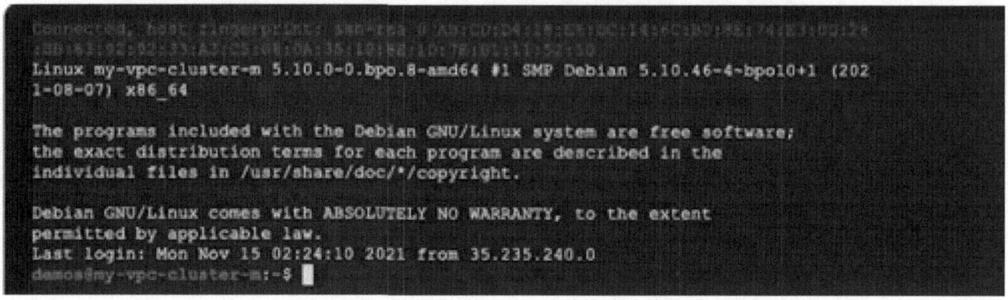

Figure 4.18: *Connecting to a Cluster*

Various Usage Patterns of Google Cloud Dataproc Clusters

Dataproc is capable of creating clusters in various patterns for different uses, which are mentioned here and illustrated in *Figure* 4.19:

- **Single User, Single Cluster**: A single user accesses a dedicated Dataproc cluster to run jobs or perform data analysis. This is common for isolated testing or development.
- **Multiple Users, Shared Cluster**: A small group of users can connect to a single shared Dataproc cluster. This pattern is often used in collaborative environments where users work on common datasets.

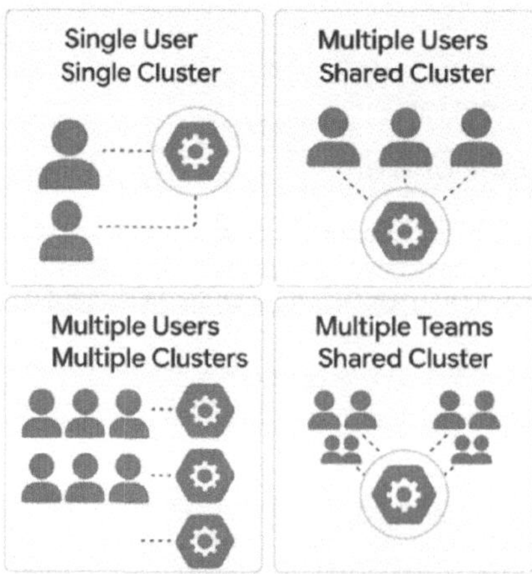

Figure 4.19: *Patterns of Dataproc Clusters*

- **Multiple Users, Multiple Clusters**: A team accesses multiple Dataproc clusters. This could be used to separate workloads by function (for example, ETL, ML, reporting) or department, enhancing performance and resource isolation.
- **Multiple Teams, Shared Cluster**: Several user groups or teams utilize a shared Dataproc cluster. This setup is efficient for cost savings and central administration, but may require careful resource and access control.

Each scenario emphasizes **flexibility and scalability**, which are the core strength of Dataproc. These strengths allow Dataproc to adapt from individual use to enterprise-wide data processing at scale.

Conclusion

In this chapter, we understood Big Data, its volume, velocity, variety, and significant challenges. We also discovered frameworks like Apache Hadoop and Apache Spark, as well as how they are crucial in distributed data processing. We then explored how Google Cloud Dataproc simplifies the deployment of these frameworks by offering a fully managed, scalable, and cost-efficient service. With features like rapid cluster provisioning, autoscaling, and seamless integration with GCP services (BigQuery, Cloud Storage), Dataproc reduces operational overhead, while optimizing performance.

We studied Dataproc's architecture and components, such as compute engine instances, persistent and pre-emptible workers, and flexible storage options (HDFS, Cloud Storage). We have ensured that they are highly efficient for diverse workloads. We understand how support for open-source tools, cost-effective pricing, and automated management make it an ideal choice for enterprises handling Big Data.

We examined the reasons for choosing Dataproc to create a cluster for modern data engineering, along with key factors such as cost efficiency, speed, and performance.

Simplified management, open-source compatibility, efficient data preprocessing, and integrated machine learning support.

We also demonstrated how to create a Dataproc Cluster with detailed steps and screenshots, aside from exploring the various usage patterns of Google Cloud Dataproc Clusters.

The next chapter will explore Google Cloud Dataflow, which is a fully managed service that supports unified batch and stream processing via the Apache Beam model. We will learn about pipeline creation, performance optimization, and real-time data handling work, while providing practical examples and use cases. By the end of the next chapter, readers will be equipped to design scalable, high-performance data pipelines tailored to diverse processing requirements, while leveraging Dataflow's serverless architecture and seamless integration with the Google Cloud ecosystem.

CHAPTER 5
Data Pipelines with Dataflow

Introduction

In the previous chapter, we explored Big Data, its characteristics of volume, velocity, and variety, and the significant challenges it presents. We discovered frameworks like Apache Hadoop and Apache Spark, as well as their importance in distributed data processing. We explored how Google Cloud Dataproc simplifies the deployment of these frameworks by offering a fully managed, scalable, and cost-efficient service. With features like rapid cluster provisioning, autoscaling, and seamless integration with GCP services (BigQuery, Cloud Storage), Dataproc reduces operational overhead while optimizing performance. We also studied Dataproc's architecture and components in detail.

This chapter offers a comprehensive guide to build and optimize scalable batch and streaming pipelines using Google Cloud Dataflow and Apache Beam. We will explore Google Cloud Dataflow, which is a unified platform that is used for designing both batch and streaming pipelines with high scalability, reliability, and efficiency. We will also understand how Dataflow's capabilities go far beyond traditional data processing. Its unified programming model streamlines development by allowing a single codebase to support diverse data scenarios, which significantly reduces complexity and operational overhead.

We will cover different Dataflow templates and understand their significance, along with how to optimize pipeline performance, follow best practices, troubleshoot issues, and explore the advanced use cases in real-time data processing.

Structure

In this chapter, we will discuss the following topics:

- Understanding Data Pipelines and Dataflow
  - Data Collection, Data Ingestion, Data Transformation
  - Data Storage and Serving Layer
- Essentials of Dataflow and Pipelines
  - Automate Data Movement, Ensure Data Quality, and so on.
- Criticality of Data Pipeline in Big Data and AI
- Overview of Google Cloud Dataflow and Key Features
- Significant challenges and limitations with Google Cloud Dataflow
- Unified Programming Model and detailed exploration
- Introduction to Apache Beam, Key Concepts and its Core Features
- Apache Beam Architecture's core components
  - Execution Model
  - Architecture Workflow
  - Simple Apache Beam Workflow Implementation
- Dataflow Templates
  - Streaming Templates, Batch Templates and Utility Templates
- Creating Pipelines with Dataflow and Cloud Storage
- Building a Workflow using the SDK
- Optimizing Pipeline Performance, Best Practices and Use Cases

Understanding Data Pipelines and Dataflow

Data pipelines are essential for modern data warehouses to manage and process large-scale data in present-day organizations with high volume data needs. The challenges in processing such data stem from its **variety, velocity, and volume**, especially while dealing with **batch** and **streaming** processing.

Batch processing can struggle with latency when immediate insights are needed. As a result, the data is put in fixed sets such as daily, nightly, weekly, and monthly reports. Streaming introduces complexity since it processes data in real-time. These metrics can include live user activity, data generated by IoT, handling out-of-order data, ensuring low latency, and maintaining high fault tolerance.

Data pipelines are constructed by enabling **Extract, Transform, Load (ETL) or Extract, Load, Transform (ELT) workflows** based on the use cases, where raw data is extracted from sources such as external databases, data warehouses, SAP, APIs and IoT. The extracted data is then transformed as cleaned, aggregated, enriched, and is finally loaded into destinations like databases, data warehouses, and data lakes. They also power **real-time analytics**, which allow businesses to react instantly and extract various insights like monitoring website traffic, or detecting fraud in financial transactions for cybersecurity. Retail companies use the pipeline to process real-time sales data, while adjusting the pricing dynamically based on the demand to retain customers.

Let us understand the common methodology of data pipelines and workflows across any cloud provider and on-premises platforms.

The process of creating a new class consists of the following stages:

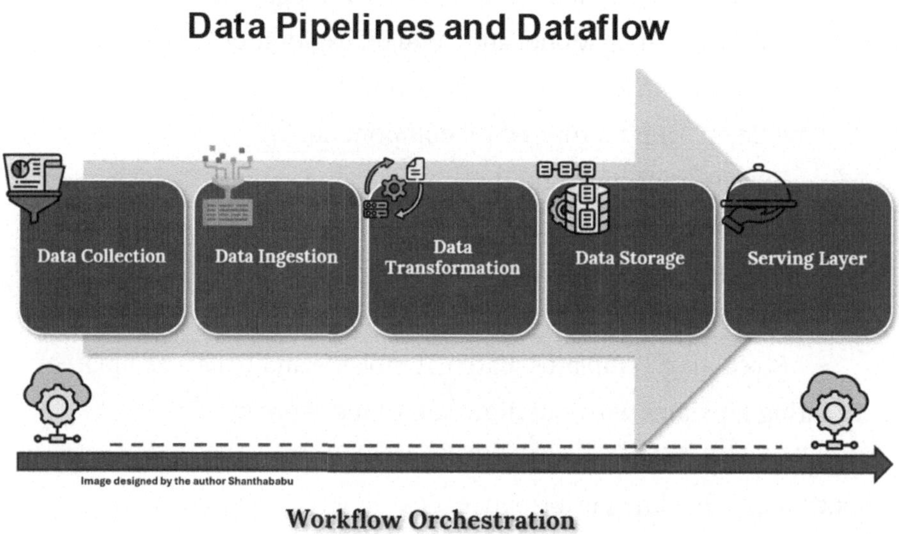

Figure 5.1: *Data Pipeline and Dataflow*

1. **Data Collection**: Collect data from various sources such as upstream applications, and define the **tables** and **columns** after a detailed discussion with stakeholders and the business team.

2. **Data Ingestion:** Data Ingestion is the process of collecting, importing, and loading data from various sources into a data storage system for further processing or analysis. Technically, this is called a **staging layer**. This data can be sourced from databases, APIs, IoT devices, logs, files, real-time streams, or other cloud storage systems. The ingestion process can be performed in batches, in real-time, or as a hybrid.

3. **Data Transformation:** Data transformation is the process of converting raw data into a structured format ready for analysis by applying a set of methods such as cleaning, filtering, aggregation, normalization, and formatting for analytics and machine learning model building. This step is crucial in **Extract, Transform, Load (ETL)** pipelines and ensures that data is consistent, accurate, and usable. This layer is the so-called **processing or transformation layer.**

4. **Data Storage:** This stage refers to using databases, data warehouses, or data lakes to store processed data efficiently for future retrieval and analysis. This layer is called the **storage layer.**

5. **Serving Layer:** From the data storage, data is served to various applications, including data science, data analytics, AI-powered products, a data warehouse, and an API for external application usage.

We have discussed **ETL** and **ELT** in detail in *Chapter 1*.

In short, *data pipelines and workflows refer to using software tools, pipelines, and orchestration frameworks to move, transform, clean, and process data across systems, while storing the data in an appropriate format without any manual intervention at each step. It also refers to adopting required business requirements, data quality, privacy, and governance as principles that underline the process.*

Automating data workflows is the backbone of operational efficiency, scalability, and reliability in modern data and AI systems.

Essentials of Dataflow and Pipelines

Figure 5.2 illustrates the essentials of dataflow and the pipeline perspective, and is detailed as follows:

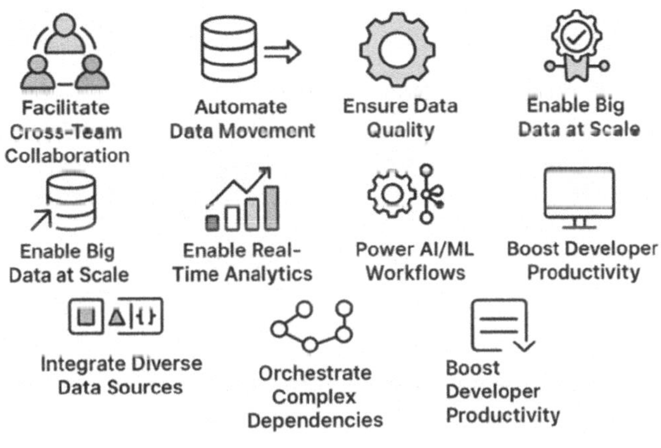

Figure 5.2: *Essentials of Dataflow and Pipelines*

To build robust, scalable, and intelligent data platforms, modern data pipelines must deliver on the following essential capabilities:

- **Facilitate Cross-Team Collaboration:** Standardized and reusable pipelines create a single version of truth, while enabling analysts, engineers, and data scientists to work on consistent datasets, reduce silos, and ensure efficient communication between teams.
- **Automated Data Movement:** Automatically extract data from diverse sources like IoT sensors, SaaS apps, cloud databases, or logs, and load it into target destinations like data lakes (for example, AWS S3, GCP Cloud Storage) or warehouses (for example, BigQuery, Snowflake) without manual effort.
- **Ensure Data Quality:** Built-in data quality checks (for example, schema validation, null handling, outlier detection, de-duplication) ensure reliable, clean datasets that reduce downstream errors in analytics and AI models.
- **Big Data at Scale:** Utilize distributed processing frameworks (for example, Apache Spark, Flink, Dataflow) to manage high volumes of data efficiently, whether they are processed in real-time or in scheduled batch jobs.
- **Enable Real-Time Analytics:** Stream data through platforms like Kafka or Pub/Sub and process it using tools like Flink or Spark Streaming. This allows dashboards and AI systems to respond instantly to events (for example, fraud detection, anomaly alerts).
- **Power AI/ML Workflows:** Provide AI systems with clean, timely, and enriched features. Pipelines ensure that model training, validation, and prediction workflows receive the most up-to-date and consistent input data.
- **Integrate Diverse Data Sources:** You can bridge siloed systems by ingesting structured (SQL databases), semi-structured (JSON, XML), and unstructured data (images, PDFs, audio) into a cohesive analytics and ML environment.
- **Support Governance and Compliance:** Pipelines can enforce security rules, enable data masking, maintain audit logs, track data lineage, and ensure compliance with GDPR, HIPAA, and SOX regulations.
- **Orchestrate Complex Dependencies:** Coordinate multi-step workflows with tools like Apache Airflow, Azure Data Factory, or Dagster. Ensure steps are executed in order, manage retries on failure, and alert stakeholders if issues arise.
- **Boost Developer Productivity:** Eliminates repetitive coding and manual data handling tasks. Developers can use low-code or code-based pipeline tools to focus on innovation, advanced analytics, and model development rather than plumbing tasks.

Criticality of Data Pipeline in Big Data and AI

The following table explains the criticality of the data pipeline in Big Data and AI solutions:

Reason	How It Helps
Handling Volume, Velocity, and Variety	Big Data involves petabytes of data flowing in real-time. As manual handling is impossible in such cases, automation ensures that there is a consistent flow of data.
Reduces Manual Errors	Automating ETL/ELT removes human errors in data prep, which boosts data quality and reliability.
Enables Real-Time AI and ML	AI systems rely on timely data. Automated workflows ensure data is always up-to-date for real-time predictions and dashboards.
Orchestrate Complex Dependencies	The different components of AI/ML pipelines such as data preprocessing, training, model deployment, and monitoring depend on each other. Tools like Apache Airflow or Azure Data Factory manage this sequencing.
Improves Scalability	As data grows, automated workflows scale horizontally (parallel execution) or vertically (higher compute), without confronting manual bottlenecks.
Enhances Collaboration and Reusability	Teams can reuse standardized pipelines for multiple use cases, which improves speed to deployment and consistency.
Support Governance and Compliance	Automation ensures that audit trails, data lineage tracking, and regulatory reporting are done consistently and securely.

Table 5.1: *Criticality of Data Pipeline in Big Data and AI*

Overview of Google Cloud Dataflow

Google Cloud offers **end-to-end data pipeline services** for building scalable, fault-tolerant ETL/ELT pipelines. The core stream and batch data processing component is **Google Cloud Dataflow**, which is a fully managed service that is based on the **Apache Beam** programming model.

Google Cloud Dataflow is a serverless data processing service designed to simplify the complexities of building and scaling data pipelines. It eliminates the need for manual infrastructure management tasks such as provisioning servers or configuring clusters and allows developers to focus on writing pipeline logic instead.

Dataflow supports a **unified model** for batch and streaming processing. This means that the same pipeline code can handle both use cases with minimal changes, which significantly reduces development overhead.

At a high level, in Google Cloud, these pipelines are built using a combination of the following services, which effectively provide excellent performance and optimization.

- **Dataflow** for compute
- **Pub/Sub** for messaging
- **BigQuery** for analytics
- **Cloud Storage** for raw data
- **Cloud Functions / Composer** for orchestration

Key Features of Google Cloud Dataflow

Google Cloud Dataflow has numerous features compared to other cloud providers. Let us explore them, as shown in *Figure* 5.3.

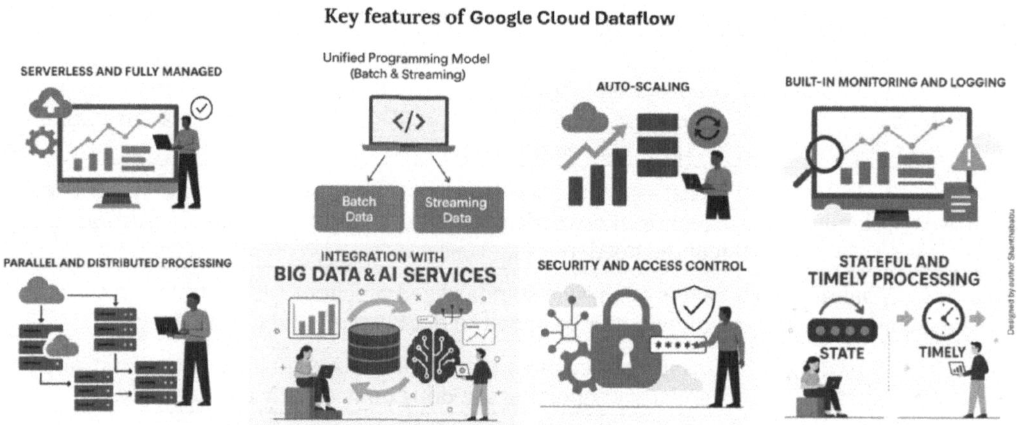

***Figure* 5.3:** *Key Features of Google Cloud Dataflow*

- **Serverless and Fully Managed:** Google Cloud Dataflow eliminates the complexity of infrastructure management by offering a fully managed and serverless data processing platform. This special feature means there is ***no need to provision, manage, or maintain clusters or virtual machines***. It can automatically handle resource ***provisioning, scaling, and cleanup***, which will allow developers to focus entirely on writing and optimizing business logic rather than worrying about underlying operational activities.
- **Unified Programming Model (Batch and Streaming):** One of Dataflow's standout features is its ***unified programming model*** that is powered by Apache Beam. Developers can use a single codebase to build pipelines that work for both **batch** and **streaming data**. Hence, whether the use case involves processing historical datasets or handling real-time data streams, the same development and operational practices are employed and executed. This key

feature reduces maintenance overhead costs and ensures consistency in logic, testing, and deployment. However, this might not be the case for other cloud providers.

- **Auto-Scaling:** It dynamically scales resources up or down based on the volume of incoming data and skewness. It also computes requirements specific to the project demand. It supports horizontal scaling ***(increasing the number of worker nodes)*** and vertical scaling ***(allocating more powerful machine types).*** This adaptive scaling ensures efficient resource utilization and maintains performance targets.
- **Parallel and Distributed Processing:** It breaks incoming data into smaller chunks known as bundles, which are then distributed across multiple worker nodes for concurrent processing. This architecture allows for ***high-throughput, low-latency processing of large-scale datasets***. It ensures that compute workloads are efficiently balanced and accelerated across a distributed infrastructure, which is ideal for handling enterprise-scale data.
- **Built-in Windowing and Triggers:** It provides advanced ***windowing*** and ***triggering*** mechanisms for stream analytics. Data can be grouped into ***fixed, sliding***, or ***session-based time*** windows. Therefore, it is easier to analyze time-sensitive patterns. Triggers allow developers to control when intermediate or final results are produced depending on business-specific data requirements.
- **Stateful and Timely Processing:** It enables stateful processing where the system maintains the state of individual keys across multiple events. This is particularly useful for complex real-time workflows like ***user sessionization, timeouts, and fraud detection***. Combined with timer-based logic, it allows pipelines to **detect patterns** or ***inactivity across event streams, while enabling highly responsive and context-aware data applications***.
- **Rich SDK and Language Support:** It supports development using Apache Beam's SDKs in ***Java*** and **Python**, with support for **Go** and **SQL** extensions on the roadmap. It seamlessly integrates with core GCP services like ***BigQuery, Cloud Pub/Sub, Cloud Storage, Cloud Spanner***, and ***Cloud SQL***. This compatibility allows developers to build comprehensive, cloud-native data workflows using their preferred tools and languages.
- **Flex Templates:** Flex Templates in Dataflow make pipelines **reusable** and **parameterized**, simplifying deployment across environments. These templates can be launched via ***Cloud Composer (Airflow), Cloud Scheduler***, or ***Cloud Functions***. These tools help in creating templates that are ideal for automated CI/CD workflows. They also support runtime parameters, which allow the same template to be reused for different datasets or logic variations.
- **Resilience and Fault Tolerance:** Built-in ***checkpointing*** and ***retry mechanisms*** ensure pipeline robustness. If a worker fails during processing, Dataflow

automatically replaces it and continues execution from the last checkpoint rather than restarting the job. This fault tolerance guarantees reliable processing with minimal data loss or duplication, which is critical for production-grade data pipelines.

- **Built-in Monitoring and Logging:** It offers powerful observability through its native UI in the Google Cloud Console. Users can monitor pipeline execution ***graphs, inspect step-level performance metrics, review worker logs***, and ***identify bottlenecks in real-time***. It also integrates with Cloud Monitoring and Cloud Logging, which allows teams to set alerts, trace failures, and perform comprehensive audits.
- **Security and Access Control:** Dataflow's security is enforced through integration with Google Cloud IAM and VPC Service Controls. These features enable fine-grained access policies and secure data processing across network boundaries. Additionally, Dataflow supports ***encryption in transit using TLS and at rest using either Google-managed*** or ***customer-managed encryption keys, while*** ensuring full compliance with enterprise security standards.
- **Integration with Big Data and AI Services:** It has native connectors to Google Cloud's ecosystem of big data and machine learning tools, including ***BigQuery*** for analytics, ***Vertex AI*** for model training, and ***Data Catalog*** for metadata management. This ability makes it a powerful engine for building end-to-end pipelines that span from raw data ingestion and real-time transformation to ML and business intelligence requirements.

Significant Challenges and Limitations with Google Cloud Dataflow

Although Dataflow has many features, it runs into challenges during the data pipeline building and complex workflows, as depicted in *Figure 5.4*.

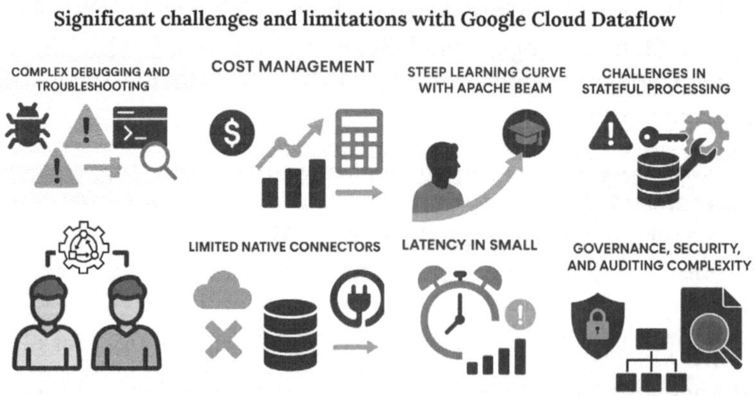

Figure 5.4: *Significant Challenges and Limitations with Google Cloud Dataflow*

- **Complex Debugging and Troubleshooting:** One of the primary challenges with Google Cloud Dataflow is the complexity involved in debugging and troubleshooting, especially in streaming pipelines. Developers often find it challenging to gain visibility into a pipeline's execution stages. While logs and stack traces are available, they are not always easy to interpret or trace back to the corresponding sections of Apache Beam code. This can significantly slow down the debugging process and increase development time, particularly in large, distributed jobs.

- **Cost Management:** Dataflow's serverless nature and auto-scaling capabilities are convenient to use, but they can also lead to unexpected costs. Jobs, especially long-running streaming ones, can accumulate high charges if they are not managed carefully. The translation of resource allocation into billing is unclear, which makes the task of forecasting costs even more difficult. Therefore, organizations must implement proactive monitoring, use budget alerts, and regularly review resource consumption and job configurations to prevent budget overruns.

- **Steep Learning Curve with Apache Beam:** Dataflow relies on Apache Beam to build pipelines, which introduces a steep learning curve for new users. Concepts such as windowing, triggers, watermarks, and side inputs are not straightforward and often require an in-depth understanding. Unlike traditional ETL tools that offer drag-and-drop or declarative interfaces, Beam's programmatic model requires strong programming skills. This makes onboarding more difficult for teams that are unfamiliar with distributed data processing.

- **Challenges in Stateful Processing:** Although Google Cloud Dataflow supports stateful processing, managing state adds a layer of complexity to the pipeline design. Developers must consider aspects like checkpointing, fault tolerance, and scalability when working with stateful DoFns (functions). Improper handling of stateful logic can result in inconsistent processing outcomes or performance degradation, which makes it a risky area for teams without prior experience in designing stateful data systems.

- **Dependency and Environment Management:** Dependency management can be a hassle for Python-based pipelines. Developers often rely on custom Docker containers or additional configuration steps, like using the extra-packages argument to include external libraries. This can lead to mismatches between local development environments and the production environment on Dataflow, resulting in runtime errors or job failures that are hard to diagnose.

- **Limited Native Connectors:** Although Dataflow integrates well with Google Cloud-native services like BigQuery and Cloud Storage, it lacks a broad set of out-of-the-box external system connectors. Integrating with non-Google data sources such as legacy databases, third-party APIs, or on-premise systems often requires writing custom connectors or transformations. This adds development overhead and can increase maintenance complexity over time.

- **Latency in Small or Short Batches:** Dataflow may not be the most efficient solution for smaller or short-duration jobs due to its relatively high cold-start times. Initializing and provisioning resources can introduce latency, which may not be acceptable for use cases requiring real-time responses or low-latency analytics. Therefore, it is not ideal for applications that rely on quick turnaround times and goals such as real-time alerting or instant data enrichment.
- **Governance, Security, and Auditing Complexity:** Implementing enterprise-grade governance, access control, and auditability in Dataflow requires careful configuration. While Google Cloud offers robust Identity and Access Management (IAM) policies, they must be finely tuned to ensure secure access to data pipelines. Additionally, Dataflow does not provide deep, built-in data lineage or audit trail features. Instead, it requires organizations to integrate external tools like Data Catalogue or Looker for complete observability and compliance tracking.

Unified Programming Model

The Unified Programming Model in Google Cloud refers to the capability of using a single framework and API for both ***batch*** and ***streaming data processing***. It is implemented through ***Apache Beam***, which powers Google Cloud Dataflow. Let us explore Apache Beam in detail.

Introduction to Apache Beam

Apache Beam is an open-source, unified programming model that abstracts the complexities of batch and streaming data processing. It allows developers to write pipelines once and execute them on multiple runners (execution engines) such as ***Google Cloud Dataflow, Apache Flink,*** *or* ***Apache Spark***. This portability makes Beam a flexible choice for tech organizations using diverse infrastructure. This enhances the pipeline's performance, and reduces the development effort and cost of building solutions.

Apache Beam is an **open-source, unified programming model** designed to define and execute both **batch and streaming data processing pipelines**. It abstracts the data processing logic from the underlying execution engine, which is known as a "runner". You can refer to the following expression to understand Beam:

"Beam" stands for: <u>B</u>atch + str<u>eam**</u> = Beam**

The expression **"Batch + Stream = Beam"** is widely used to communicate the **unified nature of Apache Beam**. Although not an official acronym, it reflects Beam's foundational goal of enabling developers to write **a single pipeline** that can handle both **batch and streaming data processing**. Instead of building and maintaining separate logic for historical datasets and real-time data, Beam allows you to use one codebase and one API. This makes it easier for developers to build consistent, scalable data solutions using the model. This simplification is particularly powerful in environments where both real-time analytics and traditional ETL pipelines are required.

Core Features of Apache Beam

- **Unified API for Batch and Streaming:** Apache Beam provides a single API that supports both batch and streaming data processing. This eliminates the need for separate tools or codebases and allows developers to write unified logic for processing both static files and real-time data streams. It also ensures consistency and reduces the development team's maintenance overhead and cost-effectiveness.

- **Portability across Runners:** Beam pipelines are portable and can run on multiple execution engines, such as ***Apache Spark, Apache Flink, Apache Apex, Google Cloud Dataflow, and Apache Samza***. This flexibility enables teams to switch environments or optimize for performance without modifying their pipeline logic.

- **Separation of Concerns:** Apache Beam separates the programming model from the execution engine. Developers focus on writing the data processing logic (Beam model), while engines like Spark or Flink handle the actual execution. This makes development simpler and infrastructure-agnostic.

Key concepts in Apache Beam include:

- **Pipelines**: The core structure that defines the data processing workflow
- **PCollections**: Immutable collections of data that flow through the pipeline (for example, a collection of log entries)
- **Transforms**: Operations applied to PCollections, such as filtering, mapping, or aggregating data
- **I/O Connectors**: Built-in utilities to read from and write to various sources/sinks such as Cloud Storage, Pub/Sub, or BigQuery

Beam's runner ecosystem allows the same pipeline to run on Dataflow for production or Spark for local testing, which provides flexibility during development.

Core Components of Apache Beam Architecture

Let us now discuss the Apache Beam architecture (refer to *Figure* 5.5) with its core components.

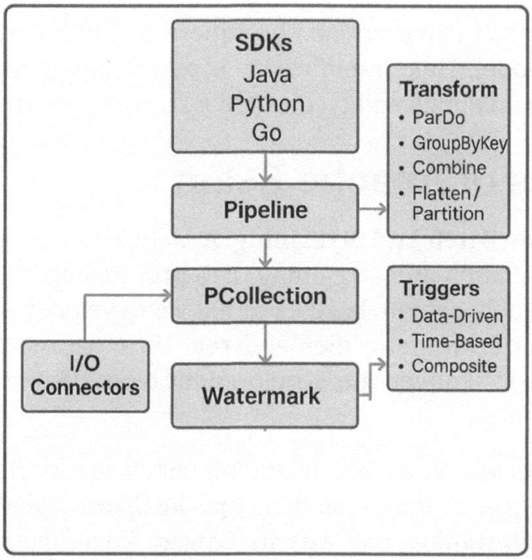

***Figure* 5.5:** *Core Components of Apache Beam Architecture*

- **SDKs:** Beam supports multiple SDKs such as **Java**, **Python**, and **Go to cater** to different developer preferences. For example, a Python developer might prefer Beam's Python SDK for its simplicity, while a Java developer might choose Java SDK for its robustness in enterprise applications.
- **Pipeline:** The pipeline is the top-level abstraction representing the entire data processing workflow. It defines the sequence of operations to be performed on the data. It acts as a blueprint that encapsulates inputs, transformations, and outputs. Developers construct a pipeline using an SDK (for example, Python, Java, Go) and submit it to a runner for execution.

  Example: A pipeline might start by reading data from a file, applying filtering and aggregation, and writing results to a database.
- **PCollection:** This is an immutable distributed dataset that represents the data as it flows through the pipeline. The result of the next transformation step serves as the input or output of each transformation step. It can be bounded (finite, for batch processing) or unbounded (infinite, for streaming processing). It is distributed across multiple workers for parallel processing and supports operations like mapping, filtering, and grouping.

Example: A PCollection might hold a stream of log entries read from a Pub/Sub topic or a set of rows from a CSV file in Cloud Storage.

- **Transform:** It helps to apply the transforming processing operation on a PCollection to produce a new PCollection. It defines the logic of the pipeline, which includes processes like ***data cleaning, enrichment***, and ***aggregation***. The following types exist to facilitate transforming data.
- **ParDo**: A general-purpose parallel processing operation that applies a user-defined function to each element (for example, parsing JSON or filtering records). *Example:* A ParDo transform can filter log entries where the error code is 500.
- **GroupByKey**: Groups elements in a PCollection by key to enable aggregation. *Example*: Grouping transaction records by customer ID to count the number of transactions per customer.
- **Combine**: Performs aggregation operations such as sum, average, or maximum across a PCollection. *Example*: Calculating the total sales amount or average order value from transaction data.
- **Flatten / Partition**: Combines multiple PCollections into one or splits a single PCollection into multiple subsets. *Example*: Flattening log data from multiple sources into a single stream, or partitioning user data based on region.
- **I/O Connectors:** I/O Connectors are pre-built utilities that handle reading from and writing to external data sources and sinks. It abstracts the complexity of interacting with diverse data systems, which ensures portability across runners.

  Examples:
  - Read from Cloud Storage, Pub/Sub, Kafka, or BigQuery.
  - Write to BigQuery, BigTable, or a file system.
- **Windowing:** It divides unbounded PCollections into finite chunks based on time or other criteria for processing streaming data. It enables time-based aggregations and handles out-of-order or late-arriving data in streaming pipelines. Here are some types of windowing:
  - **Fixed Windows**: When data is grouped into fixed time intervals (for example, 1-minute windows)
  - **Sliding Windows**: Overlapping time intervals (for example, 1-minute windows sliding every 10 seconds)
  - **Session Windows**: Groups data based on gaps between events (for example, user sessions)

Example: A pipeline might use 5-minute fixed windows to aggregate clickstream data.

- **Triggers:** Triggers control when the results of a window are emitted and encourage flexibility in handling data. They manage partial results (early firings) and late data **(late firings)** in streaming workflows. Triggers are categorized into the following types:
    - **Data-Driven**: Emits when a certain number of elements arrive
    - **Time-Based**: Emits after a time interval or when the watermark passes
    - **Composite**: Combines conditions (for example, emit early and then finalize)

  Example: A trigger might emit a partial sum every 30 seconds within a one-minute window.

- **Watermark:** A watermark is a heuristic that tracks the progress of data in a streaming pipeline. It indicates the moment when all data up to a certain point in time is expected. It helps in handling late data by allowing the pipeline to proceed while accounting for out-of-order events.

Example: If a watermark is at 08:00 PM and data arrives at 08:01 PM for 07:59 PM, it is treated as late data.

Execution Model

Now that we have discussed the core components and their roles, let us explore how the overall model execution works.

- **Runner:** A runner is the main execution engine that interprets and executes the pipeline on a distributed system. It translates the abstract pipeline into executable tasks, managing resource allocation, fault tolerance, and optimization. The Dataflow runner scales workers automatically based on pipeline load.

  Examples: Google Cloud Dataflow, Apache Flink, Apache Spark, Direct Runner (local execution)

- **SDK:** The Software Development Kit (SDK) provides the programming interface for defining data processing pipelines. Apache Beam supports Java, Python, and Go, enabling developers to write pipeline logic using familiar programming constructs, which are then executed by the selected runner.

  Example: A Python SDK script defines a pipeline that reads from Pub/Sub and writes to BigQuery.

- **Parallel Processing:** The beam pipelines are designed for parallel execution across multiple workers. The mechanism is that the runner splits PCollections into partitions, assigns them to workers, and applies transforms in parallel. This ensures scalability for large datasets by distributing the workload.

  Example: A pipeline processing 1TB of log data might split it among 100 workers.

- **Optimization:** In the optimization, there are two sub-activities; "**fusion**" combines multiple transforms into a single step to reduce overhead such as when a developer is merging a Map and Filter into one operation. Whereas, "**shuffle**" manages data movement between workers during grouping or joining operations. This improves performance and reduces latency, especially in streaming pipelines.

Architecture Workflow

The following steps outline the typical execution flow of an Apache Beam pipeline from development to data output:

1. **Pipeline Definition: A** developer uses an SDK to define a pipeline, while specifying **inputs** (for example, **`ReadFromText`**), **transforms** (for example, ParDo), and **outputs** (for example, **`WriteToBigQuery`**). Windows and triggers can be configured to handle time-based processing if needed.

2. **Submission to a Runner**: The pipeline is submitted to a runner such as **Dataflow** via a command-line tool or API call. The runner analyzes the pipeline and generates an execution plan.

3. **Execution**: This defines how the runner distributes the pipeline across a cluster of workers. PCollections are partitioned and transformations are applied in parallel. For streaming, watermarks and triggers manage the continuous flow of data.

4. **Optimization:** In Apache Beam refers to the automatic enhancements applied by the runner to improve performance and resource efficiency. It includes **fusion of adjacent transforms**, **splitting of large operations** for parallelism, and **smart scheduling** to reduce latency. The runner may also **eliminate redundant steps** and reuse computations. These optimizations ensure faster execution and lower cost without modifying pipeline logic.

5. **Output**: Processed data is written to the specified sink such as BigQuery or passed to the next stage of a multi-pipeline workflow based on the requirements.

Figure 5.6 illustrates the typical execution flow of an Apache Beam pipeline from development to data output.

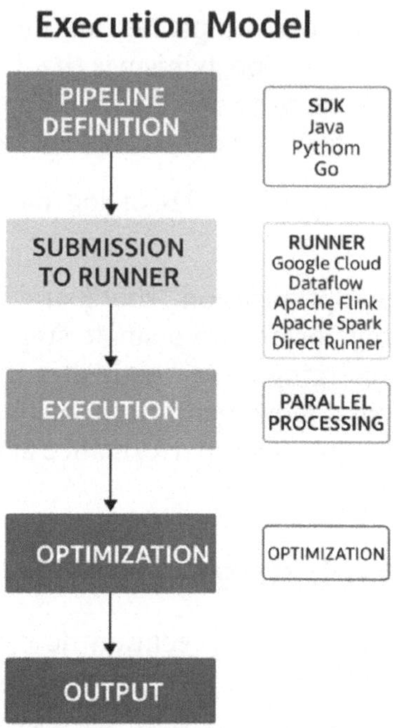

Figure 5.6: *Apache Beam Execution Model and Architecture Workflow*

Simple Apache Beam Workflow Implementation

The following steps outline a simple Apache Beam workflow for reading, filtering, and writing car data from a text file:

Step	Purpose
1	Reads car data from a CSV-style text file
2	Splits each row into a list of values
3	Filters rows for `chevrolet chevelle malibu`
4	Prints the filtered records to the console
5	Writes the filtered records to an output .txt file

Table 5.2: *A Simple Apache Beam Workflow Implementation*

Let us demonstrate a simple Apache Beam workflow implementation that reads and writes files. We can implement it with a Jupyter Notebook.

Step 1: Install the required library via the following pip:

```
!pip3 install apache_beam
```

Step 2: This Apache Beam code attempts to filter a list of car records (there are 10 records). Search for "**chevrolet chevelle malibu**" using a custom function, and print the results, as shown here:

```
import apache_beam as beam

# get the details
def get_mpg(autompg):
    return autompg['name'] == 'chevrolet chevelle malibu'

with beam.Pipeline() as pipeline:
    result = (
        pipeline
        | 'Create car data' >> beam.Create([
            {"name": "chevrolet chevelle malibu", "mpg": 18.0,
"cylinders": 8, "displacement": 307.0, "horsepower": "130", "weight":
3504, "acceleration": 12.0, "model_year": 70, "origin": 1},
            {"name": "buick skylark 320", "mpg": 15.0, "cylinders":
8, "displacement": 350.0, "horsepower": "165", "weight": 3693,
"acceleration": 11.5, "model_year": 70, "origin": 1},
            {"name": "plymouth satellite", "mpg": 18.0, "cylinders":
8, "displacement": 318.0, "horsepower": "150", "weight": 3436,
"acceleration": 11.0, "model_year": 70, "origin": 1},
            {"name": "amc rebel sst", "mpg": 16.0, "cylinders":
8, "displacement": 304.0, "horsepower": "150", "weight": 3433,
"acceleration": 12.0, "model_year": 70, "origin": 1},
            {"name": "ford torino", "mpg": 17.0, "cylinders":
8, "displacement": 302.0, "horsepower": "140", "weight": 3449,
"acceleration": 10.5, "model_year": 70, "origin": 1},
            {"name": "ford galaxie 500", "mpg": 15.0, "cylinders":
8, "displacement": 429.0, "horsepower": "198", "weight": 4341,
"acceleration": 10.0, "model_year": 70, "origin": 1},
            {"name": "chevrolet chevelle malibu", "mpg": 14.0,
"cylinders": 8, "displacement": 454.0, "horsepower": "220", "weight":
4354, "acceleration": 9.0, "model_year": 70, "origin": 1},
            {"name": "plymouth fury iii", "mpg": 14.0, "cylinders":
8, "displacement": 440.0, "horsepower": "215", "weight": 4312,
"acceleration": 8.5, "model_year": 70, "origin": 1},
            {"name": "pontiac catalina", "mpg": 14.0, "cylinders":
8, "displacement": 455.0, "horsepower": "225", "weight": 4425,
"acceleration": 10.0, "model_year": 70, "origin": 1},
            {"name": "amc ambassador dpl", "mpg": 15.0, "cylinders":
8, "displacement": 390.0, "horsepower": "190", "weight": 3850,
"acceleration": 8.5, "model_year": 70, "origin": 1}
```

```
        ])
        | 'Filter by chevrolet name' >> beam.Filter(get_mpg)
        | 'Print filtered results' >> beam.Map(print)
    )
```

Output:

```
{'name': 'chevrolet chevelle malibu', 'mpg': 18.0, 'cylinders':
8, 'displacement': 307.0, 'horsepower': '130', 'weight': 3504,
'acceleration': 12.0, 'model_year': 70, 'origin': 1}
{'name': 'chevrolet chevelle malibu', 'mpg': 14.0, 'cylinders':
8, 'displacement': 454.0, 'horsepower': '220', 'weight': 4354,
'acceleration': 9.0, 'model_year': 70, 'origin': 1}
```

Let us create a stream-style batch pipeline that reads data from a text file (auto-mpg.txt), filters it for a specific car name (chevrolet chevelle malibu), prints the results, and writes them to a text file.

```
def get_caredetails(auto):
    # Check if the car name (index 8) matches
    return auto[8].strip() == 'chevrolet chevelle malibu'

def run():
    with beam.Pipeline() as pipeline:
        car_records = (
            pipeline
            | "Read from Text File" >> beam.io.ReadFromText('auto-mpg.
txt', skip_header_lines=1)
            | "Split Record by Comma" >> beam.Map(lambda record: record.
split(','))
            | "Filter for chevrolet chevelle malibu" >> beam.Filter(get_
caredetails)
        )

        # Display matching records in the console
        car_records | "Print Filtered Records" >> beam.Map(print)

        # Write matching records to the output file
        (
            car_records
            | "Convert List to CSV String" >> beam.Map(lambda record:
','.join(record))
            | "Write to Text File" >> beam.io.WriteToText('chevrolet12',
num_shards=1)
        )
```

```
if __name__ == "__main__":
    run()
```

Function **`get_caredetails(auto)`**:

- This function considers a list called auto (which represents one row of car data split by commas).
- It checks whether the **9th column (index 8)**, which is assumed to be the **car name**, is exactly '**`chevrolet chevelle malibu`**' or not.
- **`.strip()`** is used to remove any whitespace characters from the beginning or the end.

Function **`run()`** This defines the full Beam pipeline using a context manager (with **`beam.Pipeline()`**).

Output:

['18', '8', '307', '130', '3504', '12', '70', '1', 'chevrolet chevelle malibu']

['17', '6', '250', '100', '3329', '15.5', '71', '1', 'chevrolet chevelle malibu']

Before we explore Dataflow, let us focus on Dataflow templates. Dataflow templates are significant because of the following reasons:

- They enable the separation of pipeline design from deployment and allow non-technical users to execute workflows efficiently.
- They enhance reusability by storing pre-configured pipelines that can be deployed repeatedly with customizable parameters.
- They ***reduce setup time, streamlines operations***, and eliminate the need for local **SDK *installations.***
- They support consistent execution across teams via CI/CD integration and results in scalability for recurring tasks like data import/export or real-time analytics.
- Ultimately, they lower operational overhead and accelerate data processing on the Google Cloud Platform.

Dataflow Templates

Dataflow templates in GCP are pre-packaged, reusable pipeline configurations that simplify the deployment and execution of data processing workflows. They enable developers to separate pipeline design from deployment and allow non-technical users or other teams to run pipelines without requiring them to understand the underlying code or set up a development environment. Here is a detailed breakdown:

Purpose and Benefits

- **Reusability**: Templates can be stored in a source control repository and integrated into CI/CD pipelines for consistent deployment.
- **No Local Dependencies**: Users can deploy templates via the Google Cloud Console, CLI, or REST API without locally installing the Apache Beam SDK or other dependencies.
- **Customization**: Templates support runtime parameters, which allow for flexibility in configuring inputs and outputs, as well as processing logic during deployment.

Types of Templates

The following templates are available in Dataflow. Let us explore them along with their purpose and benefits:

- **Classic Templates**: These are JSON-serialized job graphs created by running a pipeline and staging it to Cloud Storage. They require the **`ValueProvider`** interface for runtime parameters but have a static job graph.
- **Flex Templates**: As they are newer than their classic counterparts and are recommended, Flex templates package the pipeline into a Docker image stored in Artifact Registry, with a template specification file in Cloud Storage. They support dynamic job graph construction and do not require **`ValueProvider`**. Therefore, they offer greater flexibility (for example, by selecting I/O connectors at runtime).

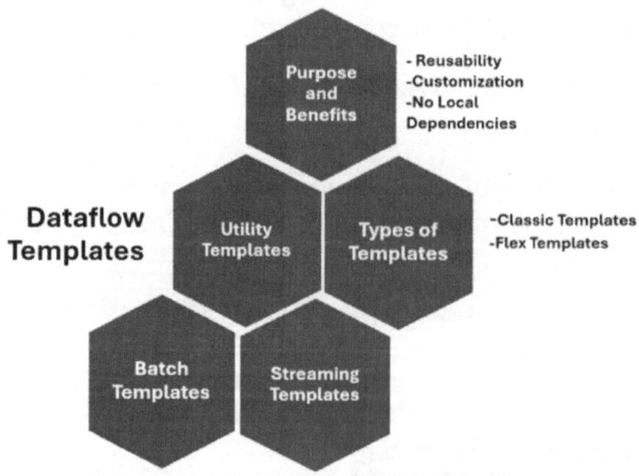

***Figure* 5.7:** *Dataflow Templates*

Creation Process:

- For **Classic templates**, developers can run the pipeline with a "–**`templateLocation`**" flag to stage the template file in Cloud Storage.

- For **Flex templates**, developers can build a Docker image, push it to Artifact Registry, and upload a JSON spec file to Cloud Storage.
- Both types of templates involve **staging** additional files (for example, dependencies) that must remain accessible to avoid runtime failures.

Deployment:

- Templates can be launched via the Google Cloud Console, gcloud CLI, or REST API. The process can take 5-7 minutes as Dataflow provisions the resources.
- Two IAM service accounts are used: a Dataflow service account (for resource manipulation) and a worker service account (for accessing pipeline files and resources).

Use Cases:

- Ideal for recurring tasks like data import/export, backup/restore bulk API operations, or real-time analytics.
- Google provides pre-built templates, which can be extended or used as-is, which reduces development time.

List of Google-Provided Dataflow Templates

Google offers a variety of open-source Dataflow templates, categorized into **Streaming**, **Batch**, and **Utility** types. These templates are hosted at gcr.io/dataflow-templates and can be found in the official documentation. The following is a list based on the available categories and examples.

- **Streaming Templates**
  - **Pub/Sub to BigQuery**: Reads JSON messages from a Pub/Sub topic and writes them to a BigQuery table in real-time
  - **Pub/Sub to Cloud Storage**: Processes messages from Pub/Sub and writes results to Cloud Storage in specified time windows
  - **Pub/Sub to Pub/Sub**: Transforms and forwards messages between Pub/Sub topics
  - **Kafka to BigQuery**: Streams data from Apache Kafka to BigQuery
  - **Datastream to BigQuery**: Ingests change data capture (CDC) from Cloud Datastream into BigQuery
- **Batch Templates**
  - **Cloud Storage to BigQuery**: Reads files from Cloud Storage, processes them and loads the data into BigQuery
  - **BigQuery to Cloud Storage**: Exports data from BigQuery to Cloud Storage in various formats (for example, CSV, JSON)

   - **Cloud Storage to Spanner**: Transfers data from Cloud Storage to Cloud Spanner
   - **BigQuery to GCS Avro**: Exports BigQuery data to Cloud Storage in Avro format
   - **JDBC to BigQuery**: Moves data from a JDBC-compatible database to BigQuery
- **Utility Templates**
   - **Text to BigQuery**: Processes text files and loads the data into BigQuery
   - **Bulk File Processing**: Handles large-scale file operations (for example, compression, transformation) in Cloud Storage
   - **Data Generator**: Generates synthetic data for testing purposes and writes it to various sinks (for example, BigQuery, Cloud Storage)

Creating Dataflow Pipelines with Cloud Storage

Step 1: Setting Up a Dataflow Environment

To begin using Dataflow, you must first set up your Google Cloud environment and have a Cloud Storage bucket. For details on creating a storage bucket, please refer to *Chapter* 3.

Follow the **Enable the Dataflow API.**

In the Google Cloud Console, navigate to the API Library, search for "Dataflow API", and enable it for your project. This allows Dataflow to interact with other Google Cloud services. Click **"`Enable`"**, as shown in *Figure* 5.8.

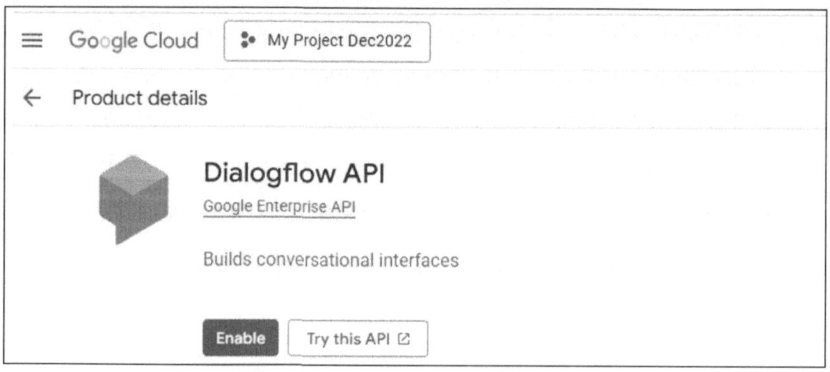

Figure 5.8: *Enabling the Dataflow API*

You can observe that the Dataflow API is enabled in *Figure* 5.9.

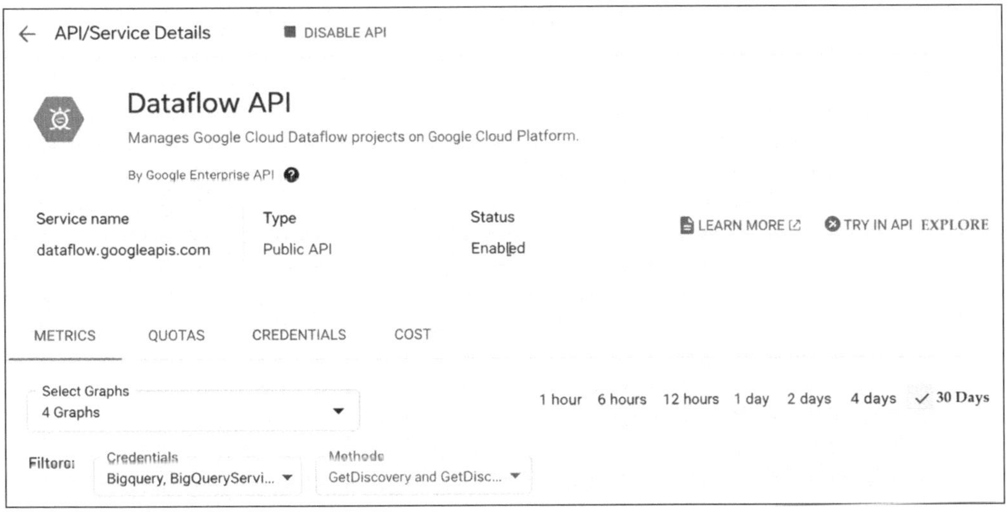

Figure 5.9: *Dataflow API Enabled for Usage*

Step 2: Search and navigate to Dataflow and the portal will take you to the screen shown in *Figure* 5.10.

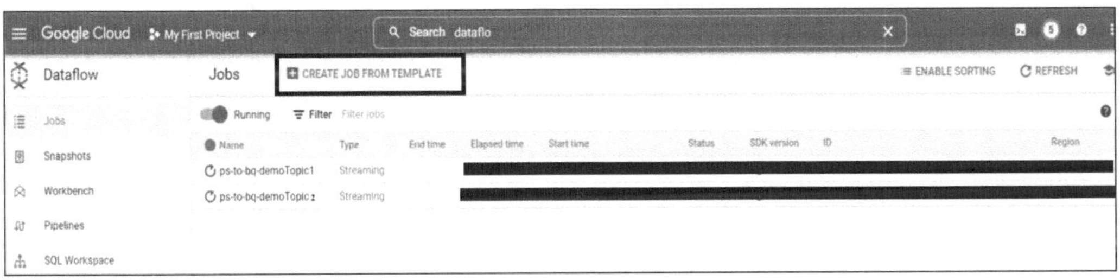

Figure 5.10: *Dataflow in the GCP Console*

To create a new flow, click "**`Create Job from template`**" seen in the top menu, as highlighted in *Figure* 5.10.

Step 3: Once you click "**`Create Job from template`**", the portal will take you to the Create job screen, as shown in *Figure* 5.11.

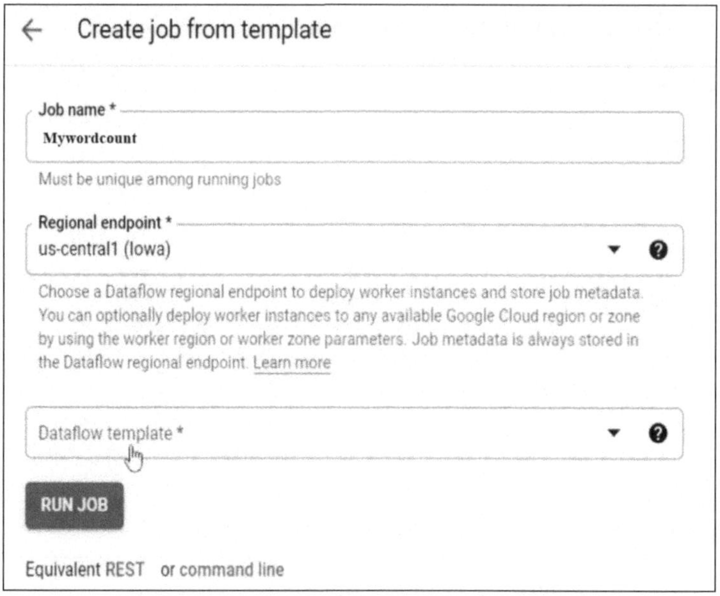

Figure 5.11: *Create a New Dataflow Template in the GCP Console*

For this demonstration, you can choose the word count template shown in *Figure* 5.12.

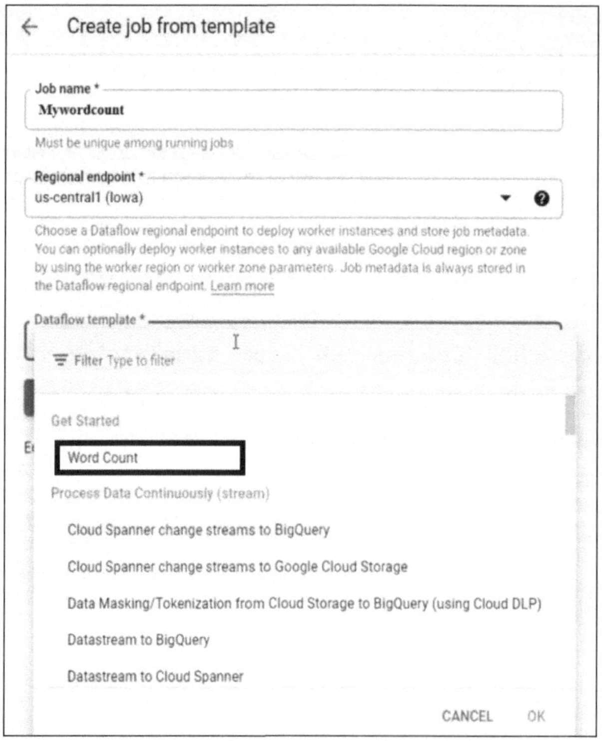

Figure 5.12: *Select the Word Count Template from the List*

Step 4: Once you select the template, the portal will display the template's workflow/Graph on the right side. This represents the flow; read each line in the given file, count the words, map the elements, and write the word count into the output file.

This is illustrated in *Figure* 5.13. You must configure the required parameters like input and output files, as well as specify the temporary location.

Figure 5.13: *Select the Word Count Template and Workflow/Graph*

Required Parameters

- **Input File(s) in Cloud Storage**:

  Select the available file from the dataflow samples.

  - gs://dataflow-samples/shakespeare/kinglear.txt
  - This is the source file from which the dataflow job reads.

- **Output Cloud Storage File Prefix (Required):**
  - Used to specify where the output (for example, word count results) should be saved
  - Example format: gs://your-bucket/counts

- **Temporary Location (Required):**
  - Location for temporary data used during pipeline execution

    - Example format: gs://your-bucket/temp
- **Encryption Options:**
    - Google-managed encryption key (default) – ***No setup required.***
    - Customer-Managed Encryption Key (CMEK) – Use Google Cloud Key Management Service (KMS) if you want to manage the encryption keys yourself.

The *Figure* 5.14 illustrates Required Parameters Dataflow to Execute the Workflow

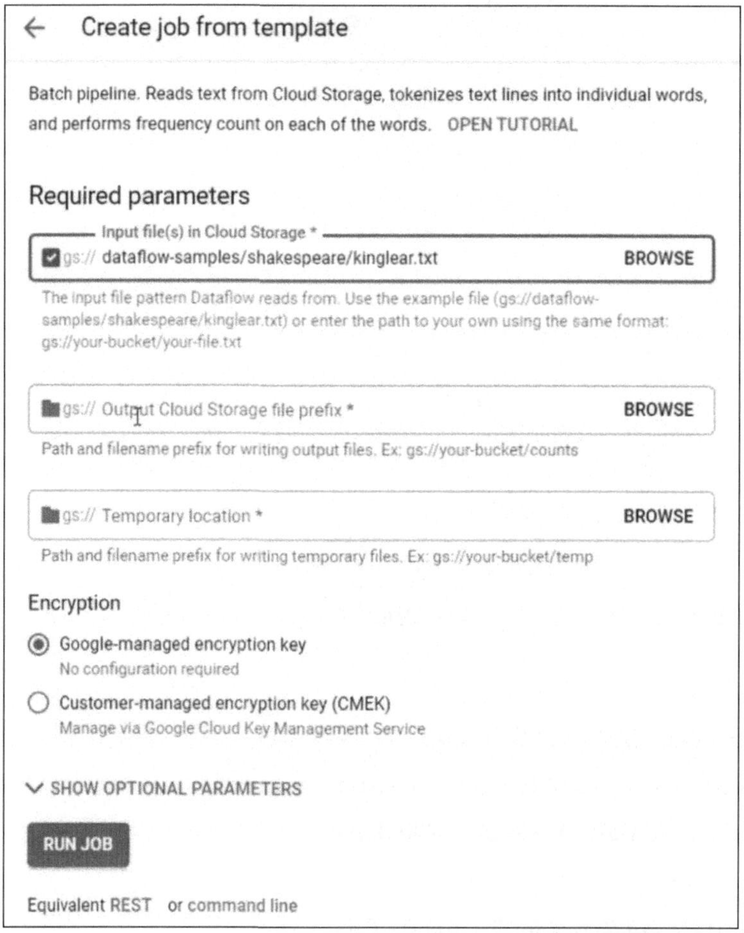

Figure 5.14: *Required Parameters Dataflow to Execute the Workflow*

Output Cloud Storage File to Temporary Location: Just like in *Figure* 5.15, you have to select the storage bucket from your cloud storage location.

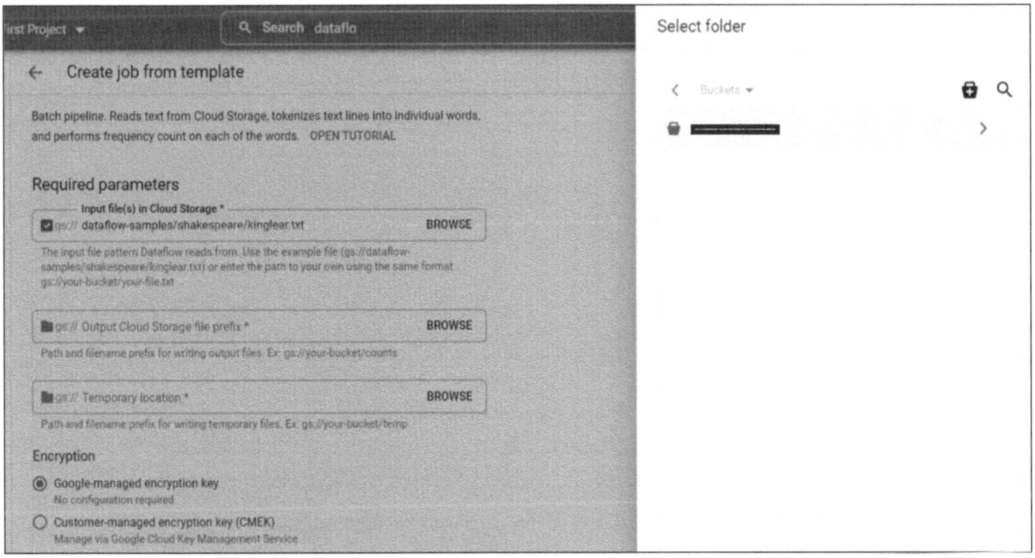

Figure 5.15: *Cloud Storage Location for Output and Temporary Storage*

Step 5: Once all the required parameters are configured, click "**Run**", and the job will be executed step by step. We can observe this in the Job Graph panel shown in *Figure 5.16*, through the job completion check mark.

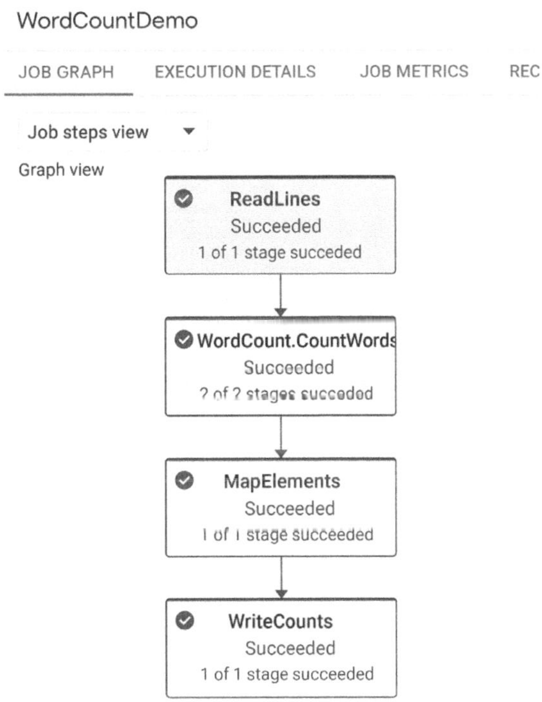

Figure 5.16: *Job Graph View in Dataflow*

Step 6: To see the job logs, click the **`Show`** menu item following the Job Graph shown in *Figure* 5.17 and highlight. You can observe the logs with the date and other key information.

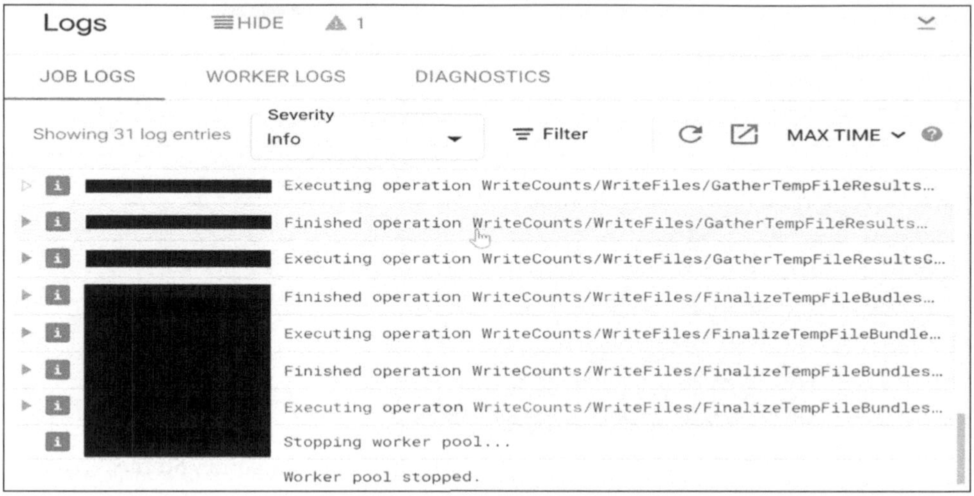

***Figure* 5.17:** *Job Logs View in Dataflow*

Step 7: Once the job is completed, the expected files will be created and stored in **`Cloud Storage`**. Now, click **`Cloud Storage`**, as shown in *Figure* 5.18.

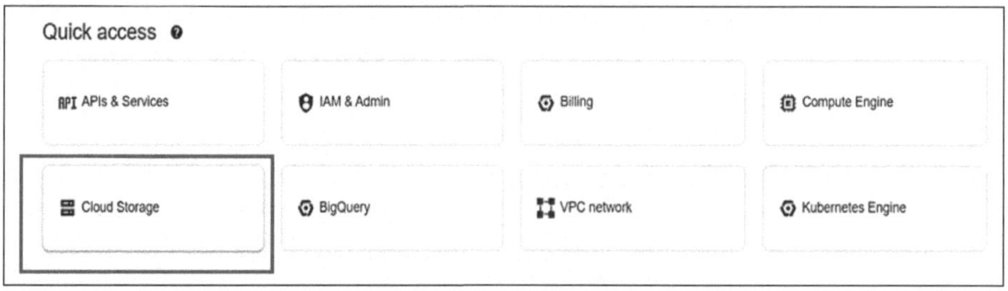

***Figure* 5.18:** *GCP – Cloud Storage Search*

Step 8: Once you click **`Cloud Storage`**, the portal will take you to your cloud storage page, where you can select the cloud storage you have configured for storing files.

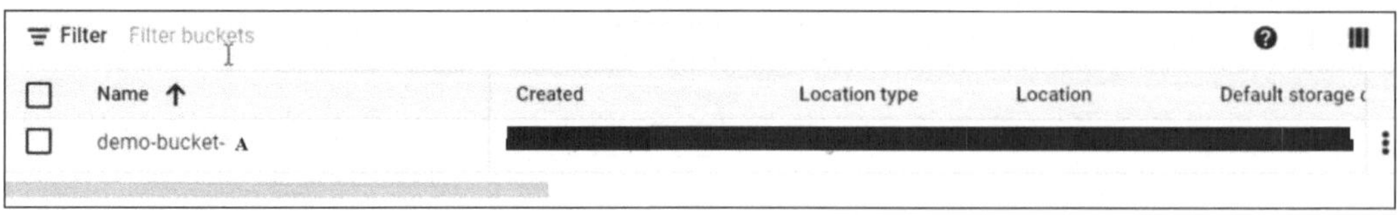

***Figure* 5.19:** *GCP – Cloud Storage -Page (Targeted Storage)*

Step 9: Once you have selected your bucket, you can find the temp folder and the job created file shown in *Figure* 5.20.

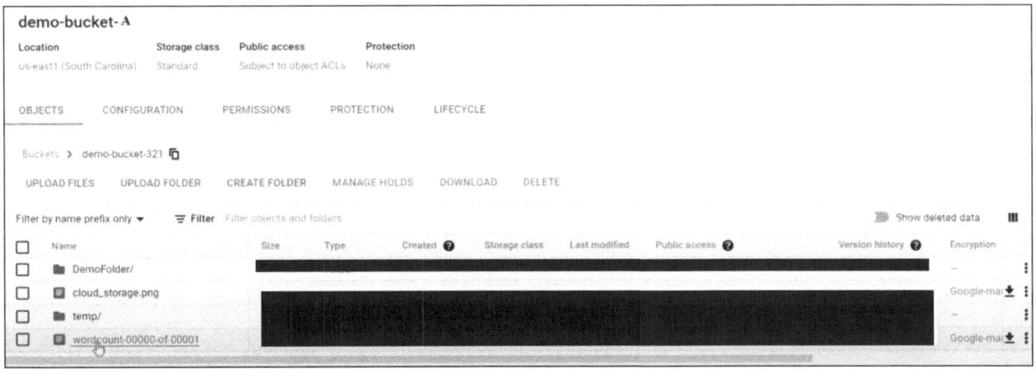

Figure 5.20: *Target File Created through the Job (Dataflow)*

Step 10: To find the file details, click the file in *Figure* 5.20. The portal will then display the screen shown in *Figure* 5.21.

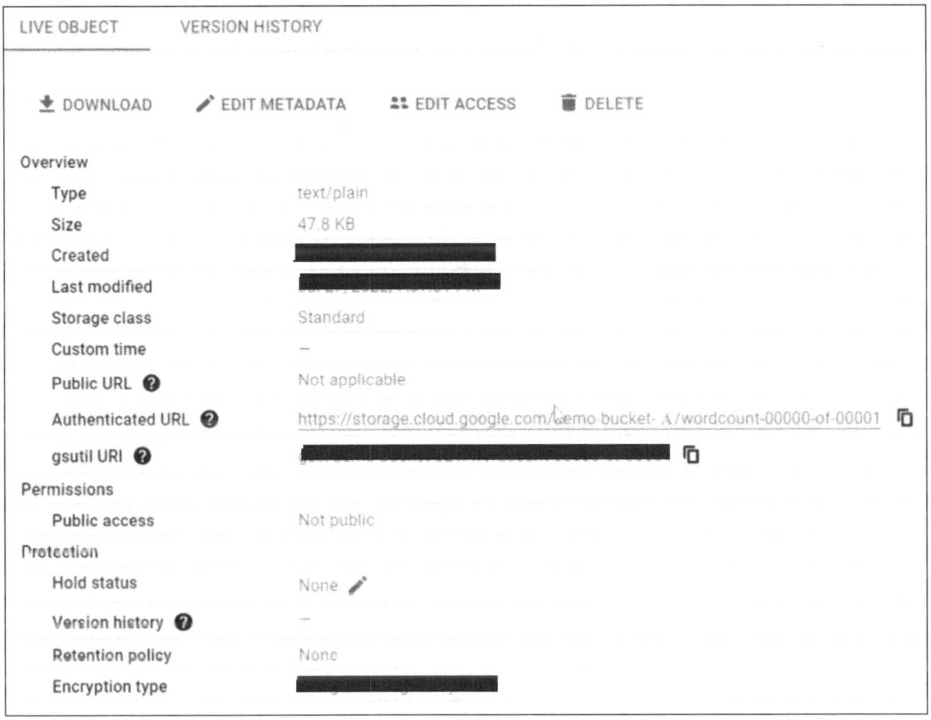

Figure 5.21: *Output File Properties (Created via Dataflow)*

The portal will open the output file as shown in *Figure* 5.22.

```
feature: 1
clock: 1
worried: 1
scattered: 1
white: 44
sudden: 1
chilly: 1
james: 3
righteous: 1
sword: 68
density:10
law: 5
underpaid: 1
clay:1
infortunate: 1
black: 12
horrible 2
forest: 8
stormy:1
```

Figure 5.22: *Output File (Created via Dataflow)*

Building a Workflow Using the SDK

We can implement the same workflow that we discussed above using the SDK dynamically. Let us explore this with a simple example illustrated in the following block diagram:

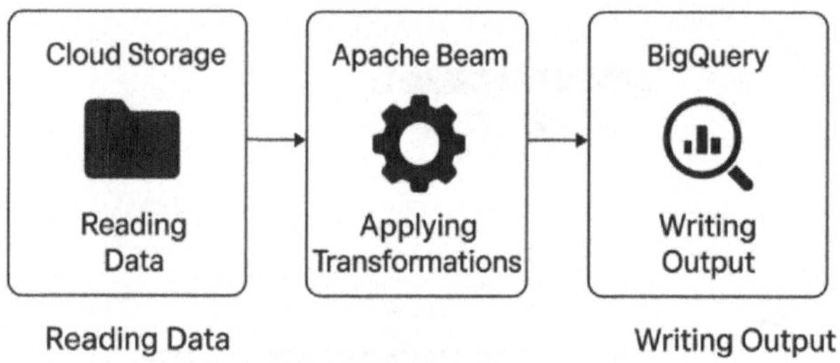

Figure 5.23: *Created via Dataflow SDK*

Install the Apache Beam SDK: Depending on your preferred language, install the SDK for Python or Java.

For Python, you can use the following pip:

```
pip install apache-beam[gcp]
```

The [gcp] extra ensures that Google Cloud-specific dependencies are included. For Java, you would typically use Maven to include the Beam dependency in your project.

You will also need to authenticate with Google Cloud using the gcloud CLI and set up a service account with appropriate permissions (for example, Dataflow Worker, BigQuery Data Editor) to allow your pipeline to access resources.

Building a Simple Batch Pipeline – Sales Report Generation

Batch pipelines process static datasets in a single execution, which makes them ideal for use cases such as generating monthly sales summaries or performing data cleansing. Here is how to construct a batch pipeline using Apache Beam and Dataflow for summarizing product sales data.

1. **Reading Data**: Use **ReadFromText** to load a CSV file from Cloud Storage (for example, gs://bucket/sales_data.csv).
2. **Applying Transformations**: Parse the CSV lines into fields, extract product names, and calculate total sales per product.
3. **Write Output**: Store the summarized results in BigQuery with appropriate schema settings.

Note: *We will be discussing BigQuery exclusively in the upcoming sections.*

Pipeline (Product Sales Summary): This pipeline processes sales records and outputs rows such as ("**Laptop**", 152000.50) and represents the total revenue by product.

```
import apache_beam as beam

def parse_csv(line):
    import csv
    from io import StringIO
    reader = csv.reader(StringIO(line))
    fields = next(reader)
    return fields[1], float(fields[2])  # (product_name, sale_amount)

with a beam.Pipeline() as pipeline:
    (pipeline
     | 'Read CSV from GCS' >> beam.io.ReadFromText('gs://bucket/sales_
data.csv', skip_header_lines=1)
      | 'Parse CSV' >> beam.Map(parse_csv)
      | 'Sum Sales' >> beam.CombinePerKey(sum)
      | 'Format for BigQuery' >> beam.Map(lambda x: {'product': x[0],
'total_sales': x[1]})
      | 'Write to BigQuery' >> beam.io.WriteToBigQuery(
          'project:dataset.sales_summary',
          schema='product:STRING, total_sales:FLOAT',
          create_disposition=beam.io.BigQueryDisposition.CREATE_IF_NEEDED))
```

Input:

- **Source**: Cloud Storage (GCS)
- **File**: gs://bucket/sales_data.csv

```
date,product,amount
2024-05-01,Laptop,1500.00
2024-05-01,Mouse,25.00
2024-05-02,Laptop,2000.00
```

Output:

- **Destination: BigQuery table project:dataset.sales_summary**

```
Laptop        | 3500.00
Mouse         | 25.00
```

Table 5.3 presents the input and output of the Batch Pipeline – Sales Report Generation for both pipelines as follows:

Stage	Details
Input Source	Google Cloud Storage (GCS)
Input Format	CSV File (gs://bucket/sales_data.csv)
Sample Input	date,product,amount2024-05-01,Laptop,1500.002024-05-01,Mouse,25.002024-05-02,Laptop,2000.00
Transformation	Parse CSV, extract product name, sum sales per product
Output Target	BigQuery Table project:dataset.sales_summary
Output Schema	product: STRING, total_sales: FLOAT
Sample Output	Laptop

Table 5.3: *Batch Pipeline – Sales Report Generation Input and Output*

Optimizing Pipeline Performance

Figure 5.24 highlights the key considerations and techniques for optimizing Apache Beam pipelines, focusing on performance tuning, efficient resource utilization, windowing strategies, optimized joins, and cost-effective execution.

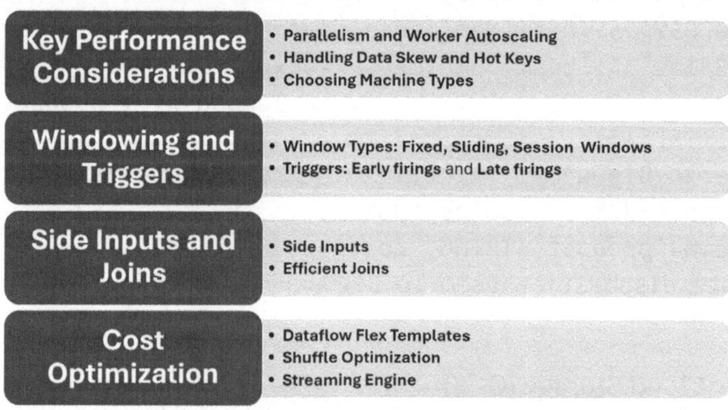

Figure 5.24: *Optimizing Pipeline Performance*

Key Performance Considerations

Key Performance Considerations

When designing data processing pipelines, optimization is a critical factor to ensure efficient execution and effective cost management. Apache Beam pipelines running on Dataflow must be carefully configured to handle varying data volumes, workloads, and resource demands.

- **Parallelism and Worker Autoscaling:** Google Cloud Dataflow automatically adjusts the number of worker nodes based on workload demands. For instance, a batch pipeline may begin with a small number of workers and scale up dynamically as input data volume increases. This behavior can be fine-tuned by defining limits such as the maximum number of workers to balance performance and cost.
- **Handling Data Skew and Hot Keys:** Uneven data distribution, where a small number of keys dominate the dataset, can lead to processing bottlenecks and underutilized workers. Techniques such as repartitioning, key sharding, or random key prefixing help distribute the workload evenly across workers and improve overall pipeline throughput.
- **Selecting Appropriate Machine Types:** Choosing the right machine configuration is essential for performance optimization. Compute-intensive operations benefit from high-CPU machines, while memory-intensive operations—such as large joins or aggregations—require high-memory machines to avoid excessive disk I/O and latency.

For example, a pipeline processing user activity logs may experience performance degradation if a single user generates a disproportionately large number of events. Repartitioning the data using a more granular key, such as a combination of user ID and time window, can help mitigate hot key issues and improve processing efficiency.

Windowing and Triggers

Windowing and triggers are critical for streaming pipelines.

- **Window Types:**
  - **Fixed Windows** (for example, 1-minute intervals)
  - **Sliding Windows** (for example, 1-minute windows sliding every 10 seconds)
  - **Session Windows** (grouping events with gaps less than a specified duration).
- **Triggers**: Control when results are emitted. **Early firings** emit partial results before the window closes, while **Late firings** handle delayed data. For example, a trigger might emit results every 10 seconds within a one-minute window.

Handling Late Data: Use **`allowed_lateness`** to process late-arriving data without discarding it to ensure completeness while incurring the cost of increased latency.

For instance, a pipeline tracking website's clicks might use sliding windows to compute click rates every 30 seconds, with a trigger to emit early results for real-time dashboards.

Side Inputs and Joins

- **Side Inputs**: These allow for the enrichment of streaming data that is static or changes slowly. For example, a pipeline processing orders might use a side input to look up customer details from a BigQuery table.
- **Efficient Joins**: In streaming pipelines, joins can be tricky due to infinite data streams. Use windowing to bind the join operation and ensure that both sides of the join (for example, orders and payments) are aligned in time.

For example, a pipeline might join streaming transaction data with a side input of fraud patterns to flag suspicious activity in real-time.

Cost Optimization

- **Dataflow Flex Templates**: These are pre-defined, reusable pipeline templates that simplify deployment and reduce setup costs. For example, a template for log processing can be reused across projects.
- **Shuffle Optimization and Streaming Engine**: This allows Dataflow's streaming engine to offload shuffle operations to Google's infrastructure and reduces costs by minimizing worker overhead.

For instance, enabling the streaming engine for a high-throughput pipeline might reduce costs by 20% as it optimizes data shuffling.

Best Practices and Troubleshooting

Figure 5.25 illustrates the operational best practices in Apache Beam, while focusing on pipeline monitoring, failure handling strategies, and enforcing security and compliance standards.

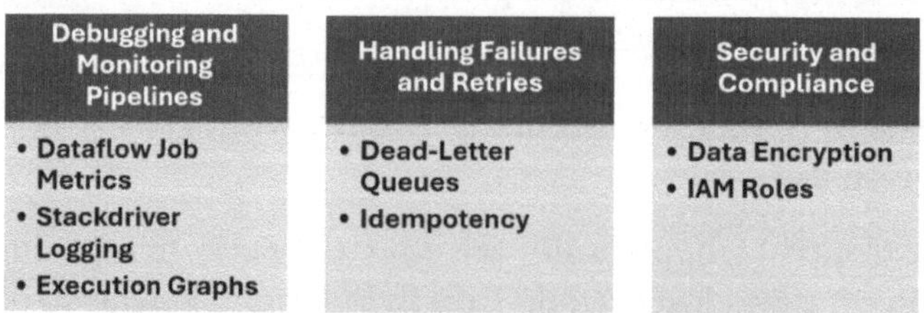

***Figure* 5.25:** *Best Practices and Troubleshooting*

Let us explore the best practices and troubleshooting:

- **Debugging and Monitoring Pipelines**
    - **Dataflow Job Metrics**: Monitor metrics like system latency, data freshness, and throughput in the Dataflow Console to ensure the pipeline is performing as expected.
    - **Stackdriver Logging**: Use logs to identify errors such as failed reads from Pub/Sub or write failures to BigQuery.
    - **Execution Graphs**: Analyze the pipeline's execution graph to spot bottlenecks such as a transform being disproportionately delayed due to data skew.

For example, if a pipeline shows high latency, the execution graph might reveal that a single worker is overloaded, which could prompt a repartitioning of the data.

- **Handling Failures and Retries**
    - **Dead-Letter Queues: For** records that fail to process (for example, malformed JSON), write them to a separate Pub/Sub topic or BigQuery table for further analysis.
    - **Idempotency**: Ensure that reprocessing the same data (for example, due to retries) does not result in duplicates. For example, use unique message IDs to deduplicate events.

A practical example can be a pipeline that fails to parse a malformed sensor reading and sends it to a dead-letter queue for manual inspection.

- **Security and Compliance**
    - **Data Encryption**: Dataflow automatically encrypts data in transit and at rest using Google Cloud's encryption mechanisms and ensures that it complies with standards like GDPR.
    - **IAM Roles**: Assign least-privilege roles to Dataflow jobs, such as **`roles/dataflow.worker`** for workers and **`roles/bigquery.dataEditor`** for BigQuery access.

For instance, a healthcare company might utilize Dataflow to process patient data, while relying on encryption and Identity and Access Management (IAM) to meet the HIPAA requirements.

Advanced Use Cases in Real-Time Data Processing

Figure 5.26 illustrates the advanced use cases in real-time data processing:

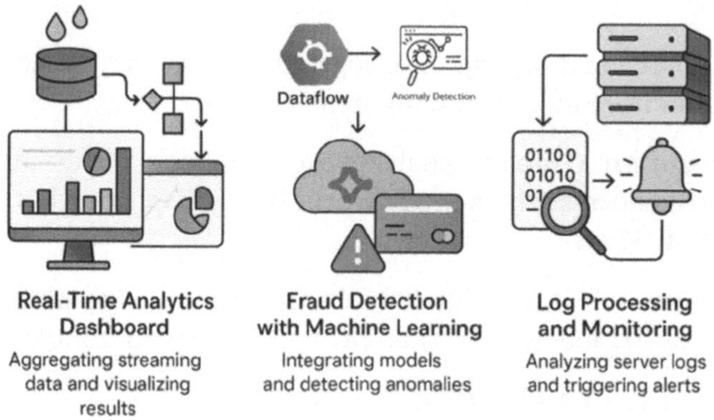

Figure 5.26: *Advanced Use Cases in Real-Time Data Processing*

Let us discuss the use case here:

- **Real-Time Analytics Dashboard:** Streaming pipelines can power dashboards for real-time insights.
    - **Aggregating Streaming Data**: Process clickstream data (for example, user clicks on a website) or IoT sensor readings (for example, temperature data) using Dataflow.
    - **Visualizing Results**: Write aggregated data to BigQuery, then use Data Studio or Looker to create interactive dashboards. For example, a dashboard might display live website traffic with metrics such as page views per minute.

A practical example is an e-commerce platform displaying real-time sales metrics, which allows managers to track performance during a flash sale.

- **Fraud Detection with Machine Learning:** Dataflow integrates with machine learning frameworks like TensorFlow.
    - **Integrating Models**: Embed a TensorFlow model in a Dataflow pipeline to score streaming data such as transaction records.
    - **Anomaly Detection**: Use the model to detect anomalies, flagging transactions that deviate from normal patterns (for example, unusually large purchases).

For example, a bank might use this to flag a $10,000 transaction from an account that typically spends $100, which might trigger an alert for further investigation.

- **Log Processing and Monitoring:**
  - **Analyzing Server Logs: Process logs in real-time** to identify errors or performance issues such as HTTP 500 errors indicating server failures.
  - **Triggering Alerts**: Utilize Cloud Monitoring to configure alerts based on log metrics and notify teams via email or Slack.

For instance, a pipeline might detect a spike in errors from a web server and alert the DevOps team to investigate the issue.

- **Event-Driven Processing**
  - **Cloud Functions with Pub/Sub**: Use lightweight Cloud Functions to perform simple transformations (for example, reformatting messages) before passing them to Dataflow for heavy processing.
  - **Chaining Dataflow Jobs**: Create workflows where one Dataflow job processes raw data and a second job performs advanced analytics such as aggregating results.

For example, a pipeline might use Cloud Functions to filter invalid messages from a Pub/Sub topic and then pass the cleaned data to Dataflow for further analysis.

Conclusion

This chapter provided a comprehensive overview of building and optimizing scalable batch and streaming data pipelines using Google Cloud Dataflow and Apache Beam. We highlighted the importance of real-time and large-scale data processing in today's analytics and AI-driven environments. Dataflow, powered by Apache Beam, offers a unified, serverless platform that simplifies the development of complex data workflows. Its ability to support both batch and streaming use cases from a single codebase reduces development effort and operational overhead, making it ideal for modern data engineering needs.

We also explored the use of Classic and Flex templates to optimize performance and the best practices for monitoring, debugging, and securing pipelines. Practical use cases such as real-time dashboards, fraud detection, and log monitoring demonstrated the platform's versatility. While Dataflow offers powerful capabilities, we noted how challenges like debugging complexity, cost management, and the Apache Beam learning curve must be addressed through clear architectural strategies, continuous performance tuning, and adopting industry best practices.

The next chapter focuses on orchestrating data workflows using Cloud Composer. It examines how automation streamlines processes, manages task dependencies through Directed Acyclic Graphs (DAGs), and leverages custom operator integrations to build dynamic, scalable, and adaptable orchestration systems.

CHAPTER 6

Orchestrating Workflows with Cloud Composer

Introduction

In the previous chapter, we discussed batch and streaming pipelines using Google Cloud Dataflow and Apache Beam. We also explored a unified platform for designing batch and streaming pipelines with high scalability, reliability, and efficiency. We now understand that Dataflow's capabilities go far beyond traditional data processing. Additionally, we covered different Dataflow templates and their significance, as well as how to optimize pipeline performance, best practices, troubleshooting, and advanced use cases in real-time data processing.

This chapter provides an in-depth exploration of workflow orchestration using Cloud Composer, while emphasizing the importance of automation in streamlining processes and managing complex dependencies. It introduces Cloud Composer as Google Cloud Platform's managed implementation of Apache Airflow for orchestrating large-scale data workflows. In this chapter, readers will learn how to design and manage Directed Acyclic Graphs (DAGs), automate task execution, and scale orchestration pipelines for enterprise-grade applications. The chapter also includes advanced topics such as building dynamic and flexible orchestration systems through custom operator integrations.

Structure

- Significance of Automating Data Workflows
- Data Pipeline Orchestration Tools and Workflow Services
    - Apache Airflow
    - Azure Data Factory (ADF)

    - AWS Step Functions
    - GCP Cloud Composer
- Exploring Directed Acyclic Graphs (DAGs)
    - DAG Setup
    - Apache Airflow Best Practices for DAGs in Airflow/Composer
- Exploring Google Cloud Composer
    - Google's Composer Architecture View
    - Key Features
    - Advantages of Cloud Composer
    - Disadvantages of Cloud Composer
    - Use Cases
- Google Cloud Composer Implementation
- Scaling Orchestration for Complex Pipelines
    - Key Considerations for Scaling Complex Pipelines
    - Best Practices for Scaling and Integration
- Integrations with Google Cloud and External Systems

Significance of Automating Data Workflows

A data workflow refers to the sequence of steps involved in collecting, processing, transforming, and delivering data from source systems such as applications, databases, SAP systems, File systems and IoT devices, to end-users, data warehouses, BI tools, data scientists, machine learning engineers or other downstream applications.

Workflow orchestration refers to the **automation and coordination of complex data tasks**. It ensures that tasks are executed in the correct order, are able to handle failures gracefully, and can scale to meet business demands. It is a foundational technical capability in the following domains:

- ETL/ELT Pipelines
- Data Lake Management
- AI/ML Model Training Workflows
- Event-Driven Architectures

Workflow orchestration is the automation and coordination of multiple interdependent tasks in a predefined sequence. It comes with the following functional capabilities:

- Correct Task Execution Order
- Dependency Resolution
- Retry and Failure Management
- Monitoring and Alerts

For example, a data pipeline may involve extracting data, transforming it, storing it in a warehouse, and triggering a ML job. Orchestration ensures that each task runs only when its prerequisites have been met.

Automating data workflows is crucial for ***streamlining processes*** and managing dependencies, as it enhances efficiency, accuracy, and scalability in data-driven operations. These qualities are in high demand across all industries that want to leverage data-driven solutions to enhance their respective sustainability.

Automating data workflows is essential for improving **efficiency, reliability, and scalability** in modern data operations. Firstly, it helps **streamline processes** by removing manual intervention. This accelerates execution and reduces bottlenecks across the data pipeline. Second, automation is crucial for **managing dependencies**, since many data tasks rely on the completion of prior steps such as ***loading data before transforming*** or ***analysing*** it. An automated system ensures these steps are executed in the correct sequence and accomplish the expectations from data-driven solutions.

Figure 6.1: *Significance of Automating Data Workflows*

Additionally, it significantly **reduces human error** by minimizing manual effort and associated costs. This leads to more accurate and consistent data processing.

Automation also enhances **scalability**, which allows organizations to handle increasing volumes and complexity of data without incurring significant overheads. In this case, GCP is often the best cloud provider to prefer.

Building reliable data pipelines and reproducible results is a key challenge in data analytics, AI and ML solutions; this is addressed by automating data flow by standardizing processes and ensuring ***consistent*** outcomes across runs.

Lastly, it supports **both real-time** and **scheduled executions,** which allows workflows to run automatically on a fixed schedule (such as hourly or daily) or be triggered by events such as new data arrivals, while ensuring timely and responsive data delivery.

Data Pipeline Orchestration Tools and Workflow Services

In the market, we have several tools that are designed to streamline data processes, ensure reliable execution, and handle intricate task dependencies in data pipelines across different cloud providers.

The strength of this open-source tool lies in its high customization, exposure to a large community, and support for complex dependency management. A significant challenge is that beginners might have to confront a steep learning curve with these tools, unlike other tools on the market. They also require an infrastructure setup for large-scale deployments.

Data pipeline orchestration tools and workflow services

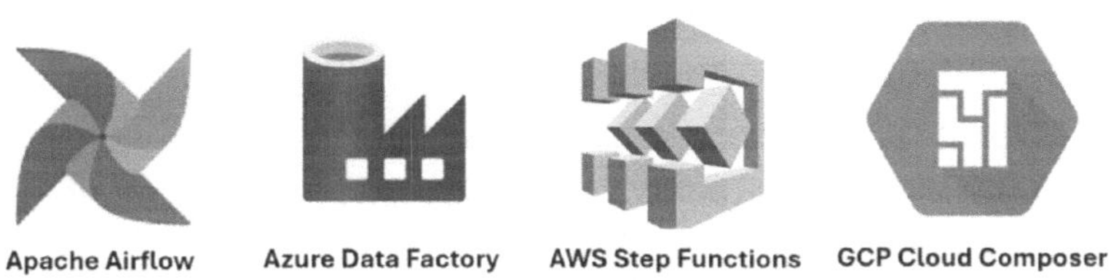

Figure 6.2: *Data Pipeline Orchestration Tools and Workflow Services*

Apache Airflow

This is an open-source platform for programmatically authoring, scheduling, and monitoring workflows. It uses **Directed Acyclic Graphs** (**DAGs**) to define tasks and their dependencies, which makes it ideal for orchestrating complex data pipelines.

- **Key Features:**
    - **DAG-Based Orchestration:** Workflows are defined as **Directed Acyclic Graphs (DAGs)**, where nodes represent **tasks** (for example, data extraction, transformation) and **edges** represent dependencies, while ensuring that tasks execute in the correct order.

    - **Extensibility:** Supports complex integrations with numerous systems (for example, SQL databases, cloud services, APIs) via operators and hooks
    - **Scheduling and Monitoring:** Provides robust scheduling (for example, cron-based) and a web-based UI to monitor pipeline execution, track failures, and retry tasks
    - **Scalability:** Can handle large-scale workflows with distributed task execution using executors like Celery or Kubernetes
- **Use Case:** Ideal for data engineers managing ETL (Extract, Transform, Load) pipelines such as aggregating data from multiple sources, transforming it, and loading it into a data warehouse

Azure Data Factory (ADF)

ADF is a cloud-native data integration service from Microsoft Azure, which is designed for orchestrating and automating data movement and transformation workflows. It is a user-friendly, serverless solution that is tightly integrated with Azure services. Cost-wise, it is expensive for large-scale pipelines and less flexible for highly customized workflows compared to Airflow.

- **Key Features**
    - **Visual Pipeline Design:** Offers a drag-and-drop interface for building pipelines, which makes it accessible for non-programmers while also supporting code-based configurations (for example, JSON)
    - **Hybrid Data Integration:** Supports data movement across on-premises and cloud environments with connectors to various data sources (for example, SQL Server, Blob Storage, Snowflake)
    - **Dependency Management:** Defines dependencies between activities (for example, run a transformation only after data ingestion completes) with built-in retry and error-handling mechanisms
    - **Integration with Azure Ecosystem:** Seamlessly integrates with Azure services like Databricks, Synapse Analytics, and ML for advanced analytics workflows
- **Use Case:** Best for organizations using Azure for data lakes, analytics, or hybrid cloud environments such as orchestrating ETL processes for business intelligence

AWS Step Functions: Overview

This is a serverless orchestration service from Amazon Web Services (AWS) that coordinates multiple AWS services into workflows using state machines. It is a fully managed, cost-effective solution for serverless workloads, which simplifies the orchestration of AWS services. As it is limited to the AWS ecosystem, it is not suited well for non-AWS or highly complex workflows.

- **Key Features**
  - **State Machine Workflow:** Defines workflows as state machines, where each state represents a task or decision point, with clear dependency management (for example, branching, parallel execution)
  - **Serverless Architecture:** Eliminates the need to manage infrastructure, while automatically scaling based on workload
  - **Integration with AWS Services:** Natively integrates with Lambda, Glue, Athena, and other AWS services, which makes it ideal for cloud-native data pipelines
  - **Error Handling and Retries:** Built-in mechanisms for handling failures, retries, and timeouts, which ensure robust dependency management
- **Use Case:** Suited for orchestrating serverless data processing pipelines such as real-time data streaming or event-driven workflows in AWS environments

GCP Cloud Composer

Google Cloud Platform's Cloud Composer is a managed workflow orchestration service built on Apache Airflow and designed for orchestrating data workflows in Google Cloud. This brings Airflow's flexibility to Google's managed infrastructure, while effectively reducing the operational burden. It is more expensive than self-hosted Airflow and has less flexibility for non-GCP integrations.

- **Key Features**
  - **Airflow under the Hood:** Inherits Airflow's DAG-based orchestration, but with Google's managed infrastructure, which reduces setup overhead
  - **Integration with GCP:** Seamlessly connects with BigQuery, Dataflow, Dataproc, and other GCP services for data processing and analytics
  - **Dependency Management:** Leverages Airflow's robust dependency handling with additional monitoring through Google Cloud's operations suite
  - **Scalability:** Fully managed, auto-scaling environment for handling large workflows
- **Use Case:** Ideal for organizations using GCP for data analytics such as orchestrating ML pipelines or ETL processes for BigQuery

Exploring Directed Acyclic Graphs (DAGs)

A **Directed Acyclic Graph (DAG)** is a graph data structure with directed edges between nodes and no cycles, which ensure a precise flow without looping back to any node. In the context of **Apache Airflow** and **Google Cloud Composer**, DAGs are central to defining and orchestrating complex workflows, particularly for data pipelines. In this section, we will explore DAGs in considerable detail, while focusing on their implementation in Airflow and Google Cloud Composer, as well as their structure, use cases, and practical examples.

A simple representation of a DAG is illustrated in *Figure* 6.3.

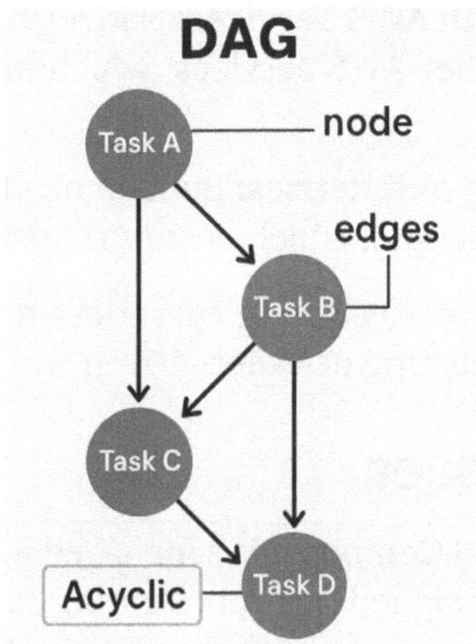

Figure 6.3: *Directed Acyclic Graph* (DAG)

DAGs in Apache Airflow

Apache Airflow is an open-source workflow orchestration platform and Directed Acyclic Graphs (DAGs) act as the fundamental structure that is used to define workflows programmatically. In Airflow, a DAG is written as a Python script that specifies a set of tasks along with their execution order and dependencies. Each DAG represents a complete workflow and contains the following characteristics:

- **Directed:** The flow of execution moves in a defined direction from one task to another.
- **Acyclic:** The workflow contains no loops or circular dependencies, which ensures that tasks do not run indefinitely.
- **Nodes (Vertices):** Represent individual tasks or operations within the workflow
- **Edges (Arrows):** Represent the dependencies and execution sequence between tasks

Core Components of a DAG

- **Tasks:** The smallest units of work that are created using operators such as `PythonOperator`, `BashOperator`, and `BigQueryOperator`
- **Dependencies:** Defined using symbols like >> and << (for example, `task1` >> `task2` indicates that `task2` runs after `task1`.)
- **DAG Object:** Configured with parameters such as `dag_id`, `schedule_interval`, `start_date`, and `catchup`
- **Scheduling:** Airflow's scheduler executes tasks based on the DAG's topological order, while strictly following all dependencies.

Key Features of DAGs

- **Dynamic:** DAGs are written in Python, which enables dynamic workflow creation and parameterization.
- **Extensible:** Supports custom operators and plug-ins to handle specialized tasks.
- **Monitoring:** Airflow provides a rich web interface to visualize DAGs, monitor task execution, track dependencies, and review execution history.

Example Use Case

A typical data pipeline may include extracting data from an external API and transform it using Python, while loading the processed data into a database and finally sending a notification upon completion.

- **Tasks:** `extract_data`, `transform_data`, `load_to_db`, `send_email`
- **Dependencies:** `extract_data` >> `transform_data` >> `load_to_db` >> `send_email`

DAGs in Google Cloud Composer

Google Cloud Composer is a fully managed version of Apache Airflow offered on Google Cloud Platform (GCP). It retains Airflow's DAG-based orchestration model while integrating seamlessly with GCP services such as BigQuery, Dataflow, Cloud Storage, and Dataproc. Cloud Composer simplifies infrastructure management, as it allows teams to focus on building and scaling reliable cloud-native workflows.

Key Differences from Airflow

- **Managed Environment:** Composer handles infrastructure setup, scaling, and maintenance, which reduces operational overhead.
- **GCP Integration:** Provides operators for GCP services (for example, `BigQueryOperator`, `DataflowCreateJobOperator`)

- **Environment Configuration:** DAGs are stored in a Cloud Storage bucket, while Composer manages Airflow workers, scheduler, and web server.
- **Monitoring:** Integrates with Google Cloud Monitoring and Logging for insights into DAG performance
- **DAG Storage:** DAGs are Python files uploaded to a specific folder in a Cloud Storage bucket (for example, gs://bucket-name/dags/), which is automatically synced to Composer's Airflow instance.

Use Cases

- **ETL Pipelines:** Extract data from Cloud Storage, transform it in BigQuery, and load results into a data warehouse.
- **Machine Learning:** Orchestrate training jobs on the AI Platform, followed by model deployment.
- **Data Integration:** Sync data across GCP services like Pub/Sub, Dataproc, and BigQuery.

Benefits

- **Scalability:** Composer auto-scales workers based on workload.
- **Security:** Integrates with GCP IAM for access control.
- **Ease of Use:** Simplifies Airflow setup with pre-configured environments.

Example DAG for Airflow/Composer

The following is a sample DAG that runs a simple ETL pipeline, which extracts data from a source, transforms it, and loads it into BigQuery. This example is compatible with both Airflow and Composer.

```
from datetime import datetime
from airflow import DAG
from airflow. operators.python import PythonOperator
from airflow.operators.dummy import DummyOperator
from airflow.contrib.operators.bigquery_operator import BigQueryOperator

# Define default arguments for the DAG
default_args =elt_pipeline {
    'owner': 'airflow',
    'depends_on_past': False,
    'email_on_failure': False,
    'email_on_retry': False,
    'retries': 1,
}

# Define the DAG
```

```
with DAG(
    dag_id='etl_pipeline',
    default_args=default_args,
    description='A simple ETL pipeline for Airflow/Composer',
    schedule_interval='@daily',
    start_date=datetime(2025, 6, 1),
    catchup=False,
) as dag:

    # Task 1: Start (Dummy task)
    start = DummyOperator(task_id='start')

    # Task 2: Extract data (Python function)
    def extract_data():
        # Simulate data extraction (for example, from an API or file)
        print("Extracting data...")
       return [{"id": 1, "value": "data1"}, {"id": 2, "value": "data2"}]

    extract = PythonOperator(
        task_id='extract_data',
        python_callable=extract_data,
    )

    # Task 3: Transform data (Python function)
    def transform_data():
        # Simulate transformation
        print("Transforming data...")
        # In practice, you'd process the extracted data here
        return "Transformed data"

    transform = PythonOperator(
        task_id='transform_data',
        python_callable=transform_data,
    )

    # Task 4: Load to BigQuery (Composer-compatible)
    load_to_bq = BigQueryOperator(
        task_id='load_to_bigquery',
            bql='SELECT * FROM `project.dataset.table` WHERE 1=0',   #
Placeholder query
        destination_dataset_table='project.dataset.transformed data',
        write_disposition='WRITE_TRUNCATE',
        use_legacy_sql=False,
    )

    # Task 5: End (Dummy task)
```

```
end = DummyOperator(task_id='end')

# Define dependencies
start >> extract >> transform >> load_to_bq >> end
```

Figure 6.4 shows the architectural representation of the above code implementation using DAG and BigQuery.

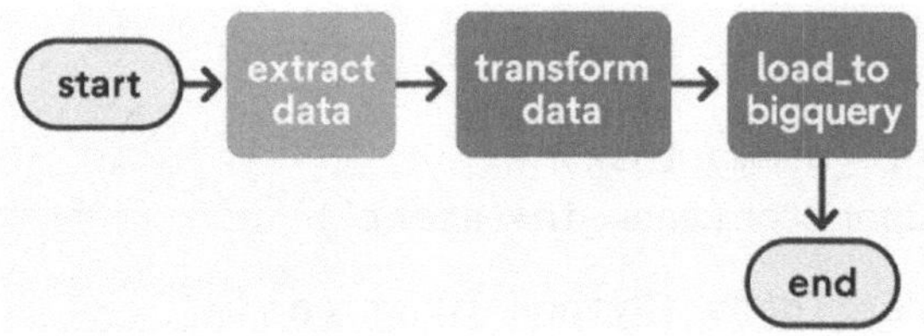

Figure 6.4: *A Simple ETL Pipeline Using DAG*

The output of the example DAG (above code) provided for **Apache Airflow** and **Google Cloud Composer** depends on how it is executed and the environment in which it runs. Since a DAG is a workflow definition, it does not produce a single "**`output`**" like a function. Instead, it executes a series of tasks in a defined order, where each task potentially produces its own results.

Code Explanation

DAG Setup: The DAG is named **`etl_pipeline`**, runs daily, and starts from June 1, 2025, without catching up on past runs.

- **Tasks**
    - **Start and End:** Dummy tasks to mark the workflow's boundaries
    - **`extract_data`:** A Python task simulating data extraction
    - **`transform_data`:** A Python task simulating data transformation
    - **`load_to_bigquery`:** A BigQuery task (relevant for Composer) to load data into a BigQuery table
- **Dependencies:** The tasks are chained in order: start → extract → transform → **`load_to_bq`** → end.
- **Composer Notes:** In Google Cloud Composer, you must ensure that the **`project.dataset.table`** is replaced with your GCP project and dataset details. The DAG file should be placed in the dags/ folder of your Composer environment's Cloud Storage bucket.

Best Practices for DAGs in Airflow/Composer

- **Idempotency:** Ensure that tasks produce the same output for the same input, enabling safe retries.

- **Modularity:** Break complex workflows into smaller, reusable DAGs or sub-DAGs.
- **Error Handling:** Use retries, `email_on_failure`, or custom callbacks to handle failures gracefully.
- **Testing:** Test DAGs locally (Airflow) or in a staging Composer environment before production.
- **Monitoring:** Use Airflow's UI or Composer's integration with Cloud Monitoring to track DAG performance and failures.
- **Resource Optimization:** In Composer, monitor resource usage (for example, GKE nodes) to avoid over-provisioning.

Exploring Google Cloud Composer

Modern data engineering pipelines require not only efficient data processing but also seamless orchestration, which involves managing the **execution order, dependencies**, and **retries of numerous tasks** as pipelines become increasingly complex, and manual scheduling and dependency tracking become unmanageable. This is where **workflow orchestration** becomes essential.

Google Cloud's **Cloud Composer**, which is a managed version of **Apache Airflow**, enables developers and data engineers to automate, schedule, and monitor workflows using code. Let us explore how to orchestrate data pipelines via Cloud Composer, starting from fundamentals and moving on to enterprise-grade customizations.

Google Cloud Composer is a fully managed workflow orchestration service built on **Apache Airflow**, designed to simplify the development, scheduling, and monitoring of data pipelines. It enables users to automate complex workflows with ease, while offering tight integration with other **Google Cloud Platform (GCP)** services for seamless data movement and processing.

By abstracting away infrastructure management, Cloud Composer allows **data engineers, analysts, and developers** to focus on building robust and scalable pipelines. It supports workflow versioning, dependency management, and the retry logic, which make it a powerful solution for end-to-end data orchestration.

Although it comes with a learning curve and cost considerations, the platform's scalability, flexibility, and native GCP integration make it a preferred choice for managing production-grade workflows in cloud environments. *Figure* 6.5 illustrates the Google Composer architecture view.

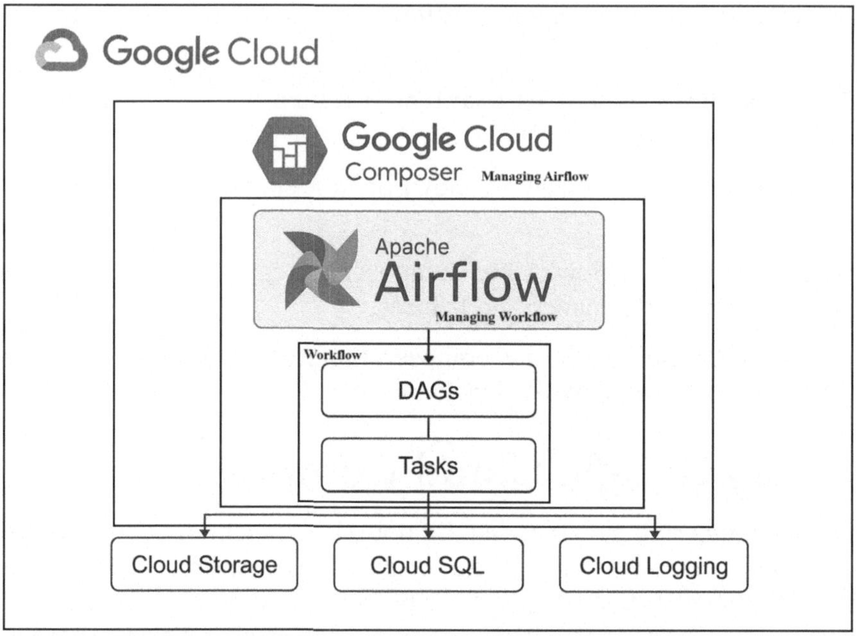

Figure 6.5: *Google Composer Architecture View*

- **Google Cloud Composer**
  - **Google Cloud Composer** is a fully managed workflow orchestration service that runs on the Kubernetes architecture.
  - Composer is **built on Apache Airflow**, an open-source project.
  - It **requires no installation or infrastructure management**, since it is completely managed by Google Cloud; we do not need to install Airflow.
  - **Airflow**
    - In **Airflow**, workflows are defined using **DAGs (Directed Acyclic Graphs)**.
    - A **DAG** is a collection of tasks with defined relationships and dependencies.
    - DAG
      - It allows users to **create, schedule, monitor, and manage workflows** across both cloud and on-premises environments.
      - It uses **Python code** to define workflows and offers flexibility and ease for developers and data engineers.
      - In data analytics, a **workflow** consists of tasks like **ingesting, transforming, analyzing, or utilizing data**.

- DAGs are written in **Python scripts** to specify the **sequence and logic** of task execution.
- This structure ensures **clarity, maintainability, and control** over complex data pipelines.

- The final data is stored in Google storage components.

Key Features of Google Cloud Composer

- **Fully Managed Service:** Simplifies the deployment, scaling, and maintenance of Apache Airflow environments and eliminates the need for manual infrastructure management
- **Seamless Integration:** Natively connects with Google Cloud services such as BigQuery, Cloud Storage, Pub/Sub, and Dataproc for streamlined data pipeline orchestration
- **Scalability:** Automatically adjusts resources based on workflow demands, while ensuring optimal performance and cost-efficiency
- **Workflow Flexibility:** Supports the creation of complex, customizable workflows using Python, which allows for greater control and adaptability
- **Robust Monitoring:** Offers detailed monitoring and logging via the Google Cloud Console for enhanced visibility and operational insights
- **Enterprise-Grade Security:** Built-in integration with IAM, VPC, Secret Manager, and Cloud KMS to ensure secure access and data protection

Advantages of Cloud Composer

- **User-Friendly and Hassle-Free:** As a fully managed service, Cloud Composer removes the complexity of setting up and maintaining Apache Airflow infrastructure, which allows teams to concentrate on designing and deploying workflows.
- **Dynamic Scalability:** Automatically scales resources up or down based on workload requirements to ensure efficient execution without the need for manual adjustments.
- **Deep Google Cloud Integration:** Seamlessly connects with a wide range of Google Cloud services such as BigQuery, Cloud Storage, and Pub/Sub, while enabling the construction of powerful, end to end data pipelines.
- **Flexible Workflow Design:** Empowers users to develop customized workflows using Python to support diverse use cases and complex orchestration logic.
- **Integrated Monitoring and Logging:** Provides built-in tools for real-time monitoring and logging via the Google Cloud Console to offer clear visibility into workflow performance and status.

Disadvantages of Cloud Composer:

- **Higher Cost for Smaller Projects:** As a managed service, Cloud Composer often incurs higher operational costs compared to self-managed Apache Airflow setups, which make it less cost-effective for small-scale or budget-sensitive projects.
- **Initial Learning Curve:** Effective use requires a good grasp of Apache Airflow concepts and proficiency in Python, which can present challenges for beginners or teams that are new to workflow orchestration.
- **Resource Optimization Expertise:** While much of the infrastructure is automated, fine-tuning resource usage for performance and cost-efficiency still demands hands-on experience and a comprehensive understanding of system behavior.

Use Cases

- **ETL Automation for Data Engineering:** Automate Extract, Transform, and Load (ETL) processes to efficiently move and process data across various storage and compute environments.
- **ML Workflow Orchestration:** Manage complex ML pipelines from data ingestion and preprocessing, to model training, evaluation, and deployment in a seamless and scalable manner.
- **Scheduled Batch Processing:** Define, schedule, and control batch jobs to run at specific times or based on predefined triggers, which ensures timely and reliable data processing.
- **Event-Driven Workflow Execution:** Automatically initiate workflows in response to real-time events from Google Cloud services such as file uploads to Cloud Storage or messages from Pub/Sub to enable responsive and dynamic data operations.

Google Cloud Composer Implementation

Access to Cloud Composer requires appropriate IAM Permissions, which can be any of the following:

Cloud Composer - IAM Permissions

- **Composer Administrator**
    - **Role:** roles/`composer.admin`
        - **Description:** Provides full control of Cloud Composer resources
        - **Scope:** This role can be granted at the **Project** level (minimum granularity).

- **Composer User**
    - **Role:** roles/**`composer.user`**
        - **Description:** Grants permissions necessary to **list** and **get** Cloud Composer environments and operations
        - **Scope:** This role can also be granted at the **Project** level (minimum granularity).

Step 1: Log into the Google Cloud Platform, search for the Cloud Composer component, and enable it by clicking the "**`Enable`**" button as shown in *Figure* 6.6:

Figure 6.6: *GCP – Enabling Cloud Composer*

Step 2: After enabling the composer, the portal takes you to the screen shown in *Figure* 6.7. Where we have to select **`Composer 3`**, as it features autoscaling with Airflow 2, modernized from the dropdown list.

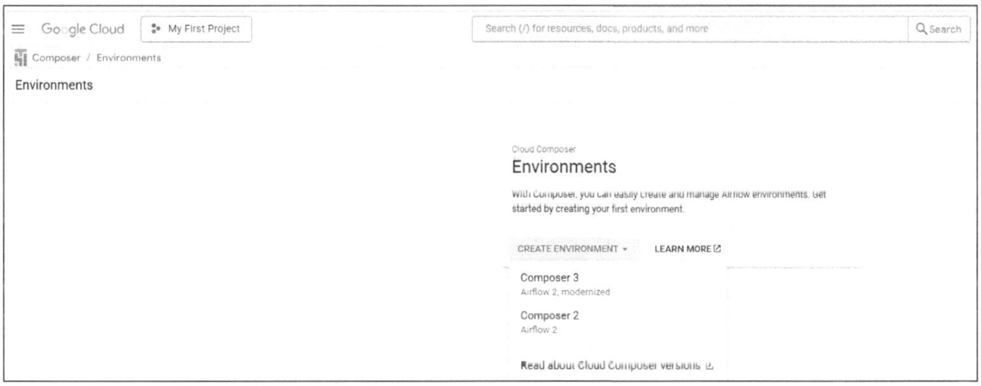

Figure 6.7: *GCP – Cloud Composer Environment*

Step 3: Once the environment is selected, the portal will take you to configure the Composer. You have to configure the following details:

- **`Name:`** <<fill name>>

- **`Location`**: < select the location>
- **`Image Version`:** Select the latest image version.
- **`Service Account`:** This service account manages the pods in your environment and performs operations such as upgrading your environment to a new version.

Figure 6.8: *GCP - Cloud Composer Configuration*

Step 4: Select the "**`Environment resources`**" based on your project requirements (such as Small, Medium, Large, and Custom). This differs from all other Workload configurations.

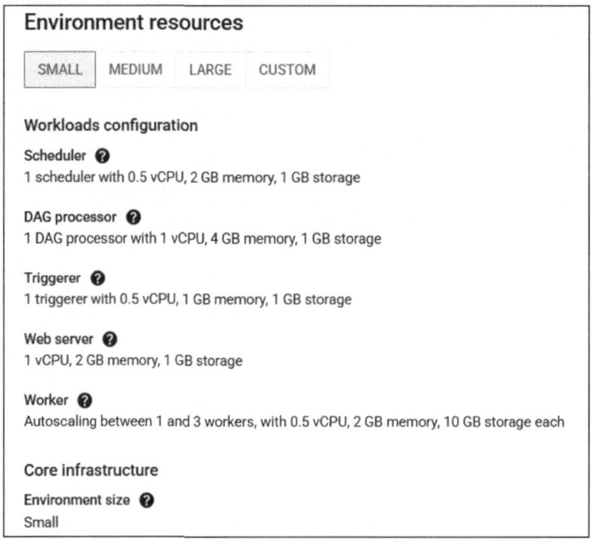

Figure 6.9: *GCP - Cloud Composer - Environment Resources Configuration*

Step 5: If you want to configure the "**`Network configuration`**" by setting up your VPC, you can create a new one or select from the provided list. Alternatively, you can skip this step since it is not mandatory. Then, click **`Create`**.

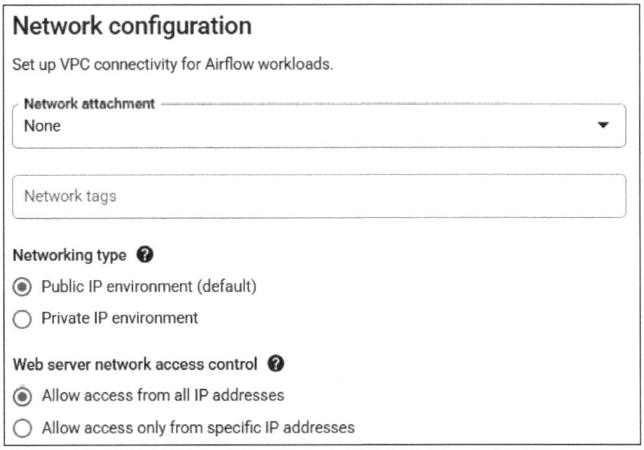

Figure 6.10: *GCP - Cloud Composer - Network Configuration (Optional)*

Step 6: Once all the required configurations are completed, the system will create the cloud composer for further operations, as shown in *Figure* 6.11.

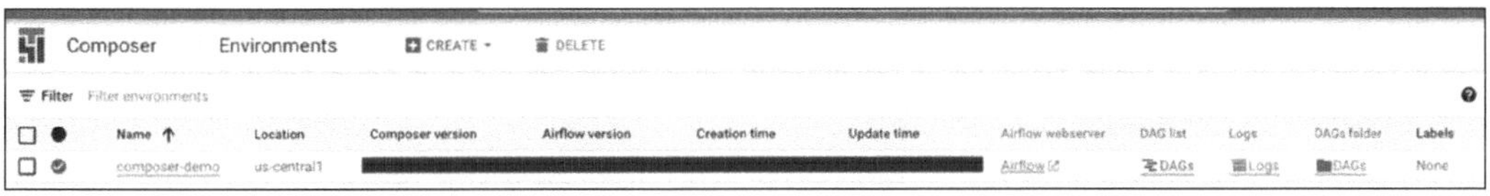

Figure 6.11: *–The Ready-to-Use GCP Cloud Composer*

The system will create three major parts, which are explained as follows:

- The Airflow web server from where we will monitor the DAGs.
- A Cloud Storage bucket under the bucket which will create a folder to store your DAGs. In this folder, you can deploy your DAGs by uploading files from your local computer.

Figure 6.12: *DAGs Folder under the Cloud Storage Bucket*

- Logs for composer-related logs, which are integrated with Log Explorer to monitor the composer's activity.

Figure 6.13: *Log Explorer to Monitor the Composer's Activity*

Step 7: Click the composer's name as indicated in Figure 6.11. The portal will take you to the screen shown in *Figure 6.14*

- **Monitoring**
  - View metrics like DAG run status, task failures, scheduler performance, and so on.
  - Integrates with **Cloud Monitoring** for performance and health tracking
- **Logs**
  - Access logs related to DAG execution, task logs, scheduler logs, and so on.
  - Pulled from **Cloud Logging (formerly Stackdriver)**

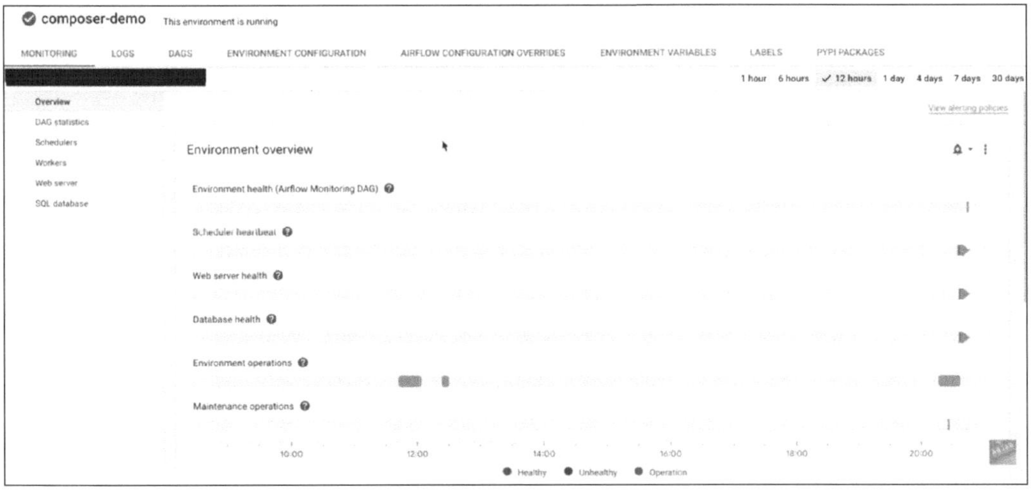

Figure 6.14: *Composer's Details*

- **DAGs**
  - Manage and view Directed Acyclic Graphs (DAGs) that are defined for workflow orchestration.
  - You can trigger DAG runs, pause, or even delete DAGs.
- **Environment Configuration**
  - Displays overall configuration including machine types, node count, image version, and so on
- **Airflow Configuration Overrides**
  - Allows you to override the default **`airflow.cfg`** settings to customize behavior like parallelism, retries, logging level, and so on
- **Environment Variables**
  - Set the environment-specific variables for DAGs or tasks, for example, API keys, paths, flags.
- **Labels**
  - Add the custom metadata to the environment for organization, billing, or access control.
- **PyPI Packages**
  - Install additional Python dependencies needed by your DAGs via public or private PyPI packages.

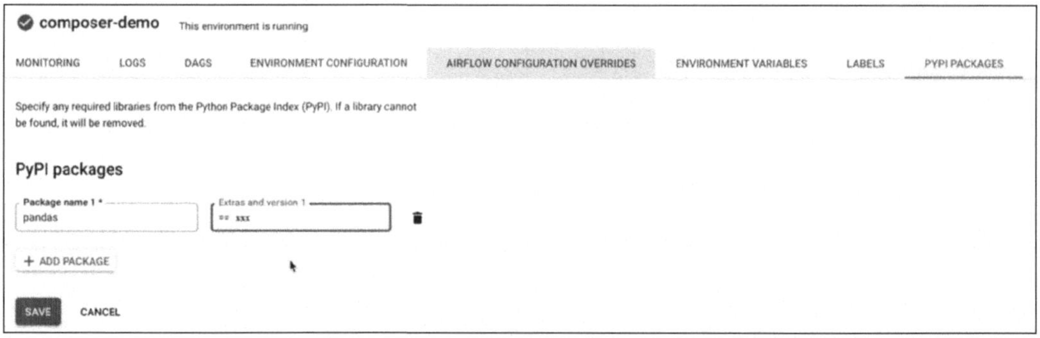

Figure 6.15: *Installing Additional Python Dependencies*

Step 8: As mentioned in step 6, you can upload your Python file to view it in the Cloud Shell Editor.

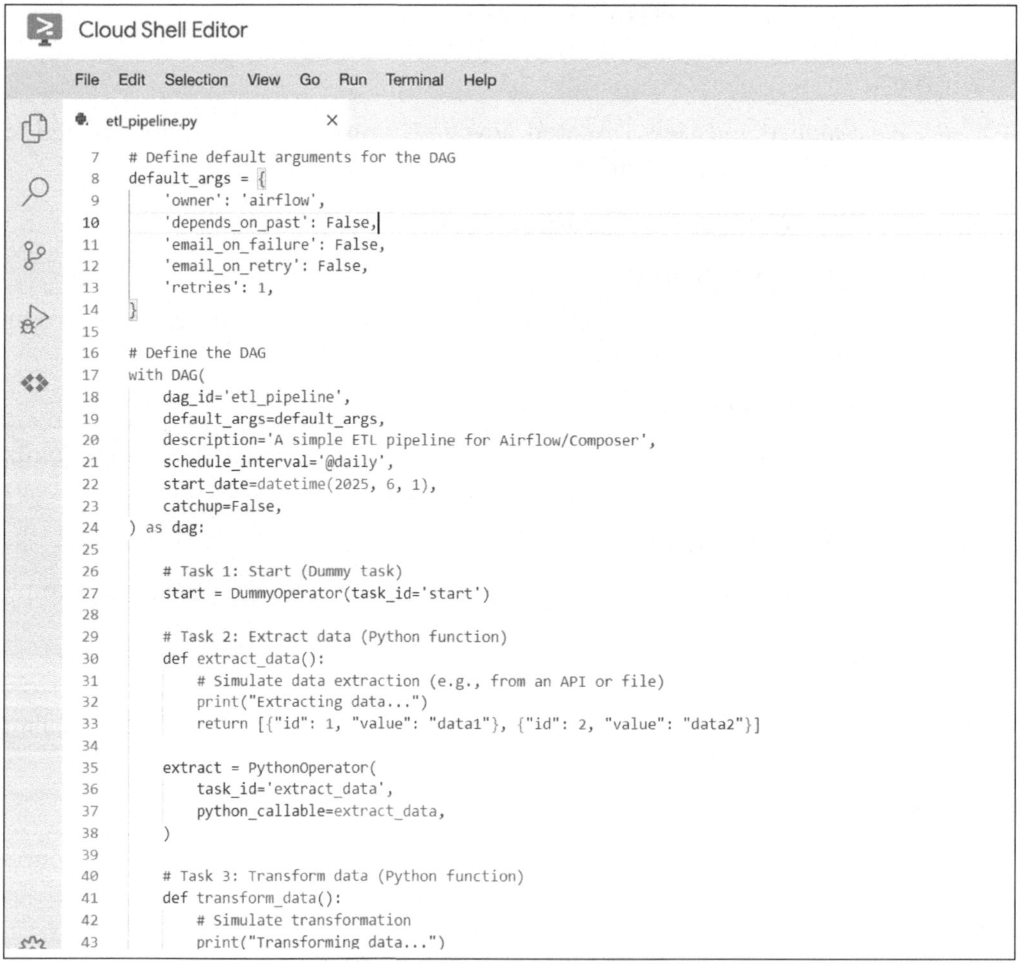

Figure 6.16: *Cloud Shell Editor*

Deploy into the Composer DAGs folder.

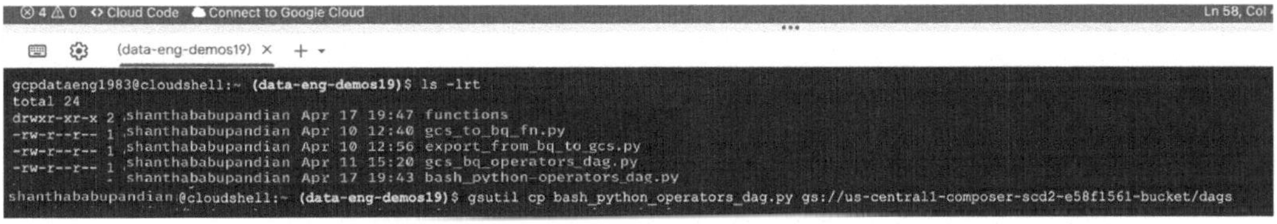

***Figure* 6.17:** *Deploying a DAG File via the Shell Editor*

Step 9: You can now go back and refresh your Composer. At this stage, you will find that your file has been successfully deployed into the Composer DAGs environment as shown in *Figure* 6.18.

***Figure* 6.18:** *Deploying a DAG File into the Composer DAGs Folder*

Step 10: Go to the Airflow environment and you can verify that your DAG has been deployed successfully (since we know that Composer is managing Airflow and DAGs internally and you can access them from the Airflow environment as well).

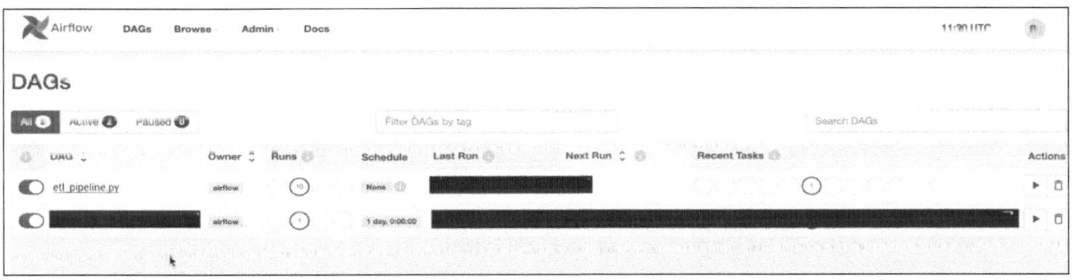

***Figure* 6.19:** *Verifying the Deployed DAG File inside the Airflow Environment*

When you click the DAG, it will take you to the screen in *Figure* 6.20, where you can see the workflow stages in **Grid View**, the status legends and DAG Details (Run summary, total success, as well as the max and min duration taken by the workflow.

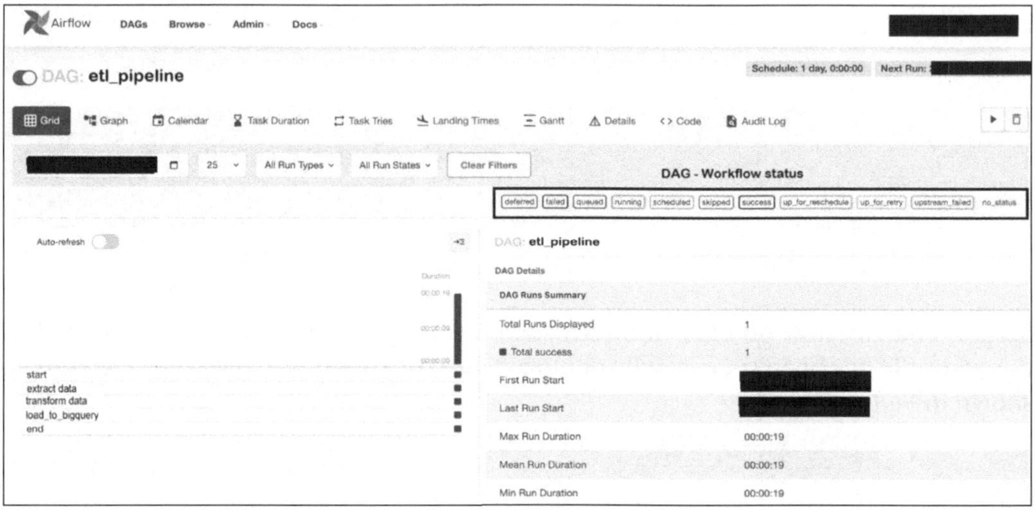

Figure 6.20: *Grid View of the DAG in the Airflow Environment*

When you select **Graph View**, you can visualize the workflow execution, one block at a time in a graphical representation. You can either click the play button in the right corner or click each block individually to trigger the task.

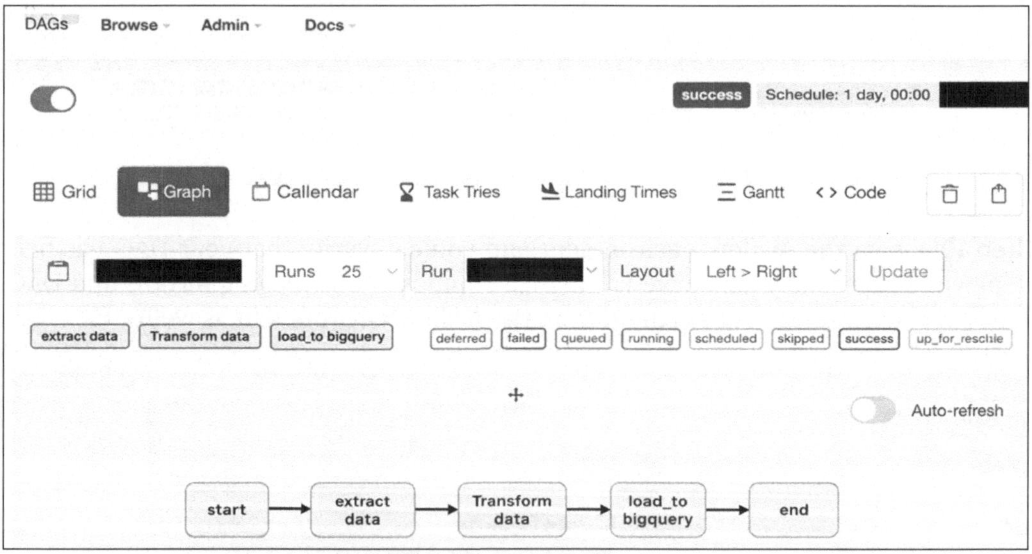

Figure 6.21: *Graph View of the DAG in the Airflow Environment*

Step 11: Check the task actions and logs of each task. Now, click any block as shown in *Figure* 6.21 and the portal will pop up a window as demonstrated in *Figure* 6.22, which shows the task actions.

Figure 6.22: *Task Actions*

Click **Log**, and the portal will direct you to the Logs screen, as shown in *Figure* 6.23.

Figure 6.23: *Task Log (Extract Data)*

Once all tasks are completed successfully, you will see the data loaded into BigQuery and all task blocks will turn green to represent successful completion.

Scaling Orchestration for Complex Pipelines

Let us discuss how to scale orchestration for complex pipelines using custom operators and integrations in Google Composer. The orchestration process involves leveraging its managed Apache Airflow environment to handle intricate workflows efficiently, based on the capabilities of Cloud Composer and the best practices for scaling, custom operators, and integrations.

As we discussed earlier, Google Cloud Composer is a fully managed workflow orchestration service built on Apache Airflow. It enables you to design, develop, schedule, and monitor complex data pipelines using Python-based DAGs. It is intended for ***orchestrating data-driven workflows, particularly ETL/ELT processes, and integrates seamlessly*** with Google Cloud services and external systems. Its managed nature eliminates infrastructure management overhead and makes it ideal for scaling complex pipelines.

Key Considerations for Scaling Complex Pipelines

Scaling orchestration in Cloud Composer involves addressing computational demands, workflow complexity, and resource efficiency. Here are some key strategies to do so:

Environment Sizing and Autoscaling

- **GKE Autoscaling:** Cloud Composer runs on Google Kubernetes Engine (GKE), which supports autoscaling of resources (nodes, CPU, memory) based on workload demands. Configure the Composer environment with appropriate worker node settings to handle peak loads.
- **Concurrency and Parallelism:** Adjust Airflow configurations like **`worker_concurrency`** and **`dag_concurrency`** to allow more tasks to run simultaneously. Use the parallelism setting to control the total number of tasks across all DAGs. Optimize these based on your pipeline's scale and resource availability.
- **Composer 3 Improvements:** The latest version of Cloud Composer (Composer 3) introduces enhanced scalability with better GKE integration and reduced operational overhead, though it still faces challenges with horizontal scaling compared to serverless solutions.

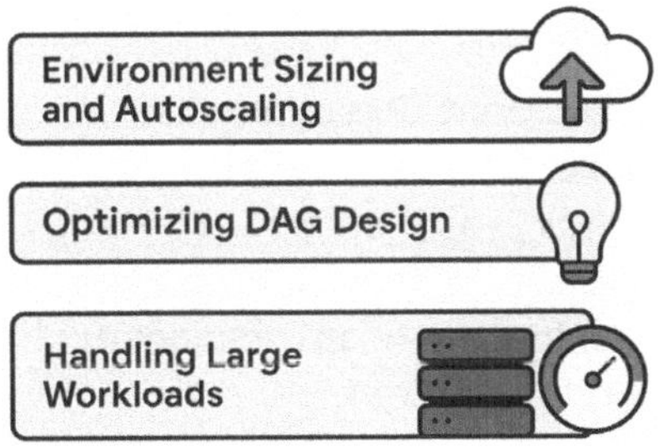

Figure 6.24: *Key Considerations for Scaling Complex Pipelines*

Optimizing DAG Design

- **Modular DAGs:** Break complex pipelines into smaller, modular DAGs to improve maintainability and reduce execution bottlenecks. Use SubDAGs and TaskGroups for logical grouping, but avoid excessive nesting to prevent performance issues.
- **Dependency Management:** Define explicit task dependencies in DAGs to enable parallel execution wherever possible to reduce the runtime for large workflows.
- **Dynamic DAG Generation:** Use Python to dynamically generate DAGs for repetitive or parameterized workflows and improve scalability for large datasets or variable pipelines.

Handling Large Workloads

- **Batch Processing:** Cloud Composer is optimized for batch workloads with acceptable latency (a few seconds between tasks). It is ideal for ETL pipelines but less suited for low-latency, real-time processing.
- **Task Distribution:** Distribute tasks across multiple worker nodes to ensure high availability and fault tolerance. Cloud Composer's managed infrastructure handles task distribution automatically.

Using Custom Operators

Custom operators in Cloud Composer extend Airflow's functionality to meet specific pipeline requirements. They also pave the way for tailored task execution and integration with custom systems.

Creating Custom Operators

- **Python-Based Operators:** Write custom operators by sub-classing Airflow's `BaseOperator` in Python. For example, create an operator to interact with a proprietary API or perform a unique data transformation. Define the operator's logic in the execute method.

Sample Code:

```
from airflow.models import BaseOperator
class CustomAPIOperator(BaseOperator):
    def __init__(self, api_endpoint, *args, **kwargs):
        super().__init__(*args, **kwargs)
        self.api_endpoint = api_endpoint
    def execute(self, context):
        # Custom logic to call the API
        Pass
```

- **Packaging and Deployment:** Package custom operators as Airflow plugins and upload them to the **`/plugins`** folder in the Cloud Composer environment's Google Cloud Storage (GCS) bucket. Install them using the Cloud Composer UI or CLI.

Use Cases for Custom Operators

- **Proprietary Systems:** Create operators to interact with internal or third-party systems not covered by Airflow's 150+ built-in Google Cloud operators (for example, BigQueryOperator, **`DataflowCreatePythonJobOperator`**).
- **Complex Transformations:** Implement operators for bespoke data processing tasks that standard operators cannot handle, such as custom ML preprocessing steps.
- **Event-Driven Triggers:** Develop sensors (a type of operator) to wait for specific conditions like the availability of a file in GCS or a message in Pub/Sub to trigger downstream tasks.

Best Practices for Scaling and Integration

- **Monitoring and Logging:** Leverage Cloud Composer's integration with Google Cloud Monitoring and Logging to track DAG performance, task failures, and resource usage. Use the Airflow UI to inspect logs and task statuses.
- **Security:** Manage access at the project level with IAM roles and use Airflow UI access control for fine-grained permissions. Ensure data encryption in transit and at rest.
- **Cost Optimization:** Monitor resource usage and adjust environment sizing to avoid over-provisioning. Use budget alerts to control costs, as Composer's pricing can be complex.
- **Error Handling and Notifications:** Configure DAGs to send notifications (for example, via Slack or email) on task failures or retries to ensure quick resolution.
- **Version Control:** Store DAGs and plug-ins in version-controlled GCS buckets to maintain consistency and enable rollback.

- **Testing and Validation:** Test DAGs and custom operators in a development Composer environment before deploying to production to avoid runtime errors.

Integrations with Google Cloud and External Systems

Cloud Composer's strength lies in its deep integration with Google Cloud services and support for multi-cloud and on-premises environments, which enables the orchestration of complex pipelines.

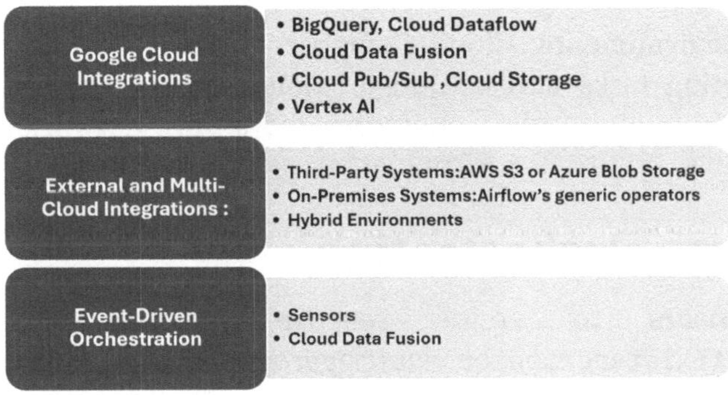

Figure 6.25: *Integrations with Google Cloud and External Systems*

Google Cloud Integrations

- **BigQuery:** Use BigQueryOperator to execute queries or load data into BigQuery tables. For example, orchestrate an ETL pipeline that extracts data from GCS, transforms it in Dataflow, and loads it into BigQuery.
- **Cloud Dataflow:** Trigger Dataflow jobs using DataflowCreatePythonJobOperator or `DataflowCreateJavaJobOperator` for stream or batch processing.
- **Cloud Data Fusion:** Use `CloudDataFusionStartPipelineOperator` to trigger and manage Data Fusion pipelines, while enabling visual pipeline design within Composer workflows.
- **Cloud Pub/Sub:** Implement event-driven pipelines with `PubSubPullSensor` to trigger tasks based on messages in Pub/Sub topics.
- **Cloud Storage:** Use `GCSObjectExistenceSensor` to monitor for new files or `GoogleCloudStorageToBigQueryOperator` to transfer data from GCS to BigQuery.
- **Dataproc:** Orchestrate Hadoop or Spark jobs with `DataprocCreateCluster Operator` and `DataprocSubmitJobOperator`.

- **Vertex AI:** Integrate with Vertex AI for ML workflows such as model training or deployment, while using custom operators or Airflow hooks.

External and Multi-Cloud Integrations

- **Third-Party Systems:** Airflow's extensive library of operators and hooks (for example, **`HttpOperator`**, S3Hook) supports integration with external APIs, databases, or cloud services like AWS S3 or Azure Blob Storage.
- **On-Premises Systems:** Use Airflow's generic operators (for example, PythonOperator, **`BashOperator`**) or custom operators to interact with on-premises databases or services via secure APIs or VPNs.
- **Hybrid Environments:** Cloud Composer supports hybrid workflows, while orchestrating tasks across Google Cloud, other clouds, and on-premises systems using appropriate operators and secure networking configurations (for example, Private IP environments).

Event-Driven Orchestration

- Use **sensors** to create reactive pipelines. For example, a **`GCSObjectExistenceSensor`** can trigger a pipeline when a new file arrives in a GCS bucket, or a **`PubSubPullSensor`** can initiate tasks based on Pub/Sub messages.
- Configure triggers in **Cloud Data Fusion** to execute downstream pipelines based on the completion status (success or failure) of upstream pipelines, while passing runtime arguments for dynamic workflows.

Conclusion

We discussed how automating data workflows is essential for modern data operations, as it enables the seamless collection, transformation, and delivery of data from diverse sources.

We explored various data pipeline orchestration tools and workflow services, including Apache Airflow, Azure Data Factory, AWS Step Functions, and Google Cloud Composer. We examine how they play a crucial role in orchestrating these workflows by managing dependencies, scheduling tasks, and ensuring scalability.

Among these, Google Cloud Composer stands out as a fully managed Airflow-based service that integrates deeply with GCP tools like BigQuery, Dataflow, Pub/Sub, and Vertex AI, while providing flexibility and reducing operational overhead.

We understand the core of workflow orchestration using Directed Acyclic Graphs (DAGs) and how to define task sequences and dependencies programmatically.

Thus, Composer enables developers to build modular, scalable, and dynamic Dataflow graphs (DAGs) using Python, allowing for parallel execution, error handling, and easy monitoring through the Airflow UI, as well as discovering best practices.

We explore Google Cloud Composer in detail, examining its architecture, key features, advantages, disadvantages, and classic use cases. This was followed by a detailed demonstration of Google Cloud Composer implementation using Airflow and DGA.

We now understand how to scale orchestration for complex pipelines and what the key considerations are for scaling them. We also are familiar best practices for scaling and integration, as well as integrations with Google Cloud and External Systems.

In the next chapter, we will discuss analytics with BigQuery, including essential SQL syntax, advanced features such as window functions, arrays, and structs, as well as the use of stored procedures for automation. It also explores disaster recovery strategies and advanced analytics with BI Engine to help users extract meaningful insights from large datasets.

CHAPTER 7
Analytics with BigQuery

Introduction

In the previous chapter, we discussed the detailed orchestration of workflows with Cloud Composer and how automating data workflows is critical for streamlining processes as well as managing dependencies. This chapter explores Cloud Composer, GCP's implementation of Apache Airflow, as a tool for orchestrating complex data workflows. Readers will learn how to design Directed Acyclic Graphs (DAGs), automate task scheduling, and scale workflows for enterprise-level applications. Advanced users will also be able to explore custom operator integrations for building dynamic and adaptable orchestration systems.

In this chapter, we will discuss how BigQuery stands as one of GCP's most powerful tools for data analytics. This chapter introduces the core SQL syntax and features that make BigQuery a leader in Big Data analytics. Readers will learn to write optimized queries, leverage advanced SQL functions such as windowing, arrays, and structs, and use stored procedures for automation. Additionally, it covers disaster recovery techniques and advanced analytics with BigQuery BI Engine, which will empower readers to derive actionable insights from their data.

Structure

In this chapter, we will cover the following topics:

- Understanding BigQuery
- Serverless Architecture of BigQuery
- Exploring the BigQuery Environment
- SQL for BigQuery: Core Syntax, Optimization, and Advanced Features

- Advanced Query Optimization Techniques in BigQuery
- Exploring Stored Procedures in BigQuery
- Advanced SQL Features in BigQuery
- Disaster Recovery in BigQuery
- Advanced Analytics with BigQuery BI Engine

Understanding BigQuery

BigQuery is Google Cloud Platform's (GCP) serverless data warehouse and analytics tool. Let us understand BigQuery's core SQL syntax, advanced features, optimization techniques, automation with stored procedures, disaster recovery strategies, and advanced analytics using BigQuery BI Engine.

BigQuery allows users to analyze massive datasets using SQL queries and focuses on scalability and performance. It handles infrastructure management, which allows users to focus on data analysis and gaining valuable insights.

Core Functions of BigQuery

Let us discuss the core functions of BigQuery in detail.

Data Storage and Management

BigQuery serves as a fully managed data warehouse system, which is capable of storing both structured and unstructured data to build a robust data platform. Its columnar storage format and advanced features ensure the efficiency of the data warehouse for the organization, thereby facilitating retrieval and excellent management.

Key Features

- **Columnar Storage**: Data is stored in a column-oriented format, optimized for complex analytical queries that scan specific columns rather than entire rows. This reduces the amount of data scanned, thereby improving query performance.
- **Structured Data**: Supports tables with defined schemas, such as `STRING`, `INTEGER`, ***and*** `DATE`, which makes it ideal for relational data, like sales records
- **Unstructured Data**: It is capable of handling semi-structured data, such as `JSON`, ***arrays, and structs***. It integrates with Cloud Storage for unstructured data such as images or logs.
- **Partitioning**: One of the key features is dividing tables into partitions (for example, by date) to ***limit the amount of data scanned*** during queries and ***speed operational performance***.

- **Clustering**: It organizes data within partitions based on specified columns (for example, region, product) for ***faster filtering*** and ***grouping***.
- **Data Lifecycle Management**: It supports time-travel **7-day snapshot retention**, automated expiration policies, and integration with Cloud Storage for long-term archiving.
- **Security and Governance**: It offers encryption at ***rest*** *and* ***in transit***, ***Identity*** and ***Access Management*** **(IAM)** controls, and audit logging for compliance.
- **SQL Querying:** BigQuery enables users to query data using ***Standard*** **SQL**, and makes it accessible to data analysts, engineers, and data scientists familiar with SQL. Its rich function library and advanced features support complex analytical queries.

Key Features:

- **Standard SQL Support**: It uses **ANSI SQL 2011** with extensions for arrays, structs, geospatial data, and so on.
- **Core Functions**: This includes ***aggregate*** (for example, `SUM`, `COUNT`), ***string*** (for example, `CONCAT`, `REGEXP_CONTAINS`), ***date/time*** (for example, `DATE_TRUNC`, `EXTRACT`), and ***mathematical functions***.
- **Advanced Features**: It supports window ***functions, arrays, structs, JSON querying***, and ***geospatial functions***.
- **Query Optimization**: It leverages ***partitioning, clustering***, and ***caching*** to reduce costs and improve performance.
- **Scripting**: The language supports stored ***procedures, variables***, and ***control flow*** (for example, IF, WHILE) for automation.

Figure 7.1 illustrates the core functions of BigQuery.

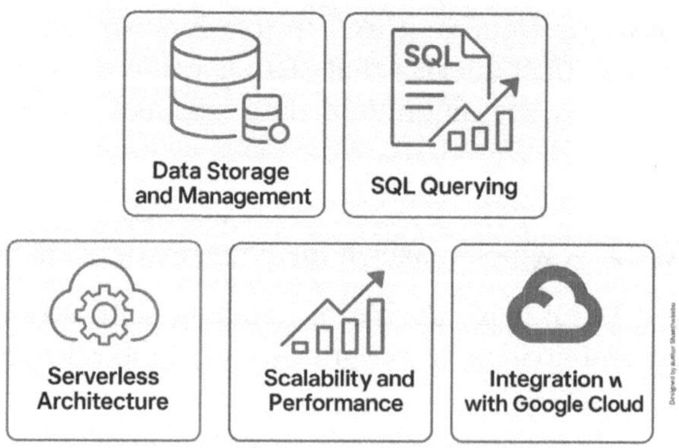

Figure 7.1: *BigQuery's Core Functions*

Scalability and Performance

BigQuery is designed for **high scalability**, which allows users to efficiently query large volumes of data in minutes. Its distributed architecture and optimization features ensure fast performance even for complex analytical workloads.

Key Features:

- **Distributed Query Engine**: It uses a **Massively Parallel Processing (MPP)** architecture to distribute queries across thousands of nodes.
- **Decoupled Compute and Storage**: It scales compute resources independently of storage, which allows for flexible performance tuning.
- **Partitioning and Clustering**: It reduces the data scanned by organizing tables into partitions and clusters.
- **BI Engine**: An in-memory analysis service for sub-second query performance in BI tools like Looker Studio.
- **Query Caching**: It stores results for **24 hours** to avoid redundant processing.
- **Slots**: It computes resources (slots) that can be reserved for predictable performance in high-concurrency scenarios.

Serverless Architecture

BigQuery's serverless architecture eliminates the need to manage infrastructure, reducing operational overhead and allowing users to focus on data analysis.

Key Features

- **No Infrastructure Management**: It handles the ***provisioning, scaling***, and ***maintenance of compute*** and ***storage resources***.
- **Automatic Scaling**: It dynamically allocates ***resources*** based on query complexity and data size.
- **Pay-as-You-Go Pricing**: It charges based on data scanned **($6/TB *as of* 2025)** and storage **($0.02/GB/*month for active storage*).**
- **Flat-Rate Pricing**: This offers reserved slots for predictable costs in high-volume scenarios.
- **High Availability**: It supports multi-region datasets to ensure data access during outages.

Integration with Google Cloud

It seamlessly integrates with other Google Cloud services for a comprehensive data analytics platform for ingestion, processing, visualization, and Machine Learning.

Key Integrations:

- **Cloud Storage**: It is capable of storing raw data (for example, **CSV, *Parquet,* JSON**) and querying it directly or loading it into BigQuery.
- **Dataflow**: It streams and batch processes data before loading it into BigQuery.
- **Dataproc**: It runs ***Apache Spark*** and ***Hadoop jobs***, writing results to BigQuery.
- **Looker Studio**: We can build interactive dashboards with sub-second query performance via ***BI Engine***.
- **BigQuery ML**: It is capable of training and deploying ***Machine Learning*** models within BigQuery.
- **Cloud Pub/Sub**: It is capable of ingesting streaming data for ***real-time analytics*** with Pub/Sub.
- **Cloud Functions**: We can build triggers in BigQuery jobs based on events (for example, new file in Cloud Storage).
- **Vertex AI**: It is capable of integrating with advanced **AI/ML** models for predictive analytics.

Supplementary Features and Utilities

Let us focus on the supplementary features and utilities of BigQuery.

- **Built-in Machine Learning (BigQuery ML):** BigQuery ML enables the building and deployment of ML models using standard SQL, which eliminates the need for external **ML tools**. It supports models such as linear ***regression, classification, and time-series forecasting*** for tasks like sales prediction. Models are trained directly on BigQuery data, thereby making ML accessible to SQL users with seamless integration.
- **Geospatial Analysis:** SQL Server Spatial includes geospatial data types and functions such as `ST_DISTANCE` and `ST_CONTAINS` that enable spatial data analysis. It supports ***location-based insights*** for use cases such as ***logistics optimization*** and ***retail planning***. Geospatial queries process coordinates and polygons efficiently, thus leveraging BigQuery's scalability.
- **Data Sharing and Governance:** It offers tools such as authorized views, IAM roles, and column-level security for secure data sharing and governance. Data Catalog integration enables dataset discovery and metadata tagging for compliance. These features ensure the maintenance controlled access and traceability across teams and organizations.

Figure 7.2 illustrates the supplementary features and utilities of BigQuery:

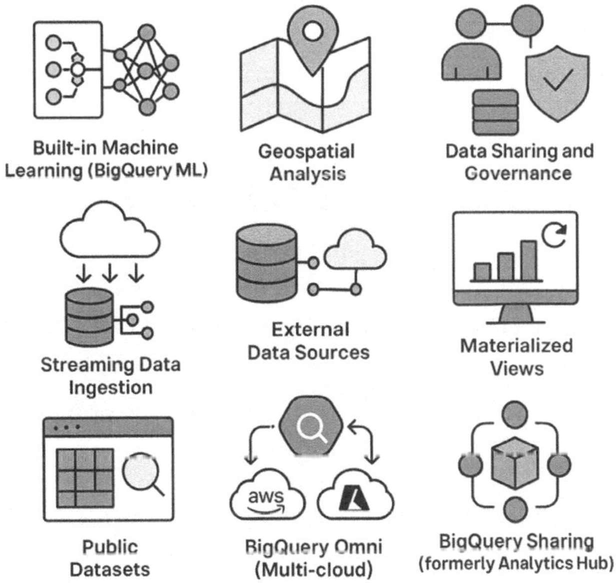

Figure 7.2: *BigQuery's Supplementary Features and Utilities*

- **Streaming Data Ingestion:** It supports real-time data ingestion via streaming inserts, while enabling continuous analytics on live data. It integrates with Cloud Pub/Sub and Dataflow for low-latency processing of event-driven data. This is ideal for applications such as real-time dashboards or fraud detection.
- **External Data Sources:** Its federated queries enable querying external data in ***Cloud Storage, Cloud Spanner, Bigtable***, or other clouds such as **AWS S3**. This eliminates the need to ingest data, reducing ETL overhead. Secure connections and schema definitions ensure structured access to heterogeneous sources.
- **Materialized Views:** These views, a beta feature, pre-compute and cache query results, improving performance for repetitive queries. They automatically refresh when source data changes, optimizing BI workloads. This feature enhances efficiency for dashboards and reports in tools like ***Looker Studio***.
- **Public Datasets: A** Public dataset marketplace provides access to diverse datasets, such as ***weather*** or ***census data***, for analysis. Users can query these datasets using standard BigQuery pricing for the data scanned. This supports research, prototyping, and data enrichment without additional storage costs.
- **BigQuery Omni (Multi-Cloud):** It enables querying data in **AWS (S3)** or A***zure (Blob Storage)*** using BigQuery's SQL engine. It processes data in-place, reducing transfer costs and supporting multi-cloud strategies. Setup requires configuring cross-cloud connections and IAM permissions.

- **BigQuery Sharing (Formerly Analytics Hub):** This feature enables the secure sharing of datasets and AI assets across organizations or teams. It provides a centralized hub for publishing and subscribing to curated data assets. IAM controls and Data Catalog integration ensure governance and secure collaboration.

Serverless Architecture of BigQuery

BigQuery's architecture is characterized by a separation of ***storage*** and ***compute***, which allows for the independent scaling and efficient processing of large datasets. It leverages Google's infrastructure, including ***Borg, Colossus, Jupiter****, and* ***Dremel*** to deliver high-performance analytics and manage data storage.

Here is a breakdown of the key components and concepts of BigQuery's architecture:

Separation of Storage and Compute

- BigQuery decouples ***storage*** and ***compute***, which means that the resources for storing data and processing queries can scale independently, as shown in *Figure* 7.3.
- This architecture allows BigQuery to handle ***massive workloads efficiently*** and ***cost-effectively***.
- Data is stored in **Colossus**, Google's distributed file system, while ***Dremel*** handles query execution.
- This separation also enables features such as ***on-demand scaling*** and ***flexible pricing***.

Key Infrastructure Components

- **Borg:** Google's cluster management system that manages resources and orchestrates tasks across thousands of CPU cores. This ensures resilience and handles failures, making BigQuery a robust solution.
- **Colossus:** Google's distributed file system that stores data and handles replication, recovery, and distributed management.
- **Jupiter:** Google's high-speed network that enables fast communication between storage and compute.
- **Dremel:** Google's query engine that efficiently processes queries across billions of rows. It dynamically allocates resources (slots) to queries based on demand, while ensuring fairness and performance.

Figure 7.3 illustrates the architecture of BigQuery.

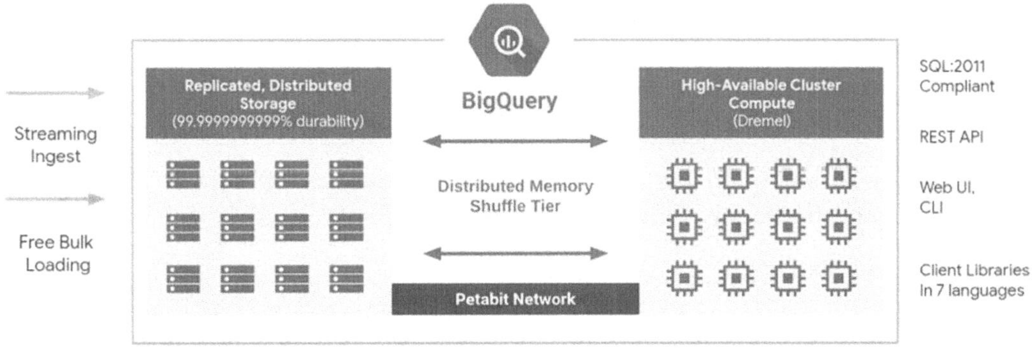

Figure 7.3: *Architecture of BigQuery (Source:* https://cloud.google.com/blog/products/data-analytics/new-blog-series-bigquery-explained-overview)

Data Storage and Processing: Let us explore how data storage and processing are handled in the BigQuery architecture.

- **Capacitor:** It uses a capacitor to store and efficiently query semi-structured data. It supports nested and repeated fields. In which each column is stored in a separate capacitor file, thereby enabling high compression and a fast-scanning process.

  Figure 7.4 illustrates the data storage structure in BigQuery:

  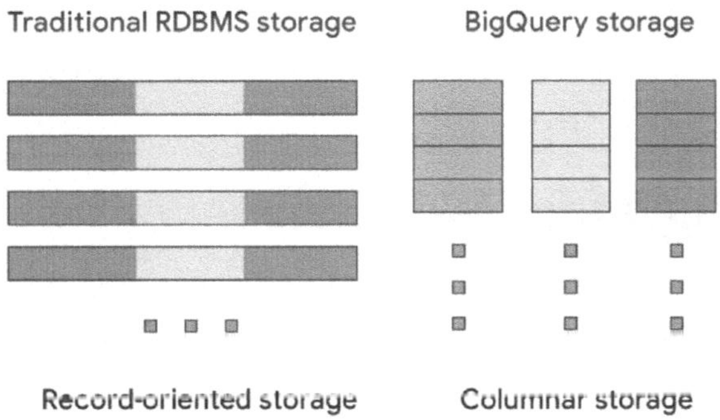

  Figure 7.4: *Data Storage in BigQuery*

- **SQL Interface:** It uses a dialect of SQL, which makes it accessible to users familiar with standard SQL statements. Users can write SQL queries without additional efforts.

- **OLAP Focus:** This is designed for Online Analytical Processing (OLAP) to enable complex data analyses and AI/ML models.

Scalability and Performance

- Its architecture allows it to scale to handle massive datasets and complex queries to achieve major industry-specific solutions.
- Since the architecture is based on the separation of storage and compute, it enables efficient scaling of each component independently.
- Dremel's ability to dynamically allocate resources effectively ensures fast query performance even under variable workloads.

Serverless and Managed

- It is a serverless platform; therefore, the developers do not need to manage infrastructure overhead challenges.
- Since this is a managed service, it handles tasks such as infrastructure management, scaling, and maintenance.

BigQuery Omni

- Omni extends BigQuery's architecture by allowing developers to run queries against data stored in other clouds such as AWS and Azure. This feature enables cross-cloud analytics and data warehousing.
- It leverages secure connections to access and process data in other clouds without physically moving it to Google Cloud.

In essence, BigQuery's architecture is designed for ***speed, scalability***, and ***efficiency*** in handling large-scale data analytics, while leveraging Google's robust infrastructure and a separation of storage and compute to deliver a ***powerful*** and ***flexible*** data warehousing solution.

Simplified BigQuery Workflow

Basically, BigQuery simplifies the process of analyzing large datasets by providing a scalable, serverless, and cost-effective data warehouse solution with powerful built-in features and integrations.

- **Data Loading:** Data can be loaded into BigQuery from various sources such as Cloud Storage, databases, or directly from applications.
- **Query Execution:** Users write SQL queries to analyze the data stored in BigQuery.
- **Result Storage:** Query results can be stored in new or existing tables, either temporarily or permanently.
- **Scalable Processing:** BigQuery's distributed query engine efficiently processes large datasets, leveraging Google's infrastructure.

Figure 7.5 illustrates the simplified BigQuery workflow:

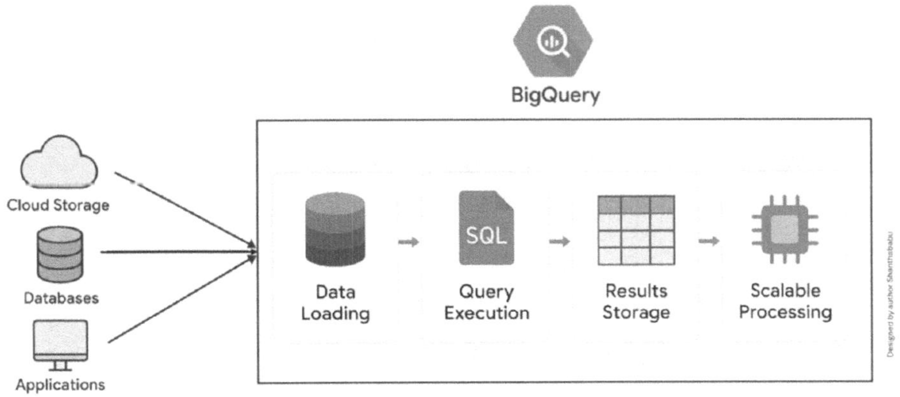

***Figure* 7.5:** *Simplified BigQuery Workflow*

Exploring the BigQuery Environment

Let us explore the BigQuery environment.

Step 1: Log into the GCP portal.

***Figure* 7.6:** GCP Landing Page

Step 2: Click **`Left Navigation Menu`** and select "**`BigQuery`**", followed by selecting "**`Studio`**", as highlighted in *Figure* 7.7.

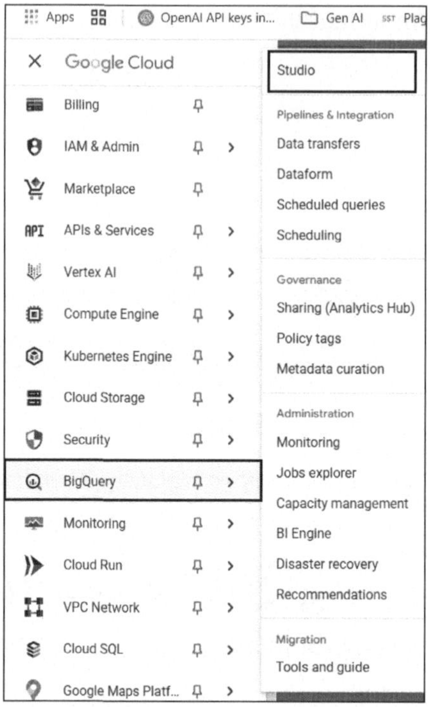

Figure 7.7: GCP – *BigQuery*

Step 3: Once you select "**BigQuery-Studio**", the system will take you to the **BigQuery-Editor**, as shown in *Figure 7.8*.

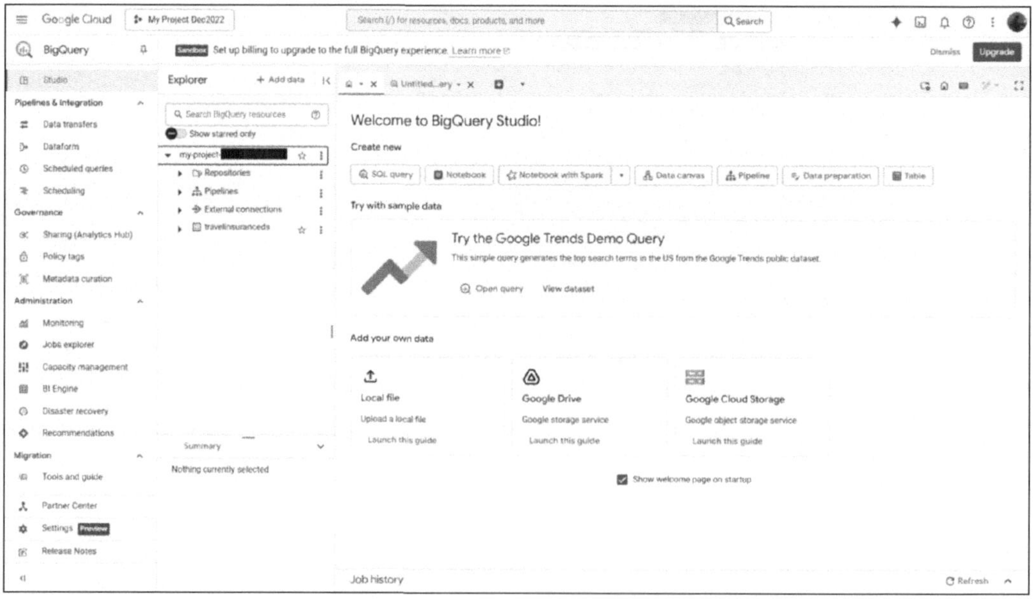

Figure 7.8: GCP – *BigQuery Editor*

Explorer Panel (Left Sidebar)

- **Resources and Tools**: Lists various BigQuery and related GCP services such as:
  - **Pipelines and Integration**: Manages data pipelines
    - **Data Transfers**: Handles data import/export schedules
    - **Dataform**: A tool for data transformation and modeling
    - **Scheduled Queries**: Manages automated query executions
    - **Scheduling**: Related to query scheduling options
    - **Governance**: Includes sharing (Analytics Hub) and:
    - Policy tags for data governance
    - **Metadata**: Manages metadata for datasets
  - **Administration**: Covers ***monitoring, jobs, capacity management, BI Engine, disaster recovery, recommendations***
  - **Migration**
    - Tools and partner center settings
    - Release notes

Selected Project: "`my-project-xxxx`" is selected, where sub-items such as "`Repositories`", "`Pipelines`", and "External connections" are expanded.

Main Workspace (Welcome to BigQuery Studio!)

- **Welcome Message**: Greets the user and offers options to get started
- **Create New**: Consists of the following for creating new resources:
  - **SQL Query**: Opens a new SQL editor for writing queries
  - **Notebook with Spark**: Launches a notebook environment with Apache Spark support
  - **Data Canvas**: A visual tool for data exploration
  - **Pipeline**: Sets up data processing pipelines
  - **Data Preparation**: Tools for cleaning and preparing data
  - **Table**: Creates a new table
- **Add your own data**: This is where you can add data from local, Google Drive, or Google Cloud Storage.

Step 4: To load the **Google Trends** dataset and other default datasets, use the View Dataset/Open Query option. The system will take you to Google Trends, where the available dataset is ready for you.

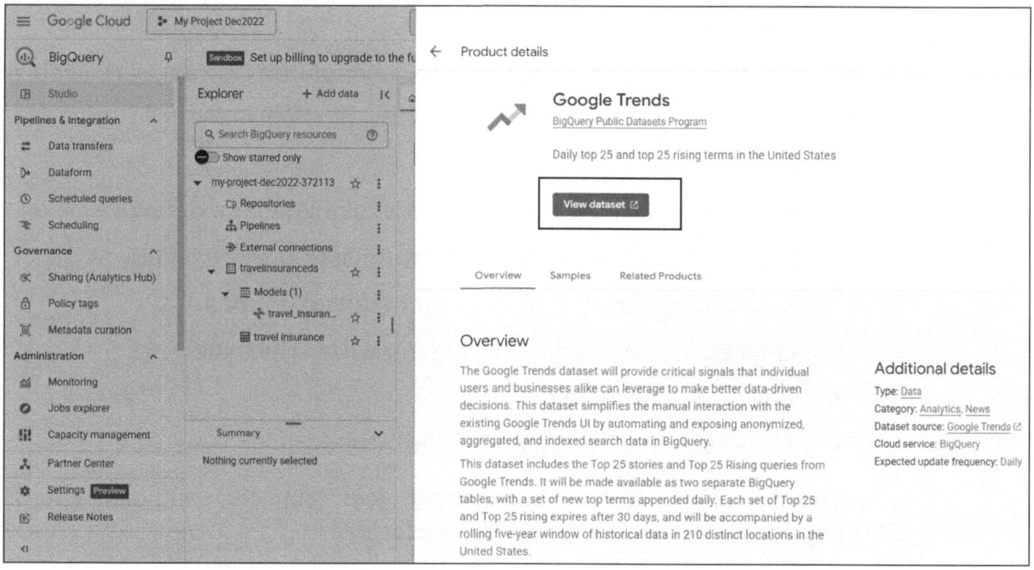

Figure 7.9: *GCP – BigQuery Editor – Google Trends Dataset*

Understanding the Explorer: In the BigQuery environment, there are significant resources for multiple purposes under each project. The resource categories are as follows:

- **Repositories**: Manage version-controlled data assets or scripts (for example, for Dataform)
- **Queries**: Access saved SQL queries for reuse
- **Notebooks**: Open interactive environments (for example, with Spark) for data analysis and visualization
- **Data Canvases**: Provide a visual interface for exploring and transforming data
- **Data Preparation**: Cleaning and preparing data before analysis
- **Pipelines**: Manages data processing workflows
- **External Connections**: Configures connections to external data sources (for example, Cloud Spanner)

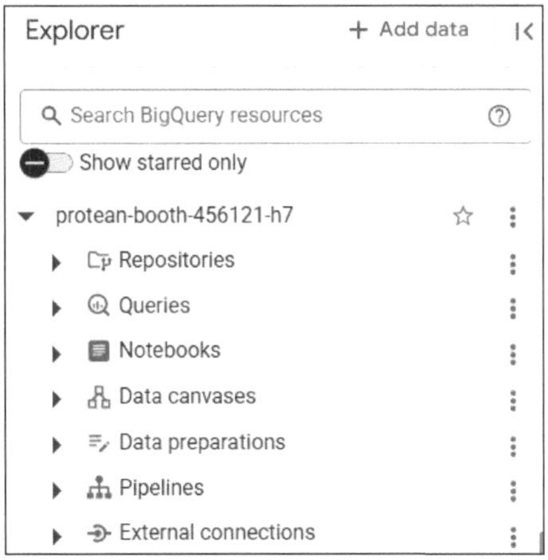

Figure 7.10: GCP – *BigQuery Editor – Project Resources*

Step 5: Select the database or table from the public data that is loaded by default in the BigQuery environment. You can observe the following details mentioned about the selected dataset:

- **Schema**: Displays the structure of the table, including column names, data types, and modes (for example, REQUIRED, NULLABLE).
- **Details**: Offers general information about the table, such as creation date, size, and ownership.
- **Preview**: Shows a sample of the table's data for quick inspection (not fully visible in this image).
- **Table Explorer**: Likely provides a hierarchical view of the table's contents or related tables

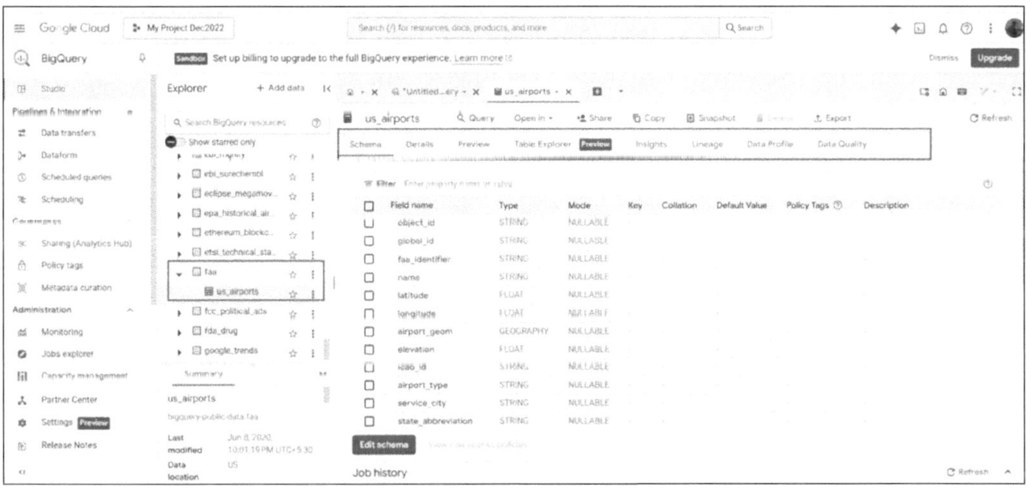

Figure 7.11: GCP – *BigQuery Editor – Google Trends Dataset – Features*

- **Insights**: Offers analytical insights or recommendations based on the table data.
- **Lineage**: Tracks the data lineage, showing the origin and transformations of the data
- **Data Profile**: Provides a statistical overview of the data, such as value distributions and null counts.
- **Data Quality**: Focuses on data quality metrics and validation (currently highlighted but disabled)

Create New Dataset

Step 6: Click the three dots shown in *Figure* 7.12 and select "**`Create Dataset`**".

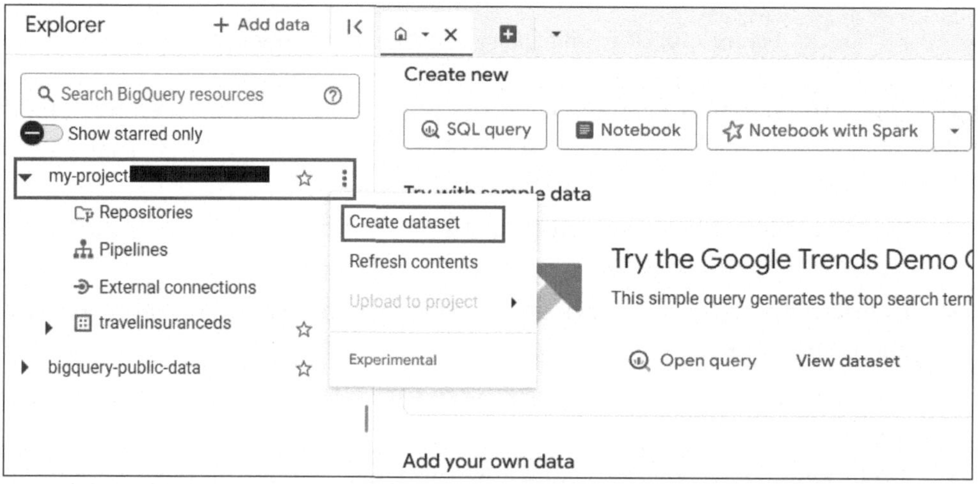

Figure 7.12: GCP – *BigQuery Editor – Creating a New Dataset*

Step 7: Once you click "**`Create Dataset`**", the system will take you to the new dataset configuration pop-up, where you have to configure the following:

Dataset ID

- **Value**: <<name of the dataset>>
- **Location Type**
    - **Options**:
        - **Region**: Allows you to specify a single geographic region (for example, us-central1) to collocate your datasets with other Google Cloud services for lower latency and cost efficiency
        - **Multi-region**: Enables BigQuery to distribute data across multiple regions within a group (for example, US for multiple regions in the United States) to increase quota limits and improve availability

- **Select**: **Multi-region US** (multiple regions in the United States). This provides higher scalability and redundancy, but it may have higher latency compared to a single region.

External Dataset

- **Supported Type**: Cloud Spanner
- It indicates that the dataset can be linked to an external data source, specifically Google Cloud Spanner, which is a fully managed relational database service. This allows you to query external data without importing it into BigQuery.
- **Link to an External Dataset**: Provides an option to connect to an existing Cloud Spanner database

Tags

- Tags allow adding metadata tags to the dataset for better organization, searchability, and governance. No specific tags are set in this configuration.

Advanced Options

- **Encryption**:
  - **Google-Managed Encryption Keys: The default** option where Google handles encryption keys to provide security without user management.
  - **Cloud KMS Key**: Allows customers to use their own encryption keys managed via Cloud Key Management Service (KMS) for greater control
- **Case Insensitive**:
  - **Enable Case-Insensitive Table Names**: If enabled, table names can be referenced regardless of case (for example, Table1 and table1 are treated as the same).
- **Default Collation**:
  - Defines the default sorting and comparison rules for string data (not specified here)
- **Default Table Expiration**:
  - **Enable Table Expiration**: If enabled, tables are automatically deleted after a set period.
  - **Default Maximum Table Age**: Specifies the number of days (not set here) after which tables expire
- **Default Rounding Mode**:
  - Sets the default rounding behavior for numerical operations (not specified here)

- **Storage Billing Model**:
    - **`STORAGE_BILLING_MODEL_UNSPECIFIED`**: Indicates that no specific billing model was selected; defaults to standard storage billing based on data size and retention
- **Time Travel Window**:
    - Defines the duration (not set here) for which historical data versions are retained for recovery or auditing, enhancing data reliability

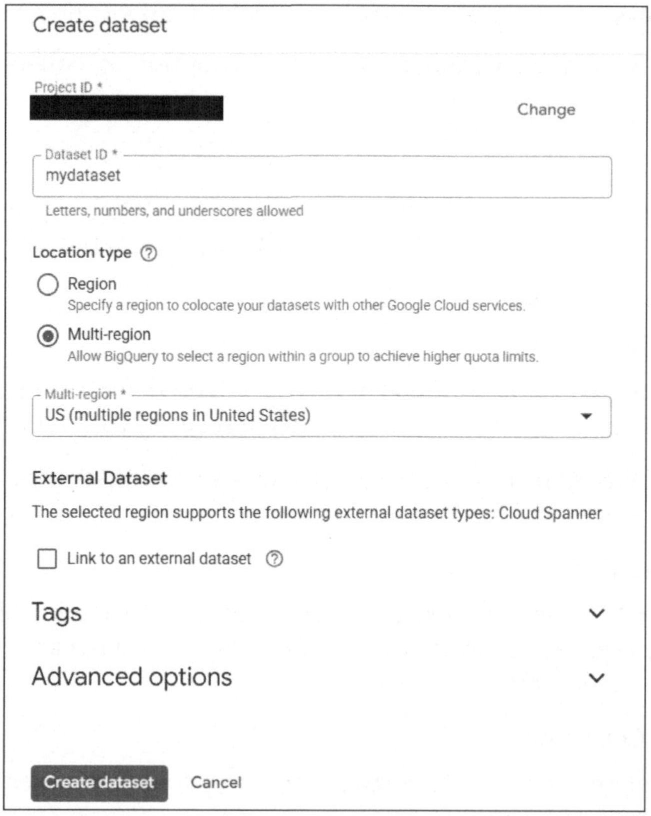

Figure 7.13: GCP – *BigQuery Editor – Configuring a New Dataset*

Step 8: After successful creation of the Dataset, it will be available under the project. Here, you can add a new table under this dataset, as shown in *Figure* 7.14.

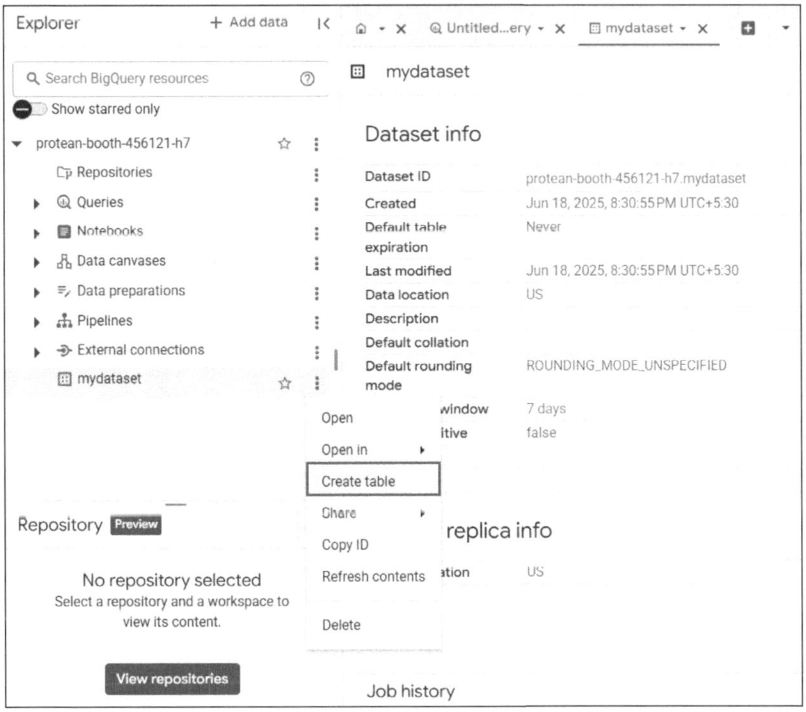

Figure 7.14: GCP – *BigQuery Editor – New Table*

Step 9: Once you click "`Create table`" under this dataset, you will see a pop-up screen shown in *Figure 7.15*.

Figure 7.15: GCP – *BigQuery Editor – Configuring a New Table*

Source:

- **Create a table from**:
    - **Empty Table**: Selected option, which indicates that the table will be created without initial data. This allows you to define the schema manually and populate it later.
    - Other options (not selected) might include uploading data from a file, Google Cloud Storage, or another table.

Destination:

- **Project*: Selected** project
- **Dataset***: Selected dataset
- **Table***: table name
- **Table Type**:
    - **Native Table**: Selected, which indicates a standard BigQuery table stored and managed natively
    - **Create a BigQuery Table for Apache Iceberg**: Unchecked; an option for creating a table compatible with Apache Iceberg, a table format for large analytical datasets (not applicable here)

Schema:

- **Edit as Text**: Toggled on, allowing schema definition via a text editor (though the graphical editor is shown). This can be switched to a text-based JSON format for advanced users.
- **Field Configuration** (for the first field):
    - **`Field Name*`**: Blank, requiring a unique name for the column (for example, column1)
    - **`Type*`**: Set to STRING, defining the data type (other options might include **`INTEGER`**, **`FLOAT`**, **`BOOLEAN`**, and so on)
    - **`Mode`**: Set to NULLABLE, indicating that the field can contain null values (alternatives include **`REQUIRED`** or **`REPEATED`**)
    - **`Max Length`**: Blank, optional field to specify the maximum length for STRING types
    - **`Description`**: Blank, optional field for adding notes about the column's purpose.
    - **`Add Field`**: Button to add another field (for example, field 2 is listed but not configured)
    - **`Trash Icon`**: Removes the field

- **Field Count**: Indicates that two fields are defined (only one is configured on the visible interface).
- **Partitioning Settings:** You can set the partitioning settings based on the project requirements like No partitioning, Partition by ingestion time, and Partition by field.

Action Buttons:

- **Create Table**: Blue button to finalize and create the table with the specified configuration.
- **Cancel**: Button to discard changes and exit the creation process.

Step 10: After all the field names and required information have been provided, you will be returned to the editor screen as shown in *Figure* 7.16.

Figure 7.16: GCP – *BigQuery Editor – New Table View*

Step 11: Inserting data using the insert statement (DDL) as shown in *Figure* 7.17.

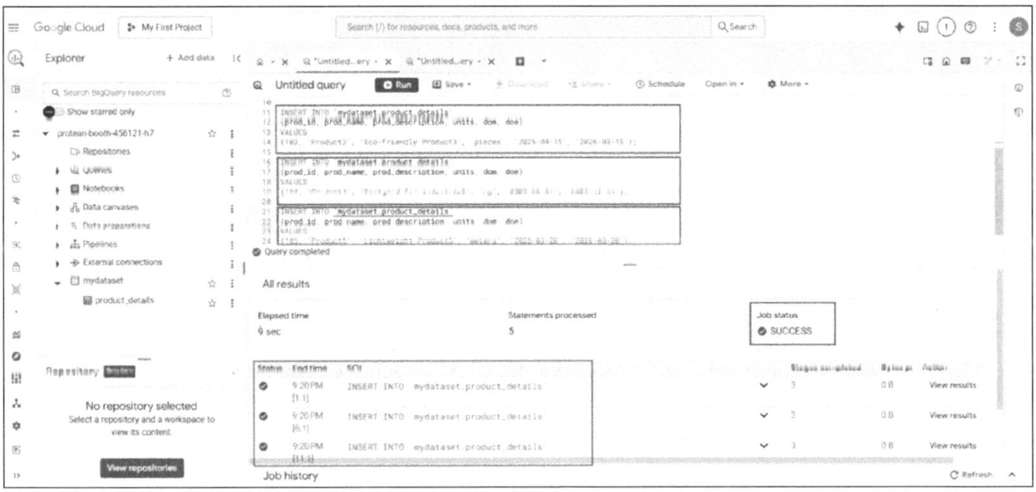

Figure 7.17: GCP – *BigQuery Editor – Adding Data to the Table*

Select the inserted data in the new table.

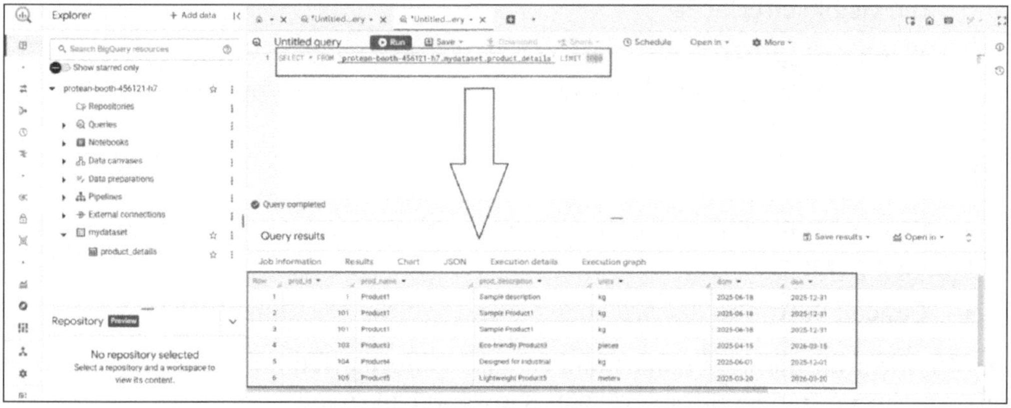

Figure 7.18: GCP – *BigQuery Editor – Select the Inserted Data*

Similarly, you can import data from Google Cloud Storage, Amazon S3, and Azure Blob Storage, or upload a file from the local machine, as shown in *Figure* 7.19. This allows you to integrate BigQuery with external and internal data sources.

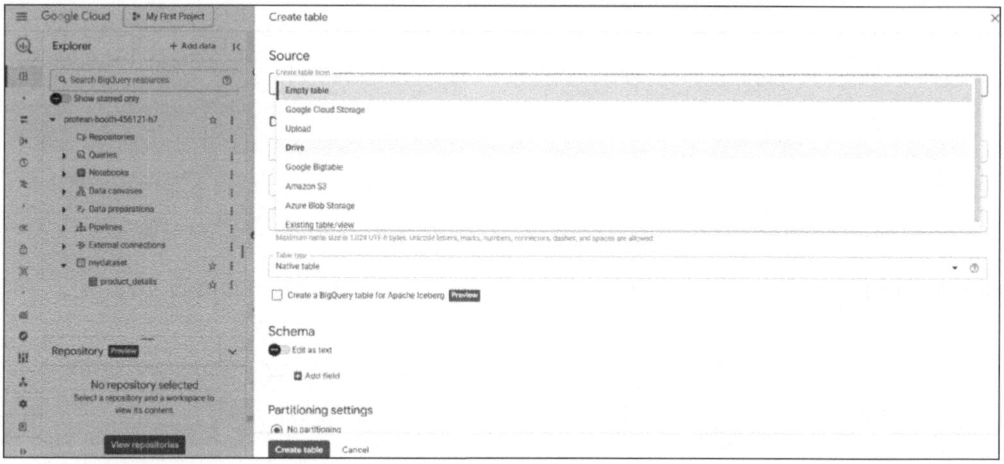

Figure 7.19: GCP – *BigQuery Editor – Multiple Sources for Importing Data*

Let us focus on the technical features of BigQuery.

SQL for BigQuery: Core Syntax, Optimization, and Advanced Features

BigQuery, Google Cloud Platform's serverless data warehouse, is a **POWERHOUSE** for big data analytics and enables users to process petabyte-scale datasets using Standard SQL (ANSI SQL 2011).

Its columnar storage, distributed architecture, and advanced features make it ideal for analytical workloads. By mastering these elements, you can write efficient queries, leverage BigQuery's full capabilities, and derive actionable insights from your data.

Core SQL Syntax and Functions

BigQuery utilizes **Standard SQL**, which is intuitive for users familiar with SQL and offers a comprehensive set of functions for data manipulation and analysis. Next, we will cover essential SQL syntax and commonly used functions, with examples based on the `sales_data` dataset.

Basic SELECT Queries

The SELECT statement retrieves data from tables. Always use fully qualified table names.

```
in the format project_id.dataset.table.
SELECT order_id, customer_id, product, quantity * price AS total_price
FROM `my-project.sales_dataset.sales_data`
WHERE region = 'US' LIMIT 10;
```

- **Explanation**: This query selects order details, calculates the total price per order, filters for the US region, and limits output to 10 rows.
- **Best Practice**: Use backticks (") for table names to handle special characters or reserved words. Avoid `SELECT *`` to minimize the amount of data scanned and reduce costs.

Filtering and Sorting: Use `WHERE` to filter rows and ORDER BY to sort results.

```
SELECT product, SUM(quantity) AS total_quantity
FROM `my-project.sales_dataset.sales_data`
WHERE order_date BETWEEN '2025-01-01' AND '2025-01-31'
  AND quantity > 0
ORDER BY total_quantity DESC;
```

- **Explanation**: Aggregates the total quantity sold per product in January 2025, except for zero-quantity orders, and sorts by quantity descending
- **Tip**: Use BETWEEN for date ranges and explicit conditions to reduce scanned data.

Aggregations: BigQuery supports standard aggregate functions: **`SUM`**, **`COUNT`**, **`AVG`**, **`MIN`**, **`MAX`**, and more.

```
SELECT
  region,
  COUNT(DISTINCT customer_id) AS unique_customers,
```

```
  AVG(price) AS avg_price,
  SUM(quantity * price) AS total_revenue
FROM `my-project.sales_dataset.sales_data`
GROUP BY region
HAVING total_revenue > 100000
ORDER BY total_revenue DESC;
```

- **Explanation**: Groups data by region, counts unique customers, calculates average price, and sums revenue, while filtering for regions with over $100,000 in revenue.
- **Optimization Tip**: Use APPROX_COUNT_DISTINCT for faster, approximate counts on large datasets.

Joins: BigQuery supports **`INNER JOIN`**, **`LEFT JOIN`**, **`RIGHT JOIN`**, **`FULL OUTER JOIN`**, and **`CROSS JOIN`**.

- **Explanation**: Joins sales and customer data, while retrieving orders from 2025 onward, including unmatched sales records (via **`LEFT JOIN`**)
- **Performance Tip**: Place smaller tables on the right side of the **`LEFT JOIN`** to optimize execution. Minimize joins by de-normalizing data when possible.

Common SQL Functions in BigQuery: The following table illustrates the common SQL functions in BigQuery.

Category	SQL Query Example Snippet	Common Functions Used
String Functions	sql SELECT product, UPPER(product) AS product_upper, CONCAT('Product: ', product) AS product_label FROM `my-project.sales_dataset.sales_data` WHERE STARTS_WITH(product, 'Widget'); 	UPPER, LOWER, CONCAT, STARTS_WITH, REGEXP_CONTAINS
Date/Time Functions	sql SELECT order_date, EXTRACT(YEAR FROM order_date) AS order_year, DATE_TRUNC(order_date, MONTH) AS order_month FROM `my-project.sales_dataset.sales_data` WHERE order_date >= DATE_SUB(CURRENT_DATE(), INTERVAL 1 YEAR); 	EXTRACT, DATE_TRUNC, DATE_ADD, DATE_SUB
Mathematical Functions	sql SELECT product, ROUND(price, 2) AS rounded_price, CEIL(quantity * price) AS ceiling_value FROM `my-project.sales_dataset.sales_data`; 	ROUND, CEIL, FLOOR, LOG, SQRT

Table 7.1: *Common SQL Functions in BigQuery*

Advanced Query Optimization Techniques in BigQuery

BigQuery, a serverless data warehouse within the Google Cloud Platform, is designed for petabyte-scale analytics and utilizes a pricing structure based on the volume of data scanned and stored. Crafting efficient queries is the key to reducing costs and enhancing performance. Given that BigQuery's pricing depends on the amount of data scanned per query, optimization is crucial for both cost management and speed. The following are the practical strategies for writing efficient queries, illustrated with examples from the **sales_data** dataset.

Figure 7.20 illustrates the advanced query optimization techniques in BigQuery:

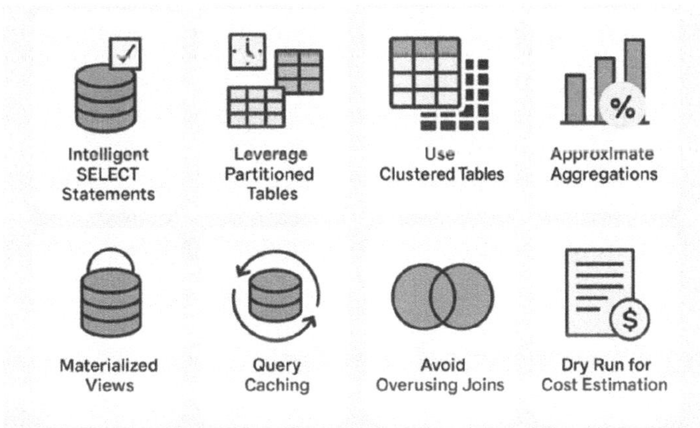

***Figure* 7.20**: *Advanced Query Optimization Techniques in BigQuery*

Intelligence Select Statements

Let us explore the types of intelligence-select-statements and sample queries:

Minimize Data Scanned: BigQuery scans entire columns for selected data and reduces the scope of scanned data, which is important.

Select Specific Columns

Avoid **SELECT *** to reduce unnecessary data scanning.

```
-- Inefficient: Scans all columns
SELECT * FROM `my-project.sales_dataset.sales_data` WHERE region = 'US';

-- Efficient: Scans only needed columns
SELECT order_id, product, quantity * price AS total_price
FROM `my-project.sales_dataset.sales_data`
WHERE region = 'US';
```

- **Explanation**: Selecting only **`order_id`**, product, and a calculated **`total_price`**, reduces the data scanned compared to **`SELECT *`**.

Tip: *Always list specific columns unless all columns are required.*

- **Filter Early with `WHERE`:** Apply filters in the **`WHERE`** clause to limit the rows scanned before processing.

```
SELECT product, SUM(quantity) AS total_quantity
FROM `my-project.sales_dataset.sales_data`
WHERE order_date >= '2025-01-01' AND order_date < '2025-02-01'
  AND region = 'US';
```

- **Explanation**: Filters for January 2025 and the US region, while reducing the dataset before aggregation

  Use `LIMIT` for Testing: Limit output during query development to save costs.

  ```
  SELECT order_id, product
  FROM `my-project.sales_dataset.sales_data`
  WHERE region = 'US'
  LIMIT 10;
  ```

- **Explanation**: Returns only 10 rows for quick validation without scanning the entire table

Leveraging Partitioned Tables

Partitioning divides a table into segments (partitions) based on a column, typically a date or timestamp, which allows for the scanning of only relevant data.

- **Creating a Partitioned Table:** Partitions the table by **`order_date`**, while enabling queries to scan only specific date ranges

  ```
  CREATE TABLE `my-project.sales_dataset.sales_data_partitioned`
  PARTITION BY DATE(order_date)
  AS
  SELECT * FROM `my-project.sales_dataset.sales_data`;
  ```

- **Querying a Partitioned Table:** Scans only the January 1, 2025 partition, significantly reducing the amount of data processed

  ```
  SELECT order_id, product, quantity
  FROM `my-project.sales_dataset.sales_data_partitioned`
  WHERE order_date = '2025-01-01';
  ```

Tip: *Use* **`DATE_TRUNC`** *or range filters for broader partition pruning.*

```
WHERE order_date BETWEEN '2025-01-01' AND '2025-01-31';
```

- **Range Partitioning:** Partitions by **customer_id** in ranges of 1,000, while optimizing queries filtering on **customer_id.**

  For non-date columns, use range partitioning.

```
CREATE TABLE `my-project.sales_dataset.sales_data_range_partitioned`
PARTITION BY RANGE_BUCKET(customer_id, GENERATE_ARRAY(0, 100000,
1000))
AS
SELECT * FROM `my-project.sales_dataset.sales_data`;
```

Using Clustered Tables

Clustering co-locates data based on specified columns, while improving performance for queries with filters or joins on those columns.

- **Creating a Clustered Table:** Partitions by **order_date** and clusters by region and product, optimizing queries filtering or grouping on these columns.

```
CREATE TABLE `my-project.sales_dataset.sales_data_clustered`
PARTITION BY DATE(order_date)
CLUSTER BY region, product
AS
SELECT * FROM `my-project.sales_dataset.sales_data`;
```

- **Querying a Clustered Table:** Clustering ensures that data for region = 'US' and product is physically co-located, which reduces scan time.

```
SELECT product, SUM(quantity) AS total_quantity
FROM `my-project.sales_dataset.sales_data_clustered`
WHERE region = 'US' AND order_date = '2025-01-01'
GROUP BY product;
```

  ***Tip**: Choose clustering keys based on frequently filtered or grouped columns (up to four keys allowed).*

Approximate Aggregations

For large datasets, use approximate functions to reduce processing time and cost.

```
SELECT
  region,
  APPROX_COUNT_DISTINCT(customer_id) AS approx_unique_customers
FROM `my-project.sales_dataset.sales_data`
GROUP BY region;
```

- **Explanation**: Uses APPROX_COUNT_DISTINCT for faster, approximate counts of unique customers

- **Other Functions**: `APPROX_QUANTILES, APPROX_TOP_COUNT` for percentiles and top values

Materialized Views

Materialized views store pre-computed query results, which is ideal for frequently accessed aggregations.

```
CREATE MATERIALIZED VIEW `my-project.sales_dataset.region_summary`
PARTITION BY DATE(month)
AS
SELECT
  DATE_TRUNC(order_date, MONTH) AS month,
  region,
  SUM(quantity * price) AS total_revenue
FROM `my-project.sales_dataset.sales_data`
GROUP BY month, region;
```

- **Explanation**: Pre-computes monthly revenue by region and updates automatically when the source table changes
- **Querying**:

  ```
  SELECT month, region, total_revenue FROM `my-project.sales_
  dataset.region_summary` WHERE month = '2025-01-01';
  ```

  Tip: *Use materialized views for dashboards or reports to reduce query costs.*

Query Caching

BigQuery caches query results for 24 hours if the underlying data has not changed.

```
SELECT region, SUM(quantity * price) AS total_revenue
FROM `my-project.sales_dataset.sales_data`
WHERE order_date >= '2025-01-01' AND order_date < '2025-02-01';
```

- **Explanation**: If this query runs multiple times within 24 hours and the data is unchanged, BigQuery serves cached results, thereby saving costs.

  Tip: *Avoid table modifications (for example,* ***`INSERT`***, ***`UPDATE`****) to leverage caching.*

Avoid Overusing Joins

Joins can be expensive, especially on large tables. Denormalize data when possible.

-- Denormalized table to avoid joins.

```
CREATE TABLE `my-project.sales_dataset.sales_data_denormalized`
AS
```

```
SELECT
  s.order_id,
  s.customer_id,
  s.order_date,
  s.product,
  s.quantity,
  s.price,
  s.region,
  c.customer_name
FROM `my-project.sales_dataset.sales_data` AS s
LEFT JOIN `my-project.sales_dataset.customer_data` AS c
  ON s.customer_id = c.customer_id;
```

- **Explanation**: Pre-joins sales and customer data into a denormalized table, which reduces query-time joins.

  ***Tip**: Use materialized views for pre-computed joins if denormalization is not feasible.*

Dry Run for Cost Estimation

Use `OPTIONS(dry_run=true)` to estimate the data scanned without executing the query.

```
SELECT order_id, product
FROM `my-project.sales_dataset.sales_data`
WHERE region = 'US'
OPTIONS(dry_run=true);
```

- **Explanation**: Returns the estimated number of bytes to be scanned and helps in optimizing queries before execution

Optimize Subqueries and Common Table Expressions

Common Table Expressions (CTEs) improve query readability and maintainability, especially for complex logic. Use CTEs instead of nested sub-queries for clarity and easier debugging. Use CTEs for readability and to avoid redundant computations.

```
WITH MonthlySales AS (
  SELECT
    DATE_TRUNC(order_date, MONTH) AS month,
    region,
    SUM(quantity * price) AS total_revenue
  FROM `my-project.sales_dataset.sales_data`
```

```
  GROUP BY month, region
)
SELECT
  month,
  region,
  total_revenue,
  total_revenue / SUM(total_revenue) OVER (PARTITION BY month) AS
revenue_share
FROM MonthlySales
WHERE month = '2025-01-01';
```

- **Explanation**: Uses a CTE to compute monthly revenue; calculates each region's revenue share

  Tip: *Avoid deeply nested sub-queries, as they can be harder to optimize.*

Best Practices for Query Efficiency:

- **Monitor Costs**: Use the BigQuery Pricing Calculator and Query Execution Details to track expenses.
- **Use Labels**: Apply the following labels to queries for cost allocation:
  - `SELECT * FROM `my-project.sales_dataset.sales_data` OPTIONS(labels=['department:analytics', 'project:sales']);`
- **Reserve Slots**: For high-concurrency workloads, reserve compute slots. These result in a more predictable performance.
- **Analyze Query Plans**: Use `EXPLAIN` to understand query execution, as demonstrated here:
  - `EXPLAIN SELECT * FROM `my-project.sales_dataset.sales_data` WHERE region = 'US';`
- **Avoid Unnecessary DISTINCT**: Use `APPROX_COUNT_DISTINCT` or redesign queries to minimize `DISTINCT`.

Exploring Stored Procedures in BigQuery

While stored procedures enable automation and modularity for repetitive or complex tasks, stored procedures in ***BigQuery*** are reusable SQL scripts that encapsulate complex logic and enable automation, modularity, and error handling.

They are written in BigQuery's scripting language, which supports variables, loops, conditionals, and exception handling.

- **Creating Stored Procedures:** Stored procedures are defined via the **`CREATE PROCEDURE`** statement.

Example: Calculate Monthly Revenue

```
CREATE PROCEDURE `my-project.sales_dataset.
CalculateMonthlyRevenue`(IN target_month DATE, OUT total_revenue
FLOAT64)
BEGIN
  -- Calculate total revenue for the specified month
  SET total_revenue = (
    SELECT SUM(quantity * price)
    FROM `my-project.sales_dataset.sales_data`
    WHERE DATE_TRUNC(order_date, MONTH) = target_month
  );

  -- Insert result into a summary table
  INSERT INTO `my-project.sales_dataset.monthly_summary` (month,
revenue)
  VALUES (target_month, total_revenue);

  -- Log success
  SELECT FORMAT('Processed revenue for %t: %f', target_month,
total_revenue) AS status;
END;
```

- **Explanation**:
  - Takes an input parameter **`target_month`** (**`DATE`**) and an output parameter **`total_revenue (FLOAT64)`**
  - Calculates revenue for the specified month and inserts it into the **`monthly_summary`**
  - Outputs a status message
- **Calling the Procedure:**
  - `DECLARE revenue FLOAT64;`
  - `CALL `my-project.sales_dataset.CalculateMonthlyRevenue`('2025-01-01', revenue);`
  - `SELECT revenue;`

- **Using Control Flow in Stored Procedures:** BigQuery supports **`IF`**, **`WHILE`**, **`FOR`**, and **`EXCEPTION`** blocks for advanced logic.

  Example: Process Multiple Months

```
CREATE PROCEDURE `my-project.sales_dataset.
ProcessMultipleMonths`(IN start_month DATE, IN end_month DATE)
BEGIN
```

```
  DECLARE current_month DATE DEFAULT start_month;
  DECLARE total_revenue FLOAT64;

  -- Loop through months
  WHILE current_month <= end_month DO
    BEGIN
      -- Calculate revenue for current month
      SET total_revenue = ( SELECT SUM(quantity * price)
        FROM `my-project.sales_dataset.sales_data`
        WHERE DATE_TRUNC(order_date, MONTH) = current_month
      );

      -- Insert into summary table
      INSERT INTO `my-project.sales_dataset.monthly_summary`
(month, revenue)
      VALUES (current_month, total_revenue);

      -- Move to next month
      SET current_month = DATE_ADD(current_month, INTERVAL 1
MONTH);
    EXCEPTION WHEN ERROR THEN
      -- Log error and continue
      SELECT FORMAT('Error processing %t: %s', current_month,
ERROR_MESSAGE()) AS error_status;
    END;
  END WHILE;

  -- Log completion
  SELECT 'Processing complete for all months' AS status;
END;
```

- **Explanation**:
  - Loops through months from **`start_month`** to **`end_month`**
  - Calculates and stores revenue for each month
  - Handles errors with an EXCEPTION block to log issues without stopping execution
- **Calling the Procedure:**

```
CALL `my-project.sales_dataset.
ProcessMultipleMonths`('2025-01-01', '2025-06-01');
```

- **Scheduling Stored Procedures:** Automate stored procedures using BigQuery Scheduled Queries

Example: Schedule Monthly Revenue Calculation

a. Go to the BigQuery console.

b. Navigate to "**`Scheduled Queries`**" and create a new schedule.

c. Set the query to:

```
DECLARE revenue FLOAT64;
                CALL `my-project.sales_dataset.
CalculateMonthlyRevenue`(DATE_TRUNC(CURRENT_DATE(), MONTH),
revenue);
```

d. Configure a daily or monthly recurrence schedule.

e. Enable notifications for failures via Cloud Monitoring.

Explanation: Automates monthly revenue calculations at the start of each month

Tip: *Use Cloud Logging to monitor execution and troubleshoot failures.*

- **Error Handling in Stored Procedures:** Use **`EXCEPTION`** blocks to handle errors gracefully.

```
CREATE PROCEDURE `my-project.sales_dataset.SafeUpdateSummary`()
BEGIN
  DECLARE total_revenue FLOAT64;
  BEGIN
    -- Attempt to calculate revenue
    SET total_revenue = (
      SELECT SUM(quantity * price)
      FROM `my-project.sales_dataset.sales_data_nonexistent` --
Table doesn't exist
    );
    INSERT INTO `my-project.sales_dataset.monthly_summary`
(month, revenue)
    VALUES (CURRENT_DATE(), total_revenue);
    EXCEPTION WHEN ERROR THEN
    -- Log error and insert the default value
    INSERT INTO `my-project.sales_dataset.error_log` (error_time,
error_message)
    VALUES (CURRENT_TIMESTAMP(), ERROR_MESSAGE());
    INSERT INTO `my-project.sales_dataset.monthly_summary`
(month, revenue)
    VALUES (CURRENT_DATE(), 0.0);
  END;
END;
```

Explanation: Attempts to calculate revenue; if the table does not exist, **`EXCEPTION`** logs an error and inserts a default value

Tip: *Always include error handling for robust automation.*

- **Clean Up Old Data:** Deletes records older than the specified retention period and logs the number of deleted rows

```
CREATE PROCEDURE `my-project.sales_dataset.CleanOldData`(IN
retention_days INT64)
BEGIN
  DECLARE cutoff_date DATE;
  SET cutoff_date = DATE_SUB(CURRENT_DATE(), INTERVAL retention_
days DAY);

  -- Delete old records
  DELETE FROM `my-project.sales_dataset.sales_data`
  WHERE order_date < cutoff_date;

  -- Log cleanup
  INSERT INTO `my-project.sales_dataset.cleanup_log` (cleanup_
date, records_deleted)
  SELECT CURRENT_TIMESTAMP(), @@row_count;
END;
```

Optimization: Uses partitioning on **`order_date`** to efficiently delete data

Best Practices for Stored Procedures:

- **Use Meaningful Names**: Name procedures descriptively (for example, **`CalculateMonthlyRevenue`**).
- **Parameterize Logic**: Use **`IN`** and **`OUT`** parameters for flexibility.
- **Handle Errors**: Always include **`EXCEPTION`** blocks for robustness.
- **Optimize Queries inside Procedures**: Apply the same optimization techniques (for example, partitioning, clustering) that you use for stored procedures.
- **Test Incrementally**: Test procedures with small datasets before scheduling.
- **Document Logic**: Add comments to explain complex steps:
    - Calculate revenue and update the summary table through:

      `SET total_revenue = (...);`

Advanced SQL Features in BigQuery

BigQuery extends Standard SQL with powerful features for advanced analytics, including window functions, arrays, structs, and more. These enable complex computations and data transformations within SQL.

- **Window Functions:** Window functions perform calculations across a set of rows (the "window") relative to the current row, without collapsing the result set.

```
SELECT  customer_id,  order_id,  order_date,  quantity * price
AS order_value,
RANK() OVER (PARTITION BY customer_id ORDER BY quantity * price
DESC) AS order_rank,
SUM(quantity * price) OVER (PARTITION BY customer_id) AS total_
customer_spend,
AVG(quantity * price) OVER ( PARTITION BY region ORDER BY order_
date    ROWS BETWEEN 6 PRECEDING AND CURRENT ROW ) AS moving_
avg_7days
FROM `my-project.sales_dataset.sales_data`;
```

  - **Explanation**:
    - **`RANK()`** assigns a rank to each order per customer based on order value.
    - **`SUM`** calculates the total spend per customer across all their orders.
    - **`AVG`** computes a 7-day moving average of order values within each region.
  - **Key Clauses:**
    - **`PARTITION BY`**: Groups rows into partitions (for example, by **`customer_id`** or region)
    - **`ORDER BY`**: Defines the order within the window
    - **`ROWS BETWEEN`**: Specifies the window frame (for example, the previous six rows and the current row)
  - **Use Cases**: Ranking, running totals, moving averages, and cumulative sums

- **Arrays**: Arrays store ordered lists of values in a single column, which is idcal for grouping related data.

Creating Arrays with `ARRAY_AGG`

```
SELECT
  customer_id,
  ARRAY_AGG(product ORDER BY product) AS purchased_products
FROM `my-project.sales_dataset.sales_data`
GROUP BY customer_id;
Explanation: Aggregates all products purchased by each customer
into an ordered array.
```

```
Tip: Use LIMIT within ARRAY_AGG to cap the number of elements:
ARRAY_AGG(product ORDER BY product LIMIT 5)
```

Flattening Arrays with UNNEST

```
SELECT
  customer_id,
  product
FROM `my-project.sales_dataset.sales_data`,
UNNEST(
  ARRAY_AGG(product ORDER BY product) OVER (PARTITION BY
customer_id)
) AS product;
```

- **Explanation**: Flattens the array of products per customer into individual rows
- **Use Case**: Analyze individual elements of an array, such as generating a list of products for further processing.

- **Structs:** Structs are nested records that store multiple fields within a single column, which can create complex data structures.

```
SELECT
  customer_id,
    STRUCT(
     SUM(quantity * price) AS total_spend, COUNT(DISTINCT order_
id) AS order_count,
     MAX(order_date) AS last_order_date    ) AS customer_summary
    FROM `my-project.sales_dataset.sales_data`
   GROUP BY customer_id;
```

- **Explanation**: Creates a struct with total spend, order count, and last order date per custo truct fields as follows:

```
SELECT
customer_id,  customer_summary.total_spend,  customer_
summary.order_count
FROM (   SELECT     customer_id,
STRUCT(SUM(quantity * price) AS total_spend, COUNT(DISTINCT
order_id) AS order_count
) AS customer_summary
```

- `FROM `my-project.sales_dataset.sales_data` GROUP BY customer_id);`
- **Use Case**: Organize related metrics into a single column for reporting or further analysis.

- **Nested and Repeated Fields:** BigQuery supports nested and repeated fields (arrays of structs), enabling complex data models.

```
CREATE TABLE `my-project.sales_dataset.customer_orders`
(
  customer_id STRING,
  orders ARRAY<STRUCT<order_id STRING, order_date DATE, total_
price FLOAT64>>
)
AS
SELECT  customer_id, ARRAY_AGG(
    STRUCT(  order_id,  order_date, quantity * price AS total_
price )
             ) AS orders
FROM `my-project.sales_dataset.sales_data` GROUP BY customer id;
```

  - **Explanation**: Creates a table with nested orders arrays, where each order is a struct containing **order_id**, **order_date**, and **total_price**.
  - **Querying Nested Data**:

```
SELECT
  customer_id,
  order.order_id,
  order.total_price
FROM `my-project.sales_dataset.customer_orders`,
UNNEST(orders) AS order
WHERE order.total_price > 1000;
```

  - **Explanation**: Flattens the orders array and filters for high-value orders

- **JSON Functions:** BigQuery supports querying and manipulating JSON data using functions such as `JSON_EXTRACT and JSON_VALUE.`

```
SELECT
  order_id,
  JSON_VALUE(json_column, '$.status') AS order_status
FROM `my-project.sales_dataset.sales_data`
WHERE JSON_VALUE(json_column, '$.status') = 'Completed';
```

  - **Explanation**: Extracts the status field from a JSON column and filters for completed orders

    Tip: *Use **JSON_EXTRACT_SCALAR** for simpler scalar extraction.*

- **Geospatial Functions:** BigQuery's GEOGRAPHY data type and geospatial functions enable location-based analytics.

```
SELECT
  store_id,
  ST_DISTANCE(
    ST_GEOGPOINT(store_longitude, store_latitude),
    ST_GEOGPOINT(customer_longitude, customer_latitude)
  ) AS distance_meters
FROM `my-project.sales_dataset.store_locations`
CROSS JOIN `my-project.sales_dataset.customer_locations`
WHERE ST_DISTANCE(
  ST_GEOGPOINT(store_longitude, store_latitude),
  ST_GEOGPOINT(customer_longitude, customer_latitude)
) < 10000; -- Within 10 km
```

- **Explanation**: Calculates the distance between stores and customers, and filters for the ones located within 10 km
- **Functions**: **`ST_GEOGPOINT, ST_DISTANCE, ST_CONTAINS, ST_BUFFER.`**
- **Use Cases**: Retail location planning and logistics optimization

Disaster Recovery in BigQuery

Disaster recovery for BigQuery aims to restore data and query access after events such as accidental data deletion, table corruption, user errors, or regional infrastructure failures. BigQuery's serverless architecture and built-in features simplify Disaster Recovery (DR), but automation is the key to rapid and reliable recovery.

Key Disaster Recovery Features

- **Cross-Region Replication**: Multi-region datasets (for example, US and EU) automatically replicate data across zones for high availability.
- **Point-in-Time Recovery (PITR)**: BigQuery retains table snapshots for up to 7 days, which allows it to recover from user errors.
- **Automated Backups**: Export data to Cloud Storage for long-term retention and cross-region redundancy.
- **IAM and Audit Logs**: Restrict destructive actions and track changes for accountability.
- **Stored Procedures and Scheduled Queries**: Automate recovery tasks and monitoring.

Disaster Recovery Goals

- **Minimize Data Loss**: Recover data to the most recent consistent state.
- **Minimize Downtime**: Restore query access quickly during outages.

- **Automate Processes**: Reduce manual intervention to improve reliability and speed.
- **Ensure Compliance**: Meet regulatory requirements for data retention and recovery.

Automated Recovery Techniques: The following are detailed automated recovery techniques, which are accompanied by examples using the **`sales_data`** dataset.

Cross-Region Replication: BigQuery's multi-region datasets automatically replicate data across multiple zones within a region (for example, US or EU), which make it more resilient against zone-level outages.

BigQuery provides robust features for data resilience and recovery.

- **Data Replication**
    - **Cross-Region Replication**: Enables multi-region datasets (for example, US and EU) for automatic replication of data across regions
    - **Manual Backups**: Export tables to Cloud Storage in formats such as Parquet or Avro.

    ```
    bash
    CollapseWrapRun
    Copy
    bq extract my-project:sales_dataset.sales_data gs://my-bucket/backup/sales_data_*.parquet
    ```

- **Point-in-Time Recovery (PITR):** BigQuery retains table snapshots for 7 days by default, which allows for recovery from accidental deletions or overwrites.

  ```
  sql
  CollapseWrap
  Copy
  CREATE TABLE `my-project.sales_dataset.sales data restored`
  AS SELECT *
  FROM `my-project.sales_dataset.sales_data`
  FOR SYSTEM_TIME AS OF TIMESTAMP_SUB(CURRENT_TIMESTAMP(), INTERVAL 1 HOUR);
  ```

    - **Explanation**: Restores the table to its state from an hour ago

- **Failover Strategies:**
    - Use multi-region datasets to query data from replicated regions during outages.
    - Implement retry logic in client applications to handle transient failures.

Advanced Analytics with BigQuery BI Engine

BigQuery BI Engine is an in-memory analysis service that accelerates queries for BI tools and enables sub-second response times for dashboards and reports.

- **Enabling the BI Engine**
  - Reserve the BI Engine capacity in the GCP Console (for example, 1 GB or 10 GB).
  - Integrate with BI tools such as Looker Studio or Tableau via BigQuery connectors.
- **Optimizing for BI Engine**
  - **Use of Aggregated Tables**: Pre-compute results for common queries.
  - **Enable Query Acceleration**: BI Engine automatically accelerates eligible queries.
  - **Monitor Usage**: Use the BI Engine dashboard to track memory allocation and query performance.

  Example: Real-Time Dashboard Query

  ```
  sql
  CollapseWrap
  Copy
  SELECT
    DATE_TRUNC(order_date, DAY) AS order_day,
    region,
    SUM(quantity * price) AS daily_revenue
  FROM `my-project.sales_dataset.sales_data`
  WHERE order_date >= DATE_SUB(CURRENT_DATE(), INTERVAL 7 DAY)
  GROUP BY order_day, region;
  ```

  - **Explanation**: Aggregates daily revenue by region for the past week and is optimized for BI Engine's in-memory processing
  - **Use Case**: Powers a real-time sales dashboard in Looker Studio
- **Benefits of BI Engine**
  - Sub-second query latency for interactive dashboards
  - Seamless integration with the existing BigQuery workflows
  - Cost-effective for high-concurrency BI workloads

Conclusion

Through this chapter, we have gained a deep understanding of BigQuery, Google Cloud Platform's serverless data warehouse and have explored its core SQL syntax, advanced features, and optimization techniques. We analyzed its scalability and performance, appreciating the distributed architecture powered by Borg, Colossus, Jupiter, and Dremel, which allows us to efficiently handle petabyte-scale analytics. Additionally, we experimented with its serverless architecture, eliminating infrastructure management, and explored its seamless integration with services such as Cloud Storage, Dataflow, and Looker Studio, which enhances our ability to build a robust data platform. Supplementary features such as geospatial analysis, BigQuery ML, and multi-cloud capabilities via BigQuery Omni further enriched our analytical toolkit as we navigated their potential.

We have also explored stored procedures to automate complex tasks, analyzed disaster recovery strategies such as cross-region replication and point-in-time recovery to ensure data resilience, and experimented with advanced analytics using BigQuery BI Engine for sub-second dashboard performance. By delving into advanced query optimization techniques and SQL features, including window functions, arrays, and structs, we harnessed BigQuery's full capabilities to derive actionable insights. Our journey through creating datasets, leveraging materialized views, and utilizing public datasets has equipped us to tackle diverse analytical challenges and positioned BigQuery as a powerful, adaptable solution for future data-driven endeavors.

In the next chapter, we will explore event-driven architectures and Pub/Sub, including how to create topics and subscriptions for real-time data integration, as well as how to build fault-tolerant systems using Pub/Sub and Dataflow. We will learn how to develop topics and subscriptions, build fault-tolerant architectures, and integrate Pub/Sub with Dataflow for seamless data processing. With hands-on examples, this chapter demonstrates how Pub/Sub enables robust event-driven systems for modern data platforms.

CHAPTER 8

Managing Data Integration with Cloud Pub/Sub

Introduction

In this previous chapter, we discussed how BigQuery is one of Google Cloud Platform's (GCP's) most powerful tools for data analytics. This chapter introduces the core SQL syntax and features that make BigQuery a leading tool for Big Data analytics. Readers will learn to write optimized queries, leverage advanced SQL functions such as windowing, arrays, and structs, besides exploring the potential of stored procedures for automation. Additionally, it covers disaster recovery techniques and advanced analytics with BigQuery BI Engine, which will empower readers to derive actionable insights from their data.

In this chapter, we will discuss the era of real-time data, where integrating and processing data streams are critical actions. This chapter introduces Cloud Pub/Sub, GCP's messaging and event-driven service, as a solution for real-time data integration. Readers will learn how to create topics and subscriptions, build fault-tolerant architectures, and integrate Pub/Sub with Dataflow for seamless data processing. With hands-on examples, this chapter demonstrates how Pub/Sub enables robust event-driven systems for modern data platforms.

Structure

In this chapter, we will cover the following topics:

- Understanding Google Cloud Pub/Sub
- Interactions between Components
- Key Features and Benefits of the Pub/Sub Components
- Cloud Pub/Sub Architecture

- Understanding Event-Driven Architecture
- Role of Pub/Sub in Event-Driven Architectures
- Enabling Event-Driven Architectures with Pub/Sub
- Comparison with other EDA Approaches
- Integrating Pub/Sub with GCP Services
- Creating Pub/Sub in GCP Environment

Understanding Google Cloud Pub/Sub

Google Cloud Pub/Sub (Publish/Subscribe) is a **real-time messaging service** by Google Cloud Platform (GCP) that enables **asynchronous communication** between **independent services**. It acts as a **middleware for event-driven architectures** and decouples message producers (publishers) and message consumers (subscribers).

Google Cloud Pub/Sub is a fully managed messaging service and acts as a scalable and reliable middleware for event-driven architectures within the ***Google Cloud Platform (GCP)***.

As described previously, it facilitates asynchronous communication between distributed services by decoupling message publishers and subscribers through topics and subscriptions.

Its seamless integration with various **GCP *services*** makes it a cornerstone for building loosely coupled, scalable, and resilient systems.

Key Components

Google Cloud Pub/Sub's components, including Publisher, Subscriber, Topic, Message Broker, and Message/Event, form a powerful and scalable messaging system for ***event-driven architectures***. In simple terms, the publishers generate events, topics organize them, the message broker ensures reliable delivery, subscribers process the data, and the messages carry the information. Together, they enable decoupled, real-time communication across GCP services and beyond, while supporting use cases from IoT to analytics to CI/CD. By leveraging Pub/Sub's managed infrastructure and best practices, developers can build resilient, scalable systems while incurring minimal operational overhead.

Publisher: A publisher is an entity, such as an application, service, or device that generates and sends messages (events) to a Pub/Sub topic. Publishers are responsible for creating the data or events that need to be communicated to other components in the system. It creates messages containing **data payloads** and **optional metadata,** and then publishes them to a specific topic in Cloud Pub/Sub.

Essentially, it utilizes the Pub/Sub client libraries (available in languages such as ***Python, Java, Go, and Node.js***) or the REST and gRPC APIs to send messages. For security reasons, the Publishers must authenticate with GCP credentials (for example, service account keys) and have the necessary IAM permissions (**`pubsub.topics.publish`**) to publish to a topic.

Additionally, it is capable of handling high-throughput publishing, supporting millions of messages per second per topic. It is capable of publishing messages in various formats like **JSON, *text, and binary***. Messages can be arbitrary data encoded as a byte string, with optional attributes for metadata.

Subscriber: A subscriber is an entity that receives messages by subscribing to one or more Pub/Sub topics. Subscribers can be applications, services, or serverless functions that process messages for tasks like analytics, notifications, or data processing.

There are two different subscription types available and are explained as follows:

- **Pull Subscription**: The subscriber actively polls the Pub/Sub service to retrieve messages. It is suitable for controlled, low-latency processing.
- **Push Subscription**: Pub/Sub pushes messages to an HTTP endpoint (for example, Cloud Run, App Engine) via POST requests. Ideal for serverless or event-driven architectures.

From a functional perspective, the system must acknowledge (ack) messages to confirm processing, ensuring at least once delivery. Unacknowledged messages are redelivered after a timeout. It supports multiple subscribers per topic, allowing parallel processing. Subscriptions can be scaled independently of publishers. It features filtering and dead letter queues.

- **Filtering**: Subscribers can filter messages based on attributes (for example, **`event_type="user_action"`**).
- **Dead Letter Queues**: Misprocessed messages can be sent to a dead letter topic for debugging or retry.

Topic: A topic is a logical channel or category in Pub/Sub where publishers send messages and subscribers receive them. It acts as a named resource that decouples message producers from consumers. Topics are created in a GCP project (for example, projects/project-id/topics/my-topic) using client libraries, the GCP Console, or G-Cloud commands.

Ideally, publishers send messages to a topic and Pub/Sub routes them to all subscriptions associated with that topic. It supports high throughput, with no practical limit on the number of messages or subscribers. During retention, it does not store messages; the retention is handled by subscriptions (**default:** 7 days, **configurable from 10 minutes to 7 days**). It is secured by access controls such as IAM roles (for example, **`pubsub.publisher`**, **`pubsub.subscriber`**) that determine who can publish to or subscribe to a topic.

Message Broker: The message broker in Cloud Pub/Sub is the underlying system that manages the routing, storage, and delivery of messages between publishers and subscribers. Unlike self-hosted brokers such as Apache Kafka or RabbitMQ, it is a fully managed service that abstracts infrastructure complexity, unlike self-hosted brokers such as Apache Kafka or RabbitMQ. Pub/Sub is a distributed system running on Google's infrastructure and is designed for high availability and scalability. It routes messages from topics to subscriptions, while ensuring that at least once delivery. In which messages are temporarily stored in subscriptions (not topics) until acknowledged or until the retention period expires. It replicates messages across multiple regions for fault tolerance and ensures delivery even during failures.

- **Comparison with Other Brokers**
  - **Apache Kafka**: Offers more control over partitioning and consumer groups, but requires manual cluster management
  - **RabbitMQ**. Focuses on queue-based messaging with flexible routing, but lacks GCP's managed scalability
  - **Redis**: Lightweight for simple pub/sub, but not suited for durable, high-throughput messaging like Google Pub/Sub
- **Key Features**
  - **Global Availability**: Can be used to publish and consume messages from any region, with low-latency delivery
  - **At-Least-Once Delivery**: Ensures that messages are delivered to subscribers, with retries for unacknowledged messages
  - **Push and Pull Models**: Supports both push (HTTP delivery) and pull (polling) subscriptions
  - **Monitoring**: Integrates with Cloud Monitoring to provide metrics such as message backlog and delivery latency

Sample Workflow:

1. A publisher sends a message to a topic.
2. The Pub/Sub broker stores the message and routes it to all subscriptions.
3. Subscribers (pull or push) receive the message, process it, and acknowledge it, after which the broker removes it from the subscription.

Message/Event: A message (or event) is the data payload sent by a publisher to a Pub/Sub topic, often accompanied by metadata attributes. It represents an event or piece of information that needs to be communicated.

In which the primary payload is encoded as a byte string (**for example, JSON, text, binary**), with a maximum size of 10 MB.

The data is represented by key-value pairs (strings) for metadata, such as **`event_type`**, **`timestamp`**, or **`source`**. These strings are optional, but helpful for filtering or routing. For uniqueness identification, a string assigns a message ID by Pub/Sub for tracking, along with a timestamp that indicates when the message was published.

- **Delivery**: Messages are delivered to all subscriptions of a topic, with at least once semantics.
- **Ordering**: Pub/Sub supports ordered delivery if the **`ordering_key`** attribute is used, while ensuring that messages with the same key are delivered in order.
- **Retention**: Messages are retained in subscriptions until acknowledged or until the retention period (up to 7 days) expires.

Interactions between Components

Let us briefly discuss how the components interact with each other to create a robust messaging system.

- **Publisher → Topic**: Publishers send messages to a topic, which acts as a named channel.
- **Topic → Message Broker**: The Pub/Sub broker stores and routes messages from the topic to all associated subscriptions.
- **Message Broker → Subscriber**: The broker delivers messages to subscribers via pull (polling) or push (HTTP POST) mechanisms.
- **Subscriber → Message**: Subscribers process the message's data and attributes and then acknowledge the message to confirm processing.
- **Message Lifecycle**: Messages are retained in subscriptions until they are acknowledged or the retention period expires, which ensures reliable delivery.

Figure 8.1 illustrates a simple Pub/Sub workflow.

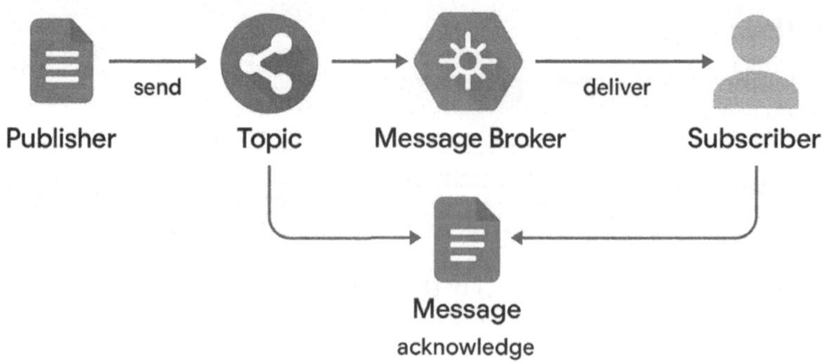

Figure 8.1: *A Simple Pub/Sub Workflow*

Example Workflow:

1. An e-commerce app (publisher) sends a "**purchase**" event to the order's topic.
2. The Pub/Sub broker routes the message to two subscriptions: analytics-sub (**pull**, for Dataflow processing) and notifications-sub (**push**, for a Cloud Run notification service).
3. The Dataflow pipeline processes the message for analytics and acknowledges it.
4. The Cloud Run service sends a confirmation email and returns a 200 status to acknowledge the message.

Key Features and Benefits of the Pub/Sub Component

The following are the key features and benefits of the Pub/Sub component:

- **Scalability**: Publishers, subscribers, and topics scale independently to handle massive workloads.
- **Decoupling**: Topics decouple publishers from subscribers, allowing independent development and scaling.
- **Reliability**: The message broker ensures at-least-once delivery with retries and persistence.
- **Flexibility**: Pub/Sub supports diverse use cases with pull/push subscriptions, filtering, and ordered delivery.
- **Integration**: Pub/Sub seamlessly connects with GCP services like Cloud Functions, Dataflow, and BigQuery.

Decoupling: In this Pub/Sub architecture, decoupling plays a significant role, and we have multiple options for these decoupling aspects. The following are the best choices.

- **Time Decoupling:** Publishers and subscribers do not need to be active simultaneously. Messages can be queued or stored until subscribers are ready.
- **Space Decoupling:** Publishers and subscribers do not need to know each other's locations or identities.
- **Control Decoupling:** Publishers do not control what happens to the messages after they are published.

Cloud Pub/Sub Architecture

***Event-Driven Architectures* (EDA)** are a powerful design paradigm for building scalable, decoupled, and resilient systems, particularly in distributed environments such as cloud platforms. Google Cloud Pub/Sub is a powerful enabler of event-driven architectures and provides a scalable, reliable, and decoupled messaging system for distributing events across various systems.

By leveraging publishers, subscribers, topics, and the message broker, Pub/Sub supports choreography over orchestration, while enabling services to respond independently to events such as "`OrderPlaced`" or "`PaymentProcessed`." Its integration with GCP services, low-latency delivery, and resilience make it ideal for building modern, cloud-native applications, from e-commerce platforms to IoT systems to real-time analytics pipelines.

Understanding Event-Driven Architecture

Event-Driven Architecture (EDA) is a design pattern where system components communicate by producing and consuming *events*. An event is a record of a significant change in state within a system, such as **"`UserSignedUp`," "`PaymentProcessed`," "`OrderPlaced`".** Instead of components directly invoking each other, they call each other via a REST API and react to events asynchronously. This enables loose coupling and independent operation.

Key Characteristics of EDA

- **Event-Centric**: Systems are built around events that represent facts about what has happened, not commands to perform actions.
- **Asynchronous Communication**: Components do not wait for immediate responses, improving responsiveness and fault tolerance.
- **Loose Coupling**: Producers and consumers of events do not need to know about each other's implementation or location, reducing dependencies.
- **Immutability**: Events are immutable records of past occurrences, which ensures a reliable audit trail.
- **Scalability**: EDA supports horizontal scaling by distributing event processing across multiple consumers.
- **Resilience**: Asynchronous processing and message persistence enable systems to tolerate failures or delays.

Figure 8.2 illustrates the key characteristics of event-driven architecture (EDA).

Figure 8.2: *Key Characteristics of EDA*

Role of Pub/Sub in Event-Driven Architectures

Google Cloud Pub/Sub is a natural fit for EDA because it provides a robust, scalable, and managed messaging system that decouples event producers from consumers. It acts as a message broker, which ensures reliable event distribution while supporting the core principles of EDA. The following are the key roles Pub/Sub plays in EDA:

Figure 8.3: *Role of Pub/Sub in Event-Driven Architectures*

- **Event Distribution**: Pub/Sub routes events from producers (publishers) to consumers (subscribers) via topics, ensuring that all interested parties receive relevant events. It supports *fan-out*, where a single event is delivered to multiple subscribers and enables parallel processing.

- **Loose Coupling**: Producers publish events to topics without knowledge of who consumes them, and subscribers listen to topics without needing to know the producers. This decoupling allows services to evolve independently, thus simplifying development and deployment.
- **Scalability**: Pub/Sub handles high event volumes (millions of messages per second) with automatic scaling, which makes it suitable for large-scale, distributed systems. Topics and subscriptions scale independently, thereby supporting dynamic workloads.
- **Resilience**: Pub/Sub's message persistence (up to 7 days by default) ensures events are not lost, even if subscribers are temporarily offline. At least one delivery with retries ensures reliable processing, even in the face of transient failures.
- **Flexibility**: New subscribers can be added to a topic without modifying the producer, enabling easy extensibility (for example, adding a new analytics service to process existing events). Pub/Sub supports both pull and push delivery models, accommodating diverse consumer types (for example, serverless functions, containerized services).

Enabling Event-Driven Architectures with Pub/Sub

Pub/Sub enables EDA by providing a structured framework for producing, distributing, and consuming events. The following is a detailed breakdown of how the components, publishers, subscribers, topics, and the message broker work together to support EDA, with practical examples:

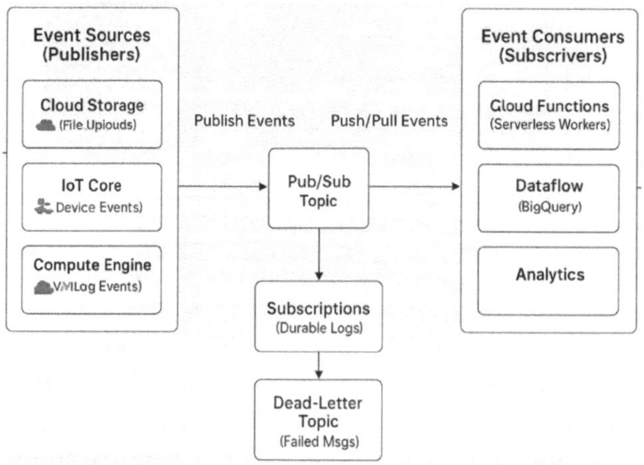

Figure 8.4: *Pub/Sub Enables Event-Driven Architectures*

How Pub/Sub Works?

Here is a step-by-step explanation of the Pub/Sub process:

1. **Publisher Creates a Message.**
    a. The publisher generates a message (for example, "`OrderPlaced`" event with data like '`{ orderId: 123, amount: 50 }`').
    b. The message is tagged with a topic (for example, "`orders`").
2. **Publisher Sends Message to Broker.**
    a. The publisher sends a message to the message broker, specifying the topic.
    b. The publisher does not know or care who receives the message.
3. **Broker Receives and Stores Message.**
    a. The message broker stores the message in the specified topic.
    b. Depending on the broker, messages may be persistent (for example, Kafka stores messages for a configurable time) or transient (for example, Redis may discard messages if no subscribers are active).
4. **Subscribers Register Interest.**
    a. Subscribers register with the broker, indicating which topics they want to listen to (for example, "`orders`").
    b. Subscriptions can be:
        - **Topic-based**: Subscribe to a specific topic (for example, "`orders`").
        - **Pattern-based**: Subscribe to topics matching a pattern (for example, "`orders.*`" for "`orders.created`" and "`orders.updated`").
        - **Content-based**: Subscribe based on message content (for example, messages where '`amount > 100`').
5. **Broker Routes Messages.**
    a. The broker matches incoming messages to subscriptions and forwards them to the appropriate subscribers.
    b. Delivery can be:
        - `Push`: The broker actively sends messages to subscribers.
        - `Pull`: Subscribers periodically request new messages from the broker.
6. **Subscribers Process Messages.**
    a. Subscribers receive messages and process them (for example, update a database, send a notification).

   b. Subscribers may acknowledge receipt (for reliable delivery) or process messages without acknowledgement (for at-most-once delivery).

7. **Error Handling and Retries**

   a. If a subscriber fails to process a message, the broker may retry delivery (depending on configuration).

   b. Dead-Letter Queues (DLQs) store unprocessable messages for later analysis.

Event Producers (Publishers)

Producers are applications, services, or devices that generate events when significant state changes occur. They publish these events to a Pub/Sub topic, which acts as a logical channel for distributing events.

How it Works

- **Event Creation**: Producers create events as messages with a data payload (for example, JSON, text) and optional attributes (for example, event type, timestamp).
- **Publishing**: Producers send messages to a specific topic through Pub/Sub client libraries or APIs.

Example: In an e-commerce system, when a customer places an order, the order service publishes an "`OrderPlaced`" event to a topic named orders.

Sample Code (Python Publisher):

```
from google.cloud import pubsub_v1
import json

project_id = "your-project-id"
topic_id = "orders"

publisher = pubsub_v1.PublisherClient()
topic_path = publisher.topic_path(project_id, topic_id)

# Event data
order_data = {
    "order_id": "12345",
    "user_id": "user789",
    "item_id": "item456",
    "timestamp": "2025-06-29T19:44:00Z"
}
data = json.dumps(order_data).encode("utf-8")
attributes = {"event_type": "OrderPlaced"}
```

```
# Publish the event
future = publisher.publish(topic_path, data, **attributes)
print(f"Published OrderPlaced event, message ID: {future.result()}")
```

Explanation: The order service publishes a JSON-encoded "**`OrderPlaced`**" event with attributes to the orders topic.

Event Consumers (Subscribers)

Consumers are services or applications that subscribe to Pub/Sub topics to react to events. Each consumer processes events independently, while performing tasks like updating databases, sending notifications, or triggering workflows.

How it Works

- **Subscriptions**: Consumers subscribe to a topic via a subscription, which can be pull (polling for messages) or push (delivering messages to an HTTP endpoint).
- **Processing**: The consumer processes the event's data and attributes and then acknowledges the message to prevent redelivery.

Example: In an e-commerce system, multiple services subscribe to the orders topic such as:

- A payment service processes payments
- An inventory service updates stock levels
- A notification service sends order confirmation e-mails

Sample Code (Pull Subscriber in Python):

```
from google.cloud import pubsub_v1
import json

project_id = "your-project-id"
subscription_id = "payment-sub"

subscriber = pubsub_v1.SubscriberClient()
subscription_path = subscriber.subscription_path(project_id,
subscription_id)

def callback(message):
    data = json.loads(message.data.decode("utf-8"))
    print(f"Processing payment for order {data['order_id']}")
    # Example: Call payment gateway API
    message.ack()  # Acknowledge the message

# Subscribe to the topic
streaming_pull_future = subscriber.subscribe(subscription_path,
callback=callback)
print(f"Listening for messages on {subscription_path}...")
```

```
try:
    streaming_pull_future.result()
except KeyboardInterrupt:
    streaming_pull_future.cancel()
```

Explanation: The payment service subscribes to the payment-sub subscription, processes "**`OrderPlaced`**" events, and acknowledges them.

Example (Push Subscriber to Cloud Run):

```
from flask import Flask, request

app = Flask(__name__)

@app.route("/notify", methods=["POST"])
def notify():
    envelope = request.get_json()
    message = envelope["message"]
    data = json.loads(message["data"].decode("utf-8"))
    print(f"Sending email for order {data['order_id']}")
    # Example: Send email via SMTP or notification service
    return ("Notification sent", 200)  # Acknowledge with 2xx status
```

Explanation: A Cloud Run service receives push messages from a subscription, sends an e-mail, and acknowledges the message with an HTTP 200 response.

Broker Mediates Communication

The Pub/Sub message broker is the core infrastructure that manages event routing, storage, and delivery. It ensures that events are reliably delivered from producers to consumers, even in distributed or failure-prone environments.

How it Works

- **Routing**: The broker routes messages from a topic to all associated subscriptions, while supporting fan-out to multiple subscribers.
- **Persistence**: Messages are stored in subscriptions (not topics) for up to 7 days (configurable), which ensures delivery even if subscribers are temporarily unavailable.
- **Delivery Semantics**: Pub/Sub guarantees *at-least-once* delivery, with retries for unacknowledged messages.
- **Ordering**: Supports ordered delivery using an **`ordering_key`** to ensure messages with the same key are processed in order.
- **Load Balancing**: Distributes messages across multiple subscriber instances for parallel processing.

Example Workflow:

- The order topic receives an "**`OrderPlaced`**" event.
- The broker delivers the event to three subscriptions: payment-sub, inventory-sub, and notification-sub.
- If the notification service is temporarily down, the broker retains the message until it is back online or the retention period expires.

Benefits:

- Ensures reliable delivery across distributed systems
- Supports high-throughput event processing with low latency
- Handles temporary subscriber failures with message persistence

Choreography over Orchestration

EDA's Pub/Sub enables *choreography*, where services react to events independently, rather than in a synchronous manner. Then *there is orchestration*, where a central controller dictates the sequence of actions. This decentralized approach enhances flexibility and reduces complexity.

How it Works

- **Orchestration Example**: A central controller (for example, a workflow engine) explicitly calls the payment service, then the inventory service and then the notification service after an order is placed. This creates tight coupling and a single point of failure.
- **Choreography with Pub/Sub**:
  - The order service publishes an "**`OrderPlaced`**" event to the orders topic.
  - The payment, inventory, and notification services subscribe to the topic and react independently, while processing the event in parallel.
  - No central controller is required, each service determines how to handle the event based on its own logic.

Example Workflow (Choreography):

- **Event**: An "**`OrderPlaced`**" event is published to the orders topic.
- **Reactions**:
  - The payment service processes the payment and publishes a "**`PaymentProcessed`**" event to the payments topic.
  - The inventory service updates stock levels and publishes an "**`InventoryUpdated`**" event.
  - The notification service sends an email and logs the action.

- **Outcome**: Each service operates independently and reacts to events without direct coordination, while improving scalability and resilience.

Benefits of Choreography:

- **Decoupling**: Services do not depend on each other's APIs or availability.
- **Flexibility**: New services can subscribe to existing events without modifying producers.
- **Resilience**: Failures in one service do not block others, as events are processed asynchronously.

Example Setup: Create a topic and subscriptions for choreography such as:

```
# Create the orders topic
gcloud pubsub topics create orders

# Create subscriptions for different services
gcloud pubsub subscriptions create payment-sub --topic=orders
gcloud pubsub subscriptions create inventory-sub --topic=orders
gcloud pubsub subscriptions create notification-sub --topic=orders
--push-endpoint=https://notification-service.example.com/notify
```

Explanation: The orders topic is created, and three subscriptions are set up: two pull subscriptions (payment-sub, inventory-sub) and one push subscription (notification-sub) for a Cloud Run service.

Benefits of Pub/Sub in EDA

- **Scalability**: Pub/Sub handles massive event volumes, enabling systems to scale with demand.
- **Decoupling**: Producers and consumers are independent, which simplifies development and deployment.
- **Resilience**: Message persistence and retries ensure that events are processed even during failures.
- **Flexibility**: New consumers can subscribe to the existing topics, supporting system evolution.
- **Integration**: Native integration with GCP services (for example, Cloud Functions, Dataflow, BigQuery) streamlines EDA implementation.

Best Practices for Pub/Sub in EDA

- **Event Design**:
  - Use clear, domain-specific event names (for example, "`OrderPlaced`" instead of "`Event1`").

  - Include metadata in the attributes (for example, `event_type`, `timestamp`) for filtering and context.
  - Keep payloads small (<10 MB) and encode complex data as JSON or `Protobuf`.
- **Topic and Subscription Management**:
  - Create one topic per event type or domain (for example, orders, payments).
  - Use separate subscriptions for each consumer to isolate processing logic.
  - Configure retention periods (for example, 1 day for transient events, 7 days for critical ones).
- **Error Handling**:
  - Use dead letter topics for messages that fail processing after retries.
  - Implement exponential backoff for transient errors in subscribers.
- **Monitoring and Observability**:
  - Use Cloud Monitoring to track subscription backlogs, delivery latency, and error rates.
  - Log message IDs and attributes for debugging and auditing.
- **Security**:
  - Apply IAM roles (`pubsub.publisher`, `pubsub.subscriber`) to restrict access.
  - Enable encryption for sensitive event data.

Challenges and Considerations

- **Message Ordering**: Pub/Sub does not guarantee message ordering unless an ordering key is used, which may introduce latency. Use ordered delivery only when necessary.
- **Duplicate Messages**: At-least-once delivery may result in duplicates. Implement idempotent processing in subscribers (for example, by checking the `message_id`).
- **Cost Management**: High message volumes or long retention periods can increase costs. Optimize message sizes and clean up unused topics/subscriptions.
- **Latency**: While Pub/Sub is low-latency, push subscriptions may introduce slight delays due to HTTP overhead. Use pull subscriptions for latency-sensitive workloads.

Comparison with Other EDA Approaches

Pub/Sub excels in managed, cloud-native EDA with tight GCP integration, while Kafka offers more control for complex streaming pipelines, and RabbitMQ suits simpler, queue-based workflows. *Table* 8.1 provides a comparison between Pub/Sub (GCP), Kafka, and RabbitMQ.

Approach	Pub/Sub (GCP)	Kafka	RabbitMQ
Management	Fully managed	Self-managed	Self-managed
Scalability	Global, auto-scaling	High, manual scaling	Moderate
Delivery Semantics	At-least-once	At-least-once, exactly-once	At-least-once
GCP Integration	Native, seamless	Limited	Limited
EDA Fit	Ideal for cloud-native EDA	Suited for custom pipelines	Best for queue-based systems

Table 8.1: *Comparison between Pub/Sub (GCP), Kafka, and RabbitMQ*

Integrating Pub/Sub with GCP Services

Google Cloud Pub/Sub offers powerful integration capabilities that make it a central component in building scalable, event-driven systems. It supports both **push and pull delivery** models, which allows messages to be delivered either through HTTP endpoints or through client-side polling.

Pub/Sub integrates seamlessly with **serverless services**, such as Cloud Functions and Cloud Run, which automatically trigger backend logic in response to published events. It also connects with **stream processing tools** such as Dataflow and Apache Beam, which makes it ideal for real-time ETL and analytics workloads. Pub/Sub can **orchestrate workflows** by triggering Cloud Workflows or Composer DAGs, while enabling automated, event-driven processing pipelines. Failed messages are handled efficiently through **dead-letter topics**, which capture undelivered events for further analysis or retry mechanisms.

Furthermore, Pub/Sub is tightly integrated with **Cloud Logging and Monitoring** and offers observability into tracking message flow, latency, and delivery success. Its **high scalability** ensures reliable performance even in globally distributed, high-throughput systems, which make it suitable for a wide range of cloud-native applications.

Common Integration Patterns

Pub/Sub enables the following integration patterns across GCP services:

- **Fan-Out:** One Pub/Sub message triggers multiple services (for example, Cloud Functions, BigQuery, Cloud Storage).
- **Data Streaming:** Real-time data from Pub/Sub to BigQuery or Dataflow for analytics.
- **Event-Driven Workflows:** Pub/Sub triggers serverless workflows in Cloud Functions, Cloud Run, or Cloud Composer.
- **Enterprise Event Bus:** Share events across services and third-party systems via Application Integration.
- **Change Data Capture:** Publish database or storage events to Pub/Sub for replication or processing.
- **Load Balancing:** Distribute tasks across Compute Engine or GKE instances.

Here is a detailed breakdown of how Pub/Sub works with major GCP services, including integration mechanisms, examples, and use cases. *Figure* 8.5 illustrates the potential Pub/Sub integration with other GCP services.

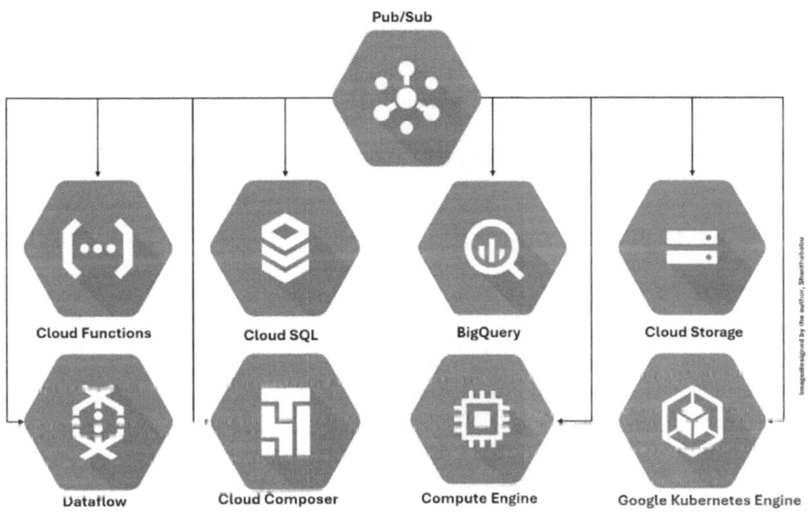

Figure 8.5: *Pub/Sub Integrates with GCP Services*

Cloud Functions (Serverless Compute)

- **How It Works:**
    - Pub/Sub triggers Cloud Functions by sending messages to a topic, which invokes a function via a push subscription (HTTP endpoint).

- Developers write event-driven functions to process Pub/Sub messages (for example, in Node.js, Python).
- **Example**: A message published to a "`user-signup`" topic triggers a Cloud Function to send a welcome email.

- **Integration Mechanism**:
  - Create a Pub/Sub topic and subscription.
  - Deploy a Cloud Function with a Pub/Sub trigger and specify the topic.
  - Pub/Sub pushes messages to the function's HTTP endpoint.
- **Use Case**
  - **Real-Time Notifications**: When a user uploads a file to Cloud Storage, Pub/Sub publishes an event and triggers a Cloud Function to notify users via email or SMS.
  - **Data Transformation**: A Cloud Function processes raw IoT data from Pub/Sub and formats it for storage in BigQuery.

Cloud Run (Containerized Serverless)

- **How It Works**:
  - Pub/Sub pushes messages to Cloud Run services via HTTP endpoints (push subscriptions).
  - Cloud Run scales containers automatically to handle message volume.
  - Example: A microservice on Cloud Run subscribes to a "`order-created`" topic to process orders.
- **Integration Mechanism**:
  - Deploy a containerized application on Cloud Run.
  - Create a Pub/Sub subscription with a push endpoint pointing to the Cloud Run service URL.
  - Authenticate Pub/Sub to invoke Cloud Run using IAM.
- **Use Case:**
  - **Microservices Communication**: A payment service on Cloud Run processes payment events published to a Pub/Sub topic.
  - **Event-Driven APIs**: Cloud Run handles webhook notifications from Pub/Sub for third-party integrations.

BigQuery (Data Warehouse)

- **How It Works**:
  - Pub/Sub streams data to BigQuery for real-time analytics using BigQuery subscriptions or Dataflow pipelines.
  - **BigQuery Subscriptions**: A special subscription type that writes messages directly to a BigQuery table, while mapping Pub/Sub schemas (for example, Avro, Protocol Buffers) to table schemas.
  - **Dataflow Integration**: Dataflow reads from Pub/Sub, transforms data and writes to BigQuery.
  - **Example**: IoT sensor data published to Pub/Sub is streamed to BigQuery for analysis.
- **Integration Mechanism**:
  - For BigQuery subscriptions:
    a. Create a Pub/Sub topic with a schema.
    b. Set up a BigQuery subscription to write to a specified table.
  - For Dataflow:
    a. Use a Dataflow template to read from Pub/Sub and write to BigQuery.
    b. **Example**: The "`Pub/Sub to BigQuery`" Dataflow template.
- **Use Case:**
  - **Real-Time Analytics**: Stream user activity logs from Pub/Sub to BigQuery for dashboards.
  - **Log Aggregation**: Centralize application logs in BigQuery for querying and monitoring.

Cloud Storage (Object Storage)

- **How It Works**:
  - Pub/Sub integrates with Cloud Storage to trigger events when objects are created, updated, or deleted.
  - Pub/Sub notifications from Cloud Storage publish events to a topic, which subscribers (for example, Cloud Functions, Dataflow) process.
  - Pub/Sub can also stream data to Cloud Storage using Dataflow or Cloud Storage subscriptions.

- **Integration Mechanism**:
  - Enable Pub/Sub notifications for a Cloud Storage bucket by specifying a topic.
  - Create a subscription to process events (for example, trigger a Cloud Function).
  - To write to Cloud Storage, use a Dataflow pipeline or Cloud Storage subscription to batch messages into files.
- **Use Case:**
  - **File Processing**: When a file is uploaded to Cloud Storage, Pub/Sub notifies a Cloud Function to process it (for example, image resizing).
  - **Data Archiving**: Stream processed Pub/Sub messages to Cloud Storage for long-term storage.

Dataflow (Stream/Batch Processing)

- **How It Works**:
  - Dataflow reads messages from Pub/Sub topics, processes them (for example, transformations, aggregations), and writes to sinks like BigQuery, Cloud Storage, or another Pub/Sub topic.
  - Dataflow supports windowing and late data handling for streaming data.
  - **Example**: Aggregate real-time sales data from Pub/Sub and write to BigQuery.
- **Integration Mechanism**:
  - Use a Dataflow template (for example, "`Pub/Sub to BigQuery`") or write a custom pipeline using the Apache Beam SDK.
  - Configure Dataflow to read from a Pub/Sub subscription and write to a sink.
- **Use Case:**
  - **Stream Analytics**: Process IoT telemetry data from Pub/Sub to compute real-time metrics
  - **ETL Pipelines**: Transform and enrich Pub/Sub messages before loading into a data warehouse

Cloud Composer (Workflow Orchestration)

- **How It Works**:
  - Cloud Composer (built on Apache Airflow) uses Pub/Sub triggers to initiate workflows.
  - Pub/Sub messages can signal the start of a Directed Acyclic Graph (DAG) in Cloud Composer.
  - **Example**: A "`data-ready`" message in Pub/Sub triggers a Cloud Composer workflow to process data.
- **Integration Mechanism**:
  - Configure a Pub/Sub sensor in a Cloud Composer DAG to listen for messages.
  - Use Pub/Sub to publish events that trigger workflows.
- **Use Case:**
  - **Big Data Orchestration**: Trigger ETL jobs when new data arrives in Cloud Storage.
  - **Scheduled Pipelines**: Use Pub/Sub to coordinate complex workflows across GCP services.

Compute Engine (Virtual Machines):

- **How It Works**:
  - Pub/Sub distributes messages to Compute Engine instances for processing, enabling load balancing and fault tolerance.
  - Instances can pull messages from subscriptions or receive them via push endpoints.
  - Example: A Compute Engine cluster processes batch jobs triggered by Pub/Sub messages.
- **Integration Mechanism**:
  - Deploy a subscriber application on Compute Engine.
  - Configure a Pub/Sub subscription (pull or push) to deliver messages to the instances.
- **Use Case**
  - **Task Distribution**: Distribute image processing tasks across Compute Engine instances.
  - **Load Balancing**: Automatically redistribute load if an instance fails.

Google Kubernetes Engine (GKE)

- **How It Works**:
  - Pub/Sub integrates with GKE by pushing messages to containerized applications or allowing them to pull messages.
  - GKE scales pods to handle message volume.
  - Example: A microservice on GKE subscribes to a Pub/Sub topic to process orders.
- **Integration Mechanism**:
  - Deploy a containerized application on GKE with an HTTP endpoint or pull client.
  - Configure a Pub/Sub subscription to deliver messages to GKE pods.
- **Use Case:**
  - **Microservices**: Enable asynchronous communication between GKE-hosted services.
  - **Event-Driven Workloads**: Process real-time events in a Kubernetes environment.

Cloud SQL and Other Databases

- **How It Works**:
  - Pub/Sub messages can trigger updates to Cloud SQL, Spanner, or other databases through intermediaries such as Cloud Functions or Dataflow.
  - Example: A "user-updated" event in Pub/Sub triggers a Cloud Function to update a Cloud SQL table.
- **Integration Mechanism**:
  - Use Cloud Functions, Cloud Run, or Dataflow to process Pub/Sub messages and write to databases.
  - No direct Pub/Sub-to-database connector exists. Therefore, an intermediate service is required.
- **Use Case**:
  - **Database Updates**: Sync user data across systems in real-time.
  - **Change Data Capture**: Replicate database changes using Pub/Sub events.

Gmail API

- **How It Works**:
  - Pub/Sub integrates with the Gmail API to publish real-time notifications for email events (for example, new emails, label changes).
  - Gmail pushes notifications to a Pub/Sub topic, which subscribers can then process.
  - Example: A new email triggers a Pub/Sub message, processed by a Cloud Function to log metadata.
- **Integration Mechanism**:
  - Configure Gmail to publish notifications to a Pub/Sub topic using the Gmail API.
  - Create a subscription to process email events.
- **Use Case:**
  - **Email Automation**: Trigger workflows based on incoming emails.
  - **Real-Time Monitoring**: Track email activity for compliance or analytics.

Cloud Monitoring and Logging

- **How It Works**:
  - Pub/Sub integrates with Cloud Monitoring to monitor message throughput, latency, and errors.
  - Logs from Pub/Sub (for example, message delivery failures) are sent to Cloud Logging for analysis.
  - **Example**: Monitor Pub/Sub subscription backlog size and alert on anomalies.
- **Integration Mechanism**:
  - Enable Cloud Monitoring for Pub/Sub metrics (for example, `pubsub.googleapis.com/subscription/num_undelivered_messages`).
  - Route Pub/Sub logs to Cloud Logging for debugging.
- **Use Case:**
  - **Operational Insights**: Track Pub/Sub performance and troubleshoot issues.
  - **Alerting**: Set up alerts for high latency or growth in the dead-letter queue.

Creating Pub/Sub in GCP Environment

Let us demonstrate how we can create a Pub/Sub in the GCP Environment.

Step 1: Logging into GCP and searching for pub/sub, as shown in *Figure* 8.6:

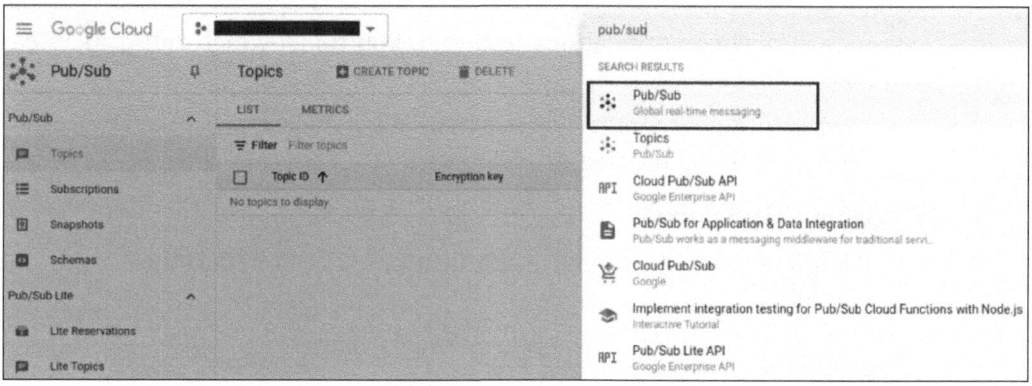

Figure 8.6: *Pub/Sub Component Search in a GCP Environment*

Step 2: After selecting Pub/Sub, the system will direct you to the screen shown in *Figure* 8.7. Click the highlighted "`Create topic`".

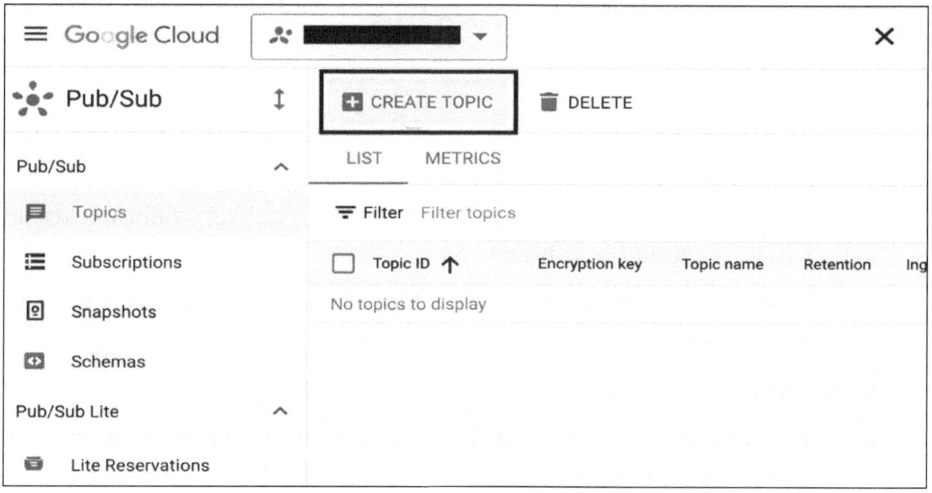

Figure 8.7: *Pub/Sub Component Environment in GCP*

Step 3: After clicking the highlighted "`Create topic`", the system will direct you to the screen shown in *Figure* 8.8. There, you have to configure the Topic for the following parameters:

- **Topic ID**: TestTopic is the name entered for the new Pub/Sub topic.
- **Topic Name (Auto-Generated):** projects/production-1800/topics/xyz

Optional Configuration Checkboxes

- **Add a Default Subscription:** Automatically creates a pull subscription tied to the topic
- **Use a Schema:** Enables schema validation for messages published to the topic (for example, Avro, Protocol Buffers)
- **Enable Ingestion:** Activates direct ingestion from external systems to Pub/Sub (for example, IoT Core or other sources)
- **Enable Message Retention:** Retains acknowledged messages beyond the default limit (useful for replaying messages)
- **Exporting Message Data to BigQuery:** Automatically routes published messages to a specified BigQuery table
- **Backup Message Data to Cloud Storage:** Creates a backup of message payloads to a Cloud Storage bucket

Encryption Options

- **Google-Managed Encryption Key (selected):** Google automatically manages and rotates the encryption keys.
- **Cloud KMS Key:** Allows customers to use their own keys from Cloud Key Management Service (KMS) for increased control

Once all the required fields are configured, click "`Create`".

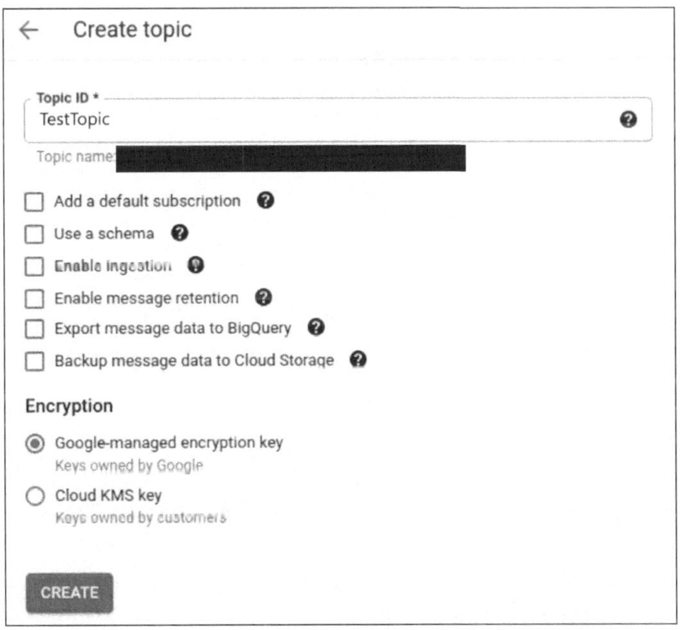

***Figure 8.8**: Pub/Sub Component – Topic Configuration*

Step 4: After configuring the system, you will be directed to the topic screen, as shown in *Figure* 8.9. To create a subscription, click "**`Subscriptions`**" in the left menu.

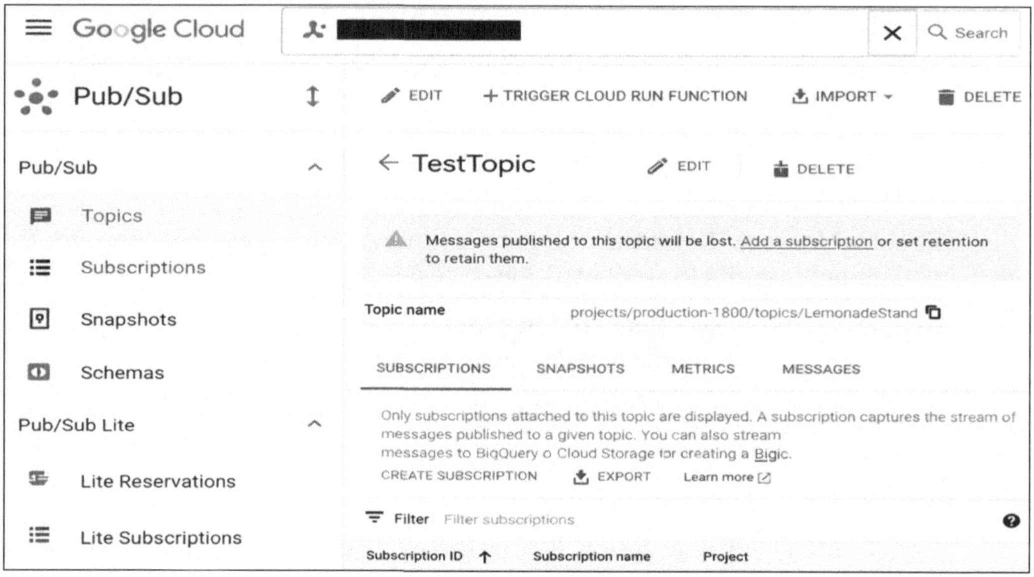

***Figure 8.9**: Pub/Sub Component – Topic Page*

Step 5: Once you click "**`Subscriptions`**" in the left menu, the system will direct you to the Subscriptions screen shown in *Figure* 8.10. There, you can create as many subscriptions as you want. Click "**`Create Subscriptions`**" menu at the top.

***Figure 8.10**: Pub/Sub Component – Subscription Page*

Step 6: Once you click **`Create Subscriptions`** menu at the top, the system will take you to the **`Create Subscriptions`** page as shown in *Figure* 8.11, and you will need to configure the details as follows:

- **Subscription ID:** A unique name to identify this subscription (required).
- **Select a Cloud Pub/Sub topic:** You must link this subscription to a **specific topic** from which it will receive messages.

Delivery Type Options: This section determines **how messages are delivered** to the subscriber.

- **Pull (Selected)**
    - The subscriber **pulls messages manually** from the subscription using an API.
    - Good for custom or batch processing.
- **Push**
    - Pub/Sub **automatically pushes messages** to an endpoint you provide (for example, a webhook).
    - Requires a secure HTTPS endpoint
- **Write to BigQuery**
    - A **push variant**
    - Messages are automatically delivered and stored in a **BigQuery table**.
- **Write to Cloud Storage**
    - Another **push variant**
    - Publishes message payloads directly into a **Cloud Storage bucket**

Message Retention Duration

- Retain unacknowledged messages for a specified time.
- You can set:
    - **Days:** Up to 31
    - **Hours/Minutes:** Fine-grained control
- **Default shown:** 7 days
- **Optional:** Retain acknowledged messages.
    - Useful if you want to reprocess messages even after they have been consumed

Expiration Period

- Subscription **expires after a number of days of inactivity**, meaning:
    - No messages are being pulled or pushed.
    - No open connections
- Max: **365 days**, Default: **31 days**

There are other configurations, but you can leave it as the default. Then click "`Create`".

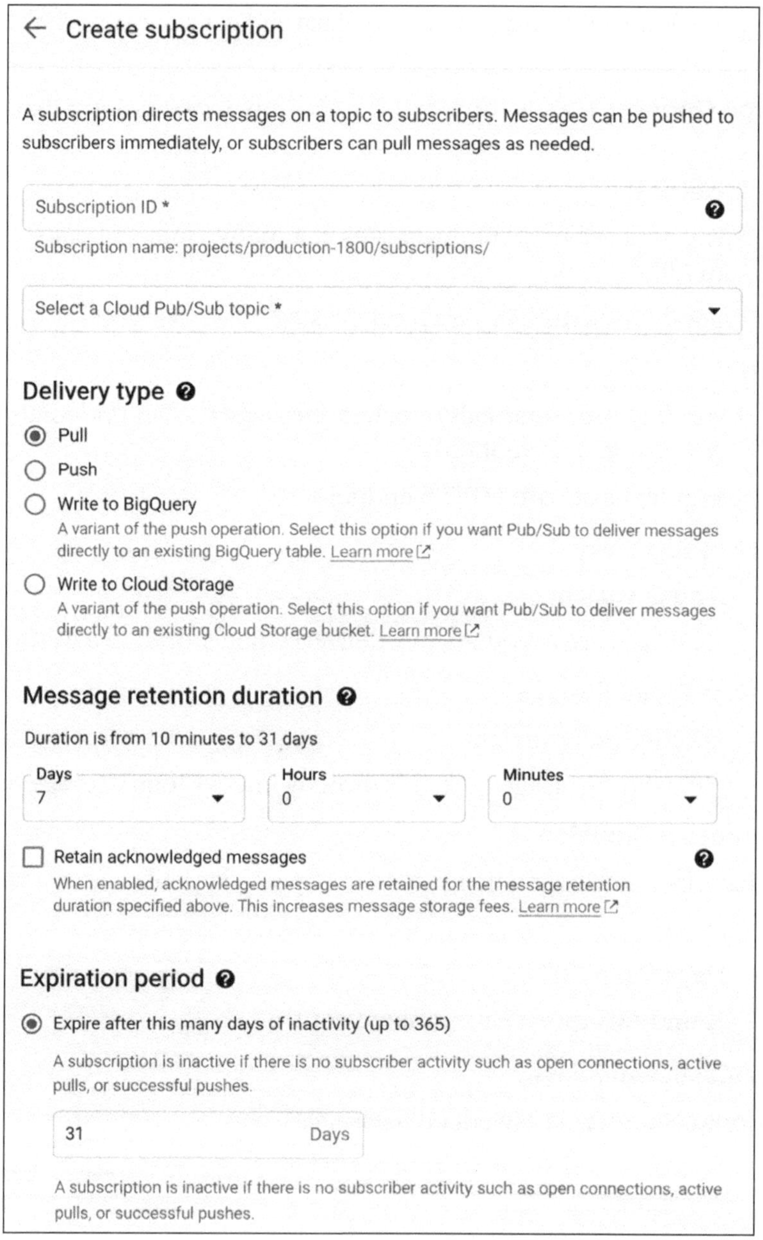

Figure 8.11: *Pub/Sub Component – Subscription Configuration*

All set, now you can see the overall status of the Pub/Sub setup as shown in *Figure 8.12*.

Figure 8.12: *Pub/Sub Component – Setup*

Step 7: Click Topics in the left menu, and you will see the list of topic(s) as shown in *Figure 8.13*.

Figure 8.13: *Pub/Sub Component – Topic – Collection(s)*

Step 8: Click "**`Messages`**" on the Topic page, and you will be directed to the Publish message screen, as shown in *Figure* 8.14. **`Message→Publish Message→Add message`** and click "**`Publish`**".

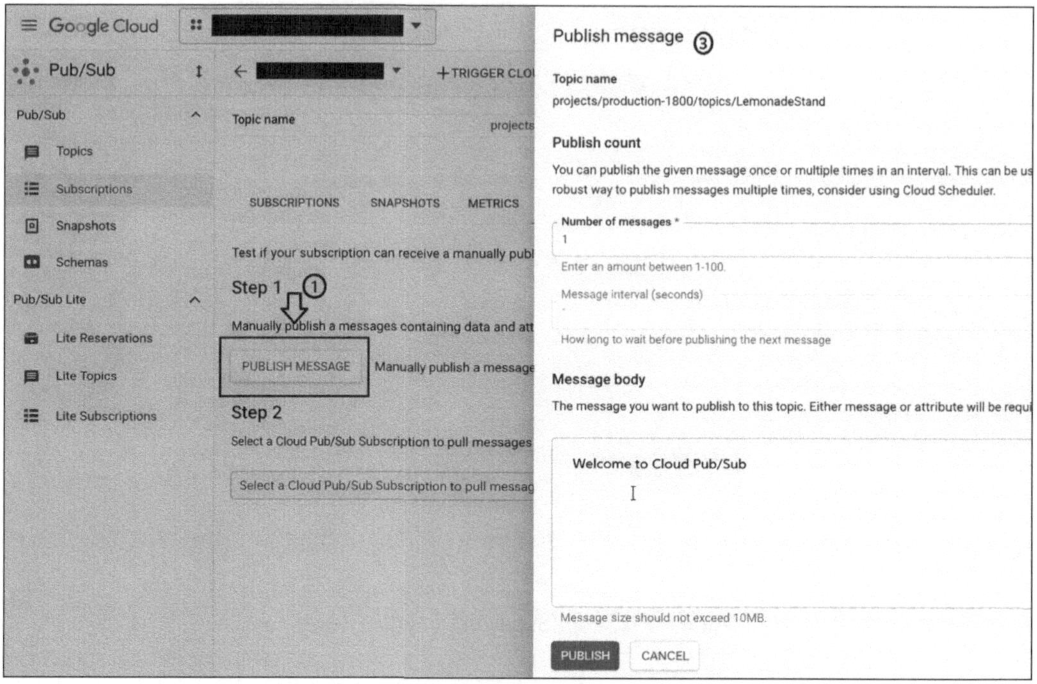

Figure 8.14: *Pub/Sub Component – Topic – Publish Message*

Step 9: Select the Subscription from the left menu and you will get the list of subscriptions as shown in *Figure* 8.15.

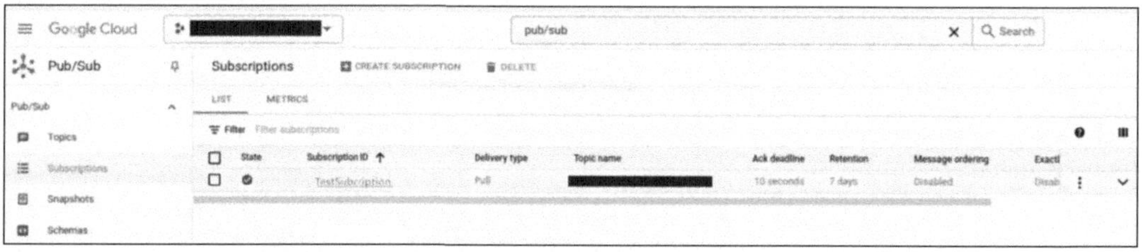

Figure 8.15: *Pub/Sub Component – Subscription List*

Step 10: When you click **`TestSubscription`**, the system will direct you to the following screen. To retrieve the message, click **"`PULL`"** if the message has not arrived yet.

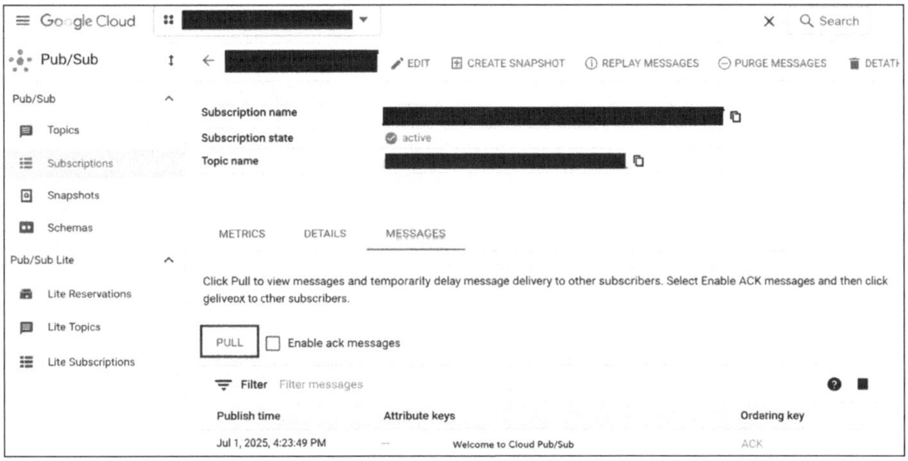

Figure 8.16: *Pub/Sub Component – Subscription – Message Pull*

You can implement the remaining delivery types similarly.

Conclusion

In this chapter, we explored the foundational concepts and architecture of Google Cloud Pub/Sub, which is a powerful messaging system for real-time, event-driven data integration. We understood how Pub/Sub enables asynchronous communication between distributed services by decoupling publishers and subscribers, which allows for scalable, resilient, and flexible system design.

We experimented with creating topics and subscriptions, configuring delivery types, and integrating Pub/Sub with a wide range of GCP services such as Cloud Functions, Cloud Run, Dataflow, and BigQuery. Through hands-on examples and practical workflows, we learned how to build fault-tolerant systems, handle message delivery and retries, and manage common challenges such as message ordering and duplication.

Additionally, we explored how Pub/Sub supports modern event-driven architectures by enabling choreography over orchestration, allowing services to independently respond to events such as "`OrderPlaced`" or "`PaymentProcessed`."

We understood the key benefits such as time, space, and control decoupling, as well as experimented with real-world integration patterns like fan-out, streaming, and automation workflows.

By the end of this chapter, you will have acquired the knowledge and practical skills that are necessary to design and implement scalable, real-time data pipelines using Cloud Pub/Sub. Throughout the chapter, the latter has been positioned as a core enabler for building intelligent, cloud-native applications.

In the next chapter, we will introduce BigQuery Machine Learning (BQML) and explain its capabilities and advantages for training and deploying models directly within BigQuery.

CHAPTER 9

BigQuery Machine Learning

Introduction

In the previous chapter, we discussed how integrating and processing data streams is critical in the ear of real-time data. This chapter introduces Cloud Pub/Sub, which is GCP's messaging and event-driven service, as a solution for real-time data integration. Readers will learn how to create topics and subscriptions, build fault-tolerant architectures, and integrate Pub/Sub with Dataflow for seamless data processing. With hands-on examples, this chapter demonstrates how Pub/Sub enables the creation of robust event-driven systems for modern data platforms.

This chapter introduces the foundational concepts of machine learning (ML) and demonstrates how BigQuery ML (BQML) leverages these capabilities within Google Cloud's data warehouse, while utilizing familiar SQL syntax. We will explore BQML's support for various models, supervised, unsupervised, time-series, and imported TensorFlow models, as well as their practical applications across domains such as retail, finance, healthcare, and marketing. We will also experiment with BQML's SQL-based interface. We will create, train, evaluate, and utilize prediction models, while benefiting from built-in features such as automatic pre-processing, hyperparameter tuning, and performance evaluation. Hands-on walkthroughs and visualizations will be used to demonstrate various metrics.

In this journey, we will explore and understand how BQML democratizes machine learning (ML) to empower data professionals to build scalable, production-ready models efficiently within the BigQuery ecosystem.

Structure

In this chapter, we will cover the following topics:

- Introduction to BigQuery ML
- Overview of Machine Learning
- Types of Machine Learning Models in BQML
- Significance of BQML within BigQuery
- Working Principle of BQML
- BQML Architecture
- Practical Use Cases of BQML
- Step-by-Step Guide to Creating and Training Models in BQML
- Model Creation and Training in the BigQuery ML Environment

Introduction to BigQuery ML

BigQuery ML (BQML) is a feature of Google Cloud's BigQuery that enables users to create, train, evaluate, and deploy Machine Learning (ML) models directly within BigQuery using standard SQL queries.

By integrating ML capabilities into **BigQuery's** data warehouse, BQML eliminates the need to export data to external ML platforms or write complex code in languages such as Python, R, or use IDEs such as Azure Databricks or AWS's SageMaker. It is designed to make machine learning accessible to data analysts, data scientists, and developers, leveraging BigQuery's serverless infrastructure for scalability and performance.

Overview of Machine Learning

Let us understand the machine learning basics before we get into the BQML.

Machine Learning (ML) is a branch of Artificial Intelligence (AI) that focuses on developing algorithms and models that enable systems to learn from data and improve over time without being explicitly programmed. ML models identify patterns in historical data and use these patterns to make predictions or decisions on new, unseen data.

Key Concepts in ML

- **Features**: The input variables (columns) used to train a model (for example, customer age, purchase history)
- **Labels**: The output variable the model aims to predict (for example, customer churn: yes/no)

- **Training**: The process of feeding data to an ML algorithm to learn patterns
- **Inference/Prediction**: Using a trained model to make predictions on new data
- **Evaluation**: Assessing model performance using metrics such as accuracy, precision, recall, or Mean Squared Error (MSE)

Types of Machine Learning

ML is broadly categorized into three types, two of which are supported by BQML. These are explained as follows:

- **Supervised Learning**: Utilizes labeled datasets (input-output pairs) to train models that predict an output based on specific input features
    - **Subtypes**
        - **Regression**: Predicts continuous values (for example, house prices, sales revenue)
        - **Classification**: Predicts discrete categories (for example, spam versus non-spam and churn versus no-churn)
    - **BQML Support**: Linear regression, logistic regression, Deep Neural Networks (DNNs), and XGBoost
    - **Use Cases**: Sales forecasting, risk assessment, and customer churn prediction
- **Unsupervised Learning**: Works with unlabeled data to discover hidden patterns or groupings
    - **Subtypes**
        - **Clustering**: Groups similar data points (for example, customer segmentation)
        - **Dimensionality Reduction**: Reduces the number of features while preserving information (for example, principal component analysis)
    - **BQML Support**: K-means clustering and matrix factorization
    - **Use Cases**: Market segmentation, recommendation systems and anomaly detection
- **Reinforcement Learning**: An agent learns to make decisions by maximizing a reward through trial and error in an environment.
    - **BQML Support**: Not currently supported
    - **Use Cases**: Robotics, game AI, and resource optimization

Types of Machine Learning Models in BQML

BigQuery ML (BQML) is a Google Cloud feature that enables users to create, train, and deploy ML models directly within BigQuery via SQL queries. It simplifies the process by eliminating the need for separate data pipelines or external tools and allows data analysts and engineers to build models with familiar SQL syntax.

BigQuery ML provides a versatile platform for building and deploying ML models using SQL, supporting a range of algorithms from simple linear models to advanced techniques such as DNNs and AutoML. Each model type is tailored to specific tasks (regression, classification, clustering, recommendation, or forecasting) and integrates seamlessly with BigQuery's data processing capabilities.

Key advantages include:

- A simplified workflow with SQL-based syntax
- Automatic preprocessing and hyperparameter tuning
- Scalability for large datasets
- Integration with Google Cloud services such as AutoML and TensorFlow

The following is an explanation of the listed machine learning models and techniques supported by BigQuery ML, which focuses on their functionality, use cases, and implementation in BQML.

BQML supports a wide range of ML models, each tailored to specific tasks. The following is a detailed breakdown of the models available:

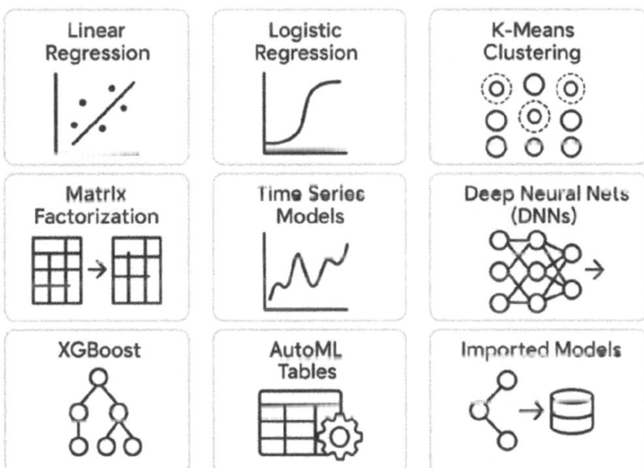

Figure 9.1: *Types of Machine Learning Models in BQML*

Linear Regression

This model is a supervised learning algorithm used for predicting a continuous numeric output (***dependent variable***) based on one or more input features (***independent variables***). It assumes a linear relationship between inputs and the output as well as models it as a straight line.

BigQuery ML Implementation

- **Model Type**: **`LINEAR_REG`**
- **Syntax:** Use **`CREATE MODEL`** with **`MODEL_TYPE = 'LINEAR_REG'`** to train the model on a dataset with labeled numeric outcomes.
- **Features:**
  - Automatically handles feature preprocessing (for example, normalization)
  - Supports L1/L2 regularization to prevent overfitting
  - Outputs coefficients and intercept for interpretability
- **Evaluation:** Use **`ML.EVALUATE`** to compute metrics such as Mean Squared Error (MSE) or R^2.
- **Prediction:** Use **`ML.PREDICT`** to generate predictions on new data.

Sample code

```
CREATE MODEL `project.dataset.model_name`
OPTIONS(MODEL_TYPE='LINEAR_REG', INPUT_LABEL_COLS=['target_column'])
AS
SELECT feature1, feature2, target_column
FROM `project.dataset.table`;
```

Use Case: Predicting numerical values such as forecasting sales, house prices, or customer lifetime value and forecasting sales, predicting website traffic, and estimating delivery times

Logistic Regression

Logistic regression is a supervised learning algorithm for binary or multiclass classification. It predicts the probability of a categorical outcome (***for example, 0 or 1***) based on input features, through a logistic function to map outputs to probabilities.

BigQuery ML Implementation

- **Model Type: `LOGISTIC_REG`** (for binary) or **`MULTICLASS_LOGISTIC_REG`** (for multiclass)

Sample Code

```
CREATE MODEL `project.dataset.model_name`
OPTIONS(MODEL_TYPE='LOGISTIC_REG', INPUT_LABEL_COLS=['label'])
AS SELECT feature1, feature2, label FROM `project.dataset.table`;
```

- **Features**
    - Supports automatic feature preprocessing (for example, one-hot encoding for categorical variables)
    - Includes regularization options (L1/L2) to improve generalization
    - Outputs probabilities for each class
- **Evaluation:** Use **`ML.EVALUATE`** for metrics such as accuracy, precision, recall, and AUC.
- **Prediction:** Use **`ML.PREDICT`** to get predicted class labels and probabilities.

Use Case: Classifying customer churn, spam detection, or disease diagnosis (for example, yes/no outcomes); churn prediction, fraud detection, and customer sentiment analysis

K-Means Clustering

K-means clustering is an unsupervised learning algorithm that partitions data into k clusters based on the similarity of features. It minimizes the variance within clusters by iteratively assigning data points to the nearest cluster centroid and grouping customers into segments based on purchasing behavior.

BigQuery ML Implementation

- Model Type: **`KMEANS`**

Sample Code

```
CREATE MODEL `project.dataset.model name`
OPTIONS(MODEL_TYPE='KMEANS', NUM CLUSTERS=3)
AS
SELECT feature1, feature2
FROM `project.dataset.table`;
```

- **Features**
    - Automatically standardizes features for consistent scaling
    - Supports specifying the number of clusters (**`NUM_CLUSTERS`**) or using AUTO to determine it
    - Uses the k-means++ initialization for better convergence

- **Evaluation**: Use **ML.EVALUATE** to compute metrics such as the Davies-Bouldin index or the mean squared distance.
- **Prediction**: Use **ML.PREDICT** to assign new data points to clusters.

Use Case: Customer segmentation, anomaly detection, or grouping similar items (for example, products, users), customer segmentation, anomaly detection, and image compression.

Matrix Factorization

Matrix factorization is an unsupervised learning technique used for recommendation systems. It decomposes a user-item interaction matrix (for example, ratings) into lower-dimensional matrices to uncover latent factors and make predictions for missing entries.

BigQuery ML Implementation

- **Model Type: MATRIX_FACTORIZATION**
- **Sample Code**

```
CREATE MODEL `project.dataset.model_name`
OPTIONS(MODEL_TYPE='MATRIX_FACTORIZATION', USER_COL='user_id',
ITEM_COL='item_id', RATING_COL='rating')
AS
SELECT user_id, item_id, rating
FROM `project.dataset.table`;
```

- **Features:**
  - Supports implicit (for example, clicks) and explicit (for example, ratings) feedback
  - Automatically tunes hyperparameters like the number of latent factors
  - Handles sparse data efficiently
- **Evaluation:** Use **ML.EVALUATE** to assess metrics like RMSE for explicit feedback.
- **Prediction:** Use **ML.PREDICT** to recommend items for users or predict ratings.

Use Case: Recommender systems for products, movies, or content personalization like product recommendations.

Time Series Models (ARIMA and ARIMA_PLUS)

Under the time series models, we have **ARIMA** and **ARIMA_PLUS**, which are designed to analyze and forecast sequential data. Here are their definitions and distinctions:

- **ARIMA**: AutoRegressive Integrated Moving Average, a statistical model for forecasting time series data based on past values and trends

- **ARIMA_PLUS**: An enhanced version that includes additional features such as trend detection, seasonality, and holiday effects

BigQuery ML Implementation

- **Model Type: ARIMA** or **ARIMA_PLUS**
- **Sample Code**

```
CREATE MODEL `project.dataset.model_name`
OPTIONS(MODEL_TYPE='ARIMA_PLUS', TIME_SERIES_TIMESTAMP_
COL='timestamp', TIME_SERIES_DATA_COL='value')
AS
SELECT timestamp, value
FROM `project.dataset.table`;
```

- **Features**
  - Automatically detects seasonality and trends
  - Supports multiple time series in a single model (for example, by region or product)
  - ARIMA_PLUS includes advanced preprocessing (for example, holiday adjustments)
- **Evaluation:** Use ML.EVALUATE for metrics such as Mean Absolute Error (MAE) or MAPE.
- **Prediction:** Use ML.FORECAST to generate future time series predictions.

Use Case: Forecasting sales, website traffic, or inventory demand over time, including demand forecasting, stock price prediction, and energy consumption forecasting

Deep Neural Networks (DNNs)

DNNs are supervised learning models with multiple layers of interconnected nodes, which are capable of learning complex patterns for regression or classification tasks.

BigQuery ML Implementation

- **Model Type**: **DNN_CLASSIFIER** (classification) or **DNN_REGRESSOR** (regression).
- **Sample Code**

```
CREATE MODEL `project.dataset.model_name`
OPTIONS(MODEL_TYPE='DNN_CLASSIFIER', INPUT_LABEL COLS=['label'],
HIDDEN_UNITS=[64, 32])
AS
SELECT feature1, feature2, label
FROM `project.dataset.table`;
```

- **Features**
    - Configurable architecture (for example, HIDDEN_UNITS for layer sizes)
    - Supports automatic feature preprocessing and regularization
    - Handles large datasets efficiently within BigQuery
- **Evaluation**: Use **ML.EVALUATE** for metrics such as accuracy (classification) or MSE (regression).
- **Prediction**: Use **ML.PREDICT** for predictions on new data.

Use Case: Advanced classification (for example, fraud detection) or regression tasks with non-linear relationships, image classification, and complex regression/classification tasks

XGBoost

XGBoost is a gradient boosting algorithm that builds an ensemble of decision trees to achieve high accuracy in regression and classification tasks. It is known for its performance and scalability.

BigQuery ML Implementation

- **Model Type: BOOSTED_TREE_CLASSIFIER** or **BOOSTED_TREE_REGRESSOR**
- **Sample Code**

```
CREATE MODEL `project.dataset.model_name`
OPTIONS(MODEL_TYPE='BOOSTED_TREE_CLASSIFIER', INPUT_LABEL_
COLS=['label'])
AS
SELECT feature1, feature2, label
FROM `project.dataset.table`;
```

- **Features**
    - Automatically optimizes hyperparameters (for example, number of trees, learning rate)
    - Supports feature importance analysis via **ML.FEATURE_IMPORTANCE**
    - Handles missing data and categorical features
- **Evaluation**: Use **ML.EVALUATE** for metrics such as AUC or RMSE.
- **Prediction**: Use **ML.PREDICT** for predictions.

Use Case: High-accuracy predictions for structured data such as customer churn, credit risk, fraud detection, customer scoring, and predictive maintenance

AutoML Tables (via BigQuery Integration)

AutoML Tables is a Google Cloud service that automates model selection and hyperparameter tuning. BigQuery ML integrates with AutoML Tables to train high-quality models with minimal configuration.

BigQuery ML Implementation

- **Model Type:** AUTOML_CLASSIFIER or AUTOML_REGRESSOR
- **Sample Code**

```
CREATE MODEL `project.dataset.model_name`
OPTIONS(MODEL_TYPE='AUTOML_CLASSIFIER', INPUT_LABEL_
COLS=['label'], BUDGET_HOURS=1.0)
AS
SELECT feature1, feature2, label
FROM `project.dataset.table`;
```

- **Features**
    - Automatically selects the best model (for example, DNN, XGBoost) based on data
    - Configurable training budget (for example, **BUDGET_HOURS**)
    - Integrates seamlessly with BigQuery data
- **Evaluation:** Use **ML.EVALUATE** for performance metrics.
- **Prediction:** Use **ML.PREDICT** for predictions.

Use Case: Builds models when minimal manual tuning is desired, such as in the case of complex datasets with many features, rapid prototyping, and complex datasets with limited ML expertise

Imported Models

BigQuery ML enables the import of pre-trained models (for example, TensorFlow models) to run predictions within BigQuery. This allows users to leverage custom models trained outside of BigQuery.

BigQuery ML Implementation

- **Model Type:** **TENSORFLOW**
- **Sample Code:**

```
CREATE MODEL `project.dataset.model_name`
OPTIONS(MODEL_TYPE='TENSORFLOW', MODEL_PATH='gs://bucket/path/to/
model')
```

- **Features**
    - Supports TensorFlow `SavedModel` format
    - Integrates with BigQuery for scalable inference
    - No training occurs in BigQuery; only predictions are supported
- **Prediction:** Use `ML.PREDICT` to run inference on imported models.
- **Limitations:** No evaluation or training capabilities for imported models.

Use Case: Using custom or third-party models for predictions on BigQuery data, such as specialized deep learning models. It leverages custom models trained outside of BigQuery.

Significance of BQML within BigQuery

BigQuery ML (BQML) is a powerful feature within Google Cloud's BigQuery that enables users to ***create, train, evaluate, and deploy*** ML models directly using SQL queries, without needing to move data to external tools.

BQML's significance lies in its ability to make ML ***accessible, scalable, and tightly integrated with BigQuery's data warehousing capabilities***. It empowers organizations to derive predictive insights from their data using familiar SQL, reduces operational complexity, and leverages Google Cloud's infrastructure for performance and scalability.

By bridging analytics and **ML, BQML *enables faster, data-driven decision-making*** across industries. BQML's integration with BigQuery offers unique advantages, making it a transformative tool for data-driven organizations. Its significance lies in the following aspects:

- **Accessibility and Democratization**
    - BQML enables users with SQL knowledge to build ML models without requiring expertise in Python, R, or ML frameworks such as TensorFlow or PyTorch.
    - Data analysts and business intelligence professionals can create models, which reduces dependency on specialized data science teams.
    - Lowers the barrier to entry for ML, which enables organizations to adopt predictive analytics more broadly.
- **Scalability and Performance**
    - As it is built on BigQuery's serverless architecture, BQML can handle petabyte-scale datasets without requiring manual infrastructure management.

- It leverages BigQuery's distributed computing capabilities for fast model training and inference, even on massive datasets.

Figure 9.2 illustrates the Significance of BQML within BigQuery:

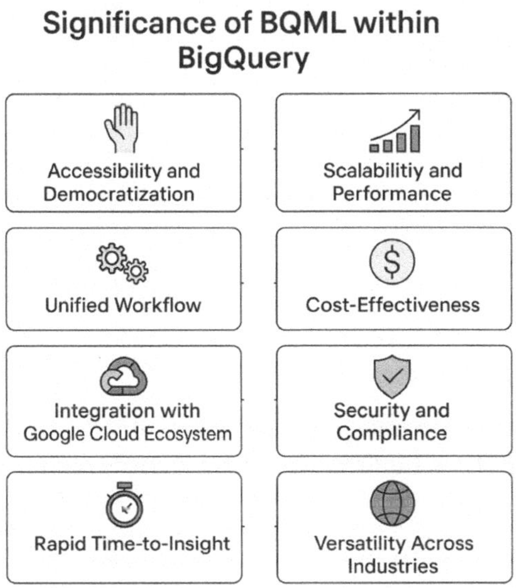

Figure 9.2: *Significance of BQML within BigQuery*

- **Unified Workflow**:
  - Combines data storage, preprocessing, modeling, and prediction within a single platform, while eliminating the need to move data between systems
  - Simplifies the ML pipeline to reduce complexity and potential errors in data handling
- **Cost-Effectiveness**
  - Operates within BigQuery's pricing model and charges according to the volume of data processed during model training and inference
  - Avoids the need for separate ML platforms or infrastructure, thereby reducing operational costs
- **Integration with Google Cloud Ecosystem**
  - Seamlessly integrates with BigQuery's data ingestion, storage, and visualization tools (for example, Looker Studio, Dataflow)
  - Supports advanced workflows through integration with Vertex AI for custom model training or deployment
  - Enables end-to-end analytics pipelines within Google Cloud

- **Security and Compliance**
    - Inherits BigQuery's enterprise-grade security features, including data encryption, Identity Access Management (IAM), and audit logging
    - Ensures compliance with data governance standards which is critical for industries such as finance and healthcare
- **Rapid Time-to-Insight**
    - Simplifies the ML lifecycle (data preparation, model training, evaluation, and prediction) using SQL, thus enabling faster development and deployment
    - Supports iterative experimentation, which allows users to refine models quickly
- **Versatility across Industries**
    - Supports a wide range of use cases, from retail (for example, demand forecasting) to healthcare (for example, patient outcome prediction) and finance (for example, fraud detection)
    - Enables organizations to embed ML into their existing data workflows

Example Workflow: This BigQuery ML code trains a logistic regression model to predict customer churn. The **`CREATE MODEL`** statement builds the model **`churn_model`** using age, **`purchase_history`**, and churn (target variable) from the **`customer_data`** table. The **`ML.EVALUATE`** function assesses the model's performance and returns metrics such as accuracy and AUC. The **`ML.PREDICT`** function applies the trained model to new data from **`new_customers`**, while predicting churn probabilities for each **`customer_id`**. The entire process of training, evaluation, and prediction is executed using SQL within BigQuery.

A typical BQML workflow might look like this:

```
-- Train a logistic regression model
CREATE MODEL `project.dataset.churn_model`
OPTIONS(MODEL_TYPE='LOGISTIC_REG', INPUT_LABEL_COLS=['churn'])
AS
SELECT age, purchase_history, churn
FROM `project.dataset.customer_data`;

-- Evaluate the model
SELECT * FROM ML.EVALUATE(MODEL `project.dataset.churn_model`);

-- Predict churn for new customers
SELECT customer_id, predicted_churn
FROM ML.PREDICT(MODEL `project.dataset.churn_model`,
                SELECT customer_id, age, purchase_history
                FROM `project.dataset.new_customers`);
```

Working Principle of BQML

BQML allows users to perform end-to-end ML tasks like data preprocessing, model training, evaluation, and prediction within BigQuery using SQL. It abstracts much of the complexity of traditional ML pipelines, which is inherent in data extraction, transformation, and model deployment, by embedding ML capabilities directly into BigQuery's serverless environment. Here is a step-by-step breakdown of its functionality (Refer to *Figure* 9.3):

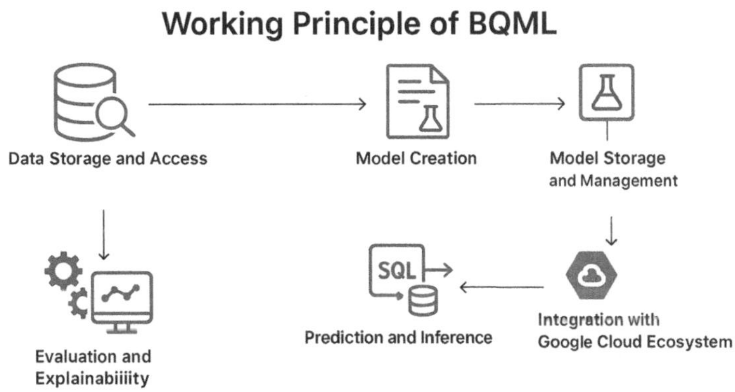

***Figure* 9.3:** *Working Principle of BQML*

- **Data Storage and Access**: BQML operates on data stored in BigQuery tables, which are optimized for large-scale analytics. Users write SQL queries to select features and labels from these tables, while leveraging BigQuery's columnar storage and query engine for efficient data retrieval.
- **Model Creation**: Users define an ML model using the **`CREATE MODEL SQL`** statement, while specifying the model type (for example, **`LINEAR_REG`**, **`LOGISTIC_REG`**, **`KMEANS`**) and options such as input features, target labels, and hyperparameters.

  BQML automatically preprocesses the data (for example, normalization, encoding categorical variables) and trains the model using Google Cloud's distributed infrastructure.
- **Training Process**: BQML leverages BigQuery's query execution engine to distribute training across multiple nodes, which enables scalability for large datasets. It uses Google's optimized implementations of algorithms (for example, TensorFlow for DNNs, custom implementations for ARIMA) to train models efficiently. Hyperparameter tuning (for example, learning rate, number of clusters) is often automated or configurable via options.
- **Model Storage and Management**: Trained models are stored as first-class objects in BigQuery, alongside tables and views, with metadata managed in the

BigQuery catalog. Models can be versioned, monitored, and accessed using standard BigQuery permissions and governance.

- **Evaluation and Explainability**: BQML provides SQL functions similar to those found in `ML.EVALUATE` to compute performance metrics (for example, accuracy, RMSE, AUC) for an `ML.FEATURE_IMPORTANCE` or `ML.EXPLAIN_PREDICT` for model interpretability. Results are returned as queryable tables that integrate seamlessly with BigQuery's analytics workflow.
- **Prediction and Inference**: Users can run predictions on new data using the ML.PREDICT function, passing a trained model and input features via SQL. Thus, BQML performs distributed inference, while scaling to efficiently handle large datasets.
- **Integration with Google Cloud Ecosystem**: BQML models can be exported to TensorFlow SavedModel format or integrated with Vertex AI for advanced workflows. Predictions can be visualized in tools like Looker Studio or used in downstream applications via BigQuery's APIs.

BQML Architecture

The architecture of BQML is tightly integrated with BigQuery's infrastructure and Google Cloud's ML capabilities. The following is a detailed breakdown of its components and how they interact:

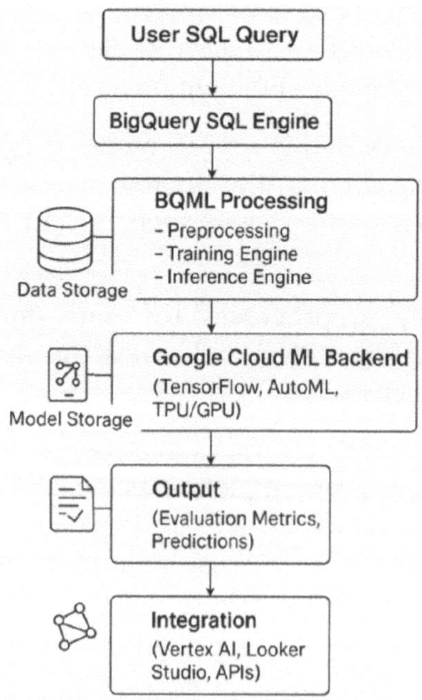

Figure 9.4: *BQML Architecture*

BigQuery Core Infrastructure

- **Storage Layer**
  - BQML operates on data stored in BigQuery's managed columnar storage, which is optimized for analytical queries.
  - Data is organized in tables, and BQML directly accesses these tables without requiring data export.
- **Query Execution Engine (Dremel)**
  - BigQuery's Dremel engine processes SQL queries, including those for BQML, using a distributed architecture.
  - It parallelizes data preprocessing, training, and inference across multiple nodes, while leveraging Google's infrastructure for scalability.
- **Compute Layer**
  - BQML uses BigQuery's serverless compute resources, while dynamically allocating resources based on dataset size and model complexity.
  - For compute-intensive tasks (for example, DNN training), BQML may offload processing to specialized hardware such as TPUs or GPUs via Google Cloud's ML backend.

BQML Processing Pipeline

- **Data Preprocessing**
  - BQML automatically handles feature engineering tasks, such as:
    - **Normalization**: Scaling numerical features for models like linear regression
    - **One-Hot Encoding**: Converting categorical variables for classification or clustering
    - **Missing Value Handling**: Imputing or excluding missing data
  - Preprocessing is performed in-memory during query execution, while leveraging BigQuery's high-performance engine.
- **Training Engine**
  - BQML maps model types to underlying ML algorithms:
    - **Linear/Logistic Regression**: Custom implementations optimized for BigQuery's distributed environment
    - **K-Means Clustering**: Uses k-means++ initialization and distributed computation

        - **Matrix Factorization**: Optimized for sparse data in recommendation systems
        - **ARIMA/ARIMA_PLUS**: Statistical models with automated seasonality and trend detection
        - **DNNs and XGBoost**: Powered by TensorFlow and custom gradient boosting implementations
        - **AutoML Tables**: Integrates with Google Cloud AutoML for automated model selection
    - Training is distributed across BigQuery's compute nodes, with hyperparameters that are either auto-tuned or user-specified.
- **Inference Engine**
    - BQML performs predictions using the same distributed query engine, while applying trained models to new data.
    - For imported TensorFlow models, BQML integrates with TensorFlow Serving for scalable inference.

Model Storage and Metadata

- **Model Artifacts**
    - Trained models are stored in BigQuery as serialized objects, with weights and metadata saved in the BigQuery catalog.
    - Models are accessible via SQL (for example, `SELECT * FROM ML.PREDICT`) and managed like other BigQuery resources.
- **Metadata Management**
    - BigQuery tracks model configurations, training statistics, and evaluation metrics, while enabling auditing and reproducibility.
    - Users can query model details using `INFORMATION_SCHEMA` or BQML-specific functions.
- **Google Cloud Ecosystem**:
    - **Vertex AI**: BQML models can be exported to Vertex AI for advanced deployment or integration with other ML workflows.
    - **AutoML**: BQML's `AUTOML_CLASSIFIER` and `AUTOML_REGRESSOR` can leverage Google's AutoML backend for model selection.
    - **TensorFlow**: Imported TensorFlow models are supported for inference, while bridging custom ML with BigQuery.

- **APIs and Tools**
    - BQML supports programmatic access via BigQuery's REST API, client libraries (for example, Python, Java), and integrations with tools such as Dataflow and Cloud Functions.
    - Visualizations can be created in Looker Studio or other BI tools connected to BigQuery.

Security and Governance

- **Access Control**: BQML inherits BigQuery's Identity and Access Management (IAM) policies, which ensures fine-grained control over model and data access.
- **Data Encryption**: Data and models are encrypted at rest and in transit, while aligning with Google Cloud's security standards.
- **Auditing**: BigQuery logs all BQML operations, while supporting compliance and monitoring.

Operational Flow with Example

To illustrate how BQML works, consider the following example of training a logistic regression model to predict customer churn:

```
-- Train a logistic regression model
CREATE MODEL `project.dataset.churn_model`
OPTIONS(MODEL_TYPE='LOGISTIC_REG', INPUT_LABEL_COLS=['churn'])
AS
SELECT age, purchase_history, churn
FROM `project.dataset.customer_data`;

-- Evaluate the model
SELECT * FROM ML.EVALUATE(MODEL `project.dataset.churn_model`);

-- Predict churn for new customers
SELECT customer_id, predicted_churn
FROM ML.PREDICT(MODEL `project.dataset.churn_model`,
                SELECT customer_id, age, purchase_history
                FROM `project.dataset.new_customers`);
```

Step-by-Step Flow in BQML Architecture

The following workflow illustrates the step-by-step execution of the BQML Architecture:

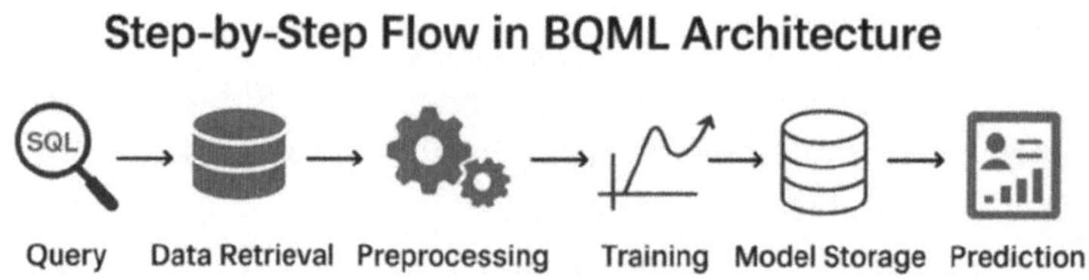

Figure 9.5: *Step-by-Step Flow in BQML Architecture*

1. **Query Parsing**
   a. The **`CREATE MODEL`** query is parsed by BigQuery's SQL engine.
   b. The model type (**`LOGISTIC_REG`**) and options (for example, **`INPUT_LABEL_COLS`**) are extracted.
2. **Data Retrieval**
   a. BigQuery retrieves age, **`purchase_history`**, and churn from the **`customer_data`** table using its columnar storage.
3. **Preprocessing**
   a. Numerical features (**`age`**, **`purchase_history`**) are normalized, and categorical features (if any) are one-hot encoded.
   b. Missing values are handled automatically based on model requirements.
4. **Training**
   a. The logistic regression algorithm is executed on BigQuery's distributed compute nodes.
   b. The model optimizes weights using gradient descent with regularization (for example, L2) applied as specified.
5. **Model Storage**
   a. The trained model (**`churn_model`**) is saved in BigQuery with its weights and metadata.
6. **Evaluation**
   a. The **`ML.EVALUATE`** query triggers a distributed computation of metrics (for example, accuracy, AUC) using the validation data.
   b. The results are returned as a BigQuery table.
7. **Prediction**
   a. The **`ML.PREDICT`** query applies the trained model to new data from **`new_customers`**.
   b. BigQuery distributes inference across nodes, while returning predicted probabilities (**`predicted_churn`**) for each **`customer_id`**.

Key Features and Benefits of BQML Architecture

Let us discuss the key features and benefits of BQML Architecture.

- **Scalability**
  - BQML leverages BigQuery's distributed architecture to handle terabytes of data, which makes it suitable for enterprise-scale ML tasks.
  - Training and inference scale seamlessly with dataset size, which eliminates the need for manual infrastructure management.
- **Serverless**
  - Users do not need to provision compute resources; BigQuery dynamically allocates resources based on workload.
- **SQL-Based Simplicity**
  - The SQL interface abstracts complex ML concepts, while enabling non-experts to build models.
  - Functions such as ML.FEATURE_IMPORTANCE and ML.EXPLAIN_PREDICT provide interpretability without external tools.
- **Extensibility**
  - Support for importing TensorFlow models and AutoML integration allows advanced users to combine custom models with BQML's simplicity.
  - Integration with Vertex AI enables deployment to production environments.
- **Cost Efficiency**
  - BQML uses BigQuery's pay-as-you-go pricing and charges according to query execution and storage, with no separate ML infrastructure costs.

Limitations and Considerations

The following parameters are the limitations and considerations of BQML Architecture:

- **Model Complexity**: BQML is optimized for structured data and specific algorithms, which limits its suitability for unstructured data (for example, images, text) or custom ML frameworks.
- **Feature Engineering**: While BQML automates preprocessing, complex feature engineering may require custom SQL queries or external tools such as Dataflow.
- **Compute Constraints**: Some advanced models (for example, DNNs) may require longer training times for vast datasets; however, BigQuery's scalability mitigates this issue.

- **Cost**: Large-scale training and inference can incur significant BigQuery query costs, especially for iterative tasks.

Practical Use Cases of BQML

BigQuery ML (BQML) is a powerful tool that enables organizations to build, train, and deploy machine learning models directly within Google Cloud's BigQuery using SQL, which make it accessible to data analysts and engineers without requiring deep ML expertise. Its integration with BigQuery's scalable infrastructure and SQL-based interface makes it ideal for a wide range of practical use cases across industries.

Figure 9.6 illustrates the practical use cases of BQML.

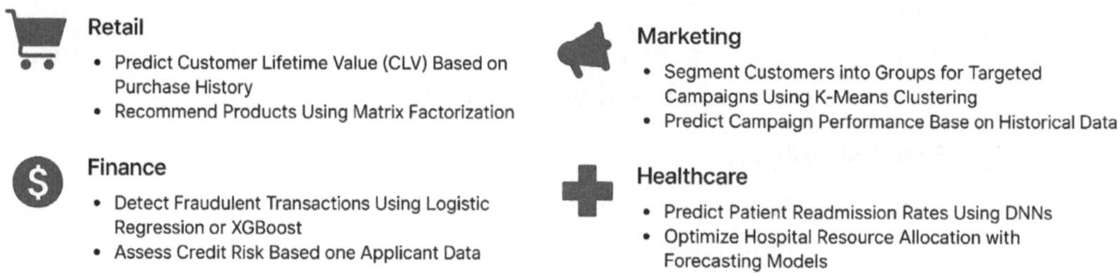

***Figure 9.6**: Practical Use Cases of BQML*

Retail

Retail organizations use data to understand customer behavior, optimize inventory, and personalize shopping experiences. Advanced analytics supports demand forecasting, dynamic pricing, and supply chain efficiency. Real-time insights help retailers improve customer satisfaction and operational performance.

Predict Customer Lifetime Value (CLV) Based on Purchase History

Customer Lifetime Value (CLV) predicts the total revenue a business can expect from a customer over their relationship. BQML can model CLV using historical purchase data, demographic information, and behavioral metrics.

- **BQML Model**: **Linear Regression** or **Deep Neural Networks** (`DNN_REGRESSOR`) for continuous value prediction.
- **How It Works**:
    - **Data**: Use customer data (for example, purchase frequency, average order value, time since last purchase, demographics).
    - **Model Training**: Train a regression model to predict CLV based on features such as total spend, number of orders, and customer tenure.

- **Example SQL**

```
CREATE MODEL `retail.clv_model`
OPTIONS(MODEL_TYPE='LINEAR_REG', INPUT_LABEL_
COLS=['lifetime_value'])
AS
SELECT customer_id, total_spent, order_count, days_since_
last_purchase, lifetime_value
FROM `retail.customer_data`;
```

- **Prediction**: Use ML.PREDICT to estimate CLV for new or existing customers.

```
SELECT customer_id, predicted_lifetime_value
FROM ML.PREDICT(MODEL `retail.clv_model`,
                SELECT customer_id, total_spent, order_
count, days_since_last_purchase
                FROM `retail.new_customer_data`);
```

- **Benefits**
    - Helps prioritize high-value customers for marketing efforts
    - Optimizes resource allocation for customer retention programs
    - Scalable to millions of customers due to BigQuery's distributed processing
- **Impact:** Retailers can focus on high-CLV customers, while improving ROI on loyalty programs and targeted promotions.

Recommend Products Using Matrix Factorization

Matrix factorization builds recommendation systems by identifying latent factors in user-item interactions (for example, purchases, ratings, or clicks) to suggest relevant products.

- **BQML Model: Matrix Factorization**
- **How It Works**
    - **Data**: A table with user IDs, item IDs, and interaction data (for example, ratings, purchase counts, or implicit feedback like clicks).
    - **Model Training**: Train a matrix factorization model to learn latent factors for users and items, while enabling predictions for unseen interactions.
    - **Example SQL**:

```
CREATE MODEL `retail.recommendation_model`
OPTIONS(MODEL_TYPE='MATRIX_FACTORIZATION', USER_COL='user_
```

```
id', ITEM_COL='item_id', RATING_COL='rating')
AS
SELECT user_id, item_id, rating
FROM `retail.user_item_interactions`;
```

- **Prediction**: Use ML.PREDICT to recommend items for users.

```
SELECT user_id, item_id, predicted_rating
FROM ML.PREDICT(MODEL `retail.recommendation_model`,
                SELECT user_id, item_id
                FROM `retail.new_interactions`);
```

- **Benefits**
  - Personalizes shopping experience, increasing customer engagement and sales
  - Handles sparse data efficiently, a common feature in retail datasets
  - Integrates seamlessly with BigQuery for real-time recommendations
- **Impact**: Boosts cross-selling and upselling, with studies showing personalized recommendations can increase conversion rates by 10-30%

Forecast Inventory Needs with Time-Series Models

Time-series forecasting predicts future inventory demand based on historical sales data, which enables retailers to optimize stock levels and minimize waste.

- **BQML Model**: **`ARIMA_PLUS`** (includes seasonality, trends, and holiday effects).
- **How It Works**
  - **Data**: Time-series data with timestamps and sales quantities (for example, daily product sales).
  - **Model Training**: Train an ARIMA_PLUS model to capture trends, seasonality, and external factors, such as holidays.
  - **Example SQL**

```
CREATE MODEL `retail.inventory_forecast`
OPTIONS(MODEL_TYPE='ARIMA_PLUS', TIME_SERIES_TIMESTAMP_
COL='sale_date', TIME_SERIES_DATA_COL='sales_quantity')
AS
SELECT sale_date, sales_quantity
FROM `retail.sales_data`;
```

  - **Prediction**: Use ML.FORECAST to predict future inventory needs.

```
SELECT forecast_timestamp, forecast_value
```

```
FROM ML.FORECAST(MODEL `retail.inventory_forecast`,
                  STRUCT(30 AS horizon));
```

- **Benefits**
    - Reduces overstocking and understocking, optimizing supply chain costs
    - Automatically accounts for seasonality and trends, improving forecast accuracy
    - Scalable for forecasting across thousands of products
- **Impact**: Minimizes stockouts and excess inventory, while potentially saving millions in supply chain costs

Finance

The finance domain relies on data analytics for risk management, fraud detection, and regulatory compliance. Real-time and historical data are used for credit scoring, trading strategies, and portfolio optimization. Secure and scalable data systems enable accurate decision-making and financial forecasting.

Detecting Fraudulent Transactions Using Logistic Regression or XGBoost

Fraud detection identifies suspicious transactions (for example, unauthorized credit card charges) by classifying them as either fraudulent or legitimate.

- **BQML Model**: **Logistic Regression** (for interpretability) or **`BOOSTED_TREE_CLASSIFIER`** (XGBoost for higher accuracy)
- **How It Works**:
    - **Data**: Transaction data with features such as amount, location, time, merchant category, and a label (fraudulent or not).
    - **Model Training**: Train a classification model to predict the probability of fraud.
    - **Example SQL**:

      ```
      CREATE MODEL `finance.fraud_model`
      OPTIONS(MODEL_TYPE='BOOSTED_TREE_CLASSIFIER', INPUT_LABEL_
      COLS=['is_fraud'])
      AS
      SELECT amount, transaction_time, merchant_category, is_fraud
      FROM `finance.transaction_data`;
      ```

    - **Prediction**: Use **`ML.PREDICT`** to flag potentially fraudulent transactions.

```
SELECT transaction_id, predicted_is_fraud, predicted_is_
fraud_proba
FROM ML.PREDICT(MODEL `finance.fraud_model`,
                SELECT transaction_id, amount, transaction_
time, merchant_category
                FROM `finance.new_transactions`);
```

- **Benefits**:
  - High accuracy with XGBoost for complex patterns; interpretable with logistic regression
  - Real-time inference for immediate fraud detection
  - Integrates with BigQuery's audit logs for compliance
- **Impact**: Reduces financial losses from fraud, with some banks reporting a 20-50% improvement in detection rates

Assessing Credit Risk Based on Applicant Data

Credit risk assessment predicts the likelihood of a loan applicant defaulting, which helps in making informed loan approval decisions.

- **BQML Model**: **Logistic Regression** or **`DNN_CLASSIFIER`** for binary classification (default or no default)
- **How It Works**
  - **Data**: Applicant data (for example, credit score, income, debt-to-income ratio, loan amount) with a label indicating default status.
  - **Model Training**: Train a model to predict default probability.
  - **Example SQL**:

```
CREATE MODEL `finance.credit_risk_model`
OPTIONS(MODEL_TYPE='DNN_CLASSIFIER', INPUT_LABEL_
COLS=['default'], HIDDEN_UNITS=[64, 32])
AS
SELECT credit_score, income, debt_to_income, loan_amount,
default
FROM `finance.applicant_data`;
```

  - **Prediction**: Use ML.PREDICT to assess risk for new applicants.

```
SELECT applicant_id, predicted_default, predicted_default_proba
FROM ML.PREDICT(MODEL `finance.credit_risk_model`,
                SELECT applicant_id, credit_score, income,
debt_to_income, loan_amount
                FROM `finance.new_applicants`);
```

- **Benefits**
  - DNNs capture non-linear patterns in complex datasets
  - Explainability via `ML.FEATURE_IMPORTANCE` helps meet regulatory requirements
  - Scalable to process large applicant pools
- **Impact**: Improves loan approval accuracy, while reducing default rates and enhancing portfolio performance

Marketing

Marketing leverages data to analyze customer preferences, campaign performance, and market trends. Predictive analytics enables targeted advertising and customer segmentation. Data-driven insights help improve customer engagement and Return on Investment (RoI).

Segment Customers into Groups for Targeted Campaigns Using K-Means Clustering

Customer segmentation groups customers based on behavior or demographics for personalized marketing campaigns:

- **BQML Model**: `KMEANS` for unsupervised clustering
- **How It Works**:
  - **Data**: Customer data with features such as purchase frequency, average spend, and demographics
  - **Model Training**: Train a k-means model to group customers into clusters based on similarity.
  - **Example SQL**:

```
CREATE MODEL `marketing.segmentation_model`
OPTIONS(MODEL_TYPE='KMEANS', NUM_CLUSTERS=5)
AS
SELECT customer_id, purchase_frequency, avg_spend, age,
region
FROM `marketing.customer_data`;
```

  - **Prediction**: Use ML.PREDICT to assign new customers to clusters.

```
SELECT customer_id, CENTROID_ID
FROM ML.PREDICT(MODEL `marketing.segmentation_model`,
              SELECT customer_id, purchase_frequency, avg_
```

```
spend, age, region
                    FROM `marketing.new_customers`);
```

- **Benefits**
  - Identifies distinct customer segments (for example, high-spenders, occasional buyers) for targeted campaigns
  - Scalable to millions of customers
  - Integrates with marketing tools for campaign execution
- **Impact**: Increases campaign ROI by 10-20% through personalized targeting.

Predict Campaign Performance Based on Historical Data

Predict the success of marketing campaigns (for example, click-through rates, conversions) using historical data.

- **BQML Model**: **Linear Regression** or **`DNN_REGRESSOR`** for continuous outcomes (for example, conversion rate), or **Logistic Regression** for binary outcomes (for example, click or no click).
- **How It Works**:
  - **Data**: Campaign data with features such as channel, budget, audience segment, and historical performance metrics
  - **Model Training**: Train a model to predict campaign outcomes.
  - **Example SQL**:

```
CREATE MODEL `marketing.campaign_model`
OPTIONS(MODEL_TYPE='LOGISTIC_REG', INPUT_LABEL_
COLS=['clicked'])
AS
SELECT channel, budget, audience_segment, clicked
FROM `marketing.campaign_data`;
```

  - **Prediction**: Use **`ML.PREDICT`** to forecast performance for new campaigns.

```
SELECT campaign_id, predicted_clicked_proba
FROM ML.PREDICT(MODEL `marketing.campaign_model`,
                    SELECT campaign_id, channel, budget,
audience_segment
                    FROM `marketing.new_campaigns`);
```

- **Benefits**:
  - Optimizes budget allocation by predicting high-performing campaigns

   - Fast iteration with real-time predictions in BigQuery
   - Supports A/B testing and campaign optimization
- **Impact**: Improves campaign effectiveness, potentially increasing conversions by 5-15%

Healthcare

Healthcare uses data to improve patient care, diagnostics, and operational efficiency. Analytics supports disease prediction, treatment optimization, and resource planning. Secure data processing ensures patient privacy, while enabling evidence-based medical decisions.

Predicting Patient Readmission Rates Using DNNs

Predict the likelihood of a patient being readmitted to a hospital within a specific time period (for example, 30 days) to improve care and reduce costs.

- **BQML Model**: `DNN_CLASSIFIER` for binary classification (readmitted or not)
- **How It Works**:
   - **Data**: Patient data with features such as age, diagnosis, length of stay, and prior admissions
   - **Model Training**: Train a DNN to predict readmission probability.
   - **Example SQL**:

```
CREATE MODEL `healthcare.readmission_model`
OPTIONS(MODEL_TYPE='DNN_CLASSIFIER', INPUT_LABEL_
COLS=['readmitted'], HIDDEN_UNITS=[128, 64])
AS
SELECT age, diagnosis_code, length_of_stay, prior_
admissions, readmitted
FROM `healthcare.patient_data`;
```

   - **Prediction**: Use `ML.PREDICT` to identify high-risk patients.

```
SELECT patient_id, predicted_readmitted_proba
FROM ML.PREDICT(MODEL `healthcare.readmission_model`,
                SELECT patient_id, age, diagnosis_code,
length_of_stay, prior_admissions
                FROM `healthcare.new_patients`);
```

- **Benefits**:
   - DNNs capture complex patterns in medical data.
   - Enables proactive interventions for high-risk patients

  - Compliant with healthcare data security via BigQuery's encryption

- **Impact**: Reduces readmission rates, which will save hospitals millions (for example, U.S. hospitals face $17B in readmission penalties annually)

Optimize Hospital Resource Allocation with Forecasting Models

Forecast patient admissions and resource needs (for example, beds, staff) to optimize hospital operations.

- **BQML Model**: **`ARIMA_PLUS`** for time-series forecasting
- **How It Works**
  - **Data**: Historical admission data with timestamps and counts (for example, daily admissions)
  - **Model Training**: Train an ARIMA_PLUS model to predict future admissions.
  - **Example SQL**:

```
CREATE MODEL `healthcare.admission_forecast`
OPTIONS(MODEL_TYPE='ARIMA_PLUS', TIME_SERIES_TIMESTAMP_
COL='admission_date', TIME_SERIES_DATA_COL='admissions')
AS
SELECT admission_date, admissions
FROM `healthcare.admission_data`;
```

  - **Prediction**: Use **`ML.FORECAST`** to predict future admissions.

```
SELECT forecast_timestamp, forecast_value
FROM ML.FORECAST(MODEL `healthcare.admission_forecast`,
                 STRUCT(30 AS horizon));
```

- **Benefits**
  - Accounts for seasonality (for example, flu season) and trends
  - Improves resource planning, reducing wait times and costs
  - Scalable for multi-hospital systems
- **Impact**: Enhances operational efficiency, while potentially reducing costs by 5-10% through optimized staffing and bed allocation

E-Commerce

Build Recommendation Systems for Personalized Shopping Experiences: Recommend products to users based on their browsing or purchasing history, which will enhance the user experience and driving sales.

- **BQML Model**: **Matrix Factorization** (similar to retail use case)
- **How It Works**
  - **Data**: User-item interaction data (for example, views, purchases, ratings)
  - **Model Training**: Train a matrix factorization model to recommend products.
  - **Example SQL**:

```
CREATE MODEL `ecommerce.recommendation_model`
OPTIONS(MODEL_TYPE='MATRIX_FACTORIZATION', USER_COL='user_
id', ITEM_COL='product_id', RATING_COL='interaction_score')
AS
SELECT user_id, product_id, interaction_score
FROM `ecommerce.user_interactions`;
```

  - **Prediction**: Use `ML.PREDICT` to generate recommendations.

```
SELECT user_id, product_id, predicted_interaction_score
FROM ML.PREDICT(MODEL `ecommerce.recommendation_model`,
                SELECT user_id, product_id
                FROM `ecommerce.new_interactions`);
```

- **Benefits**
  - Drives personalized shopping experiences, increasing customer satisfaction
  - Handles large-scale interaction data efficiently
  - Integrates with e-commerce platforms via BigQuery APIs
- **Impact**: Increases average order value by 10-20% through relevant recommendations

Forecast Sales Trends to Optimize Pricing Strategies

Predict future sales trends to inform dynamic pricing, promotions, or inventory strategies.

- **BQML Model**: `ARIMA_PLUS` for time-series forecasting
- **How It Works**:
  - **Data**: Historical sales data with timestamps and revenue or quantity metrics
  - **Model Training**: Train an `ARIMA_PLUS` model to forecast sales
  - **Example SQL**:

```
CREATE MODEL `ecommerce.sales_forecast`
```

```
OPTIONS(MODEL_TYPE='ARIMA_PLUS | model_type`, TIME_SERIES_
TIMESTAMP_COL='sale_date', TIME_SERIES_DATA_COL='revenue')
AS
SELECT sale_date, revenue
FROM `ecommerce.sales_data`;
```

  - **Prediction**: Use **ML.FORECAST** to predict future sales.

```
SELECT forecast_timestamp, forecast_value
FROM ML.FORECAST(MODEL `ecommerce.sales_forecast`,
                 STRUCT(30 AS horizon));
```

- **Benefits**
  - Enables dynamic pricing based on predicted demand
  - Improves promotional planning and inventory management
  - Scalable for forecasting across product categories or regions
- **Impact**: Optimizes pricing, while potentially increasing revenue by 5-15% through data-driven strategies

Step-by-Step Guide to Creating and Training Models in BigQuery ML

Figure 9.7 illustrates the step-by-step guide, followed by a detailed discussion of each step:

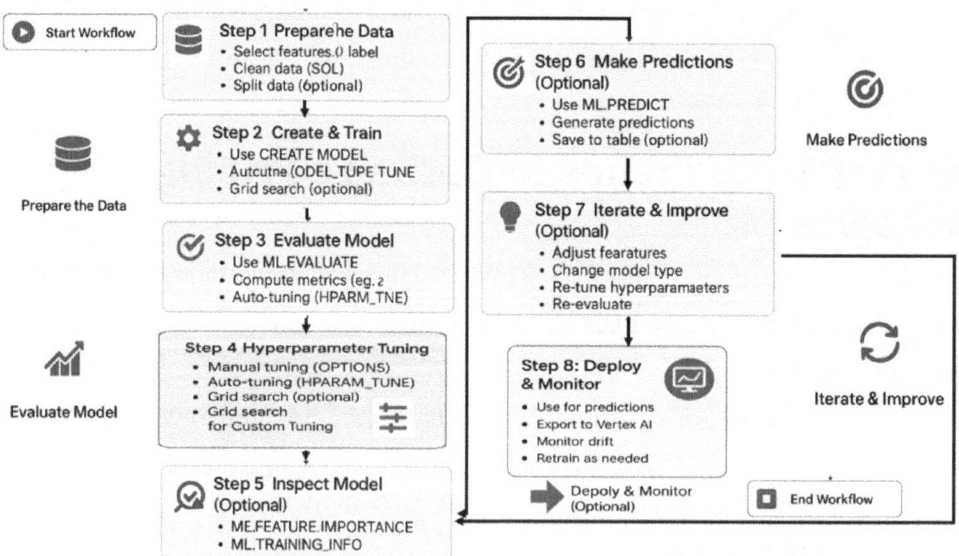

Figure 9.7: *Step-by-Step Guide to Creating and Training Models in BigQuery ML*

Step 1: Prepare the Data

Before creating a model, ensure your data is stored in BigQuery tables and is well-structured for ML. This involves selecting relevant features, handling missing values, and splitting data into training, validation, and test sets if needed.

- **Tasks**
  - Identifying input features (independent variables) and the target variable (label for supervised learning).
  - Cleaning data (for example, remove duplicates, handle nulls) using SQL or BigQuery's built-in pre-processing
  - Optionally, splitting the data into training and test sets using SQL (BQML can also perform automatic splits for some models)
- **Example SQL** (Prepare a dataset for customer churn prediction):

```
CREATE OR REPLACE TABLE `project.dataset.training_data`
AS
SELECT
customer_id,  age,  purchase_history,  days_since_last_purchase,
churn AS label
FROM `project.dataset.customer_data`
WHERE
  -- Filter out incomplete records
  age IS NOT NULL   AND purchase_history IS NOT NULL   AND churn
IS NOT NULL;
```

- **Considerations**
  - Ensure sufficient data volume for robust training (for example, thousands of rows for supervised models).
  - Use representative data to avoid bias.
  - For time series models, ensure that timestamps are properly formatted.
- **BQML Preprocessing**: BQML automatically handles tasks such as normalization (for numerical features), one-hot encoding (for categorical features), and missing value imputation during training, thereby reducing the need for manual pre-processing.

Step 2: Create and Train the Model Using SQL

BQML uses the CREATE MODEL SQL statement to define and train an ML model. You specify the model type, input features, target variable, and optional hyperparameters.

- **Tasks**
  - Choose the appropriate model type based on the problem (for example, **LOGISTIC_REG** for classification, **LINEAR_REG** for regression, **KMEANS** for clustering).
  - Define the model name and dataset.
  - Specify the target variable (for supervised learning) using **INPUT_LABEL_COLS**.
  - Provide the training data via a **SELECT** query.
- **Example SQL** (Train a logistic regression model for churn prediction):

```
CREATE OR REPLACE MODEL `project.dataset.churn_model`
OPTIONS(
  MODEL_TYPE='LOGISTIC_REG',
  INPUT_LABEL_COLS=['label'],
  DATA_SPLIT_METHOD='AUTO_SPLIT', -- Automatically splits data
into train/validation
  MAX_ITERATIONS=10, -- Optional hyperparameter
  L2_REG=1.0 -- Optional regularization
)
AS
SELECT  age,  purchase_history,  days_since_last_purchase,
label FROM `project.dataset.training_data`;
```

- **Key Components**
  - **MODEL_TYPE**: Specifies the algorithm (for example, **LOGISTIC_REG**, **BOOSTED_TREE_CLASSIFIER**, **ARIMA_PLUS**, **KMEANS**)
  - **INPUT_LABEL_COLS**: Defines the target variable for supervised learning (not needed for unsupervised models like K-means)
  - **OPTIONS**: Configures hyperparameters, data splitting, and other settings
  - **SELECT Query**: Provides the training data with features and labels
- **Model Types**
  - **Supervised**: Linear regression, logistic regression, DNNs (**DNN_CLASSIFIER**, **DNN_REGRESSOR**), XGBoost (**BOOSTED_TREE_CLASSIFIER**, **BOOSTED_TREE_REGRESSOR**), AutoML Tables
  - **Unsupervised**: K-means clustering, matrix factorization
  - **Time Series**: **ARIMA**, **ARIMA_PLUS**
  - **Imported**: TensorFlow models for inference

- **Automatic Data Splitting**
  - BQML supports **`DATA_SPLIT_METHOD`** options like **`AUTO_SPLIT`** (default, typically 80/20 train/validation), **`RANDOM`**, **`SEQ`**, or **`CUSTOM`** for manual splits.
  - Example of a custom split:

```
OPTIONS(
  DATA_SPLIT_METHOD='CUSTOM',
  DATA_SPLIT_COL='split_column' -- Column with 'TRAIN',
'VALIDATE', or 'TEST')
```

- **Considerations**
  - Ensure that the model type aligns with the problem (for example, classification versus regression).
  - Use **`CREATE OR REPLACE MODEL`** to overwrite existing models.
  - The training time depends on dataset size, model complexity, and hyperparameters (for example, DNNs take longer than logistic regression).

Step 3: Hyperparameter Tuning

Hyperparameters control the behavior of the ML algorithm (for example, learning rate, number of iterations). BQML supports manual and automated hyperparameter tuning to optimize model performance.

- **Tasks**
  - Identify model-specific hyperparameters (for example, **`L2_REG`** for regularization, **`NUM_CLUSTERS`** for K-means).
  - Manually set hyperparameters in the OPTIONS clause or use automated tuning for supported models.
  - For advanced tuning, use a grid search approach by training multiple models with different hyperparameter combinations.
- **Manual Hyperparameter Tuning**
  - Example of logistic regression:

```
CREATE OR REPLACE MODEL `project.dataset.churn_model`
OPTIONS(
  MODEL_TYPE='LOGISTIC_REG',
  INPUT_LABEL_COLS=['label'],
  L2_REG=0.1, -- Regularization strength
  MAX_ITERATIONS=20, -- Number of training iterations
```

```
  EARLY_STOP=TRUE -- Stop training if performance plateaus
)
AS
SELECT age, purchase_history, days_since_last_purchase, label
FROM `project.dataset.training_data`;
```

- Common Hyperparameters
  - **Linear/Logistic Regression**: L1_REG, L2_REG, MAX_ITERATIONS, LEARN_RATE
  - **DNNs**: HIDDEN_UNITS (for example, **[64, 32]**), DROPOUT, BATCH_SIZE
  - **XGBoost**: NUM_TREES, MAX_TREE_DEPTH, LEARNING_RATE
  - **K-Means**: NUM_CLUSTERS, INIT_METHOD
  - **ARIMA_PLUS**: HORIZON, DECOMPOSE_TIME_SERIES

- **Automated Hyperparameter Tuning**
  - BQML supports automatic tuning for some models (for example, XGBoost, DNNs) via **AUTO_TUNE=TRUE** or specific tuning options.
  - Example for XGBoost:

```
CREATE OR REPLACE MODEL `project.dataset.churn_model`
OPTIONS(
  MODEL_TYPE='BOOSTED_TREE_CLASSIFIER',
  INPUT_LABEL_COLS=['label'],
  AUTO_CLASS_WEIGHTS=TRUE, -- Balances classes
  NUM_PARALLEL_TREE=10, -- Number of trees to train in
parallel
  HPARAM_TUNE=TRUE -- Enables auto-tuning
)
AS
SELECT age, purchase_history, days_since_last_purchase,
label
FROM `project.dataset.training_data`;
```

  - BQML explores a predefined range of hyperparameters (for example, learning rate, tree depth) and selects the best combination based on validation performance.

- **Grid Search for Custom Tuning**
  - Manually train multiple models with different hyperparameter values and compare performance.

- Example Script (Simplified):

```
-- Model 1: L2_REG=0.1
CREATE OR REPLACE MODEL `project.dataset.churn_model_1`
OPTIONS(MODEL_TYPE='LOGISTIC_REG', INPUT_LABEL_
COLS=['label'], L2_REG=0.1)
AS SELECT age, purchase_history, days_since_last_purchase,
label
FROM `project.dataset.training_data`;

-- Model 2: L2_REG=1.0
CREATE OR REPLACE MODEL `project.dataset.churn_model_2`
OPTIONS(MODEL_TYPE='LOGISTIC_REG', INPUT_LABEL_
COLS=['label'], L2_REG=1.0)
AS SELECT age, purchase_history, days_since_last_purchase,
label
FROM `project.dataset.training_data`;
```

- Evaluate models to select the best one (see Step 4).

- **Considerations**
  - Automated tuning is convenient, but it may increase training time and cost.
  - Manual tuning requires domain knowledge to select relevant hyperparameters.
  - Monitor BigQuery costs, as multiple training runs can be expensive for large datasets.

Step 4: Evaluate the Model

Model evaluation assesses the trained model's performance using metrics such as accuracy, RMSE, or AUC. BQML provides the **`ML.EVALUATE`** function to compute these metrics on a validation or test dataset.

- **Tasks**
  - Use **`ML.EVALUATE`** to compute model-specific metrics.
  - Optionally, specify a custom evaluation dataset (if not using the automatic split).
  - Analyze results to determine if the model meets performance requirements.
- **Example SQL** (Evaluate the churn model):

```
SELECT * FROM ML.EVALUATE(
```

```
MODEL `project.dataset.churn_model`,
( SELECT age, purchase_history, days_since_last_purchase, label
  FROM     `project.dataset.test_data`    ) );
```

- **Output Metrics** (Example for logistic regression):
  - **Accuracy**: Proportion of correct predictions
  - **Precision/Recall**: For imbalanced datasets (for example, churn is a rare event)
  - **F1 Score**: Harmonic mean of precision and recall
  - **AUC-ROC**: Area under the receiver operating characteristic curve
  - **Log Loss**: Measures prediction confidence
  - Example output table:

Accuracy	Precision	Recall	F1 Score	ROC AUC	Log Loss
0.85	0.8	0.75	0.77	0.9	0.35

Table 9.1: *Output Metrics*

- **Model-Specific Metrics**
  - **Regression (for example, Linear Regression)**: Mean Squared Error (MSE), Root Mean Squared Error (RMSE), R^2
  - **Clustering (for example, K-Means)**: Davies-Bouldin Index, Mean Squared Distance
  - **Time Series (for example, `ARIMA_PLUS`)**: Mean Absolute Error (MAE), Mean Absolute Percentage Error (MAPE)
  - **Recommendation (for example, Matrix Factorization)**: RMSE for explicit feedback
- **Custom Evaluation Dataset**
  - If `DATA_SPLIT_METHOD='AUTO_SPLIT'` was used, BQML is evaluated on the validation set automatically.
  - For a separate test set, provide it in the `ML.EVALUATE` query (as shown earlier).
- **Additional Evaluation Tools**
  - **ML.CONFUSION_MATRIX**: For classification models, view true positives, false positives, and so on.

```
SELECT * FROM ML.CONFUSION_MATRIX(MODEL `project.dataset.
churn_model`);
```

- **ML.ROC_CURVE**: For binary classification, analyze the ROC curve.

```
SELECT * FROM ML.ROC_CURVE(MODEL `project.dataset.churn_model`);
```

- **Considerations**
  - Ensure that the evaluation dataset is representative and not used during training to avoid overfitting.
  - For imbalanced datasets (for example, fraud detection), prioritize metrics such as AUC or F1 over accuracy.
  - If performance is poor, revisit hyperparameters, feature engineering, or model type.

Step 5: Inspect Model Details (Optional)

BQML provides functions to understand the trained model, such as feature importance and training statistics, which aid in debugging and improvement.

- **Tasks**
  - Use **ML.FEATURE_IMPORTANCE** to identify which features contribute most to predictions.
  - Use **ML.TRAINING_INFO** to review training progress (for example, loss over iterations).
- **Example SQL** (Feature importance for churn model):

```
SELECT
  *
FROM
  ML.FEATURE_IMPORTANCE(MODEL `project.dataset.churn_model`);
```

  - Output example:

Features	Importance
purchase_history	0.45
days_since_last_purchase	0.35
age	0.2

Table 9.2: *Output – Feature Importance*

- **Example SQL** (Training Info):

```
SELECT  * FROM  ML.TRAINING_INFO(MODEL `project.dataset.churn_
model`);
```

  - Output includes iteration number, loss, learning rate, and duration per iteration.

- **Considerations**:
    - Feature importance helps identify irrelevant features to remove or new features to engineer.
    - Training info is useful for diagnosing convergence issues (for example, if loss plateaus early).

Step 6: Make Predictions

Once the model is trained and evaluated, use it to make predictions on new data with the **`ML.PREDICT`** function.

- **Tasks**
    - Prepare a dataset with the same features used for training (excluding the label).
    - Run **`ML.PREDICT`** to generate predictions.
- **Example SQL** (Predict churn for new customers):

```
SELECT   customer_id,   predicted_label,   predicted_label_proba
FROM
  ML.PREDICT( MODEL `project.dataset.churn_model`,     (
      SELECT          customer_id, age, purchase_history, days_
since_last_purchase  FROM
        `project.dataset.new_customers`      ) );
```

- **Output** (Example for logistic regression):
    - **`predicted_label`**: Predicted class (for example, 0 or 1 for churn)
    - **`predicted_label_proba`**: Probability for each class
    - Example:

Customer ID	Predicted Label	Predicted Label Proba 0	Predicted Label Proba 1
123	1	0.3	0.7
456	0	0.85	0.15

***Table 9.3:** Output Metrics for Prediction*

- **Considerations**
    - Ensure that the input dataset has identical feature names and types as the training data.
    - For time-series models, use **`ML.FORECAST`** instead of **`ML.PREDICT`**.

- Predictions can be saved to a table or integrated with downstream applications via BigQuery APIs.

Step 7: Iterate and Improve (Optional)

If the model's performance is unsatisfactory, iterate by adjusting features, hyperparameters, or model types to improve it.

- **Tasks**
  - Add new features or engineer existing ones (for example, create interaction terms using SQL).
  - Try a different model type (for example, switch from logistic regression to XGBoost for better accuracy).
  - Adjust hyperparameters based on evaluation results or training info.
  - Re-evaluate and compare models to select the best one.
- **Example** (Try XGBoost instead of logistic regression):

```
CREATE OR REPLACE MODEL `project.dataset.churn_model_xgboost`
OPTIONS(   MODEL_TYPE='BOOSTED_TREE_CLASSIFIER', INPUT_LABEL_
COLS=['label'],
  NUM_TREES=100,   MAX_TREE_DEPTH=5 )
AS
SELECT age, purchase_history, days_since_last_purchase, label
FROM `project.dataset.training_data`;

-- Evaluate and compare
SELECT * FROM ML.EVALUATE(MODEL `project.dataset.churn_model_
xgboost`);
```

- **Considerations**:
  - Balance model complexity with interpretability (for example, XGBoost is more accurate but less interpretable than logistic regression).
  - Monitor training costs, as iterative experiments can accumulate expenses.

Step 8: Deploy and Monitor

After achieving satisfactory performance, deploy the model for production use and monitor its performance over time.

- **Tasks**
  - Use the model for real-time or batch predictions via **`ML.PREDICT`**.

  - Export the model to Vertex AI for advanced deployment (supported for some model types).
  - Monitor model drift by periodically re-evaluating on new data.
  - Retrain the model if performance degrades (for example, due to changing customer behavior).
- **Example SQL** (Save predictions to a table):

```
CREATE OR REPLACE TABLE `project.dataset.churn_predictions`
AS
SELECT   customer_id,  predicted_label,  predicted_label_proba
FROM
ML.PREDICT(   MODEL `project.dataset.churn_model`,     ( SELECT
customer_id, age,
purchase_history, days_since_last_purchase   FROM `project.
dataset.new_customers` )  );
```

- **Export to Vertex AI** (if needed):

```
XPORT MODEL `project.dataset.churn_model`
TO 'gs://bucket/path/to/export'
OPTIONS(FRAMEWORK='TENSORFLOW');
```

- **Considerations**
  - Ensure compliance with data governance policies (for example, access controls via BigQuery IAM).
  - Schedule retraining using Cloud Scheduler and BigQuery jobs for automated updates.
  - Use **`ML.EXPLAIN_PREDICT`** for explainability in production to understand individual predictions.

So far, we have a clear understanding of the Step-by-Step Guide to Creating and Training Models in BigQuery ML. Let us now look at a similar exception in the BigQuery Environment.

Model Creation and Training in the BigQuery ML Environment

Step 1: Log in to GCP, navigate to BigQuery, and create the model. *Figure* 9.8 illustrates the model details page for an ML model created using BigQuery ML (BQML) within Google Cloud's BigQuery interface.

Figure 9.8: *Model Creation and Training in the BigQuery ML Environment*

- **Model Name: `travel_insurance_model`** – The name of the model created under the dataset **`travelinsuranceds`**
- **Model Type:** Logistic Regression – Used for binary classification problems (for example, will the customer buy travel insurance: Yes/No)

The schema shown in *Figure* 9.9 is part of the dataset '**`travelinsuranceds`**' under the project. This schema defines the structure and data types used in the table that was used to train the model.

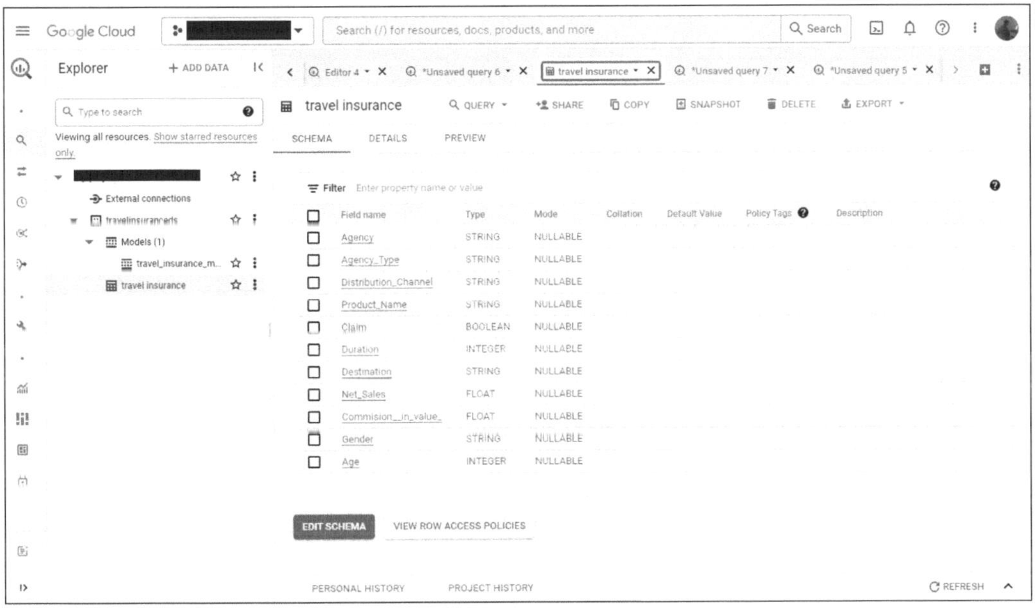

Figure 9.9: *Model Creation and Training in the BigQuery ML Environment - Schema*

Key Notes

- The Claim column is the **target label** used in model training.
- All fields are **`NULLABLE`**, meaning they can contain missing values.
- Features such as **`Net_Sales`**, Duration, and Age are numerical and suitable for logistic regression.
- Categorical variables such as **`Agency`**, **`Product_Name`**, and **`Distribution_Channel`** likely undergo encoding internally by BigQuery ML.

Step 2: You are creating a **logistic regression model** named **`travel_insurance_model`** using SQL in BigQuery. The model is trained on the dataset **`travelinsuranceds.travel_insurance`**, as shown in *Figure 9.10*.

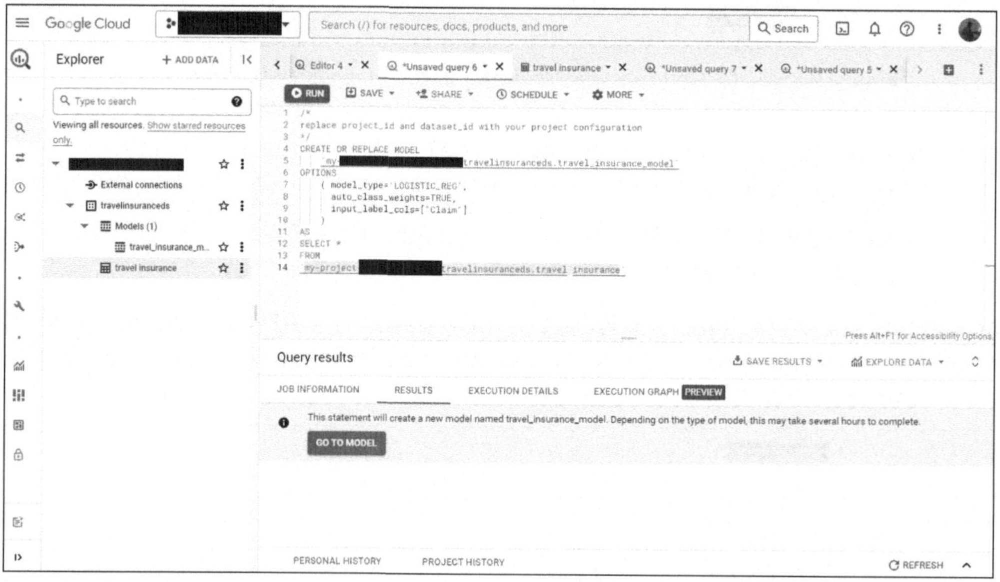

Figure 9.10: *Model Creation and Training in the BigQuery ML Environment – Step 2*

Component Explanation: Components are explained in *Table 9.4*.

`CREATE OR REPLACE MODEL`	Creates a new ML model or replaces the existing one if it exists
`model_type='LOGISTIC_REG'`	Specifies logistic regression, suitable for binary classification tasks
`auto_class_weights=TRUE`	Automatically balances class weights, which is useful when the dataset is imbalanced
`input_label_cols=['Claim']`	The target column (Claim) is what you are trying to predict.
`SELECT * FROM ...`	Uses all columns from the **`travel_insurance`** table to train the model

Table 9.4: *Component Explanation*

Step 3: Click the Run button, which shows the **model evaluation process** in **Google BigQuery ML (BQML)** after training a logistic regression model named **`travel_insurance_model`** using SQL. Evaluation Metrics (Displayed Below the Query). These are explained in *Table* 9.5 and *Figure* 9.11.

Metric	Value	Description
`precision`	0.0424	Out of all the predicted positive claims, only ~4.2% was correct. Very low precision.
`recall`	0.7023	The model successfully identified 70% of actual positive (claim) cases.
`accuracy`	0.7636	About 76.4% of all predictions (positive and negative) were correct.
`f1_score`	0.08	Combines precision and recall, but is low due to poor precision
`log_loss`	0.6889	Measures uncertainty in probability predictions (lower is better)
`roc_auc`	0.8008	Area Under the ROC Curve — good (~0.80 is considered strong); reflects the ability to rank positive over negative classes

Table 9.5: *Metrics Explanation*

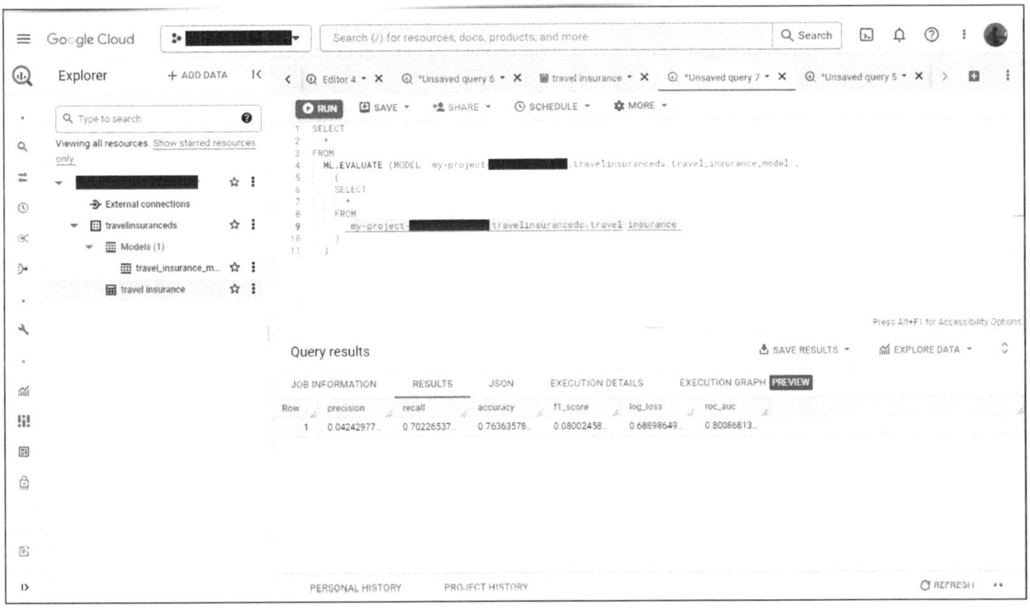

Figure 9.11: *Model Creation and Training in the BigQuery ML Environment – Step 3 (Evaluate)*

Insights

- **High recall** but **very low precision** suggests that the model is **predicting many false positives**.
- The **ROC AUC of (0.80)** is promising — the model separates positive versus negative well.

- **F1-score is low**; this means that the model might not be suitable for production without tuning.

Step 4: Prediction step using a trained model (**`travel_insurance_model`**) in **Google BigQuery ML (BQML)**. The query uses the **`ML.PREDICT`** function to apply the **logistic regression model** on the dataset **`travel_insurance`** as shown in *Figure* 9.12.

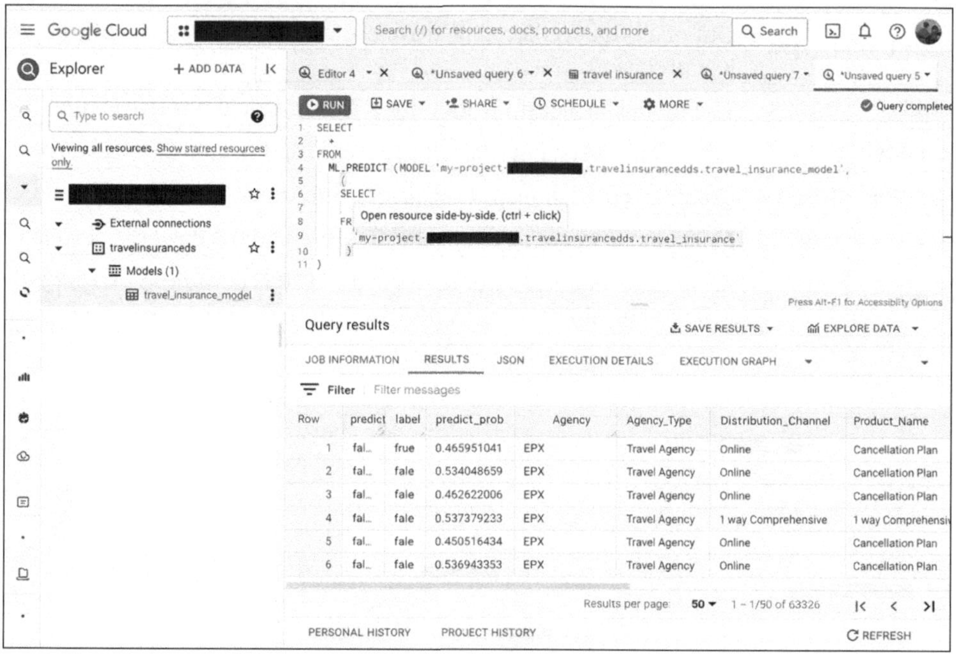

***Figure* 9.12:** *Model Creation and Training in the BigQuery ML Environment – Step 4 (Prediction)*

Query Result Explanation

Column	Description
predicted_label (`predict`)	The model's predicted outcome (true/false) for each record (likely claim or not)
actual label (`label`)	The true values from the dataset that are used to compare with the predictions
prediction probability (`predict_prob`)	Probability that the model assigns to the prediction being **true** (that is, the claim)
`Agency`, `Agency_Type`, `Distribution_Channel`, `Product_Name`	Input features used by the model, shown here to analyze prediction context

***Table* 9.6:** *Model Output Explanation*

This BigQuery ML model is designed to predict whether a travel insurance claim will be made (**`predicted_Claim`**), using logistic regression. The model was configured with a maximum of 20 iterations, but converged in just two iterations, which indicates a quick training process.

Regularization parameters L1 and L2 were both set to 0, with early stopping enabled and a learning rate strategy of line search. The data split method was set to Auto, which allowed BigQuery to manage the training and evaluation partitioning automatically.

Step 5: Navigate to the Evaluation tab of the **`travel_insurance_model`** ML model in BigQuery ML, which provides detailed insights into its performance. You can see the visualizations in *Figure* 9.13.

- **Precision-Recall with Threshold**: This method helps identify the optimal threshold where both precision and recall are acceptable.
- **Precision-Recall Curve**: Measures trade-off; low area under the curve (AUC ≈ 0.06) signals weak performance on minority class
- **ROC Curve**: Shows true positive versus false positive rates. AUC ≈ 0.779 reflects relatively good classifier behavior

The **interpretation** is as follows:

- High **recall (66.8%)**: The model excels at identifying true positives.
- **Low precision (8.9%)**: Many false positives exist.
- **ROC AUC (0.7794)** indicates decent model discrimination between classes.

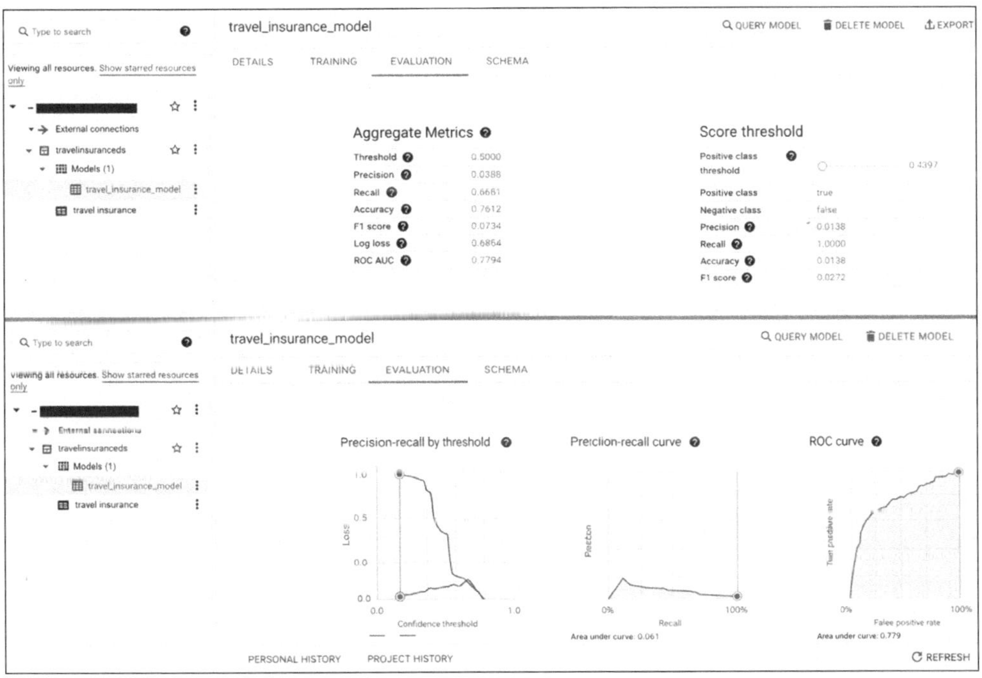

Figure 9.13: *Evaluation Visualizations*

Step 6: Navigate to the **Training tab** of the **`travel_insurance_model`** in BigQuery ML, which shows the visual metrics for model training performance over iterations as demonstrated in *Figure* 9.14.

Graph Insights

- **Loss Curve (Left)**
    - Shows the model's loss across iterations.
    - Here, the loss appears **flat**, indicating **very little change**, likely due to:
        - Early stopping
        - Limited iterations (only 2)
        - Possibly a well-fitted or undertrained model
- **Duration (Middle)**
    - Indicates the time taken for every iteration
    - Each bar shows the duration in seconds:
        - Iterations 0 and 1 have similar training times, suggesting stable computation.
- **Learning Rate (Right)**
    - Displays the **learning rate progression**
    - Since the strategy used was line search, the rate **increased** linearly over iterations.

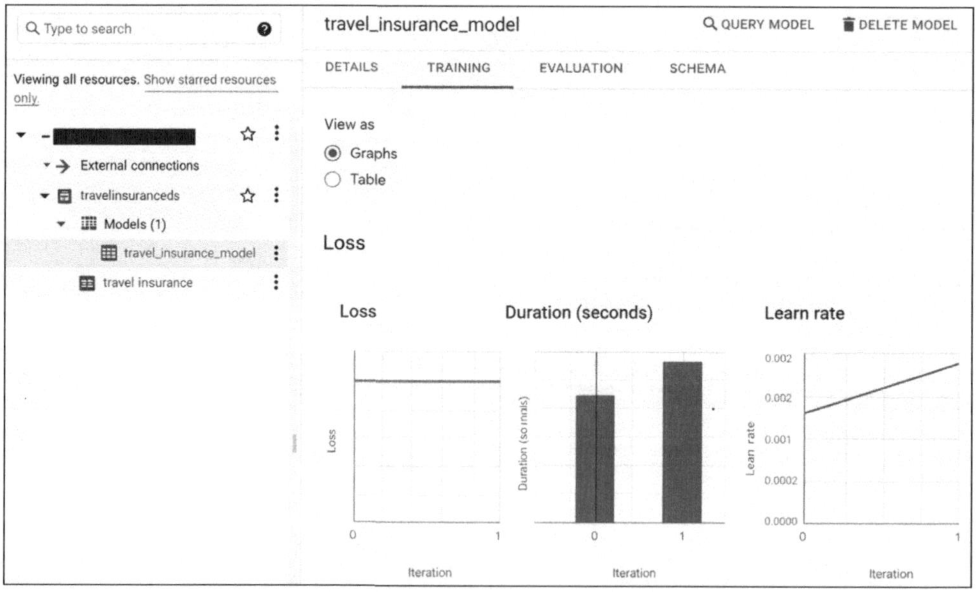

***Figure 9.14:** Model Training Performance over Iterations*

Conclusion

In this chapter, we **understood** the foundational concepts of ML and how BigQuery ML (BQML) integrates these capabilities into Google Cloud's data warehouse using familiar SQL syntax. We **explored** the range of machine learning models supported by BQML, spanning supervised, unsupervised, time-series, and imported TensorFlow models, and their real-world use cases across industries such as retail, finance, healthcare, and marketing.

We **experimented** with BQML's SQL-based interface to create, train, evaluate, and predict using various models, while observing how features such as automatic preprocessing, hyperparameter tuning, and model evaluation simplify the end-to-end machine learning workflow. Through hands-on walkthroughs and visualizations in the BigQuery ML environment, we **observed** how model performance metrics such as accuracy, ROC AUC, precision, and recall provide actionable insights into the effectiveness of our models.

Together, this journey highlighted BQML's unique ability to democratize ML, while enabling data analysts and engineers to build scalable, production-ready models within the BigQuery ecosystem. This chapter lays a solid foundation for integrating predictive intelligence into modern data platforms with minimal overhead and maximum efficiency.

In the next chapter, we will explore how BigQuery performance optimization is carried out to scale data solutions effectively.

CHAPTER 10

BigQuery Performance Optimization

Introduction

In this previous chapter, we understood the foundational concepts of Machine Learning (ML) and demonstrated how BigQuery ML (BQML) leverages these capabilities within Google Cloud's data warehouse, while utilizing familiar SQL syntax. We will now explore BQML's support for various ML models and their practical applications across domains. We have experimented with BQML's SQL-based interface. We also created, trained, evaluated, and utilized prediction models, while benefiting from built-in features such as automatic pre-processing, hyperparameter tuning, and performance evaluation. Hands-on walkthroughs and visualizations demonstrated various metrics. In this journey, we explored and understood how BQML democratizes ML, while enabling data professionals to build scalable, production-ready models efficiently within the BigQuery ecosystem.

In this chapter, we will learn what optimizing performance entails and why it is crucial for scaling data solutions effectively. This chapter focuses on techniques such as partitioning and clustering tables, schema design best practices, and query optimization to minimize costs and enhance performance. Readers will also learn strategies for managing data quality, validation, and version control, while ensuring that their BigQuery setups are efficient and reliable. By mastering these optimizations, readers can maximize the value of their data.

Structure

In this chapter, we will cover the following topics:

- Understanding Query Optimization
- Key Components of Query Optimization

- Understanding the Role of Query Optimization in Improving Performance
- The Critical Role of Query Optimization in Scaling Data Solutions
- Techniques for Query Optimization
- Exploring BigQuery Performance Optimization
- Impact of BigQuery Optimization on Other GCP Services
- Key Optimization Techniques Supporting GCP Integration
- BigQuery Schema Design
- Best Practices for BigQuery Schema Design
- Exploring BigQuery Data Quality Strategies: Data Accuracy and Control

Understanding Query Optimization

Query optimization is the process of enhancing the performance of database queries by selecting the most efficient execution plan to retrieve or manipulate data. It involves ***analyzing a query, restructuring it***, or ***leveraging database features*** to minimize resource consumption such as **CPU, *memory, disk I/O and reduce execution time***. The goal is to ensure that queries run as ***quickly*** and ***cost-effectively*** as possible while maintaining accuracy.

In database systems, a query optimizer, which is a core component of a Database Management System (DBMS), evaluates multiple execution plans for a given query and selects the one with the lowest estimated cost. The cost of this is typically measured in terms of resource usage and response time. Query optimization is critical in relational databases such as MySQL, PostgreSQL, and SQL Server, but also applies to non-relational systems such as NoSQL databases, data warehouses, and Big Data platforms.

Key Components of Query Optimization

Let us discuss the key components of query optimization techniques.

- **Query Parsing and Translation**
  - The DBMS parses the query to ensure syntactic correctness and translates it into an internal representation, such as a query tree or relational algebra expression.
  - Semantic checks ensure that the query is valid (for example, tables and columns exist).
- **Execution Plan Generation**
  - The optimizer generates multiple possible execution plans for the query. Each plan represents a distinct approach to accessing and combining data using indexes, joins, or scans.

    - Plans may involve different join orders, access methods (for example, full table scan versus index scan), or data retrieval strategies.

- **Cost Estimation**
    - The optimizer estimates the cost of each execution plan based on metrics such as CPU cycles, disk I/O, memory usage, and network latency.
    - It uses statistics about the data (for example, table size, column cardinality, index availability) to predict resource consumption.

Figure 10.1 illustrates the key components of query optimization techniques:

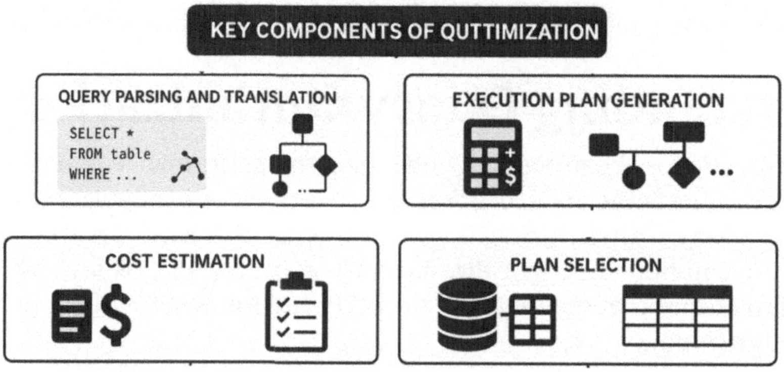

Figure 10.1: *Key Components of Query Optimization*

- **Plan Selection**
    - The optimizer selects the plan with the lowest estimated cost. This may not always be the absolute fastest plan in practice due to imperfect statistics or unpredictable workloads, but it aims to balance efficiency and reliability.
- **Execution**
    - The chosen plan is executed by the database engine, retrieving and manipulating the data as requested.

Understanding the Role of Query Optimization in Improving Performance

Query optimization has a direct impact on the performance of database operations, which is crucial for enhancing user experience, improving system efficiency, and optimizing cost management. Here is the set of factors that contribute to performance:

- **Reduced Execution Time**: Optimized queries execute faster by minimizing the number of operations, such as ***disk reads, joins, or sorts***. For example, using an index to fetch specific rows instead of scanning an entire table can reduce query time from seconds to milliseconds.

- **Lower Resource Consumption**: Efficient queries consume fewer system resources such as CPU, memory, Input and Output. This is especially important in high-concurrency environments where multiple users or applications query the database simultaneously.
- **Improved Scalability**: Optimized queries allow the system to handle larger datasets and higher query volumes without performance degradation. This is critical for scaling data solutions to support growing user bases and data volumes.

Figure 10.2 illustrates the role of query optimization in improving performance:

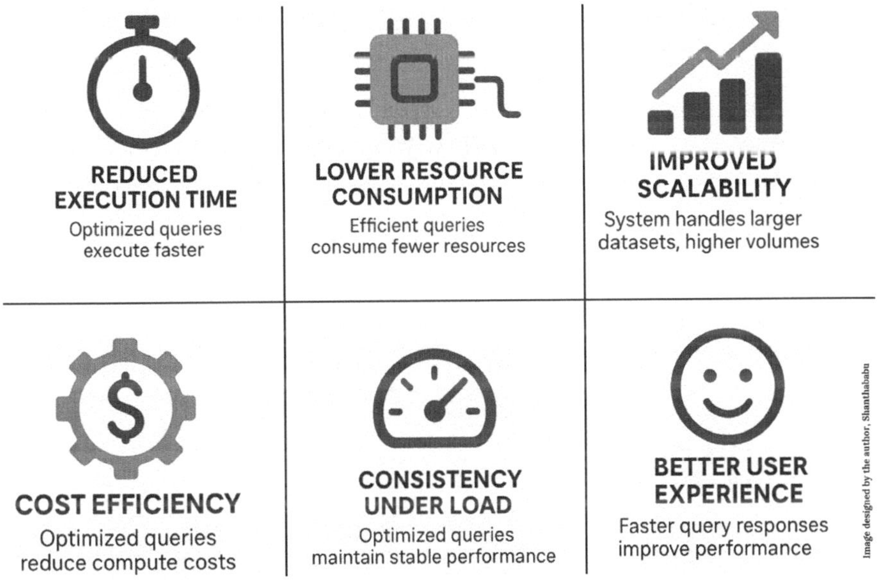

Figure 10.2: *Role of Query Optimization in Improving Performance*

- **Cost Efficiency**: In cloud-based databases (for example, AWS RDS, Google BigQuery), resource usage translates directly to costs. Optimized queries reduce compute and storage costs, which makes them essential for cost-effective operations.
- **Better User Experience**: Faster query responses improve application performance, which leads to quicker page loads, real-time analytics, or smoother user interactions.
- **Consistency Under Load**: Optimized queries maintain performance stability during peak usage, which prevents bottlenecks and ensures predictable response times.

The Critical Role of Query Optimization in Scaling Data Solutions

Scaling data solutions effectively means ensuring that a system can handle increased data volumes, user concurrency, and query complexity without compromising performance or incurring prohibitive costs. Query optimization is a cornerstone of scalability for the following reasons:

- **Handling Large Data Volumes**
  - As datasets grow (for example, from terabytes to petabytes), unoptimized queries can become exponentially slower due to increased I/O and processing requirements. Query optimization techniques such as partitioning, indexing, and materialized views enable systems to process large datasets efficiently.
  - For example, partitioning a table by date range allows queries to scan only the relevant partitions, which reduces the I/O for time-based queries.

Figure 10.3 illustrates the role of query optimization in scaling data solutions:

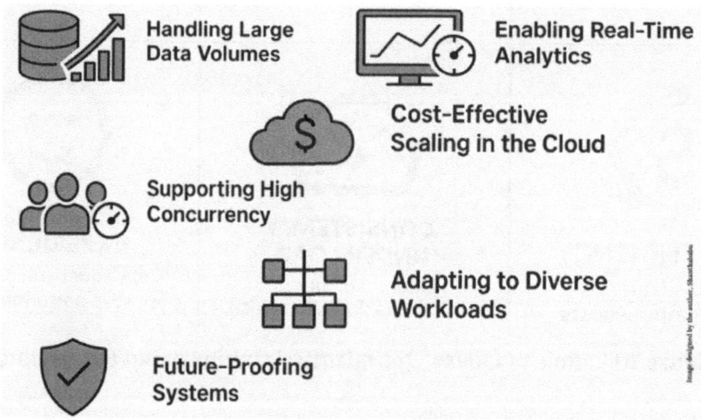

Figure 10.3: *Role of Query Optimization in Scaling Data Solutions*

- **Supporting High Concurrency**
  - In multi-user or multi-application environments, poorly optimized queries can lock resources, thereby causing contention and slowdowns. Optimized queries reduce resource contention, which enables the system to support more concurrent users.
  - **Example:** Using proper indexing and avoiding full table scans minimizes lock durations, thus improving concurrency.

- **Enabling Real-Time Analytics**
    - Modern applications often require real-time or near-real-time data processing (for example, dashboards, recommendation systems). Optimized queries ensure low-latency responses, which is critical for real-time use cases.
    - **Example**: In a data warehouse like Snowflake, query optimization ensures that complex analytical queries (for example, aggregations over billions of rows) complete quickly.
- **Cost-Effective Scaling in the Cloud**
    - Cloud databases charge based on compute and storage usage. Unoptimized queries can lead to excessive resource consumption, resulting in higher costs. Optimization ensures that scaling (for example, adding nodes or storage) remains cost-efficient.
    - **Example**: In Google BigQuery, using clustered tables and avoiding unnecessary SELECT * queries reduces billed data scans.
- **Adapting to Diverse Workloads**
    - Scalable systems must handle a mix of query types (for example, OLTP for transactional workloads, OLAP for analytical workloads). Query optimization ensures that diverse workloads run efficiently by tailoring execution plans to specific query patterns.
    - **Example**: OLTP systems benefit from indexes for point queries, while OLAP systems use columnar storage for aggregations.
- **Future-Proofing Systems**
    - As data and user demands grow, optimized queries prevent the need for frequent hardware upgrades or re-architecture. This makes the system more resilient to future scaling requirements.
    - **Example**: A well-optimized database can delay the need for sharding or distributed architectures by maximizing single-node performance.

Techniques for Query Optimization

In general, we can achieve optimal performance and scalability. The following techniques are employed in query optimization:

- **Indexing: Indexes** (for example, B-tree, hash, bitmap) allow the database to locate rows quickly without scanning entire tables. Indexes increase storage and maintenance overhead. Therefore, they must be used judiciously.

Example: A B-tree index on the `user_id` column speeds up lookups for specific users.

- **Query Rewriting**: Rewriting queries to use more efficient constructs (for example, replacing subqueries with joins) can reduce execution time.

  Example: `SELECT * FROM users WHERE id IN (SELECT user_id FROM orders)` can be rewritten as a JOIN for better performance.

- **Table Partitioning: Dividing** large tables into smaller partitions based on a key (for example, date, region) reduces the data scanned by queries.

  Example: A table partitioned by year allows queries for 2025 data to skip earlier partitions.

- **Materialized Views**: Pre-computed results stored as materialized views can speed up frequently executed queries, especially in data warehouses.

  Example: A materialized view aggregating daily sales avoids recalculating sums for every query.

- **Caching**: Caching query results (for example, in Redis or Memcached) reduces database load for repetitive queries.

  Example: Caching a leaderboard query in a gaming app avoids redundant database hits.

- **Denormalization**: In some cases, denormalizing data (for example, combining tables to avoid joins) improves query performance at the cost of increased storage.

  Example: Storing user details and order summaries in a single table for faster retrieval

- **Statistics and Histograms**: Keeping database statistics up to date ensures that the optimizer has accurate information about data distribution, which leads to better execution plans.

  Example: Updating statistics after a large data load prevents the optimizer from choosing suboptimal plans.

Figure 10.4 illustrates the techniques for query optimization:

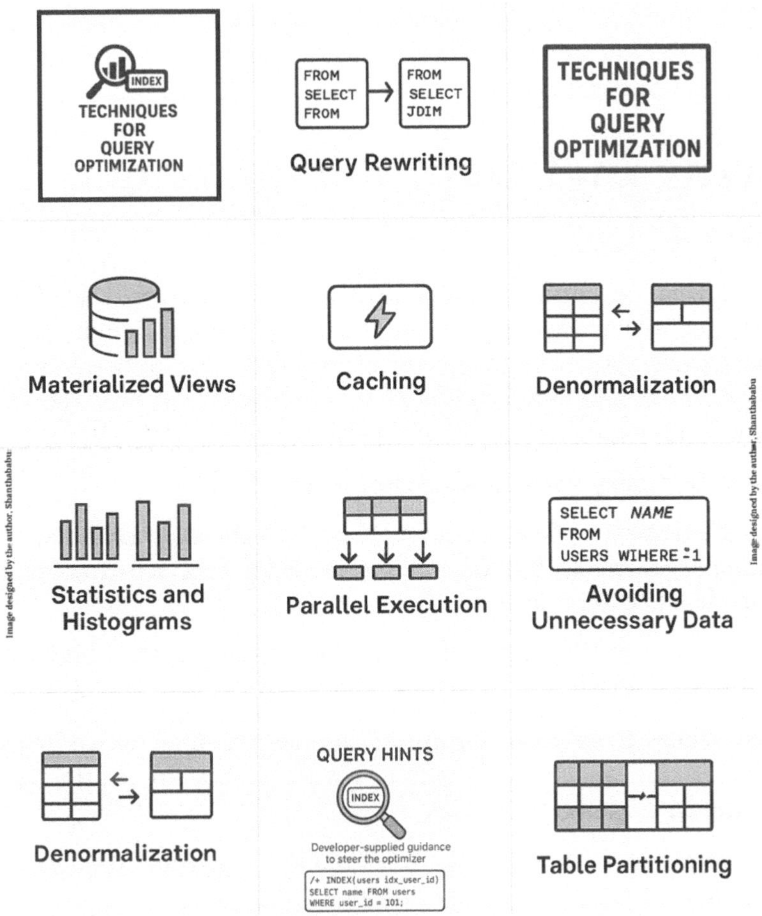

***Figure 10.4**: Techniques for Query Optimization*

- **Parallel Execution**: Distributing query execution across multiple CPU cores or nodes (in distributed systems) reduces processing time for large queries.

  Example: In Apache Spark, queries are parallelized across a cluster to handle big data workloads.

- **Avoiding Unnecessary Data**: Selecting only required columns (instead of **`SELECT *`**) and filtering early (for example, using **`WHERE`** clauses) reduces data processing.

  For example, **`SELECT name, email FROM users WHERE active = 1`** is more efficient than **`SELECT * FROM users`**.

- **Query Hints**: In some cases, developers can provide hints to the optimizer to guide plan selection (for example, forcing the use of a specific index).

Example: In PostgreSQL, `/*+ INDEX(table_name index_name) */` suggests using a particular index.

So far, we have discussed generic query optimizations; now, let us focus on how query performance and optimizations techniques work in GCP BigQuery.

Exploring BigQuery Performance Optimization

BigQuery performance optimization is critical for enhancing the efficiency, cost-effectiveness, and scalability of data processing in Google Cloud Platform's (GCP) serverless data warehouse. Beyond improving BigQuery itself, optimization significantly benefits other GCP components by enabling seamless integration, reducing resource contention, and enhancing overall system performance.

Significance of BigQuery Performance Optimization

- **Cost Efficiency**: BigQuery charges based on the data scanned. Optimization techniques such as ***partitioning, clustering, and selective column queries reduce scanned data, lowering costs.***

  For example, partitioning a 1TB table by date and clustering by `customer_id` can reduce query costs by 50-70% by scanning only relevant data.

- **Faster Query Execution**: Optimized queries ***run faster, enabling real-time or near-real-time analytics critical for time-sensitive*** applications such as ***fraud detection or customer analytics.***

  For example, a query on a partitioned table runs in seconds instead of minutes, which supports rapid decision-making.

- **Scalability**: BigQuery handles ***petabyte-scale data***, but unoptimized queries can strain resources. Optimization ensures consistent performance as data grows.

  For example, clustering minimizes data shuffling, while maintaining performance for large-scale joins.

- **Improved User Productivity**: Faster queries enhance the experience for ***data analysts, scientists, and stakeholders, while enabling quicker insights and iteration.***

  For example, dashboards powered by optimized queries load instantly, which improves user satisfaction.

- **Resource Efficiency**: Optimization reduces resource contention in shared environments, which also ensures equitable performance across users and workloads.

- For example, efficient queries free up slots for other processes in flat-rate pricing models.

Impact of BigQuery Optimization on Other GCP Services

BigQuery integrates with various GCP services, as we discussed in earlier chapters. Here, we will explore how performance optimization amplifies their effectiveness by reducing latency, costs, and resource usage. The following are the key GCP components:

Cloud Dataflow: Dataflow processes and transforms streaming or batch data, often loading results into BigQuery.

- **Benefit**: Optimized BigQuery tables (for example, partitioned by ingestion time) reduce write latency and query costs for Dataflow outputs. For example, Dataflow pipelines writing to partitioned tables enable faster downstream queries and improve ETL pipeline efficiency.
- **Example**: A Dataflow job streaming IoT sensor data into a partitioned BigQuery table allows real-time analytics with minimal query lag.

Figure 10.5 illustrates the impact of BigQuery optimization on other GCP services:

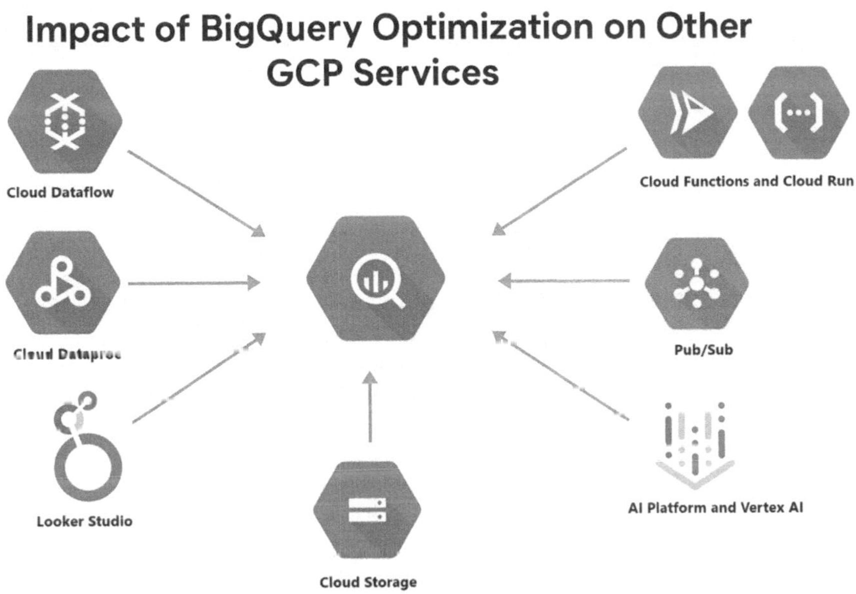

Figure 10.5: *Impact of BigQuery Optimization on Other GCP Services*

Cloud Dataproc: Dataproc runs Spark and Hadoop jobs, often querying BigQuery for analytics.

- **Benefits**: Optimized BigQuery tables reduce query execution time for Dataproc jobs, while lowering compute costs and improving job throughput. Clustering ensures that Spark queries scan less data.
- **Example**: A Spark job on Dataproc querying a clustered BigQuery table by region processes data 60% faster, which reduces cluster runtime.

Looker Studio (formerly Google Data Studio): Looker Studio creates interactive dashboards using BigQuery as a data source.

- **Benefits**: Optimized queries with BI Engine and materialized views ensure low-latency dashboard rendering to enhance user experience. Reduced data scanning lowers costs for frequent dashboard refreshes.
- **Example**: A sales dashboard using a materialized view in BigQuery refreshes in <2 seconds, which improves stakeholder access to insights.

Cloud Functions and Cloud Run: These serverless compute services trigger workflows or process data, while often interacting with BigQuery.

- **Benefits**: Optimized BigQuery queries reduce latency in event-driven workflows, which ensure faster execution of Cloud Functions and Cloud Run tasks. This minimizes compute costs and improves responsiveness.
- **Example**: A Cloud Function triggered by a new BigQuery table partition processes data faster due to clustering and complete it in half the time.

Pub/Sub: Pub/Sub handles real-time messaging, often feeding data into BigQuery via Dataflow.

- **Benefit**: Optimized BigQuery ingestion (for example, partitioned tables) ensures efficient handling of high-throughput Pub/Sub messages, which reduces backlog and processing delays.
- **Example**: A Pub/Sub stream feeding clickstream data into BigQuery benefits from ingestion-time partitioning, which enables near-real-time analytics.

Cloud Storage: Cloud Storage stores raw data before loading it into BigQuery or acts as an external table source.

- **Benefits**: Optimized BigQuery queries on external tables in Cloud Storage reduce data scanning and improve performance. Partitioned external tables align with BigQuery's optimization strategies.
- **Example**: Querying a partitioned external table in Cloud Storage reduces scan costs by 80% compared to unpartitioned data.

AI Platform and Vertex AI: These platforms use BigQuery to train ML models or run predictions.

- **Benefit**: Optimized BigQuery queries provide faster data retrieval for model training, which reduces compute time and costs. Materialized views can pre-aggregate features for ML pipelines.
- **Example**: A Vertex AI model trained on a clustered BigQuery table retrieves features 50% faster, which speeds up the training process.

BigQuery ML: BigQuery ML trains and serves ML models directly in BigQuery.

- **Benefits**: Optimized tables reduce training and prediction times as less data is scanned. This lowers costs and improves model iteration speed.
- **For example,** a logistic regression model trained on a partitioned dataset runs 40% faster, which enables quicker experimentation.

Key Optimization Techniques Supporting GCP Integration

Next, we will cover key optimization techniques in detail, including their mechanics, benefits, and specific impacts on GCP services such as ***Dataflow, Dataproc, Looker Studio, BigQuery ML, Cloud Functions, Vertex AI, and other relevant services***. The goal is to illustrate how these optimizations reduce data scanning, lower costs, improve query performance, and enhance the efficiency of integrated GCP workflows.

Partitioning and Clustering

- **Partitioning**: Divides a BigQuery table into smaller segments (partitions) based on a column, typically a date, timestamp, or integer (for example, **`transaction_date`** or **`customer_id`**). Partitions limit the data scanned by queries to only the relevant segments.
- **Clustering**: Organizes data within each partition based on one or more columns (up to four), and groups similar values. This reduces the amount of data scanned for queries that filter or aggregate on clustered columns (for example, **`store_id`** or **`region`**).

How It Works

- Partitioning splits data into logical chunks (for example, daily partitions for **`DATE(sale_date)`**), so a query like **`SELECT * FROM table WHERE sale_date = '2025-07-01'`** scans only that day's partition.
- Clustering sorts data within partitions, so queries with **`WHERE`** or **`GROUP BY`** on clustered columns (for example, **`WHERE store_id = '123'`**) scan only the relevant data blocks.
- BigQuery automatically maintains clustering, while partitioning can be time-based ***(ingestion or column-based)*** or range-based.

Figure 10.6 illustrates partitioning and clustering:

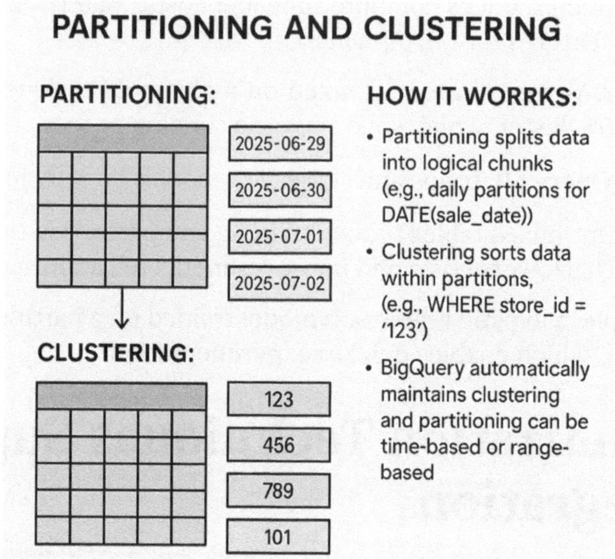

Figure 10.6: *Optimization Techniques - Partitioning and Clustering*

Benefits of GCP Integration

- **Cloud Dataflow**: Partitioned tables reduce write and read latency for Dataflow pipelines that are loading or querying BigQuery. For example, a Dataflow job that processes streaming IoT data into a partitioned table by event date enables faster downstream analytics.
- **Cloud Dataproc**: Spark and Hadoop jobs on Dataproc benefit from reduced data scanning when querying partitioned/clustered tables, which lowers compute costs and speeds up job completion.
- **Looker Studio**: Dashboards querying partitioned/clustered tables load faster as only relevant data is scanned. This improves user experience for real-time reporting.
- **Vertex AI**: ML training pipelines retrieve data faster from partitioned/clustered tables, which reduces pre-processing time.
- **Example**: A 5TB sales table partitioned by `sale_date` and clustered by `product_category` reduces the amount of data scanned by 80% for a Dataflow job aggregating sales, cutting costs and processing time from 30 minutes to 5 minutes.

Implementation Tips

- Choose partitioning keys based on common query filters (***for example,*** `DATE(timestamp)` ***for time-series data***).

- Select clustering keys with high cardinality and frequent use in filters or joins (*for example*, `customer_id`, `region`).
- Combine partitioning and clustering for maximum efficiency (*for example*, `partition by date`, *cluster by* `user_id`).
- Monitor query execution details to ensure partitions/clusters are leveraged.

Materialized Views

Materialized views are pre-computed, stored query results that automatically refresh when the underlying table changes. They are ideal for repetitive aggregations or complex queries.

Figure 10.7 illustrates materialized views:

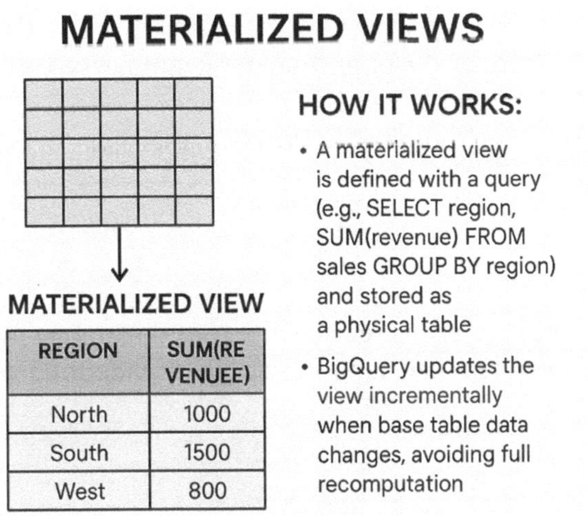

Figure 10.7: *Optimization Technique -Materialized Views*

How It Works

- A materialized view is defined by a query (for example, `SELECT region, SUM(revenue) FROM sales GROUP BY region`) and stored as a physical table.
- BigQuery updates the view incrementally when the base table data changes, while avoiding full recomputation.
- Queries on materialized views scan less data than recomputing aggregations on raw tables.

Benefits of GCP Integration

- **Looker Studio**: Materialized views pre-aggregate data for dashboards, which reduces query latency and costs. For example, a view aggregating daily sales by `store_id` ensures instant dashboard refreshes.

- **BigQuery ML**: Training ML models on materialized views is faster, as pre-aggregated features (for example, average customer spend) reduce data processing.
- **Cloud Functions/Cloud Run**: Event-driven workflows querying materialized views complete faster. This minimizes compute runtime and costs.
- **Example**: A materialized view summarizing 10TB of transaction data by date and category reduces query time for a Looker Studio dashboard from 20 seconds to 2 seconds and cuts costs by 60%.

Implementation Tips

- Create materialized views for frequently run aggregations or joins.
- Ensure that the view's query leverages partitioning/clustering for additional savings.
- Monitor view refresh costs and adjust granularity to balance freshness and expense.
- Use BigQuery's automatic refresh to keep views updated without manual intervention.

BI Engine

BI Engine is an in-memory analysis service integrated with BigQuery, which is designed to accelerate query performance for interactive applications such as dashboards or ad-hoc analysis.

How It Works

- BI Engine allocates in-memory capacity (slots) to cache and process query results, which reduces latency for complex or repetitive queries.
- It integrates seamlessly with Looker Studio, BigQuery's console, and other BI tools via JDBC/ODBC.
- Users reserve BI Engine capacity (for example, 1GB or 10GB) to enable low-latency queries.

Figure 10.8 illustrates the BI Engine:

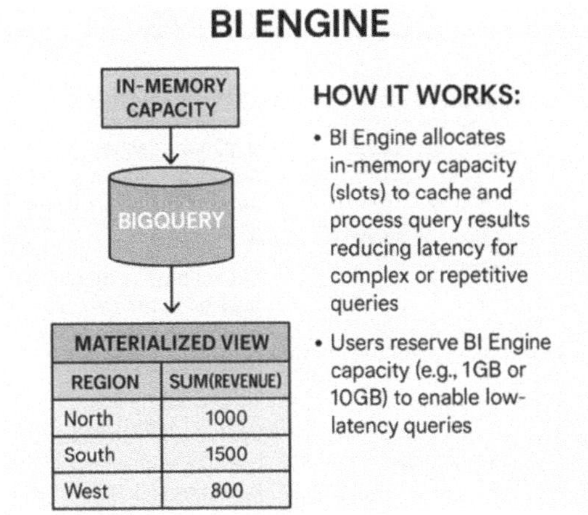

Figure 10.8: *Optimization Techniques - BI Engine*

Benefits of GCP Integration

- **Looker Studio**: BI Engine ensures sub-second query responses for dashboards, which enhances the user experience for real-time analytics.
- **Cloud Functions/Cloud Run**: Serverless applications querying BigQuery for real-time insights (for example, recommendation systems) benefit from BI Engine's low latency.
- **Vertex AI**: Faster data retrieval for feature engineering and inference queries improves ML pipeline efficiency.
- **Example**: A retail dashboard in Looker Studio using BI Engine renders a complex sales report in <1 second, compared to 10 seconds without BI Engine, which improves stakeholder decision-making.

Implementation Tips

- Reserve BI Engine capacity based on workload needs (start small, for example, 1GB, and scale up).
- Combine partitioned/clustered tables to maximize performance.
- Monitor BI Engine usage in the GCP console to optimize capacity allocation.
- Use for high-concurrency or latency-sensitive workloads such as dashboards or APIs.

Query Caching

Query caching stores the results of identical queries in BigQuery's temporary storage, which allows reuse without reprocessing.

Figure 10.9 illustrates the query caching:

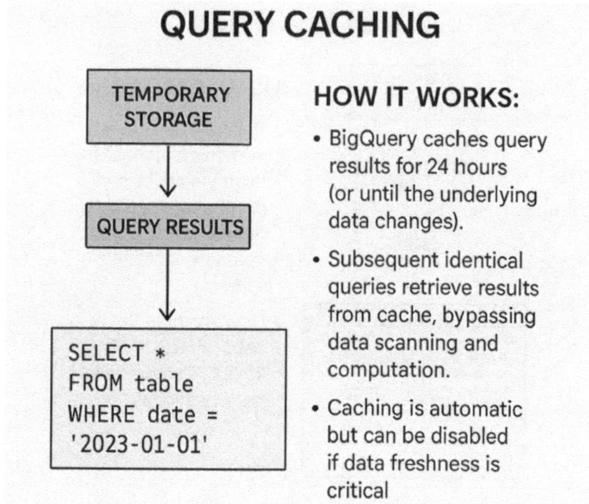

Figure 10.9: *Optimization Technique -Query Caching*

How It Works

- BigQuery caches query results for 24 hours (or until the underlying data changes).
- Subsequent identical queries retrieve results from the cache and bypass data scanning and computation.
- Caching is automatic, but it can be disabled if data freshness is critical.

Benefits of GCP Integration:

- **Looker Studio**: Dashboards that run repetitive queries (for example, daily sales summaries) use cached results, while reducing costs and load times.
- **BigQuery ML**: ML pipelines running feature extraction queries benefit from caching and speed up iterative training.
- **Cloud Functions/Cloud Run**: Event-driven workflows querying static datasets (for example, reference tables) avoid redundant processing, which lowers costs.
- **Example**: A Looker Studio report querying a 1TB table daily uses cached results reduces the query costs from $5 to $0 and cutting load time from 15 seconds to 1 second.

Implementation Tips

- Ensure that queries are deterministic (for example, avoid NOW() or random functions) to enable caching.
- Use for stable datasets or infrequently updated tables.

- Monitor cache hit rates in query execution details to assess effectiveness.
- Disable caching for real-time applications requiring fresh data.

Schema Design (Denormalization)

Denormalization involves flattening nested or related data into a single table to simplify queries and reduce the need for complex joins.

Figure 10.10 illustrates schema design:

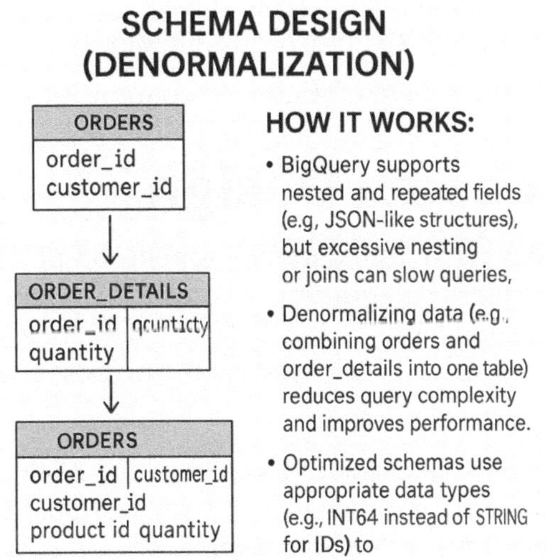

***Figure* 10.10**: *Optimization Techniques - Schema Design*

How It Works

- BigQuery supports nested and repeated fields (for example, JSON-like structures), but excessive nesting or joins can slow queries.
- Denormalizing data (for example, combining orders and **`order_details`** into one table) reduces query complexity and improves performance.
- Optimized schemas use appropriate data types (for example, **`INT64`** instead of **`STRING`** for **`IDs`**) to minimize storage and processing.

Benefits of GCP Integration

- **Cloud Dataflow**: Denormalized tables simplify ETL pipelines as Dataflow processes fewer joins and reduces compute time and costs.
- **BigQuery ML**: Flattened schemas provide faster feature access for model training, which improves iteration speed.
- **Cloud Dataproc**: Spark jobs querying denormalized tables execute faster due to fewer joins, which lowers cluster costs.

- **For example, a** denormalized 2TB table combining customer and transaction data reduced Dataflow ETL runtime by 40% and BigQuery ML training time by 30%, compared to querying normalized tables.

Implementation Tips:

- Denormalize during data ingestion (for example, via Dataflow or Cloud Data Fusion).
- Balance denormalization with storage costs as you increase table size.
- Use nested/repeated fields for related data (for example, arrays for ordered items) to maintain some structure without joins.
- Regularly review the schema for unused columns or inefficient data types.

BigQuery Schema Design

BigQuery schema design is a foundational aspect of performance optimization, cost efficiency, and seamless integration with other Google Cloud Platform (GCP) components. A well-designed schema enhances query performance, reduces data scanning costs, simplifies data processing, and ensures scalability for large-scale analytics.

The following is a detailed explanation of BigQuery schema design principles and best practices, and their impact on performance and integration, tailored to the context of performance optimization and GCP ecosystems.

Understanding BigQuery Schema Design

In BigQuery, a schema defines the structure of a table, including column names, data types, and properties like required or nullable fields. Unlike traditional relational databases, BigQuery is a columnar, serverless data warehouse optimized for analytical queries, with no indexes or primary/foreign keys. Instead, it relies on columnar storage, partitioning, clustering, and nested/repeated fields for performance. Schema design directly influences query efficiency, storage costs, and integration with GCP services such as Dataflow, Looker Studio, BigQuery ML, and Vertex AI.

Key Schema Design Considerations

- **Columnar Storage**: BigQuery stores data in a columnar format, making it efficient for analytical queries that access specific columns. Selecting fewer columns reduces the amount of data scanned, which lowers costs and improves speed.

- **Nested and Repeated Fields**: BigQuery supports nested (`STRUCT`) and repeated (ARRAY) fields, enabling semi-structured data storage (for example, JSON-like data) without requiring joins.

- **Partitioning and Clustering**: Schema design must account for columns used for partitioning (for example, date) and clustering (for example, high-cardinality fields like **user_id**) to minimize data scanned.
- **Data Types**: Choosing appropriate data types (for example, INT64 versus STRING) affects storage size and query performance.
- **Denormalization**: BigQuery performs best with denormalized schemas, which reduces the need for complex joins, which are resource-intensive.

A **schema in BigQuery** defines the structure of a table, that is, the name, data type, and mode (**NULLABLE**, **REQUIRED**, **REPEATED**) of each field. *Table* 10.1 illustrates the schema components in BigQuery.

Component	Description
Field Name	Identifier for the column
Data Type	Data types: **STRING**, **INT64**, **FLOAT64**, **BOOL**, **BYTES**, **TIMESTAMP**, **DATE**, **DATETIME**, **TIME**, **GEOGRAPHY**, **RECORD**
Mode	**NULLABLE** (default), **REQUIRED**, **REPEATED** (array)

Table 10.1: *Schema Components*

Best Practices for BigQuery Schema Design

We have mentioned the best practices for designing BigQuery schemas, along with explanations of their rationale, implementation, and impact on performance and GCP integration.

Figure 10.11 illustrates best practices for BigQuery schema design:

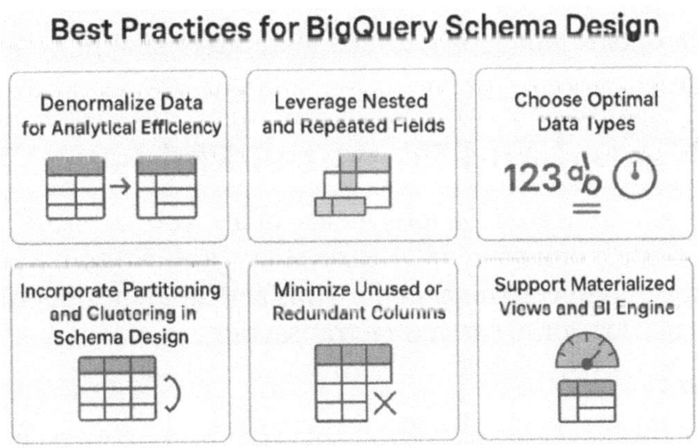

Figure 10.11: *Best Practices for BigQuery Schema Design*

Denormalize Data for Analytical Efficiency

BigQuery is optimized for analytical queries, not transactional ones. Joins across multiple tables are computationally expensive and increase data scanning costs. Denormalization flattens related data into a single table and reduces query complexity and improving performance.

How to Implement

- Combine related tables (for example, **`orders`** and **`order_details`**) into one table during data ingestion through tools such as Cloud Dataflow or Cloud Data Fusion.
- Use nested/repeated fields to store related data hierarchically (for example, an order with an array of **`order_items`**).
- **Example**: Instead of separate customers and orders tables, create a single table with a customer **`STRUCT`** containing fields like **`customer_id`** and name, and a repeated orders **`ARRAY`** containing fields like **`order_id`** and **`amount`**.

Benefits

- Simplifies queries by eliminating joins, which reduces query execution time and costs
- Enhances performance for GCP services such as Dataflow (fewer transformations) and BigQuery ML (faster feature access)
- Example: A denormalized 10TB table combining events and users reduces Dataflow ETL runtime by 40% and BigQuery ML training time by 30% compared to normalized tables

Considerations:

- Denormalization increases storage size, so it must be balanced with cost constraints.
- Use nested fields judiciously to maintain query simplicity without excessive complexity.

Leverage Nested and Repeated Fields

Nested (**`STRUCT`**) and repeated (**`ARRAY`**) fields allow you to store semi-structured data efficiently, while mimicking JSON-like structures without requiring separate tables. This approach reduces the need for joins and simplifies queries, especially for hierarchical data like logs or e-commerce transactions.

How to Implement

- Use **`STRUCT`** for one-to-one relationships (for example, a customer field with a name and email subfields).

- Use **ARRAY** for one-to-many relationships (for example, an **order_items** array with **item_id** and price for each order).
- **Example** Schema:

```
CREATE TABLE dataset.sales (
  sale_id INT64,
  sale_date DATE,
  customer STRUCT<customer_id INT64, name STRING, email STRING>,
  items ARRAY<STRUCT<item_id INT64, product_name STRING, price
FLOAT64>>
)
PARTITION BY sale_date;
```

Benefits

- Reduces query complexity by embedding related data, improving performance for services such as Looker Studio (dashboards) and Vertex AI (ML feature extraction)
- Minimizes data scanning by keeping related data together, lowering costs
- **Example**: Querying a nested items array for the total order value is 50% faster than joining the separate orders and order_items tables

Considerations

- Avoid excessive nesting (for example, >3 levels), as it can complicate queries and reduce readability.
- Use **UNNEST** sparingly, as it can increase the amount of data scanned if not combined with filtering.

Choose Optimal Data Types

Data types impact storage size and query performance. For example, storing IDs as STRING instead of INT64 increases storage but slows comparisons. BigQuery's columnar storage benefits from compact, precise data types.

How to Implement

- Use numeric types (**INT64**, **FLOAT64**) for IDs, counts, or metrics instead of **STRING**.
- Prefer **DATE**, **DATETIME**, or **TIMESTAMP** for time-based data to enable partitioning and efficient filtering.
- Use **STRING** for unstructured or variable-length data, but avoid overuse for structured fields.
- Example: Change a **customer_id** column from STRING (for example, "**12345**") to **INT64** (**12345**) to reduce storage by 20% and speed up comparisons.

Benefits

- Reduces storage costs, as compact data types use less space
- Speeds up query operations (for example, filtering, grouping) for services such as BigQuery ML and Dataproc
- **Example**: Converting a `product_id` column from `STRING` to `INT64` in a 5TB table saves 10% storage and reduces query time by 15% for a Dataflow pipeline.

Considerations

- Validate data consistency before changing types to avoid errors (for example, non-numeric values in a `STRING` column).
- Use BigQuery's schema auto-detection for initial loads, but manually refine types for production.

Incorporate Partitioning and Clustering in Schema Design

Partitioning and clustering reduce the amount of data scanned by queries, directly lowering costs and improving performance. Schema design must include columns suitable for partitioning (for example, time-based) and clustering (for example, high-cardinality filters).

How to Implement

- **Partitioning**: Choose a column to use for partitioning, typically `DATE`, `TIMESTAMP`, or `INTEGER`. Common choices include `created_at` or `transaction_date`.
  - **Example**: `PARTITION BY DATE(sale_date)` for daily partitions
  - **Types**: Ingestion-time (based on load time) or column-based (for example, `DATE` or `INTEGER` range)
- **Clustering**: Select up to four columns frequently used in `WHERE`, `GROUP BY`, or `JOIN` clauses (for example, `customer_id`, `region`).
  - **Example**: `CLUSTER BY customer_id`, `region`.

Example Schema:

```
CREATE TABLE dataset.transactions (
  transaction_id INT64,
  transaction_date TIMESTAMP,
  customer_id INT64,
  region STRING,
  amount FLOAT64
)
```

```
PARTITION BY DATE(transaction_date)
CLUSTER BY customer_id, region;
```

Benefits:

- Reduces data scanned by 50-80% for queries filtering on partitioned/clustered columns, benefiting Dataflow, Looker Studio, and Vertex AI.
- Speeds up query execution, for example, a query on a 1TB partitioned/clustered table runs in 5 seconds versus 30 seconds unoptimized.
- Example: A Dataproc Spark job querying a clustered table by **`customer_id`** completes 60% faster, reducing cluster costs.

Considerations:

- Choose partitioning keys with moderate cardinality (for example, daily partitions, not hourly, to avoid excessive partitions).
- Cluster on high-cardinality columns (for example, **`user_id`**) for maximum efficiency.
- Monitor partition/clustering effectiveness via query execution details.

Minimize Unused or Redundant Columns

BigQuery charges based on data scanned, so unused or redundant columns increase costs without adding value. A lean schema improves query performance and simplifies maintenance.

How to Implement

- Audit schemas to identify columns not used in queries or reports (use BigQuery audit logs or query history).
- Remove or archive unused columns during data ingestion or transformation (for example, via Dataflow).
- Avoid duplicating data across columns (for example, storing both **`full_name`** and **`first_name`** + **`last_name`**).
- Example: Drop a **`legacy_id`** column no longer used in a 2TB table to reduce storage by 5% and query costs by 10%.

Benefits

- Lowers storage and query costs, which impacts all GCP services querying BigQuery
- Simplifies schema for downstream processing in Dataflow or BigQuery ML
- Example: Removing unused columns from a table saves $100/month in query costs for a Looker Studio dashboard

Considerations

- Archive dropped columns to Cloud Storage for future reference.
- Validate with stakeholders before removing columns to avoid data loss.

Supporting Materialized Views and BI Engine

Materialized views and BI Engine rely on well-designed schemas to maximize performance for repetitive or interactive queries. Schema design should anticipate pre-aggregation or in-memory processing needs.

How to Implement

- Design schemas with columns suited for aggregation in materialized views (for example, SUM(amount) by date and region).
- Ensure that partitioning/clustering aligns with materialized view queries to minimize refresh costs.
- Use compact data types and denormalized structures to optimize BI Engine's in-memory processing.
- **Example**: A materialized view on a table with **`DATE(sale_date)`** partitioning and **`store_id`** clustering refreshes 50% faster.

Benefits

- Materialized views speed up Looker Studio dashboards and BigQuery ML training by pre-aggregating data.
- BI Engine ensures sub-second query responses for Cloud Functions or Vertex AI real-time applications.
- Example: A materialized view reduces Looker Studio query time from 20 seconds to 2 seconds, saving 70% in costs.

Considerations

- Limit materialized views to high-value, repetitive queries to control refresh costs.
- Reserve BI Engine capacity based on workload (for example, 1GB for small dashboards, 10GB for enterprise use).

Exploring BigQuery Data Quality Strategies: Data Accuracy and Control

Let us explore key techniques for maintaining ***data accuracy, ensuring validation integrity***, and ***implementing effective version control*** within Google BigQuery environments. These strategies are essential for developing reliable, high-performance data pipelines and analytics solutions.

Data Accuracy

Data accuracy ensures that the data stored and processed in BigQuery is correct, consistent, and trustworthy.

Figure 10.12 illustrates the key techniques to achieve this:

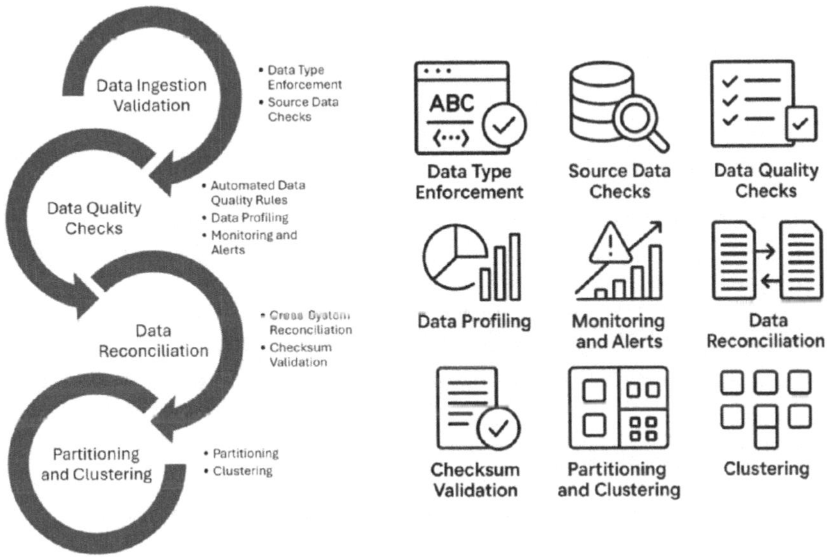

***Figure 10.12**: BigQuery's Data Accuracy Strategies*

Data Ingestion Validation

- **Schema Validation**: Define strict table schemas in BigQuery using JSON schema definitions or explicit column definitions. Use **`REQUIRED`** fields for critical columns to prevent null values.
    - **Example**: When creating a table, specify the following:

    ```
    CREATE TABLE my dataset.my_table (
      id STRING NOT NULL,
      timestamp TIMESTAMP NOT NULL,
      value FLOAT64 );
    ```

- **Data Type Enforcement**: Ensure that incoming data matches the expected data types. Use BigQuery's built-in type casting or preprocessing scripts to validate and transform data before loading.
- **Source Data Checks**: Implement checks at the data source (for example, ETL pipelines) to verify data formats, ranges, and completeness before ingestion.
    - **Example**: Use Apache Airflow or Cloud Composer to validate CSV files before loading them into BigQuery.

Data Quality Checks

- **Automated Data Quality Rules**: Create SQL-based data quality checks to run after data ingestion. These checks can identify anomalies, missing values, or duplicates.
    - **Example**: Check for duplicate records through the following:

    ```
    SELECT id, COUNT(*) as count
    FROM my_dataset.my_table
    GROUP BY id
    HAVING count > 1;
    ```

- **Data Profiling**: Use tools such as Dataform or custom SQL scripts to profile data distributions, detect outliers, and ensure data conforms to expected patterns.
- **Monitoring and Alerts**: Set up Cloud Monitoring to track data quality metrics (for example, row counts, null percentages) and trigger alerts for anomalies.

Data Reconciliation

- **Cross-System Reconciliation**: Compare data between BigQuery and source systems (for example, CRM, ERP) to ensure consistency.
    - **Example**: Reconcile row counts between a source database and BigQuery via:

    ```
    SELECT COUNT(*) as source_count FROM source_db.table
    -- Compare with
    SELECT COUNT(*) as bq_count FROM my_dataset.my_table
    ```

- **Checksum Validation**: Compute checksums or hashes for critical columns in both the source and BigQuery to verify data integrity during transfers.

Partitioning and Clustering

- **Partitioning**: Use time-based or integer-based partitioning to improve query performance and reduce the risk of processing incorrect data.
    - **Example**: Partition a table by date, as shown:

    ```
    CREATE TABLE my_dataset.my_table (
      id STRING,
      event_date DATE
    )
    PARTITION BY event_date;
    ```

- **Clustering**: Apply clustering on frequently queried columns to optimize performance and reduce costs, while ensuring accurate results for filtered queries.
    - **Example**: Cluster by a customer ID, as shown:

```
CREATE TABLE my_dataset.my_table
CLUSTER BY customer_id;
```

Validation Integrity

Validation integrity ensures that data processing and transformations in BigQuery produce correct and consistent results. *Figure* 10.13 illustrates the techniques to maintain validation integrity.

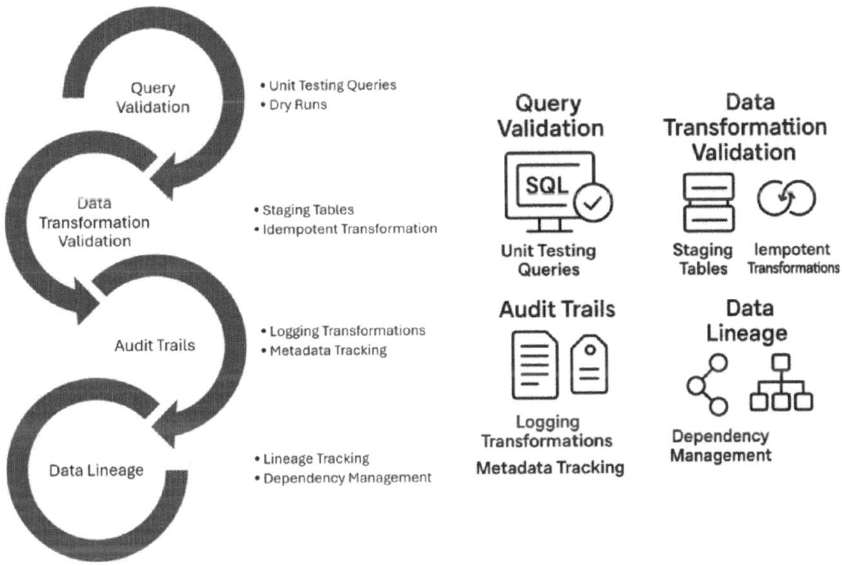

***Figure* 10.13:** *BigQuery's Validation Integrity Strategies*

Query Validation

- **Unit Testing Queries**: Use tools like dbt (Data Build Tool) to create unit tests for SQL queries. Test edge cases, null values, and expected outputs.
    - **Example** dbt test:

```
models:
name: my_table
tests:
not_null:
column_name: id
unique:
column_name: id
```

- **Dry Runs**: Use BigQuery's **--dry_run** flag to validate query syntax and estimate costs without executing the query.
    - **Example**:

      ```
      bq query --dry_run "SELECT * FROM my_dataset.my_table WHERE
      event_date = '2025-07-12'"
      ```

Data Transformation Validation

- **Staging Tables**: Use staging tables to load raw data before applying transformations. Validate the transformed data against the staging data to ensure correctness.
    - **Example**: Compare row counts before and after a transformation through:
        - `SELECT COUNT(*) as staging_count FROM my_dataset.staging_table`

          Compare with
        - `SELECT COUNT(*) as transformed_count FROM my_dataset.transformed_table`
- **Idempotent Transformations**: Design transformations to be idempotent and ensure that running them multiple times produces the same result. This prevents data corruption during retries.

Audit Trails

- **Logging Transformations**: Log all data transformation steps, including the SQL queries executed and their parameters, via BigQuery's audit logs or custom logging tables.
    - **Example**: Create a logging table just like shown here:

      ```
      CREATE TABLE my_dataset.audit_log (
      query_id STRING,
      query_text STRING,
      execution_time TIMESTAMP,
      user STRING );
      ```
- **Metadata Tracking**: Use BigQuery's **INFORMATION_SCHEMA** to track table and column metadata changes over time.

Data Lineage

- **Lineage Tracking**: Use tools such as Dataform or Google Cloud Data Catalog to track data lineage, while ensuring that transformations are traceable back to their source.

- **Dependency Management**: Document dependencies between tables and queries to prevent unintended changes from breaking downstream processes.

Version Control

Version control ensures that changes to BigQuery schemas, queries, and pipelines are tracked, reversible, and reproducible. *Figure 10.14* illustrates the best practices for implementing version control in BigQuery environments:

Schema Versioning:

- **Schema Evolution**: Use BigQuery's schema evolution capabilities to add new columns without disrupting existing queries. Avoid destructive changes (for example, deleting columns) unless absolutely necessary.
  - **Example**: Add a new column through:

```
ALTER TABLE my_dataset.my_table
ADD COLUMN new_field STRING;
```

- **Schema Snapshots**: Store schema definitions in a version control system (for example, Git) as JSON or SQL files.
  - Example Schema File (**`my_table_schema.sql`**):

```
CREATE TABLE my_dataset.my_table (
  id STRING NOT NULL,
  timestamp TIMESTAMP NOT NULL );
```

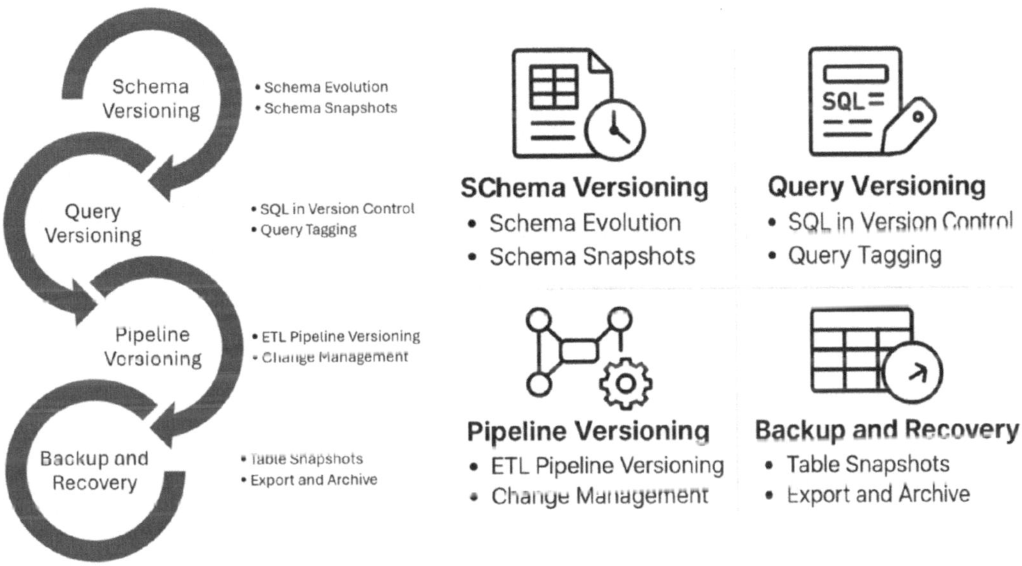

Figure 10.14: *BigQuery's Version Control Strategies*

Query Versioning:

- **SQL in Version Control**: Store all SQL queries in a Git repository, organized by dataset or project. Use tools such as **dbt** or Dataform to manage and version SQL code.
  - **Example** dbt Model Structure:

    ```
    models/
      my_dataset/
        my_table.sql
        my_view.sql
    ```

- **Query Tagging**: Tag queries with version numbers or commit hashes in the metadata or comments to track their history.
  - **Example**:

    ```
    -- Version: v1.2, Commit: abc123
    SELECT * FROM my_dataset.my_table;
    ```

Pipeline Versioning

- **ETL Pipeline Versioning**: Version ETL pipelines (for example, Apache Airflow DAGs, Cloud Composer workflows) in Git. Use tags or branches to manage different pipeline versions.
  - Example Airflow DAG Versioning:

    ```
    from airflow import DAG
    dag = DAG(
        'my_bigquery_etl',
        description='ETL pipeline for my_dataset, v1.0',
        schedule_interval='@daily')
    ```

- **Change Management**: Implement a change management process to review and test pipeline changes before deployment. Use CI/CD pipelines to automate testing and deployment.

Backup and Recovery

- **Table Snapshots**: Use BigQuery's table snapshot feature to create point-in-time backups of tables.
  - **Example**:

    ```
    CREATE TABLE my_dataset.my_table_snapshot
    AS SELECT * FROM my_dataset.my_table
    WHERE _PARTITIONTIME = TIMESTAMP('2025-07-12');
    ```

- **Export and Archive**: Periodically export critical tables to Google Cloud Storage in formats such as Avro or Parquet for long-term storage and recovery.
  - **Example**:
    ```
    bq extract my_dataset.my_table gs://my-bucket/my_table_
    backup/*.avro
    ```

Performance Optimization

To ensure high performance in BigQuery environments while maintaining data accuracy and validation integrity, consider the following strategies illustrated in *Figure* 10.15.

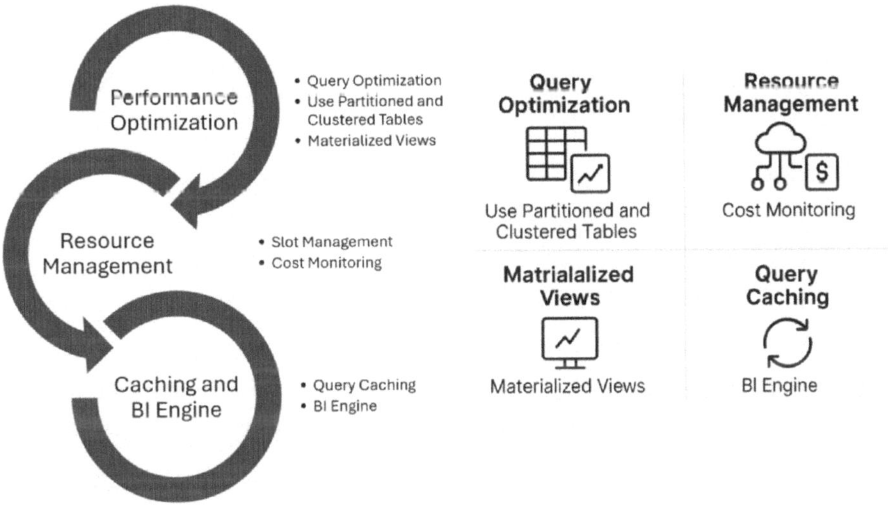

Figure 10.15: *BigQuery's Performance Optimization Strategies*

Query Optimization:

- **`**Avoid SELECT ***`**: Specify only the required columns in queries to reduce data scanned and improve performance.
- **Use Partitioned and Clustered Tables**: Leverage partitioning and clustering to minimize query costs and improve execution times.
- **Materialized Views**: Use materialized views for frequently accessed query results to reduce computation overhead.
  - **Example**:
    ```
    CREATE MATERIALIZED VIEW my_dataset.my_mv
    AS SELECT id, COUNT(*) as event_count
    FROM my_dataset.my_table
    GROUP BY id;
    ```

Resource Management:

- **Slot Management**: Monitor and manage BigQuery slots to ensure sufficient resources for critical workloads. Use reservations for high-priority jobs.
- **Cost Monitoring**: Use BigQuery's billing reports and Cloud Monitoring to track query costs and optimize expensive queries.

Caching and BI Engine:

- **Query Caching**: Enable query caching for repetitive queries to reduce costs and improve performance.
- **BI Engine**: Use BigQuery BI Engine for low-latency analytics, especially for dashboards and interactive queries.

Security and Access Control

- **IAM Policies**: Use Google Cloud IAM to restrict access to datasets and tables based on roles and responsibilities.
    - **Example**: Grant read-only access as shown here:

    ```
    bq add-iam-policy-binding \
    --member='user:analyst@example.com' \
    --role='roles/bigquery.dataViewer' \
    my_dataset
    ```

- **Data Encryption**: Ensure data is encrypted at rest and in transit using Google Cloud's default encryption or customer-managed encryption keys (CMEK).
- **Row-Level Security**: Implement row-level security using BigQuery's row access policies to restrict data access based on user attributes.

Monitoring and Maintenance

Monitoring and Maintenance are significant factors in this strategy journey, as shown in *Figure* 10.16.

Figure 10.16: *BigQuery's Monitoring and Maintenance Strategies*

- **Scheduled Refresh**: Schedule regular data quality checks and table refreshes through Cloud Scheduler or Airflow.

- **Performance Audits**: Periodically audit query performance using BigQuery's query execution details and optimize slow queries.
- **Data Retention Policies**: Set expiration dates for temporary or staging tables to manage storage costs.
    - **Example**:

```
CREATE TABLE my_dataset.temp_table
OPTIONS(expiration_timestamp=TIMESTAMP_ADD(CURRENT_
TIMESTAMP(), INTERVAL 7 DAY));
```

Conclusion

In this chapter, we have understood the vital role played by query optimization in modern data systems. We **explored** a wide range of optimization techniques such as indexing, query rewriting, partitioning, clustering, materialized views, caching, and denormalization—all of which contribute to reduced query execution time, lower resource consumption, and improved system performance.

We also **investigate** how these principles are explicitly applied within **Google BigQuery**, while emphasizing techniques such as BI Engine, query caching, and schema design best practices that significantly enhance analytics performance and reduce operational costs. Beyond performance gains, we examined strategies to maintain data accuracy, validation integrity, and version control, while ensuring that BigQuery-based systems remain reliable and audit-ready. We also explored the broader impact of optimization across GCP services such as Dataflow, Dataproc, Looker Studio, Cloud Functions, and Vertex AI, while demonstrating how query efficiency results in better integration, faster processing, and more intelligent decision-making.

Ultimately, this exploration provided a 360-degree view of how query optimization is not just a performance enhancer, but a core architectural discipline that shapes everything from system responsiveness and analytical agility to cloud cost control and long-term scalability. By mastering these optimization techniques, we are better equipped to build robust, intelligent, and future-ready data systems across cloud-native environments.

In the next chapter, we will explore the critical role of data security and compliance in today's regulatory landscape. Additionally, we will highlight GCP's tools for user permissions, encryption, and data masking, along with governance best practices such as access control, cataloguing, and retention policies, which are all aimed at building secure and compliant data platforms.

CHAPTER 11

Data Security and Compliance on GCP

Introduction

In the previous chapter, we learned what optimizing performance entails and why it is crucial for scaling data solutions effectively. This chapter focuses on techniques such as partitioning and clustering tables, schema design best practices, and query optimization to minimize costs and enhance performance. Readers will also learn about strategies for managing data quality, validation, and version control to ensure that their BigQuery setups are efficient and reliable. By mastering these optimizations, readers can maximize the value of their data.

In this chapter, we will discuss how data security and compliance are non-negotiable in today's regulatory landscape. This chapter explores GCP's tools for managing user permissions, encryption, and data masking. It delves into best practices for data governance, including access control, data cataloguing, classification, and retention policies. By implementing these practices, readers can build secure, compliant, and trustworthy data platforms that align with business and regulatory requirements.

Structure

In this chapter, we will cover the following topics:

- Data Security in Data Engineering
- Data Compliance in Data Engineering
- Understanding Data Masking and Governance
    - Data Masking and Data Governance
    - GCP's IAM - Encryption, Data Masking and Data Governance

- Data Masking in GCP
- Data Governance in GCP

Data Security in Data Engineering

Data security and compliance in data engineering refer to the practices, technologies, and policies implemented to protect data from unauthorized access, breaches, or misuse while ensuring that they adhere to legal, regulatory, and organizational standards. These are critical components of data engineering, as data pipelines and systems often handle sensitive information such as ***personal, financial, or proprietary data.***

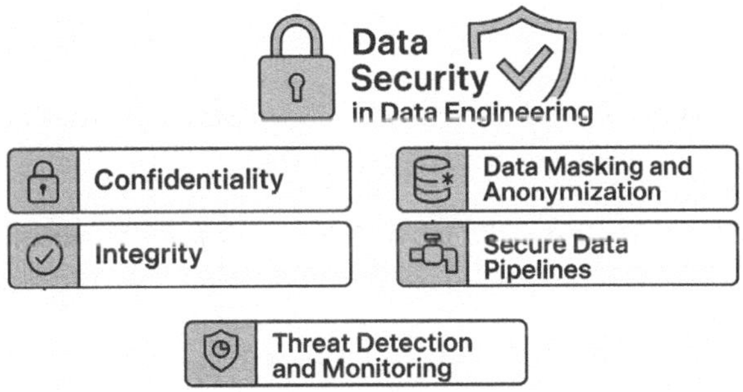

Figure 11.1: *Data Security in Data Engineering*

Data security focuses on safeguarding data throughout its lifecycle and includes stages like ***ingestion, storage, processing, transformation, and delivery***. Data engineers must design and maintain systems that protect data confidentiality, integrity, and availability (the CIA triad). The key aspects include:

- **Confidentiality**: Ensuring that only authorized users or systems can access data through encryption, access control, and authentication and authorization
- **Encryption**: Data should be encrypted at rest (for example, using AES-256) and in transit (for example, TLS/SSL). For example, data stored in cloud platforms like AWS S3 or databases like Snowflake should use encryption by default.
- **Access Controls**: Implement Role-Based Access Control (RBAC) or Attribute-Based Access Control (ABAC) to restrict data access. Tools such as Apache Ranger or AWS IAM help enforce fine-grained permissions.
- **Authentication and Authorization**: Use strong authentication mechanisms (for example, multi-factor authentication) and tools such as OAuth or Kerberos to verify user identities and permissions.

Integrity

Ensuring that data remains accurate and unaltered during processing or storage

- **Data Validation**: Data engineers implement checks (for example, checksums, hash functions) to detect corruption or tampering during data ingestion or transformation.
- **Auditing and Logging**: Track data access and modifications using tools such as AWS CloudTrail or Azure Monitor to detect unauthorized changes.

Availability

Ensuring that data and systems are accessible to authorized users when needed.

- **Redundancy and Backups**: Design fault-tolerant systems with data replication and backups to prevent data loss (for example, using distributed storage such as Hadoop HDFS or cloud-native solutions).
- **Disaster Recovery**: Implement strategies such as automated failover or geo-redundant storage to ensure data availability during outages.

Data Masking and Anonymization

For sensitive data, techniques such as tokenization, pseudonymization, or data masking (for example, replacing personally identifiable information with synthetic data) are used to protect privacy during testing or analytics.

Secure Data Pipelines

- Data engineers secure ETL/ELT pipelines by using secure APIs, encrypted connections, and monitoring for vulnerabilities.
- Tools such as Apache Kafka or AWS Kinesis can be configured with security features like SSL/TLS and access controls.

Threat Detection and Monitoring

- Implement monitoring tools to detect anomalies or breaches (for example, Splunk, Datadog).
- Use intrusion detection systems and regularly patch systems to address vulnerabilities.

Data Compliance in Data Engineering

Compliance entails adhering to laws, regulations, and industry standards governing the handling, storage, and processing of data. Data engineers must design systems that meet these requirements, which vary by industry, region, and data type. Key compliance considerations include:

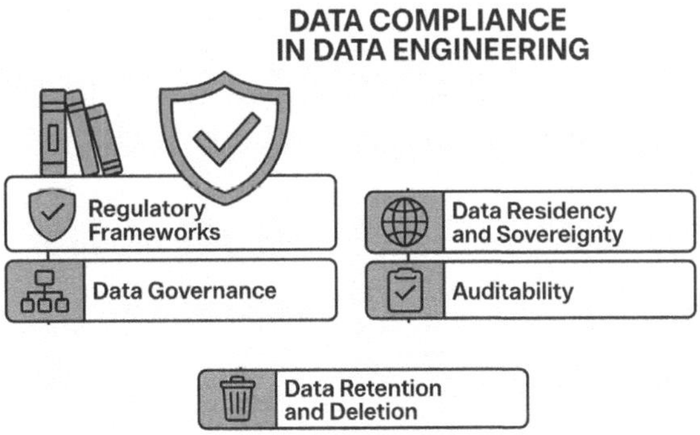

Figure 11.2: *Data Compliance in Data Engineering*

Regulatory Frameworks

- **General Data Protection Regulation (GDPR)**: Applies to organizations handling EU residents' data. Data engineering requires consent for data collection, data minimization, and the right to erasure (for example, deleting user data upon request)
- **California Consumer Privacy Act (CCPA/CPRA)**: Grants California residents rights over their personal data, including the right to know, delete, and opt out of data sales
- **Health Insurance Portability and Accountability Act (HIPAA)**: Governs healthcare data in the U.S. and requires strict controls on Protected Health Information (PHI)
- **Payment Card Industry Data Security Standard (PCI DSS)**: Applies to organizations handling credit card data, mandating encryption, access controls, and regular audits
- **SOC 2**: Focuses on security, availability, processing integrity, confidentiality, and privacy for service providers handling customer data

Data Governance

Data engineers implement governance frameworks to ensure compliance with policies.

This includes:

- **Data Classification**: Labeling data (for example, public, confidential, restricted) to apply appropriate controls
- **Data Lineage**: Tracking data flow through pipelines to ensure transparency and compliance (for example, using tools such as Apache Atlas or Collibra)

- **Metadata Management**: Documenting data sources, schemas, and transformations to support audits

Data Residency and Sovereignty

- Some regulations require data to be stored in specific geographic regions (for example, the GDPR mandates that EU data stays within the EU unless adequate protections are in place).
- Data engineers configure cloud storage (for example, AWS regions, Azure Geo-Zones) to comply with residency requirements.

Auditability

- Systems must maintain audit trails to demonstrate compliance during regulatory reviews. This includes logs of data access, modifications, and pipeline activities.
- Tools such as AWS Glue or Apache Airflow can integrate with logging systems to track pipeline execution.

Data Retention and Deletion

- Compliance often requires defining retention periods (for example, GDPR's "*right to be forgotten*" or HIPAA's 6-year retention for certain records).
- Data engineers implement automated retention policies and secure deletion processes (for example, using AWS S3 lifecycle policies).

Modern Regulations Require Robust Data Protection and Compliance Measures

Data security and compliance are crucial in today's regulatory landscape and are driven by the convergence of escalating cyber threats, stringent legal frameworks, and increasing expectations from consumers and stakeholders. The following is a deeper dive into why these elements are non-negotiable, with additional context and examples to illustrate their importance.

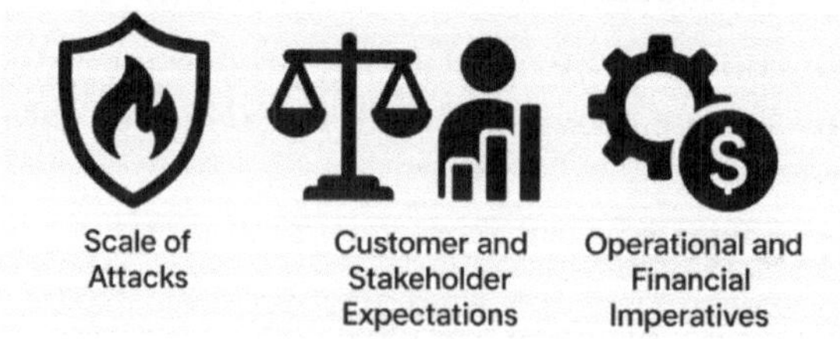

Figure 11.3: *Data Security and Compliance in Today's Regulatory Environment*

Escalating Cyber Threats

The digital world is increasingly vulnerable to sophisticated cyberattacks, which makes robust data security measures essential. These threats include:

Scale of Attacks

- **Claim**: According to a 2024 report by IBM, the average cost of a data breach reached $4.45 million, with ransomware attacks alone increasing by 13% year-over-year. High-profile incidents, like the 2023 MOVEit breach affecting millions of records, highlight the scale of the problem.
    - **Reference**: IBM, "*Cost of a Data Breach Report 2024*," https://www.ibm.com/reports/data-breach
    - **Justification**: The IBM report, based on 604 organizations, confirms the average data breach cost of $4.88 million in 2024, a 10% increase from 2023's $4.45 million, with ransomware attacks rising by 13%. The MOVEit breach was noted as a significant third-party vulnerability that affected over 94 million users.
- **Claim**: Cybercriminals use advanced techniques such as AI-driven phishing, zero-day exploits, and supply chain attacks. For example, the 2021 SolarWinds attack compromised multiple organizations, including government agencies, by exploiting a single vulnerability.
    - **Reference**: Cybersecurity and Infrastructure Security Agency (CISA), "*SolarWinds Orion Supply Chain Attack*," https://www.cisa.gov/solarwinds
    - **Justification**: CISA's documentation details the SolarWinds attack, where a single vulnerability in the Orion software allowed attackers to compromise government and private sector organizations, which highlights the use of supply chain attacks as an advanced tactic.
- **Claim**: Beyond financial losses, breaches lead to operational downtime, intellectual property theft, and eroded customer trust. Small and medium-sized businesses are particularly vulnerable, with 60% failing within six months of a significant cyberattack, as noted by the U.S. National Cybersecurity Alliance.
    - **Reference**: U.S. National Cybersecurity Alliance, "*Small Business Cybersecurity Statistics*", https://staysafeonline.org/resources/small-business-cybersecurity/
    - **Justification**: The National Cybersecurity Alliance cites studies showing that 60% of small businesses fail within six months of a cyberattack due to financial and operational impacts, including downtime and trust erosion.

Stringent Regulatory Frameworks

- **Claim**: GDPR mandates strict data handling practices, including user consent, data minimization, and breach notifications within 72 hours. Non-compliance can result in fines of up to €20 million or 4% of the company's annual global turnover. For instance, Google was fined €50 million in 2019 for violating the GDPR.
    - **Reference**: European Data Protection Board (EDPB), "*GDPR Enforcement Tracker*," https://www.enforcementtracker.com/
    - **Justification**: The EDPB's tracker documents GDPR requirements and fines, including the €50 million penalty against Google in 2019 for lack of transparency in user consent processes. It confirms the GDPR's fine structure, which is up to €20 million or 4% of the global turnover.
- **Claim**: CCPA grants consumers the right to access, delete, and opt out of data sharing. Violations can lead to fines of $7,500 per intentional violation. Similar state laws, such as Virginia's CDPA and Colorado's CPA, are further expanding this trend.
    - **Reference**: California Attorney General, "*California Consumer Privacy Act (CCPA) Enforcement*," https://oag.ca.gov/privacy/ccpa
    - **Justification**: The California AG's website outlines CCPA's consumer rights and penalties, including $7,500 per intentional violation, and notes the emergence of similar laws such as Virginia's CDPA and Colorado's CPA.
- **Claim**: Industry-specific regulations such as HIPAA and PCI DSS have tailored requirements. HIPAA violations can cost up to $1.5 million annually, as seen in cases like the 2022 Advocate Aurora Health breach settlement.
    - **Reference**: U.S. Department of Health and Human Services, "*HIPAA Enforcement Actions*," https://www.hhs.gov/hipaa/for-professionals/compliance-enforcement/enforcement-results/settlements/index.html
    - **Justification**: HHS details HIPAA violation penalties, with a maximum of $1.5 million per violation type annually. The 2022 Advocate Aurora Health settlement is cited as an example of enforcement action for improper handling of data.
- **Claim**: Regulations often apply extraterritorially. GDPR affects any company handling data of EU citizens, while the CCPA applies to businesses with California customers, regardless of their location.

- **Reference**: GDPR.eu, "What is GDPR, the EU's Data Protection Regulation?" https://gdpr.eu/what-is-gdpr/
- **Justification**: GDPR.eu explains GDPR's extraterritorial scope, which applies to any organization processing EU residents' data. Similarly, the California AG's CCPA page confirms its applicability to businesses serving California residents, regardless of location.

Customer and Stakeholder Expectations

- **Claim**: A 2023 Pew Research survey found that 64% of consumers avoid companies with poor security records, and 81% believe they have little control over how their data is used. High-profile breaches, such as the 2021 T-Mobile incident that exposed data for 50 million customers, erode trust.
  - **Reference**: Pew Research Centre, "*Americans and Privacy: Concerned, Confused and Feeling Lack of Control Over Their Personal Information*," https://www.pewresearch.org/internet/2023/09/27/americans-and-privacy-concerned-confused-and-feeling-lack-of-control-over-their-personal-information/
  - **Justification**: The Pew survey confirms 64% of consumers avoid companies with weak security, and 81% feel they lack data control. The 2021 T-Mobile breach, which exposed data for 50 million customers, was documented in news reports as a trust-damaging incident.
- **Claim**: Partners and vendors increasingly demand proof of compliance (for example, SOC 2 or ISO 27001 certification) before engaging. Non-compliance can lead to lost contracts or partnerships.
  - **Reference**: Varonis, "157 *Cybersecurity Statistics and Trends [updated 2024]*," https://www.varonis.com/blog/cybersecurity-statistics
  - **Justification**: Varonis notes that 66% of companies report compliance mandates driving spending, indicating that partners and vendors require certifications such as SOC 2 or ISO 27001 to ensure secure business relationships.
- **Claim**: A single breach can devastate a brand. For example, Equifax's 2017 breach resulted in a $1.4 billion settlement and long-term reputational damage.
  - **Reference**: U.S. Federal Trade Commission (FTC), "*Equifax Data Breach Settlement*," https://www.ftc.gov/enforcement/cases-proceedings/refunds/equifax-data-breach-settlement
  - **Justification**: The FTC details Equifax's 2017 breach, which exposed 147 million people's data, resulting in a $1.4 billion settlement and significant reputational damage due to widespread public and media backlash.

Operational and Financial Imperatives

- **Claim**: Cyberattacks can halt operations. The 2021 Colonial Pipeline ransomware attack disrupted fuel supplies across the U.S. East Coast and highlighted the operational stakes.
    - **Reference**: Bloomberg, "*Colonial Pipeline Shuts Major U.S. Fuel Line After Cyber Attack*," https://www.bloomberg.com/news/articles/2021-05-08/colonial-pipeline-shuts-major-u-s-fuel-line-after-cyber-attack
    - **Justification**: Bloomberg's coverage confirms that the Colonial Pipeline attack disrupted fuel supplies for days, illustrating the operational impact of cyberattacks on critical infrastructure.
- **Claim**: Beyond direct costs (for example, ransom payments, legal fees), breaches lead to lost revenue and customer churn. A 2024 Verizon study found that 73% of breached organizations faced significant revenue losses.
    - **Reference**: Verizon, "2024 *Data Breach Investigations Report*," https://www.verizon.com/business/resources/reports/dbir/
    - **Justification**: Verizon's 2024 DBIR, analyzing 30,458 incidents, states that 73% of breached organizations experienced significant revenue losses due to customer churn and operational impacts.
- **Claim**: Cyber insurance premiums are rising, and insurers often require proof of compliance with standards such as NIST or ISO 27001 to offer coverage.
    - **Reference**: Varonis, "157 *Cybersecurity Statistics and Trends [updated 2024]*," https://www.varonis.com/blog/cybersecurity-statistics
    - **Justification**: Varonis highlights that compliance with standards like ISO 27001 is increasingly required for cyber insurance, with 66% of companies noting compliance-driven spending, reflecting insurer demands.

Understanding Data Masking and Governance

Data masking and governance are essential components of modern data security and compliance strategies. Data masking involves replacing sensitive information with fictitious but realistic data to protect it from unauthorized access during development, testing, or analytics. Governance ensures that data is managed responsibly, adhering to policies, regulations, and quality standards. Together, they safeguard data privacy, enhance compliance, and build trust in data-driven systems.

Data Masking

Data masking is a security technique used to protect sensitive data by transforming it into a form that is not identifiable or usable by unauthorized parties, while preserving its utility for legitimate purposes. It is particularly valuable in scenarios where sensitive data, such as Personally Identifiable Information (PII), financial records, or proprietary information, needs to be used in non-production environments (for example, development, testing, or analytics) or shared with third parties without exposing the original data.

Core Objectives

- **Protect Sensitive Data**: Prevent unauthorized access to sensitive information to reduce the risk of data breaches.
- **Maintain Usability**: Ensure that the masked data mimics the structure and format of the original data, so that it remains functional for its intended purpose.
- **Ensure Compliance**: Align with data protection regulations such as General Data Protection Regulation (GDPR), Health Insurance Portability and Accountability Act (HIPAA), Payment Card Industry Data Security Standard (PCI-DSS), and California Consumer Privacy Act (CCPA).

Key Characteristics of Data Masking

This section highlights three critical characteristics of data masking. Let us explore each in detail.

- **Irreversibility (in Static Masking):** In static data masking (SDM), the masked data cannot be reverse-engineered to retrieve the original data. This ensures that even if the masked data is exposed, it will pose no security risk. Techniques such as substitution, shuffling, or redaction replace sensitive data with fictitious values that have no direct correlation to the original data. Unlike encryption, which is reversible with a key, static masking is designed to be permanent.
    - **Example**: A real Social Security Number (SSN) like 123-45-6789 is replaced with a random but valid-looking SSN like 987-65-4321. There is no way to trace the masked SSN back to the original without a separate mapping (which is typically not stored in the static masking).
    - **Use Case**: Static masking is ideal for creating secure copies of production databases for use in non-production environments like testing or training.

- **Data Usability:** Masked data retains the format, structure, and statistical properties of the original data, which ensures it can be used for its intended purpose without breaking application functionality. Applications often rely on specific data formats (for example, a 16-digit credit card number or a valid email address). Masking preserves these formats to avoid errors in testing or analytics.
    - **Example**: A masked credit card number like ****-****-****-1234 maintains the 16-digit format and may pass basic validation checks (for example, Luhn algorithm) to ensure compatibility with payment processing systems.

  Techniques Supporting Usability:
    - **Format-Preserving Encryption (FPE)**: Ensures that encrypted data retains the same format (for example, a phone number like 123-456-7890 becomes 987-654-3210).
    - **Substitution**: Replaces data with realistic alternatives from a lookup table (for example, replacing "John Smith" with "Jane Doe").
    - **Use Case**: A development team testing an e-commerce application needs realistic but safe data to simulate transactions without exposing real customer information.
- **Compliance:** Data masking helps organizations meet regulatory requirements by reducing the exposure of sensitive data, thereby lowering the risk of non-compliance penalties.

  Relevant Regulations
    - **GDPR**: Requires protection of personal data and mandates measures like pseudonymization (a form of masking) to safeguard EU citizens' data
    - **HIPAA**: Protects patient health information and requires safeguards for data used in non-production environments
    - **PCI-DSS**: Mandates protection of cardholder data such as credit card numbers
    - **CCPA**: Grants California residents rights over their personal data, which requires organizations to secure it during processing or sharing
- **How Masking Helps**: By replacing sensitive data with non-sensitive equivalents, masking ensures that even if data is accessed improperly, it does not result in a compliance violation.
    - **Example**: A company masks customer email addresses in a test database to comply with GDPR, which ensures that developers cannot access real PII.

Types of Data Masking

The excerpt lists four types of data masking: ***Static Data Masking (SDM), Dynamic Data Masking (DDM), On-the-Fly Masking, and Tokenization***. Let us explore each in depth, including their technical implementation and use cases.

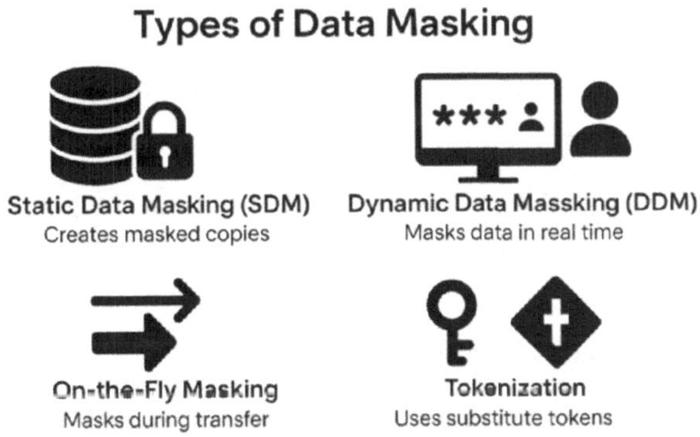

Figure 11.4: *Types of Data Masking*

Static Data Masking (SDM)

SDM creates a permanent, masked copy of a production database for use in non-production environments such as development, testing, or training.

- **How It Works**
    - A copy of the production database is created.
    - Masking rules apply to sensitive fields (for example, replacing names, SSNs, or credit card numbers).
    - The masked database is deployed to non-production environments.
- **Key Features**
    - **Irreversible**: The masked data cannot be traced back to the original.
    - **One-Time Process**: Masking is applied once, which creates a static dataset.
    - **Referential Integrity**: Masking tools ensure relationships between tables (for example, foreign keys) are preserved.
- **Use Case**: A bank creates a masked version of its customer database for developers to test a new mobile banking app, which ensures that no real customer data is exposed.
- **Tools**: Informatica Persistent Data Masking, IBM InfoSphere Optim, Oracle Data Masking and Subsetting.

- **Challenges**
    - Ensuring referential integrity across large, complex databases
    - Managing storage for large masked datasets
- **Implementation Steps**
    - Identify sensitive data using data discovery tools.
    - Define masking rules (for example, substitute names, shuffle SSNs).
    - Apply masking to a copy of the production database.
    - Validate the masked data for usability and integrity.
    - Deploy the masked database to the target environment.

Dynamic Data Masking (DDM)

DDM masks data in real-time at the application or database layer, based on user roles or permissions, without altering the underlying data.

- **How It Works**
    - Masking rules are configured in the database or application.
    - When a user queries the data, the system applies masking dynamically based on their access level.
    - For example, a customer service representative sees only the last four digits of a credit card number, while an administrator sees the full number.
- **Key Features**
    - **Real-Time**: Masking occurs at query time, not in the stored data.
    - **Role-Based**: Different users see different levels of masked data.
    - **No Data Modification**: The original data remains unchanged in the database.
- **Use Case**: A hospital's database allows nurses to see patient names and medical conditions but masks SSNs and addresses unless accessed by authorized personnel.
- **Tools**: Microsoft SQL Server Dynamic Data Masking, Oracle Virtual Private Database, and IBM Guardium.
- **Challenges**
    - Performance overhead due to real-time masking
    - Complex configuration for role-based access

- **Implementation Step**
    - Define user roles and permissions.
    - Configure masking rules in the database (for example, `MASKED WITH (FUNCTION = 'partial(4)')` in SQL Server).
    - Test the masking behavior for different user roles.
    - Monitor performance and adjust rules to minimize latency.

On-the-Fly Masking

Masks data during transfer between systems, typically during Extract, Transform, Load (ETL) processes, without storing a masked copy.

- **How It Works**
    - Data is masked as it is extracted from a source system and loaded into a target system.
    - Often used in data integration pipelines where sensitive data moves between environments.
- **Key Features**
    - **Transient Masking**: No permanent masked copy is created.
    - **Real-Time**: Masking occurs during data transfer.
    - **ETL Integration**: Commonly integrated with ETL tools such as Talend or Informatica.
- **Use Case**: A company transfers customer data from a production database to a cloud-based analytics platform, while masking PII during the transfer.
- **Tools**: Informatica PowerCenter, Talend Data Integration, Apache NiFi with custom masking scripts, and so on.
- **Challenges**
    - Ensuring that masking does not slow down ETL processes
    - Maintaining data consistency during transfer
- **Implementation Steps**
    - Identify sensitive data in the ETL pipeline.
    - Configure masking rules in the ETL tool.
    - Test the pipeline to ensure masked data is usable in the target system.
    - Monitor ETL performance and data integrity.

Tokenization

Replaces sensitive data with unique tokens that can be mapped back to the original data using a secure token vault, if needed

- **How It Works**
  - Sensitive data (for example, a credit card number) is replaced with a token (for example, a random string).
  - The mapping between the token and the original data is stored in a secure token vault.
  - Authorized systems can detokenize the data using the vault, while unauthorized systems see only the token.
- **Key Features**
  - **Reversible (with Vault)**: Unlike static masking, tokenization allows authorized users to retrieve the original data.
  - **High Security**: The token vault is heavily secured and encrypted.
  - **Format Preservation**: Tokens often match the format of the original data.
- **Use Case**: A payment processor tokenizes credit card numbers to secure transactions, while allowing merchants to process payments without storing sensitive data.
- **Tools**: Protegrity, Voltage SecureData, TokenEx
- **Challenges**
  - Managing and securing the token vault
  - Performance overhead for tokenization/detokenization
- **Implementation Steps**
  - Set up a secure token vault.
  - Integrate tokenization into applications or databases.
  - Define access controls for detokenization.
  - Test tokenization workflows and vault security.

Common Data Masking Techniques

As we discussed, specific sets of common masking techniques are available. The excerpt lists six common data masking techniques. Let us explore each with examples, technical considerations, and use cases.

Substitution

Replaces sensitive data with realistic but fake data from a lookup table or generator

- **Example**: Replace "*John Smith*" with "*Jane Doe*" from a name database, or replace 123-45-6789 with 987-65-4321 from a valid SSN generator.
- **Technical Considerations**
    - Use a large, diverse lookup table to avoid repetitive or predictable data.
    - Ensure that the substituted data maintains business rules (for example, valid email formats).
- **Use Case**: Masking customer names in a CRM database for testing
- **Tools**: Informatica, IBM InfoSphere Optim, or custom scripts with libraries like Faker (Python)

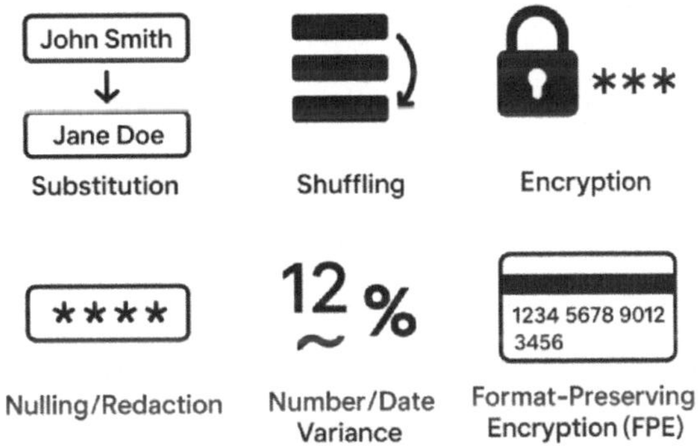

***Figure 11.5**: Types of Data Masking*

Shuffling

Randomly reorders data within a column while preserving the dataset's structure

- **Example**: Shuffle SSNs in a customer table so each record gets a different (but real, for understanding purposes) SSN from the same dataset.
- **Technical Considerations**
    - Ensure that shuffling does not break referential integrity (for example, matching records across tables).
    - Avoid shuffling small datasets, as patterns may still be identifiable.
- **Use Case**: Masking employee IDs in an HR database to prevent identification
- **Tools**: Database-specific scripts (for example, SQL RAND() function) or masking tools like Oracle Data Masking

Encryption

Encrypts sensitive data using an algorithm, which makes it unreadable without a decryption key

- **Example**: Encrypt the credit card number 1234-5678-9012-3456 into a ciphertext like XyZ9kPq....
- **Technical Considerations**
  - Requires secure key management to prevent unauthorized decryption
  - May not preserve data format, which can break application functionality
- **Use Case**: Securing data in transit or production environments (less common for non-production masking)
- **Tools**: AES encryption libraries, Oracle Transparent Data Encryption, Microsoft Always Encrypted

Nulling/Redaction

Replaces sensitive data with null values or removes it entirely

- **Example**: Replace a customer's address with `NULL` or **** in a test database.
- **Technical Considerations**
  - This can disrupt application logic that expects non-null values.
  - Suitable for data that is not critical for testing or analytics
- **Use Case**: Redacting medical diagnoses in a research dataset to protect patient privacy
- **Tools**: SQL scripts (for example, `UPDATE table SET column = NULL`) or masking tools

Number/Date Variance

Adjusts numerical or date values slightly to obscure the original data while preserving its utility

- **Example**: Change the birthdate from 1990-05-15 to 1990-05-12 or adjust the salary from $50,000 to $49,800.
- **Technical Considerations**
  - Ensure that variance does not affect statistical analysis or business logic.
  - Define acceptable ranges (for example, ±5 days for dates, ±10% for numbers).

- **Use Case**: Masking financial data for analytics while preserving trends
- **Tools**: Custom scripts or masking tools with variance functions

Format-Preserving Encryption (FPE)

Encrypts data while maintaining its original format and length

- **Example**: A 16-digit credit card number 1234-5678-9012-3456 becomes 9876-5432-1098-7654, which is still a valid 16-digit number.
- **Technical Considerations**:
    - Requires specialized algorithms (for example, FF1 or FF3 in NIST standards)
    - Balances security and usability but requires key management
- **Use Case**: Masking credit card numbers in a payment processing system for testing
- **Tools**: Voltage, SecureData, Protegrity, or open-source FPE libraries

Implementation Considerations

We have discussed the types of data and common techniques to mask the data. Let us understand how to implement data masking effectively by considering the following:

- **Data Discovery**: Utilize tools such as Informatica Data Privacy or Microsoft Purview to identify sensitive data across databases, files, and applications.
- **Masking Rules**: Define rules based on data type, sensitivity, and use case.

  For example:
    - PII (names, SSNs): Use substitution or shuffling.
    - Financial Data (credit cards): Use FPE or tokenization.
    - Dates: Use variance.
- **Referential Integrity**: Ensures that masking preserves relationships between tables (for example, a customer ID in one table matches the same ID in another)
- **Performance**: Dynamic masking can introduce latency; optimize rules and test performance.
- **Scalability**: For large datasets, use parallel processing or cloud-based masking tools.
- **Security**: Secure masking tools and token vaults to prevent unauthorized access.
- **Testing**: Validate masked data to ensure it meets application requirements and complies with relevant standards and regulations.

Tools and Technologies

- **Commercial Tools**
    - **Informatica Persistent Data Masking**: Supports static and dynamic masking with robust data discovery
    - **IBM InfoSphere Optim**: Comprehensive solution for masking and test data management
    - **Oracle Data Masking and Subsetting**: Ideal for Oracle databases
    - **Microsoft SQL Server Dynamic Data Masking**: Built-in DDM for SQL Server
    - **Delphix**: Combines masking with data virtualization for efficient test data management
- **Open-Source Tools**
    - **ARX**: An open-source anonymization tool for structured data
    - **OpenPseudonymiser**: A lightweight tool for Pseudonymizing PII
    - **Faker (Python)**: A library for generating realistic fake data for substitution
- **Custom Solutions**: Use Python, Java, or SQL scripts for specific masking needs, but ensure thatthey meet compliance requirements.

Real-World Scenario: Securing Customer Data through Data Masking

Let us consider a practical way to implement data masking by examining the following scenario:

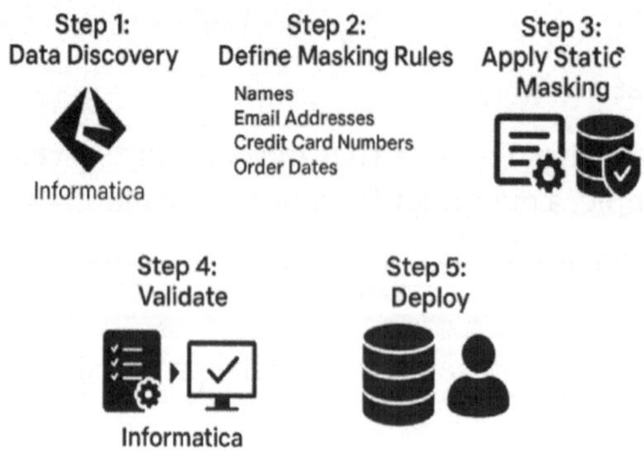

Figure 11.6: *Practical Example - Data Masking*

Scenario: A retail company needs to provide a test database to developers without exposing customer PII.

Step 1: Data Discovery: Use Informatica to identify sensitive fields (for example, names, email addresses, credit card numbers) in the customer database.

Step 2: Define the Masking Rules.

a. **Names**: Substitute with random names from a lookup table.

b. **Email addresses**: Use FPE to generate valid-looking email addresses (for example, john.doe@example.com becomes jane.smith@sample.com).

c. **Credit card numbers**: Use tokenization or FPE to preserve the 16-digit format.

d. **Order dates**: Apply date variance (±7 days).

Step 3: Apply Static Masking.

a. Create a copy of the production database.

b. Use Informatica to apply masking rules, ensuring referential integrity (for example, customer IDs remain consistent across tables).

Step 4: Validate.

a. Test the masked database with the application to ensure it supports order processing and reporting.

b. Verify that masked data cannot be reverse-engineered.

Step 5: Deploy: Provide the masked database to developers and monitor access to ensure compliance with GDPR.

Challenges and Solutions

Data masking is a mandatory process, and various tools and techniques are available to implement it. Of course, we might face challenges and subsequent solutions. Let us focus on them now.

Challenges	Solutions
Performance Overhead: Dynamic masking can slow down queries	Optimize masking rules and use efficient database engines. Cache frequently accessed data to reduce latency.
Referential Integrity: Masking can break relationships between tables	Use tools that support consistent masking across related fields (for example, masking a customer ID the same way in all tables).
Compliance Complexity: Regulations like GDPR require specific masking techniques (for example, pseudonymization)	Align masking strategies with regulatory requirements and consult legal experts.
Data Volume: Masking large datasets can be time-consuming	Use parallel processing or cloud-based tools to scale masking operations.

Table 11.1: *Challenges and Solutions*

Data masking is a crucial technique for safeguarding sensitive data and can also be used in non-production environments or for analytics purposes. By understanding the types of masking ***(static, dynamic, on-the-fly, tokenization)*** and techniques ***(substitution, shuffling, encryption, and so on),*** organizations can implement robust solutions tailored to their needs. Effective data masking requires careful planning, the use of appropriate tools, and alignment with relevant compliance requirements. By addressing challenges such as performance, integrity, and scalability, organizations can safeguard data, reduce risks, and maintain trust with stakeholders.

Data Governance

Data governance refers to the framework of policies, processes, roles, and tools that ensure data within an organization is managed, secure, and used responsibly. It establishes standards and guidelines for ***data quality, security, privacy, and compliance, which enable organizations to maintain trust, meet regulatory requirements, and derive value from their data assets.***

Key Purposes

- Ensure data is accurate, consistent, and reliable.
- Protect sensitive data from unauthorized access or misuse.
- Align data management practices with organizational goals and legal/regulatory requirements.
- Facilitate accountability and transparency in data handling.

Key Components of Data Governance

There are six critical components or pillars of data governance. Let us explore each in detail; *Figure* 11.7 illustrates the same concept.

***Figure* 11.7:** *Key Components of Data Governance*

Data Policies: It provides a clear framework for consistent data handling and ensures compliance with regulations such as GDPR, HIPAA, PCI-DSS, and CCPA. It consists of a set of rules and guidelines that dictate how data is accessed, used, stored, and protected within an organization.

- **Examples**
  - Only authorized personnel can access sensitive data (for example, PII or financial records).
  - All non-production environments (for example, testing or development databases) must use masked data.
  - Data retention policies outline the duration for which sensitive data can be stored before it is deleted.
- **Implementation**
  - Draft policies in collaboration with legal, compliance, and IT teams.
  - Document policies in a centralized repository (for example, a governance platform like Collibra).
  - Communicate policies to all employees and enforce them through access controls and audits.

Data Stewardship: Ensures accountability for data management and compliance at every level of the organization. Assigning individuals or teams (data stewards) to oversee data quality, compliance, and adherence to governance policies.

- **Roles and Responsibilities**
  - **Data Stewards**: Manage specific datasets, ensure data quality, and resolve issues such as inconsistencies or inaccuracies.
  - **Data Owners**: Senior stakeholders accountable for specific data domains (for example, customer data, financial data).
  - **Governance Committees**: Oversee the overall governance programme and align it with business objectives.
- **Implementation**
  - Identify and train data stewards for each business unit or data domain.
  - Define clear responsibilities such as monitoring data quality or approving access requests.
  - Use tools such as Alation or Collibra to track stewardship activities.

Data Quality: Ensuring that data is accurate, consistent, complete, and reliable for its intended use is an important step. High-quality data supports reliable analytics, reporting, and decision-making.

- **Key Metrics**
    - **Accuracy**: Data reflects real-world values (for example, correct customer addresses).
    - **Consistency**: Data is uniform across systems (for example, the same customer ID in CRM and billing systems).
    - **Completeness**: No critical data is missing.
    - **Timeliness**: Data is up-to-date for decision-making.
- **Implementation**
    - Use data profiling tools (for example, Informatica Data Quality, Talend) to assess and improve data quality.
    - Implement data cleansing processes to correct errors or inconsistencies.
    - Establish data quality KPIs and monitor them regularly.

Data Security and Privacy: Protecting data from unauthorized access, breaches, or misuse while ensuring compliance with privacy regulations helps in safeguarding sensitive information and maintain compliance with regulations like GDPR's "*right to be forgotten*" or HIPAA's patient privacy rules.

- **Key Practices**
    - Implement access controls (for example, role-based access control (RBAC) or attribute-based access control (ABAC)).
    - Encrypt sensitive data at rest and in transit.
    - Use data masking (as described in the original text) to protect sensitive data in non-production environments.
- **Implementation**
    - Deploy security tools such as IBM Guardium or Splunk for real-time monitoring and threat detection.
    - Integrate data masking into governance policies to protect PII, financial data, or intellectual property.
    - Conduct regular security audits to identify vulnerabilities.

Metadata Management: Maintaining metadata (data about data) is critical to track data lineage, ownership, usage, and transformations. It provides transparency and traceability, while enabling organizations to understand and trust their data.

- **Examples of Metadata**
    - **Lineage**: Tracks the origin and transformations of data (for example, how customer data flows from CRM to analytics)

- **Ownership**: Identifies who is responsible for specific datasets
- **Usage**: Documents how data is used in reports, applications, or analytics

- **Implementation**
    - Use metadata management tools such as Collibra, Alation, or Microsoft Purview to catalogue metadata.
    - Automate metadata collection to track data lineage across systems.
    - Ensure metadata is accessible to data stewards and analysts for governance and analytics.

Compliance and Auditing: This step refers to adhering to internal policies and external regulations through regular audits and tracking mechanisms. It demonstrates compliance, identifies gaps, and mitigates risks of non-compliance penalties.

- **Key Activities**
    - Conduct audits to verify compliance with regulations (for example, GDPR, CCPA).
    - Maintain audit trails to track who accesses sensitive data and when.
    - Report compliance status to regulators or stakeholders.
- **Implementation**
    - Use tools such as Splunk or IBM Guardium for real-time audit trail monitoring.
    - Schedule regular compliance audits (for example, quarterly or annually).
    - Document audit findings and remediation plans for transparency.

Importance of Data Governance

Of course, we should understand why data governance is critical, particularly in conjunction with data masking aspects:

- **Regulatory Compliance**: Governance ensures that data handling practices align with regulations such as GDPR, HIPAA, PCI-DSS, and CCPA. For example, governance policies may mandate the use of data masking in non-production environments to protect sensitive data.
- **Risk Mitigation**: By defining clear policies, roles, and monitoring mechanisms, governance reduces the likelihood of data misuse, errors, or breaches.

Figure 11.8: *Importance of Data Governance*

- **Customer Trust**: Responsible data management builds trust with customers, partners, and stakeholders by demonstrating a commitment to data protection.
- **Operational Efficiency**: Governance provides a structured approach to data management and reduces inefficiencies caused by poor data quality or inconsistent practices.
- **Support for Data Masking**: As noted in the text, "*data masking is a tactical component of a broader data governance strategy*." Governance ensures that masking is applied consistently, monitored for compliance, and aligned with organizational policies.

Relationship between Data Governance and Data Masking

The following factors influence the relationship between data governance and data masking. Let us explore them.

- **Integration**: Data masking is a practical implementation of governance policies, which ensures that sensitive data is protected in accordance with defined rules.
- **Consistency**: Governance ensures that masking techniques (for example, substitution, tokenization) are applied uniformly across systems and environments.
- **Compliance**: Governance frameworks monitor masking activities to ensure that they meet regulatory requirements such as the GDPR's pseudonymization mandates.

- **Risk Reduction**: Together, governance and masking reduce the risk of data breaches, regulatory fines, and reputational damage by ensuring that sensitive data is protected at all stages of its lifecycle.

Implementation Steps for Data Governance in GCP

Let us explore the steps to implement data governance as part of a broader strategy with data masking.

Implementing an effective data governance framework ensures that data is managed securely, compliantly, and efficiently across an organization. The following steps establish a robust data governance program, which are designed to align with organizational goals and regulatory requirements:

Step 1: Establish a Governance Framework.

- **Objective**: Create a structured foundation for data governance by defining its scope, objectives, and policies.
- **Actions**
    - Define the scope of governance (for example, customer data, financial data, or all enterprise data).
    - Develop clear policies for data access, usage, retention, and protection (for example, "*All non-production environments must use masked data*" or "*Sensitive data access is restricted to authorized roles*").
    - Align policies with regulations such as GDPR, HIPAA, PCI-DSS, or CCPA.
    - Document policies in a centralized, accessible repository.
- **Tools**: Use governance platforms such as Collibra or Microsoft Purview to store and manage policies.
- **Example**: A retail company creates a policy mandating that customer PII (for example, names, addresses) is accessible only to verified employees and must be masked in test environments.

Step 2: Assign Roles and Responsibilities.

- **Objective**: Establish accountability by designating individuals and teams to oversee data governance.
- **Actions**
    - Appoint **data stewards** to manage specific data domains (for example, customer data, HR data) and ensure compliance with policies.
    - Designate **data owners** (for example, department heads) to take accountability for data quality and security within their domains.

    - Form a **data governance committee** to provide strategic oversight and align governance with business objectives.
    - Define clear responsibilities, such as monitoring data quality, approving access requests, or resolving compliance issues.
- **Tools**: Use role management features in platforms such as Alation or Okta to assign and track responsibilities.
- **Example**: A healthcare organization assigns a data steward to oversee patient data, ensuring compliance with HIPAA through regular quality checks and access monitoring.

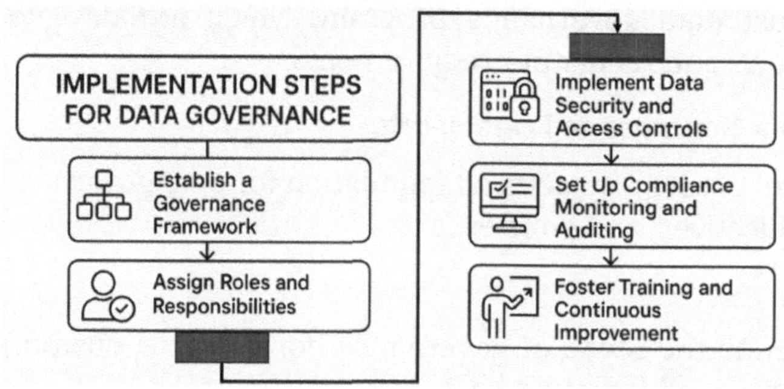

***Figure 11.9:** Implementation Steps for Data Governance in GCP*

Step 3: Implement Data Quality and Metadata Management.

- **Objective**: Ensure data is accurate, consistent, and traceable to support governance goals.
- **Actions**:
    a. Conduct data profiling to assess data quality (for example, accuracy, completeness, consistency) using automated tools.
    b. Establish data quality standards and KPIs (for example, "*Customer records must have 99% accuracy*").
    c. Implement metadata management to track data lineage, ownership, and usage (for example, document how customer data flows from CRM to analytics).
    d. Automate metadata collection to maintain a comprehensive data catalogue.
- **Tools**: Use Talend Data Quality for profiling, Collibra for metadata management or Apache Atlas for open-source metadata tracking.
- **Example**: A financial institution uses Microsoft Purview to catalogue metadata, while ensuring that data lineage for transaction records is traceable across systems.

Step 4: Enforce Data Security and Access Controls.

- **Objective**: Protect sensitive data and ensure only authorized users can access it.
- **Actions**
    a. Implement role-based access control (RBAC) and attribute-based access control (ABAC) to restrict data access based on user roles or attributes (for example, location, purpose).
    b. Integrate data masking (for example, static or dynamic masking) into governance policies to protect sensitive data in non-production environments.
    c. Encrypt sensitive data at rest and in transit using industry-standard algorithms (for example, AES-256).
    d. Deploy monitoring tools to detect unauthorized access attempts.
- **Tools**: Use IBM Guardium for security monitoring, Okta for access control, or Microsoft SQL Server for dynamic masking.
- **Example**: A bank restricts access to credit card data to compliance officers and masks it for developers using Informatica Persistent Data Masking.

Step 5: Set Up Compliance Monitoring and Auditing.

- **Objective**: Ensure ongoing adherence to governance policies and regulatory requirements.
- **Actions**
    a. Establish audit trails to track data access and usage (for example, who accessed customer PII and when).
    b. Schedule regular compliance audits (for example, quarterly) to verify adherence to policies and regulations.
    c. Use automated tools to monitor compliance in real-time and generate reports for regulators or stakeholders.
    d. Document audit findings and remediation plans for transparency.
- **Tools**: Use Splunk for real-time monitoring, IBM Guardium for audit trails, or Collibra for compliance reporting.
- **Example**: An e-commerce company uses Splunk to monitor access to customer data, while ensuring GDPR compliance by tracking and auditing all access events.

Step 6: Foster Training and Continuous Improvement.

- **Objective**: Build a culture of data governance through education and iterative refinement.
- **Actions**
    a. Provide training programs to educate employees on governance policies, data protection, and their roles in compliance.
    b. Collect feedback from audits, incidents, and stakeholders to identify gaps in governance processes.
    c. Update policies and practices to address new regulations, technologies, or organizational changes.
    d. Automate governance tasks (for example, data discovery, classification) to reduce manual effort and improve efficiency.
- **Tools**: Use e-learning platforms for training, Collibra for policy updates, or Microsoft Purview for automated data discovery.
- **Example**: A tech company trains its developers on governance policies while emphasizing the use of masked data and updates policies annually to align with CCPA updates.

Best Practices for Data Governance

Organizations must adhere to certain best practices that are applicable to data governance. Here are the governance-specific ones:

- **Start Small**: Begin with high-risk data domains (for example, PII, financial data) to establish governance policies and processes before scaling to other areas.
- **Align with Business Needs**: Ensure that governance supports business objectives, such as enabling analytics or ensuring compliance, without creating unnecessary barriers.
- **Document Everything**: Maintain detailed documentation of policies, roles, audit results, and metadata for transparency and compliance.
- **Leverage Automation**: Use tools such as Microsoft Purview or Collibra to automate data discovery, classification, and monitoring, reducing manual errors and effort.
- **Stay Compliant**: Regularly review regulations (for example, GDPR, CCPA) and update governance policies to remain compliant.
- **Educate and Train**: Provide ongoing training to employees on governance policies and their role in data protection.

Challenges and Solutions

The following factors are the challenges that are relevant to data governance, along with their proposed solutions:

- **Evolving Regulations**
  - **Issue**: Compliance requirements change frequently and require updates to governance policies.
  - **Solution**: Stay informed about regulatory changes through legal counsel or industry updates. Use flexible governance platforms that can adapt to new requirements (for example, Collibra's customizable policy frameworks).
- **Employee Resistance**
  - **Issue**: Teams may resist new governance policies due to perceived complexity or restrictions.
  - **Solution**: Provide training to highlight the benefits of governance (for example, reduced risk, improved trust). Simplify policies and use user-friendly tools to minimize friction.
- **Data Consistency**
  - **Issue**: Inconsistent data across systems can undermine governance efforts.
  - **Solution**: Implement data quality tools (for example, Talend) and metadata management to ensure consistency and traceability.

Tools and Technologies for Data Governance

To implement Data Governance, multiple tools and technologies are available in the marketplace. Let us explore a few of them.

- **Data Governance Platforms**
  - **Collibra**: It is a leading platform for managing policies, metadata, and compliance. It supports data cataloguing, lineage tracking, and policy enforcement.
  - **Alation**: It focuses on data cataloguing and collaboration, while enabling data stewards to manage metadata and ensure data quality.
  - **Microsoft Purview**: It provides data discovery, classification, and governance for cloud and on-premises environments.
  - **Talend Data Fabric**: It integrates data quality, governance, and integration for comprehensive data management.

- **Monitoring and Auditing Tools**
  - **Splunk**: Real-time monitoring and audit trail analysis for data access and usage
  - **IBM Guardium**: Security and compliance monitoring for databases and applications
- **Open-Source Options**
  - **Apache Atlas**: An open-source metadata management and governance platform for the Hadoop ecosystem
  - **Custom Scripts**: Python or Java scripts for specific governance tasks such as metadata extraction or policy enforcement

Data governance is a strategic framework that ensures data is managed responsibly, securely, and in compliance with regulations. By defining policies, assigning roles, ensuring data quality, securing data, managing metadata, and monitoring compliance, organizations can mitigate risks, maintain trust, and derive value from their data. Governance is essential for supporting tactical measures such as data masking to ensure that sensitive data is consistently protected and aligned with organizational and regulatory standards. Implementing governance requires careful planning, the right tools (for example, Collibra, Microsoft Purview), and ongoing monitoring to adapt to evolving needs and regulations.

GCP's IAM - Encryption, Data Masking and Data Governance

Google Cloud Platform (GCP) provides a comprehensive suite of tools to manage user permissions, encryption, data masking, and data governance, which enables organizations to secure sensitive data, ensure compliance, and maintain operational efficiency.

Managing User Permissions in GCP: GCP's Identity and Access Management (IAM) system provides granular control over who can access resources. It ensures that only authorized users or services interact with data and applications. IAM is central to securing GCP resources and enforcing the principle of least privilege (PoLP), which minimizes the risk of unauthorized access.

Key Tools and Features

Identity and Access Management (IAM)

- **Functionality**: IAM allows administrators to define roles and permissions for users, groups, and service accounts at various levels (for example, project, dataset, or table). It supports fine-grained access control, enabling organizations to assign specific permissions based on job functions.

- **Roles**
    - **Predefined Roles**: GCP provides roles like **`roles/bigquery.dataViewer`** for read-only access to BigQuery datasets or **`roles/storage.objectAdmin`** for managing Cloud Storage objects.
    - **Custom Roles:** Organizations can create tailored roles for specific needs, while ensuring precise permission assignments.

      Example: A developer might be granted **`roles/compute.instanceAdmin`** to manage virtual machines, but not **`roles/compute.networkAdmin`** to modify the network configurations.cadosecurity.com
- **Principle of Least Privilege (PoLP)**: IAM enforces PoLP by ensuring that users have only the permissions necessary for their tasks, which reduces the attack surface. For example, a data analyst might have access to BigQuery tables, but not to encrypted keys.
- **Audit Logging**: IAM integrates with Cloud Audit Logs to track who accesses resources and when. It provides a record for compliance and incident investigation.
- **Implementation**: Use the GCP Console, gcloud CLI, or APIs to assign roles. Regularly audit permissions using tools like Policy Analyzer to detect over-provisioned accounts.

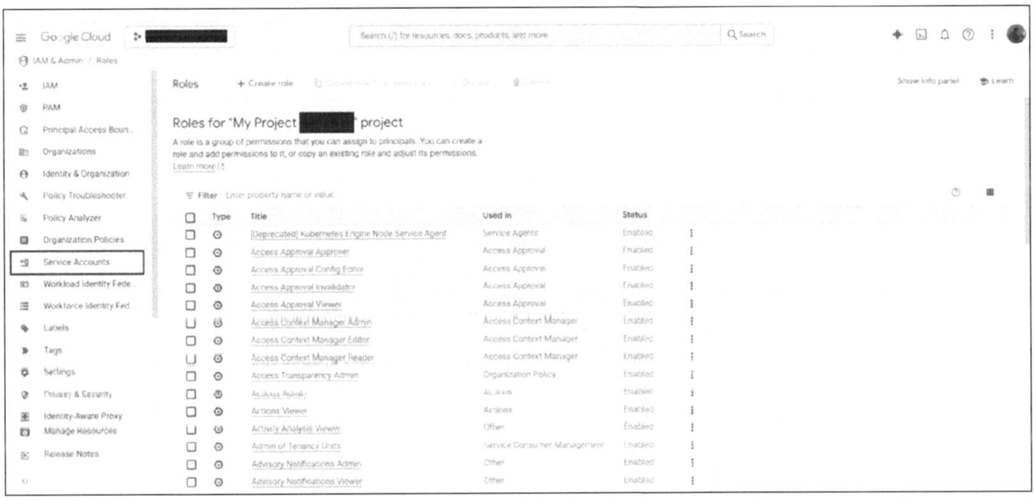

Figure 11.10: Roles in the GCP Console – Service Accounts

Encryption in GCP

GCP provides comprehensive encryption mechanisms to protect data at rest and in transit, while ensuring confidentiality and compliance with regulations such as GDPR,

HIPAA, and PCI-DSS. Encryption is a cornerstone of GCP's security framework and offers options for both Google-managed and customer-managed keys. *Figure 11.11* illustrates this:

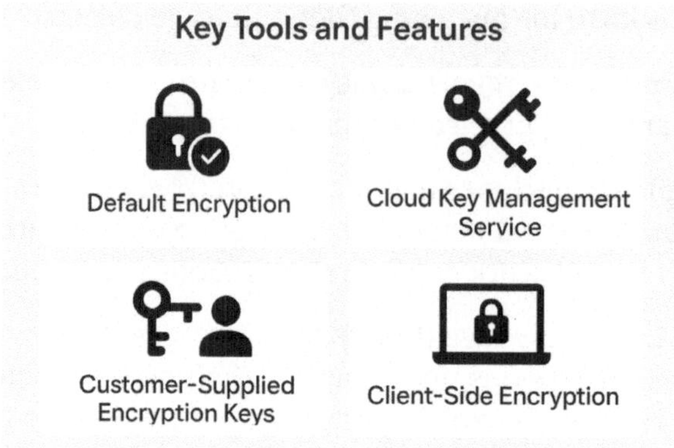

Figure 11.11: *Encryption in GCP*

Key Tools and Features

- **Default Encryption**
  - **Functionality**: All data in GCP is encrypted by default at rest (for example, in Cloud Storage, BigQuery, Cloud SQL) through Google-managed keys (AES-256 standard) and in transit using Transport Layer Security (TLS). No additional configuration is required.
  - **Use Case**: A retail company stores customer data in Cloud Storage, which is automatically encrypted without manual intervention.
- **Cloud Key Management Service (KMS)**
  - **Functionality**: This is a cloud-hosted service for creating, managing, rotating, and destroying encryption keys (symmetric and asymmetric, for example, AES-256, RSA 2048). It supports Customer Managed Encryption Keys (CMEK) for greater control.
  - **Features**
    - **Key Rotation**: Automatically rotates keys or allows manual adjustments to meet compliance needs.wiz.io
    - **Integration**: Works with services such as BigQuery, Cloud Storage, and Compute Engine to encrypt data with CMEK
    - **Hardware Security Modules (HSMs)**: Provide industry-standard HSMs for high-security key storage

    - **Use Case**: A healthcare organization uses CMEK to encrypt patient data in BigQuery, which ensures that only authorized systems with access to the keys can decrypt it.
    - **Example**: Create a key ring and key in KMS using G-Cloud KMS. You can then create and apply them to a BigQuery dataset for encryption.
- **Customer-Supplied Encryption Keys (CSEK)**
    - **Functionality**: Allows users to provide their encryption keys for services like Compute Engine, while offering complete control over encryption without storing keys on GCP servers
    - **Use Case**: A government agency uses CSEK to encrypt virtual machine disks, which ensures that Google cannot access the data without the provided key.
    - **Challenge**: CSEK requires manual key management, which can be complex. Users must securely store and provide keys for decryption.
- **Client-Side Encryption**
    - **Functionality**: Encrypts data before it is sent to GCP, using keys managed by the customer. It is supported on Google Workspace and other services.
    - **Use Case**: Airbus uses client-side encryption in Google Workspace to protect critical company data, controlling encryption keys independently.

Data Masking in GCP

Data masking in GCP protects sensitive data by obfuscating it while maintaining its usability for analytics, testing, or development. GCP's primary tool for data masking is Cloud Data Loss Prevention (DLP), which comes with additional capabilities in BigQuery for column-level masking.

Key Tools and Features

- **Cloud DLP**
    - **Functionality**: Automatically detects, classifies, and masks sensitive data (for example, PII, credit card numbers) in text, images, or structured data using predefined or custom detectors
    - **Masking Techniques**
        - **Redaction**: Replaces sensitive data with asterisks or null values (for example, 123-45-6789 becomes ***-**-****)

    - **Tokenization**: Replaces data with unique token while preserving format (for example, a credit card number maps to a token in a token vault)
    - **Format-Preserving Encryption**: Encrypts data while maintaining its format (for example, a phone number remains a valid phone number)
    - **Hashing**: Uses SHA-256 to hash data; although deterministic hashing may be vulnerable to brute-force attacks if not combined with other measures.
  - **Integration**: Works with BigQuery, Cloud Storage, and Dataflow for real-time or batch masking; supports DLP templates for reusability configurations
  - **Use Case**: A company scans a Cloud Storage bucket for Chilean National IDs using DLP's `CHILE_CDI_NUMBER` infoType and applies masking to redact them before loading them into BigQuery.
    - **Example**: Create a DLP inspection template to detect PII and a de-identification template to mask it, then apply these in a Dataflow pipeline.
- **BigQuery Policy Tags and Dynamic Data Masking**
  - **Functionality**: Policy tags provide column-level access control and dynamic data masking in BigQuery. They allow administrators to define masking rules (for example, redaction, nullification, and custom UDFs) based on user roles.
  - **Roles**
    - **BigQuery Masked Reader**: Users can view masked data (for example, only the last four digits of a credit card).
    - **Data Catalogue Fine-Grained Reader**: Users can see unmasked data.
    - **No Role**: Users are denied access to the column.
  - **Masking Rules**
    - **Default Masking**: Replaces data with a fixed value (for example, `XXXXX` for phone numbers)
    - **Last Four Characters**: Shows only the last four characters (for example, `XXXX-XXXX-XXXX-1234`)

    - **Date Year Mask**: Truncates dates to the year (for example, 2025-07-16 becomes 2025-01-01)
    - **Custom UDFs**: Apply user-defined functions for complex masking (for example, masking Japanese names, though standard rules may struggle with non-Latin characters)
  - **Use Case**: A fintech company uses policy tags to mask Social Security Numbers in BigQuery to allow analysts to view masked data while administrators see unmasked data.
    - **Example**: Assign a `High_Sensitivity` policy tag to a column containing SSNs, set a masking rule to show only the last four digits, and grant the BigQuery Masked Reader role to analysts.

Data Governance in GCP

Data governance in GCP ensures data is managed securely, compliantly, and efficiently across the organization. GCP provides tools such as Dataplex, Data Catalogue, and partner integrations (for example, Collibra, Informatica) to centralize metadata, enforce policies, and promote data democratization while maintaining compliance. Please refer to the GCP page for detailed steps (https://cloud.google.com/dataplex/docs/lake-security).

Key Tools and Features

- **Dataplex**
  - **Functionality**: A centralized platform for managing and governing data across GCP services (for example, BigQuery, Cloud Storage). It supports data discovery, metadata management, and policy enforcement.
  - **Features**
    - **Data Catalog**: A fully managed, scalable metadata repository that auto-indexes datasets and enforces access controls. Users cannot search for data they lack permission to access.
    - **Data Lineage**: Tracks data origins and transformations, while ensuring traceability for compliance and analytics.
    - **Analytics Hub**: Enables secure sharing of data assets across teams or organizations while maintaining governance controls.
  - **Use Case**: A retail company uses Dataplex to catalogue customer data, track its lineage from CRM to BigQuery, and enforce access policies.

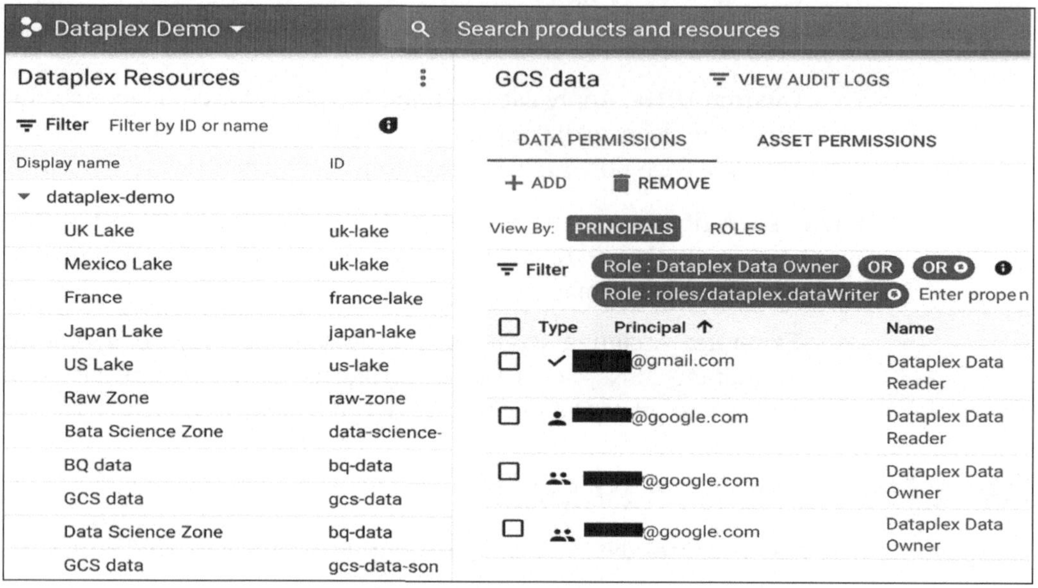

***Figure 11.12**: Dataplex in GCP*

- **Cloud Data Loss Prevention (DLP)**
  - **Functionality**: Supports governance by identifying and classifying sensitive data, enabling policies for masking or tokenization to ensure compliance
  - **Use Case**: A bank uses DLP to scan BigQuery tables for PII and apply governance policies to mask sensitive columns for non-authorized users.
- **Security Command Center (SCC)**
  - **Functionality**: A centralized security and governance tool that monitors vulnerabilities, misconfigurations, and threats across GCP resources. It provides actionable recommendations and integrates with DLP and Chronicle for threat detection.
  - **Features**
    - **Cloud Identity and Entitlement Management (CIEM)**: Identifies excessive or dormant permissions using ML
    - **Audit Logs**: Tracks security events and data access for compliance reporting
  - **Use Case**: A healthcare provider uses SCC to detect misconfigured IAM roles and ensure compliance with HIPAA.

- **Partner Integrations**:
  - **Functionality**: GCP integrates with third-party governance platforms such as Collibra and Informatica for unified governance across on-premises and multi-cloud environments.
  - **Use Case**: A multinational company uses Collibra with GCP's Data Catalog to manage metadata across GCP and on-premises systems.

Critical Evaluation of Data Security and Governance Components in GCP

- **Strengths**
  - **Integrated Ecosystem**: GCP's tools (IAM, DLP, KMS, Dataplex) are tightly integrated and provide a seamless approach to permissions, encryption, masking, and governance.
  - **Automation**: Features like DLP's automated data discovery and Data Catalog's auto-indexing reduce manual effort.
  - **Compliance Support**: GCP certifications (for example, ISO 27001, HIPAA) and audit logging support compliance with global regulations.
- **Weaknesses**
  - **Complexity of IAM**: Fine-grained IAM roles can be difficult to manage, especially for large organizations. Users report frustration with over-permissive roles or complex configurations.
  - **Masking Limitations**: BigQuery's masking rules may struggle with non-Latin data (for example, Japanese characters), which often requires custom solutions.
  - **Key Management Overhead**: CMEK and CSEK require careful key management, which can be resource-intensive for smaller teams.
- **Critical Perspective**: While GCP's tools are robust, the shared responsibility model places a significant burden on users to configure security and governance correctly. Misconfigurations (for example, overly permissive IAM roles) can compromise security, as is noted in user feedback. Organizations must invest in training and automation to maximize the effectiveness of these tools.

Conclusion

In this chapter, we understood the fundamental importance of data security and compliance in the context of modern cloud-based data engineering. We explored how Google Cloud Platform (GCP) provides a rich ecosystem of tools such as IAM, DLP, KMS, and Dataplex to effectively manage encryption, access control, data masking, and governance.

We comprehended the layered approach GCP adopts to ensure the confidentiality, integrity, and availability of data, while aligning with regulatory mandates such as GDPR, HIPAA, CCPA, and PCI-DSS.

We also **investigated** the technical nuances of data masking strategies, including their types and implementation best practices, as well as the symbiotic relationship between data masking and governance. Additionally, we examined GCP's support for auditability, metadata management, policy enforcement, and automated compliance monitoring.

Thus, by integrating these capabilities and frameworks, we now understand how organizations can proactively secure sensitive data, minimize risk, meet stakeholder expectations, and maintain operational resilience in an increasingly complex digital and regulatory environment.

Index

A

B

C

D

H

I

K

L

M

N

O

P

S

T

X